BETTER REASONING

TECHNIQUES FOR HANDLING ARGUMENT, EVIDENCE, AND ABSTRACTION

BETTER REASONING

TECHNIQUES FOR HANDLING ARGUMENT, EVIDENCE, AND ABSTRACTION

Larry Wright

University of California, Riverside

HOLT, RINEHART AND WINSTON

New York   Chicago   San Francisco   Philadelphia
Montreal   Toronto   London   Sydney
Tokyo   Mexico City   Rio de Janeiro   Madrid

For Emily

Library of Congress Cataloging in Publication Data

Wright, Larry.
  Better reasoning.

  Includes index.
    1. Reasoning. 2. Evidence. 3. Abstraction.
  4. Analysis (Philosophy). I. Title.
  BC177.W74   160   81-6203
  ISBN 0-03-056218-X   AACR2

CBS COLLEGE PUBLISHING
Holt, Rinehart and Winston
The Dryden Press
Saunders College Publishing

Preface

This text grew out of a long-running project attempting to say something systematic and helpful about a broad range of reasoning problems naturally encountered in the course of a college education, or just in everyday life. These problems tended to cluster around two central topics: one was the evaluation of *evidence,* the other was general or abstract *characterization.* Unfortunately, treatments of reasoning available in textbooks encouraged a rather heavy-handed treatment of these issues. In attempting to modify and supplement those treatments I gradually—almost inadvertently—began the project that resulted in this book. It is published in the hope that others who feel the need for a more sensitive treatment of language and empirical inference will benefit from the results of the struggle this project has entailed.

The overriding strategy of the project has been to develop technique and apparatus to engage the best skills we already have. Since all reasoning—every argument—must stop somewhere, we should try to stop with, to proceed from, the best, most certain judgments we can bring to bear. A bit of structure is valuable if it shows how a difficult question may be resolved into easier ones. And what is easy or difficult depends on our human abilities: what we naturally do well or badly. Accordingly, the general organization and particular schemata offered in this text are explicitly designed to rest on our best perceptions, our clearest diagnoses, our most intersubjective judgments. Further structure is added only when it can be used to replace a shaky judgment with more secure ones. Occasionally, alternative schemata are provided to allow varying degrees of analysis, depending on the case and the need. This strategy enables us to bring some powerful skills to bear on a surprisingly broad range of topics and issues, in a practically useful way.

The body of the text is divided into two sections: Argument Analysis (Chapters 1–5) and Language (Chapters 6–8). The first part is more orthodox, taking off from a roughly standard induction/deduction distinction. But it devotes most of its attention to *inductive* argument, taking as central one particular type of inductive argument, on which our skills have the most direct purchase (diagnostic arguments). Part Two departs further from orthodoxy in being primarily an exploration of the linguistic institutions spawned by the nature of our skills and practical interests. The premise of this exploration is that when reasoning becomes abstract, the greatest hazard is misunderstanding our own linguistic skill, and the value of the linguistic institutions to which it gives rise. The second part of the text has a slightly more philosophical cast than the first, and is therefore of primary interest to those students who are naturally drawn to more abstract rumination.

The two parts of the text are unified by an underlying appeal to our basic perceptual and diagnostic skills. In fact, Part Two might have been included in Chapter 4 as just one more application of diagnostic induction. But it is such an important application, justifying such extensive treatment, that a separate section was clearly desirable. This obviously accounts for the unusual order of presentation (language usually being treated first). Our diagnostic skills and related schemata are best studied in their relatively simple application to normal evidence evaluation, before taking on the complex difficulties in our handling of language. Only when we have a pretty good grasp of them can they be of much help in the subtle and abstract issues we examine in Part Two.

The notions doing the most pedagogic work in the two parts of the text are, in Part One, 'rival conclusions', and in Part Two, 'substantive context'. Focusing argument analysis on rival conclusions serves to direct and stimulate a student's imagination to think of the plausible competition for an inductively supported hypothesis, and to think up counterexamples to alleged deductions. 'Substantive context' is used to capture the role of our perceptual skill and general understanding in our use of language. It essentially ties the two parts of the text together.

This text owes a great deal to Jeff Johnson and Jim Hearne, who shared the teaching of my critical thinking course during the gestation of the central notions used here. Special thanks are due David Harrah and Ray Lyons for their careful reading and helpful criticisms of earlier versions of the manuscript. The original inspiration of much that is contained here was provided by Michael Scriven when I was his student. The typescript was prepared with superhuman flawlessness by Clara Dean.

L. W.

Contents

ONE

ARGUMENT ANALYSIS

1

Arguments: General Background

SEMANTIC AND LEXICAL PRELIMINARIES

Occasionally we encounter a statement in need of support—an opinion expressed in a newspaper column, perhaps, or some view offered by a friend in conversation. Even something you have said yourself may have trouble standing by itself. Something must be said in its behalf if it is to be taken seriously: other statements must be marshaled around to prop it up. I say to you, "Joe plagiarized his term paper." You are skeptical: "Why do you think so? He's never done anything like that before." I reply, "Much of it is nearly word-for-word the same as an article in last week's *Time* magazine: a few minor changes here and there, but for the most part identical." Here I offer my second statement in support of my first. This is a simple example of what is called offering an *argument* for a statement. It is a useful procedure to the

3

extent that the supporting statements are more secure than—or more easily made secure than—the original statement.

In normal, everyday contexts the word 'argument' refers to other sorts of things, of course. Often enough an argument is something two people *have,* or something you got into because you couldn't keep your mouth shut, and is invariably unpleasant. "Well, you see, officer, Jeff and Jim got into an argument, there was a lot of yelling and swearing, terrible accusations about each other's parents, one thing led to another, and, well, you know the rest." There is doubtless some relation between this sense of 'argument' and the sense of 'argument' we will be discussing here; but the connection is tenuous and largely unhelpful. In discussions of reasoning, 'argument' refers very specifically to the (usually) dispassionate *marshaling of support for some statement* (or viewpoint, or conclusion, or position). It is not at all like a fight, and need not even involve a disagreement. This sense of 'argument' even has its own vocabulary: arguments here are not something one gets into, but rather something one constructs, offers to someone, brings to bear on an issue, or evaluates. To offer an argument for a statement is, typically, to provide reason to believe the statement is correct. The bracing exchange between Jim and Jeff is meant to emphasize what is *not* meant by 'argument' in this context.

The basic schematic picture of an argument is this:

$$S_1$$
$$S_2$$
$$S_3$$
$$====$$
$$C$$

C represents the *conclusion* of the argument: the statement being argued *for.* S_1, S_2, and S_3 represent the statements offered in *support* of the conclusion. Obviously there may be any number of supporting statements; the number chosen in this illustration is arbitrary. The pair of broken lines is used primarily to separate the two kinds of statements from each other. However, the separating lines may also be taken to represent the supporting relationship that the Ss are alleged to bear to C. Support comes in different forms, and shortly we will use different separating lines to stand for different kinds of support.

So an argument consists basically of two things, a top (support claims) and a bottom (conclusion), offered as having a certain relationship to one another (one supports the other). Anything that can be broken into these components is an argument. Since most of what we call giving reasons may be put in argumentative form, much of the general topic of *reasoning* consists of argument analysis; thus does a book on reasoning begin with several chapters on argument.

Closely related to the concept of argument is the sometimes tricky notion of inference. The verb 'to infer' is often confused with the verb 'to imply,' and this confusion is worth avoiding if we can. The distinction may be kept straight by remembering two things. First, inferring is always done by people, not by facts or statements; and second, when we infer, we always infer *from* something or other, usually facts or statements. "From the wreckage strewn about the room, Holmes inferred there had been a struggle." Holmes did the inferring, and he did it *from* the fact that the room was a mess. By contrast, facts and statements imply things, and of course they do not imply them "from" anything: the expression 'imply from' is nonsensical. "The wreckage in the room implied that there had been a struggle." The condition of the room is what does the implying here. We do sometimes speak of people implying things, but only when we are indirectly referring to their statements.

Applying these suggestions to the abstract argument model pictured above, we may see how to talk about arguments in general, using either verb. It takes somebody to infer the conclusion from the support claims, but the support claims themselves, if they are good enough, imply the conclusion. Philosophers have jargonized inference talk a bit and speak of our inferring *from* the support claims (sometimes called premises) *to* the conclusion. So when philosophers say they are examining an inference, they are examining what we would call an argument. In this context philosophers use the words 'argument' and 'inference' almost interchangeably: they are practically synonyms here.

CRITICAL PRELIMINARIES

Thus arguments are just a very important kind of reasoning: reasoning that involves supporting a position or drawing a conclusion. To criticize or evaluate that sort of reasoning is simply to do argument analysis. But the arguments we will want to examine—most interesting arguments—are not found lying around neatly separated into the components of our little schema: a top and a bottom and a clear relationship between them. Quite usually the reasoning under scrutiny is expressed in a passage of standard English prose, and there is often some question at the outset concerning just what is being inferred from what. So the first step in analyzing an argument is normally to rewrite the argument in schematic form, to think through the inferential structure of the passage before attempting any evaluation. This is nearly always helpful, and sometimes enormously revealing. People who should know better have made mistakes they could have avoided by careful schematization of an argument. It is important to get clear at the outset precisely what is being asked to support what; otherwise a criticism may fall quite wide of the mark.

Accordingly, when facing a passage of prose—a sentence, a paragraph, even an entire essay—and considering whether to attack it as an argument, there are four important questions to ask about it:

1. Is it an argument (or does it contain one)?
2. What is it an argument for (that is, what is the conclusion)?
3. What support does it provide (that is, what are the support statements)?
4. How strong is this support (that is, how *good* is the argument)?

Asking these four questions *in this order* will structure the entire critical enterprise, and Part One of this book may be viewed as a detailed examination of these four questions. A preliminary look at them will serve to get us started.

Question One. It may sound silly to reserve a whole question—one fourth of the mnemonic—for the elementary issue of whether what we have is actually an argument. But it is an important point; and it is so commonly overlooked that it is worth a little extra attention. Part of the reason for this no doubt has something to do with the nature of human disagreement. We are quick to call mistakes fallacies when they involve certain kinds of subject matter. Any important disagreement that requires reflection we are inclined to think must be traceable to flawed reasoning, some fallacious argument. We allow that the identification of simple objects, or a preference for one kind of ice cream, requires no argument; our disagreements about such things may be simple mistakes, or matters of taste. But when the disagreeable opinion concerns a relatively complex social or political issue we are tempted to view it not simply as wrong or even perverse, but rather as bad thinking, faulty reasoning. Whatever the cause, it is common to find people objecting to the 'reasoning' in a passage (often an editorial or letter to the editor) when the passage merely expresses an (obnoxious) opinion that has no inferential structure at all. In such a case the target of the objection is not an argument, whatever else it may be. For something to be an argument there must be two things, a conclusion and some support. If such a division cannot be made, there is no argument. The opinion may be true, it may be false, but there is no *inference* to evaluate.

The context within which this mistake is most tempting and most regrettable is the one we currently occupy: philosophical courses in reasoning. Casting about for illustrations of new argumentative tricks, we sometimes allow enthusiasm to overwhelm perception and force examples into required forms whether they fit or not. It is a temptation to which we all are prone, and one we must constantly guard against.

Questions Two and Three. In answering question one we have already begun to address questions two and three. In deciding that what we have is an argument, we need not actually state and distinguish a conclusion and supporting statements, but we do have to assure ourselves that such a distinction is possible. Now we must flesh out that distinction and actually specify C and the Ss. In the easiest cases there are key words (flag terms) pointing to the major components (Ss, C) of an argument. The words 'therefore', 'thus', 'hence', 'so', 'it follows that' are the most common clues that the conclusion is coming up. The words 'since', 'if', 'because' are the most frequent indicators of support claims.

> Since proposal A on the November ballot contains a provision allowing the city council to alter any part of it on a majority vote, it follows that those who think the passage of proposal A would be a disaster must have a very low opinion of our city council.

There is as clear a case as can be constructed. The support claim and the conclusion fall in the proper order, are separated by the only internal punctuation, and are each flagged by an appropriate expression. To schematize would require merely dropping the flags, writing the first clause above the second, and drawing separating lines between them.

Very seldom are both the support claims *and* the conclusion flagged by characteristic terms, however: usually one or the other is all you get. Even in the 'proposal A' illustration, the second flag ("it follows that") is a bit forced and the passage would read better without it. (Check this by reading it aloud without the offending phrase.) But dropping it raises no real difficulty because the example is such a simple one, and in any case, one flag is usually enough.

Flag terms become slightly more important when the order in which the elements occur is inverted or jumbled.

> Those who think the passage of proposal A would be a disaster must have a very low opinion of our city council, because that proposal contains a provision allowing the council to alter any part of it on a majority vote.

This is of course exactly the same argument, but the order of the major components is inverted and there is only one flag: "because." None of this bears on the structure of the argument—it would be schematized in exactly the same way as the first version.

Except in the very simplest cases, there is no reliable, purely mechanical way to schematize arguments using devices such as punctuation, order of presentation, and typical indicator terms. These devices are helpful, but usually we must also rely on our basic understanding of what an argument is—that is, some statements being offered in support of another. The guiding principle of schematization is simply to *make the most plausible sense of the* *passage under analysis.* * Is it plausible, in the context, to suppose the author intended an argument? Is it plausible to suppose she meant to conclude what we have concluded? Would she have reasonably thought the support claims we have selected were firm enough to use in this way? If the answers to questions like these are not clearly 'yes', that raises difficulties for the analysis. In complicated cases, several attempts at schematization will often be required before we can accommodate the entire passage. And, of course, some passages will be so obscure on crucial points that a confident judgment on its structure cannot be made.

There are nevertheless two aspects of the tougher sort of passage that we can say something useful about. The first concerns padding. Most argumentative prose contains asides and embellishments that are neither part of the conclusion nor essential to the support: they are comfortable padding on the argument's bare bones. Padding like this is usually not frivolous or gratuitous; it may have any of a large number of functions: dramatic effect, humor, apology, explanation, illustration, insult, expression of disgust, ego trip, irresistible cheapshot, and doubtless many more. And it may, in some cases, be a misunderstood irrelevancy. But since the analysis aims to extract the barebones structure of the argument, such padding does not appear in the schematization. Whether something should be treated as padding depends on how it fits into the most thoughtful reconstruction of the argument. Hence it is a matter of judgment for which the analyzer is responsible.

> Walking into the room, Holmes observed a shambles. Furniture was overturned, the draperies torn, books were scattered about and the lamps were broken. Any ordinary chap would have suspected a fight: an attack on somebody or a struggle over some thing. But Holmes was too astute. He noted the contents of the dresser drawers, dumped out and ground into the floor with nearly Carthaginian vindictiveness. "A warning," he muttered, almost to himself, as he relit his pipe.

If our interest is simply in extracting Holmes's argument, there is much here that counts as padding. All of it may be an interesting and important part of the story, but most of it may be omitted in reconstructing Holmes's inference. Some parts are totally irrelevant (his walking in, the speculation about the ordinary chap, his relighting his pipe). Some are illuminating but need not be explicitly mentioned in the schematic reconstruction (details of the shambles and the epochal assessment of the vindictiveness). A plausible schematization would run:

*This principle is at work even in the use of flag terms because those terms have other jobs too: in some contexts they are *not* flag terms, although it is usually easy to recognize when this is so. "If you touch that again I'll beat your head in" uses 'if' to introduce a threat, not a support claim. And 'because' often signifies a *causal* connection, not an *inferential* one: "The boat capsized because everybody rushed to starboard when the commotion started."

(S)   The shambles bears signs of vindictive vandalism.

==================================

(C)   The room was purposely wrecked to make a point, perhaps to strike fear into someone's heart.

It would be just as correct to include a second supporting statement giving further detail: what sort of room it was, perhaps even whose room, if we knew, and possibly details of the shambles. In the usual context all this is probably unnecessary, however, since we have the passage to consult and thus what "the shambles" refers to is perfectly clear.

The crucial thing to notice in this example is that much of the analytical burden is placed on our simple understanding of a passage of prose. There are no flag terms, yet it is pretty clear that something is being inferred from something else. It is not difficult to identify what those two things are—although several different characterizations of them are possible. And, finally, categorizing the omitted bits as the prosy embellishments of a detective story is quite plausible on its face. This is a relatively easy case, but it is a useful illustration. Harder cases of this type differ from this one merely in requiring more effort and imagination in exactly the same task: plausibly accounting for all the details of an inferential passage. That is, finding C, finding the Ss, and making reasonable sense of all the rest as various sorts of padding.

Editor,

I wonder if the employees of the Department of Motor Vehicles could stop complaining about having to work on Saturdays long enough to realize who is footing the bill for their paychecks.

As a taxpayer, I'm getting more than a little tired of government—federal, state, county, and city—employees who are too busy thinking of themselves to give a "tinker's dam" about the general public for whom they are supposed to work.

If hospital services can be available 24 hours a day, 365 days of the year, I would hope the DMV could stay open 4 hours on Saturday. They certainly get more than enough holidays to compensate.

Although the sentiment expressed in this letter comes close to the pure expression of opinion discussed under question one, there is a hint of inferential structure which may charitably be schematized as follows.

(S_1)   The DMV is a public service wholly supported by taxes.
(S_2)   Keeping the DMV open on Saturdays would be a substantial convenience for many taxpayers.

==================================

(C)   The DMV should be open on Saturdays.

Omitting the parts about holidays and hospitals may be unfair to the author, but it is difficult to see how it would help the argument to work them into its structure. This letter was selected to represent the toughest sort of case, however, and part of what that means is that we should not expect to have complete confidence in our reconstruction of it. Improvement on the above rendering may well be possible, and that is left as an exercise for the reader. The object should be to represent it as well as possible before criticism, a point that will be discussed further shortly. Of course, some passages may not yield a satisfactory schematic reconstruction despite our best efforts. We may be forced (and it should take force) to conclude that the passage is inferentially unclear.

The other kind of 'tougher' case that will reward our attention is one in which something important is more or less clearly presumed, but not explicitly stated in the passage itself. Sometimes the conclusion itself is merely implicit:

It is distressing to see drivers with the wrong license plate number blithely disobeying the law at gas stations. Observing the odd/even regulation conserves gasoline by making us conscious of our driving habits.

The most plausible statement to represent as the conclusion of this argument would be something like 'everybody should abide by the odd/even rule', or, perhaps, 'if you care about conserving energy you should abide by the odd/ even rule'. The fact that no statement of this form appears in the passage itself is relatively unimportant. The sentiment is clear.

In other cases an important part of the support is left unstated:

Current economic indicators are so bad that the wise investor will stay out of the stock market until there is a substantial change in the forecast.

The conclusion here is the claim that it is wise to stay out of the stock market; and the support offered for this is that economic indicators are down. But there are two things almost certainly taken for granted in this argument which it might be worthwhile making explicit. The first is that the bad economic indicators make it likely that the market will decline (or continue to decline) in the near future, and the second is that investors are in the market to make money. These are sometimes called 'presuppositions', because even though they are not explicitly stated in the argument, the strength of the argument depends on them: if they are challenged, the argument itself is challenged. These particular presuppositions are fairly unproblematic: they are not so subtle that the maker of the argument would be totally unaware of them, and they are not likely to be challenged in any interesting way. (There is at least one exception; can you think of it?) But occasionally, in the most surprising places, digging out a presupposition suddenly raises a difficulty with the argument that we simply had not noticed before. For example, it is often argued that the price of petroleum should be allowed to rise (say, by removing federal price controls) because that would encourage further exploration and hence increase the petroleum supply. Among other things, this argument assumes that it would be economically sensible for an oil company to plow increased profits back into the oil business. But it might well be that oil companies would be economically better off to use their profits to diversify into fast-food operations or the entertainment industry. The presuppositions must be considered, and the argument won't wash without some reason to prefer the first presupposition to the second.

Digging out presuppositions is one of the first tricks we learn when we begin to think about analyzing arguments, and it is easy to get carried away with it. Doing it well requires care and judgment (and practice!), so a couple of precautions are called for. The first precaution has a name: the principle of charity. This is not a version of the golden rule, but rather a quite specific and weighty recommendation for dealing with arguments. Namely, always reconstruct an argument as plausibly as possible before criticizing it. This point is perhaps stronger when put negatively: don't stick the arguer with a needlessly weak or flawed version of the argument. If you disregard this rule you end up criticizing an argument that is easily patched up. So you waste a lot of time and energy, and even risk misleading yourself about the strengths of the arguments you examine. (Of course, if you are only having fun making somebody mad, or just trying to reproach the arguer, then the principle of charity is clearly not relevant. But then what you are doing is not argument analysis either.)

In the stock market example, it is tempting to saddle the arguer with a number of presuppositions that are easy to attack. The zealous critic might charge the author with assuming that *all* the economic indicators are bad (which is almost never the case), or that bad indicators *always* presage lower stock prices (which is doubtful). But the argument does not require anything so sweeping (and hence vulnerable) in order to make its point. In the first place, it may well be that only *some* economic indicators are relevant to stock market prices, and it is possible that it takes only a few of these to guarantee a bad market. Second, the wise investor will worry about bad economic indicators even if they are only *usually* a reliable guide to the fortunes of the market: by the time he has a guarantee it is usually too late to do much good. The principle of charity requires taking this sort of thing into account. And this in turn requires both an acquaintance with the subject matter of the argument and, frequently, a practiced imagination. But it will become increasingly clear as we explore argument analysis that education and imagination are *the* indispensable requisites of this activity. Learning how better to use what we already have, and how to discover what else we need, is the major project of this book. But for now it is important to understand the role of charity in reconstructing arguments: ignoring it generally entails wasting time in meaningless peripheral skirmishes when there is a battle to be fought.

A second caution for enthusiastic presupposition hunters concerns the simple judgment of when to stop. Nearly any argument will allow presuppositions to be dug out almost without limit, although they quickly become trivial and uninteresting. The stock market example presupposes that there is a stock market and that investors care about its future and that the world won't be obliterated tomorrow, among other things. But these are boring distractions: in most contexts they are *simply* understood, and mentioning them misses the point of the argument. Knowing when to stop, knowing when all the useful presuppositions have been disinterred, requires a lively awareness of the context and plain good sense. This too improves with practice.

Question Four. This brings us naturally to what might be called the pragmatics of evaluation: practical considerations involved in the assessment of an argument. The two major functions of arguments are to assure oneself and to persuade someone else. Most other uses of argument are parasitic on these. Notice right away that *what* we are assuring ourself or persuading someone else of is not always that the conclusion of the argument is true. Arguments provide conclusions with support; our evaluation is to determine *how much* support has been offered. And to the question "how much?" (or "how good?") there is a *range* of answers, from "conclusive," to "a lot," "some," "a little," to "virtually none." How much is needed or useful depends on the case. On a tough theoretical question in physics a very little bit of support is not only useful but cherished, justifying enormous effort and expense. But the same amount of support offered for the proposition that the food just served is not poisonous would be wholly useless in normal circumstances.

However, the most important point to make about the two functions of argument mentioned above (assuring and persuading) is that they provide practical criteria for determining when an argument has been adequately dissected. For your own assurance, you must analyze an argument far enough for it to be clear that the judgement of support strength is one *you* can *reliably* make. Exactly what this consists of will, again, vary with the kind of argument being considered and will become clear in the following chapters. But for an example somewhat misleading in its simplicity, consider an arithmetic calculation that can be put in the form of an argument.

(S)   The number we are looking for is $(9/10)^4$.

=====================

(C)   The number is 0.6561.

In this case, as in any ordinary calculation, the support offered is alleged to be conclusive—the calculation is either conclusively right or equally wrong.

Nevertheless, as it stands, most of us are unable to judge whether it is right or wrong without interposing some steps between S and C. Which steps and how many depend on the individual. Most of us would be able to make the judgment if it were broken down as follows:

(S)   The number is $(9/10)^4$.
  1. Hence the number is $(9/10) \times (9/10) \times (9/10) \times (9/10)$.

  2. " $\dfrac{9 \times 9 \times 9 \times 9}{10 \times 10 \times 10 \times 10}$

  3. " $\dfrac{81 \times 81}{100 \times 100}$

  4. " $\begin{array}{r} 81 \\ \times\,81 \\ \hline 81 \\ 648 \\ \hline 6561 \end{array}$

  5. Hence the number is $\dfrac{6561}{10{,}000}$.

==

(C)   The number is 0.6561.

Someone who did not know that 9 X 9 is 81 would have to add at least one more step between 2 and 3. Someone never introduced to multiplication would have to have all of the steps reduced even further to additive ones. And, of course, addition can be reduced to counting if necessary. Normally educated people virtually never reduce these calculations to counting, and some could easily omit some steps included above. Some would want entirely different steps.* What you need and where you stop depend on what you know—that is, on what you are reliable at judging.

Most arguments are not very much like arithmetic calculations. This example is useful merely to illustrate the individual variation in ability to make inferential judgments. If the object of the argument is to assure yourself about something, then you stop when you reach judgments you can reliably make. This of course requires a lively awareness of your own biases, weaknesses, and limitations, and sometimes these are very difficult to detect. The explorations in this book will reveal all sorts of ways to test and sharpen judgmental prowess.

When the object of an argument is to persuade someone else, the analytical criterion is altered; how much it is altered depends on the similarities or the antagonists. The analysis must proceed until they reach common ground; the end comes only with judgments they both can make. This rule is actually just

*Step 4, for example, is easier to do in your head if you break 81 into $80 + 1$ and run through a simple binomial expansion: $(80 + 1) \cdot (80 + 1) = 6400 + 160 + 1 = 6561$.

a rudiment of civil conversation: if other people's views are important, differences in judgment must be treated as honest disagreements and resolved by working from areas of agreement. This takes patience, imagination, empathy, and (as always) practice, but it is the only civil recourse in a world in which different backgrounds yield disparate perceptions. The arithmetic example is relevant here too. If I am using the calculation to persuade someone of the answer I have reached (C), that end will not be achieved until the calculation includes steps the person is competent to judge.

EXERCISES

Review Questions
1. Why can't support claims infer a conclusion?
2. The word 'must' is sometimes a flag term.
   a. What does it flag?
   b. Make up (or find) a plausible example in which it functions as a flag term.
   c. Make up an example in which it does *not* function as a flag term.
3. Without consulting the text, describe the principle of charity in a sentence or two. What are the most important risks in violating this rule?

Arguments
1. Much of the letter concerning Saturday service at the DMV (on p. 9) was omitted from the schematization of the argument it offered. List the sentiments expressed in that letter that were thereby represented as padding. See if you can restructure the argument (expand the schematization) by including one or more of these sentiments in a way that *clearly strengthens* the argument.
2. Which of the following passages contain an argument? Identify the support and the conclusion of the ones that do. Rewrite the argument in schematic form, omitting the padding.
   a. [Background: take this passage to be a comment by an air safety official investigating a midair collision.] Since the pilots of both planes unemotionally acknowledged the presence of another aircraft in their vicinity, and made no attempt to avoid each other, they each must have seen a third plane, rather than each other. There was plenty of time between the acknowledgment and the collision to avoid hitting each other.
   b. On his way home from work, Ivan Potter lost control of his car, crashed through a freeway guardrail, and rolled into an adjoining soybean field. Examination of his corpse at the crash site by a qualified physician revealed no broken bones or external injuries. So it is reasonable to think that Ivan's death caused the accident rather than the other way around.

c. Dear Editor,

As far as I'm concerned *all* politicians are crooks. They may smile and kiss babies and say pleasant things at election time, but when they get back to Washington, or the state capital, or into their offices at city hall, you can trust them as far as you can throw a grand piano. They're all out for themselves.

d. Most items imported by AJS, Inc. are fountain pens of one kind or another, and are invariably defective. Nevertheless, because most of what AJS imports is from China, eccentric Beverly Canard buys something from every shipment. Among other things, we may glean from this that at least one fountain pen from China is defective.

e. Dear Editor,

There's not a dime's worth of difference among all the major-party candidates currently campaigning for president. It would be a step back toward meaningful democracy to add a space on the ballot marked "none of the above." It might encourage a little well-earned humility among our elected officials.

3. Schematize David Broder's argument in the following column as economically as possible. List separately the parts of the column you omitted as padding. Characterize the function of each: that is, explain why Broder included it in his column even though it does not show up in the bare-bones structure of his argument.

Move by Bell and Connally to Limit Term of President Rejected a Long Time Ago
David S. Broder

In the space of 24 hours, late last month, two men of judgment and experience in serious statecraft who share a conservative bias on constitutional questions recommended to the consideration of their fellow citizens a constitutional amendment of great consequence.

John Connally, the former governor of Texas and present candidate for the Republican nomination for president, and Griffin Bell, the former federal appeals court judge and current attorney general of the United States, endorsed the proposal for granting future presidents a single six-year term, with no possibility of re-election.

The idea is not a new one. As Bell noted in his University of Kansas lecture, it was discussed at the constitutional convention, proposed to Congress as an amendment in 1826 and has been re-introduced some 160 times since then.

That history does more than suggest antiquity of the notion; it also hints at its frailty. One would presume that if this particular change in the Constitution were really needed, it would have been made before now.

But this is a time when many are eager to rewrite the Constitution. Half a dozen proposed amendments are bumping into each other on their way to and from the legislatures, and given the eminence of Connally and Bell, it probably would be a mistake to ignore their notion.

In both cases, the avowed purpose of the proponents is to liberate the president from politics and incline his thoughts toward more elevated matters than re-election. As Bell put it, "The single, six-year term would permit the long-term, steady planning and implementation that our government needs plus saving a fourth year now lost to campaigning."

Or as Connally argued in his own announcement of candidacy, "Nothing . . . would be more conducive to the restoration of the confidence of the people in our form of government . . . than the knowledge that an American president from the day of the assumption of office has fulfilled his political role and has no future except as the historians view him as a statesman.

The operative assumption in both arguments is that it is politics—specificially the calculation of strategy for re-election—that demeans the presidency and undercuts the leadership potential of the office.

But that argument is buttressed neither by the experience of history nor the test of common sense. The Connally-Bell amendment would not strengthen the president's leadership, nor would it increase his accountability for the exercise of his power.

By arbitrarily lopping 24 months off his maximum term of service, it would limit his capacity to move policy in a sustained direction. By taking him off the ballot in all congressional elections held during his tenure in office, it would reduce his influence with the legislative branch and make him even less able to resist the encroachment of Congress on his prerogatives.

The proposal would also eliminate the use of the re-election campaign as a source of discipline on the exercise of presidential authority. By immunizing the president from receiving the voters' judgment on his stewardship in office, it would encourage him to ignore public opinion.

It is, in sum, exactly as bad an idea as Alexander Hamilton thought it was when he wrote in Federalist 72: "Nothing appears more plausible at first sight, nor more ill-founded upon close inspection than a scheme which . . . has had some respectable advocates—I mean that of continuing the chief magistrate in office for a certain time and then excluding him from it. . . . These effects would be for the most part rather pernicious than salutary."

4. Following the argument below are listed seven statements of varying relevance to the argument. Some are irrelevant in the sense that whether they are true or false does not affect the strength of the argument (call these category 3). Some might well be relevant in this sense on one natural construction of the argument, but the argument may be charitably constructed to remain strong even if they turn out to be false (call these category 2). Others are so crucial to the argument that it would inevitably be weakened if they turned out to be false. These we can reasonably include among the *presuppositions* of the argument: their truth is presupposed by the argument (call these category 1).

Exercise

Determine which category (1, 2, or 3) each of the seven statements fits into most naturally. Then, for each statement you place in category 2, describe how the argument would have to be construed to avoid being damaged if it (the statement) turned out to be false.

Argument

Dear Editor,

Since every watt of electricity we use contributes to the energy crisis, worsens our balance of payments, weakens this country's economy, and helps destabilize the civilized world, unnecessary use of electricity is not just unpatriotic, it is truly criminal. Accordingly, the frivolous use of electricity for burning strings of colored lights at Christmas should not just be discouraged, it should be banned. Lighting up trees and shrubs and doorways and windows and eaves and roofbeams irresponsibly squanders our precious resources. Harsh penalties should be instituted for such reckless profligacy.

List

a. Publishing letters in the press has some impact on public policy.
b. People using Christmas lights are consciously trying to undermine our economy.
c. The contribution Christmas lighting makes to the energy crisis is more important than the various benefits people derive from it.
d. The story of Christmas is a myth.
e. Conservation is the only way out of the energy crisis.
f. Using Christmas lights does not naturally produce a reduction in other energy use that compensates for what they consume.
g. Only lights that are strung together contribute to the energy crisis.

5. State at least one important presupposition being made in each of the following arguments. (Note: Recall that presuppositions are unstated propositions that the argument, clearly or plausibly, depends upon. What is explicitly stated in the argument does not fall under the heading of 'presupposition' precisely because it *is* explicitly stated. In digging out presuppositions we simply *accept* what is stated—for the sake of argument.)

a. Since the Warsaw Pact countries will almost certainly change from oil exporters to oil importers during the 1980s, the Middle East will doubtless remain a focus of international tensions for some time to come.
b. If you pay more than four or five hundred dollars for a stereo system you've wasted your money. You simply can't hear the differences the more expensive components make.
c. Don't buy a car without air conditioning in Southern California, even if you will never use it. Because, when the time comes, it will be very hard to sell.

2

Matters of Form:
Induction
and Deduction

TWO QUESTIONS

Consider once again the general form of an argument:

$$S_1$$
$$S_2$$
$$S_3$$
$$====$$
$$C$$

For a variety of reasons, which will become clear in this chapter, it is useful to break the evaluation of an argument into two parts—two questions—that may be treated separately. The first question we might ask about this argument is

Question I: Are the supporting statements, S_1, S_2, and S_3, true (or, at least, reasonable to believe)?

We may know the Ss are true, we may know that one or more is false, or we may not be sure one way or the other. If one of the support claims is false, this will generally reduce—and often eliminate altogether—the support provided for C by the argument. If we are not sure, answering this first question will require further investigation—perhaps other arguments.

It is the second question, however, which has dominated argument analysis, that raises the more troubling and interesting issues.

Question II: If the supporting statements *were* true, how much support *would* they provide for the conclusion, C?

This question concerns the relationship between the support and the conclusion: the link correcting them together. The strength of this link may be evaluated before we know whether or not the support claims themselves are true.

To answer this second question, we, as it were, grant the support claims —for the sake of argument—and see where that leads. We may discover that the supporting statements offered in a particular argument would provide no support for its conclusion *even if they were true*—in which case we can save ourselves the trouble of checking them out. In exploratory cases, Question II is involved in deciding what data to gather in the first place. Before we look for data, before we run tests or conduct an investigation, it is reasonable to ask whether the results would be of any value. If we found data of a certain kind, *would* they count for or against the conclusion we are interested in? If not, if they were irrelevant, it would be a waste of time to carry out that particular test. At this preliminary stage, Question II is our sole concern. Question I is not yet relevant: we have not settled on support claims to discover the truth of.

But even after we have decided on support claims, and have a full-blown argument to evaluate, it is important to keep the two questions separate: they are independent. And the principal task of a text on argument analysis is to say something useful and systematic about answering Question II. How do we recognize good support (a strong link)? Are there different kinds of good support? Are there different criteria for different kinds? Are some kinds intrinsically better than others? Some controversy and much confusion surround these issues. This chapter deals with that controversy in order to diminish the confusion.

THE BASIC DISTINCTION

Suppose you are considering various arguments for the proposition that Lee Harvey Oswald shot President Kennedy (this would be C, the conclusion of each argument). The first argument offers in support of this proposition merely the fact that Oswald was seen in the building from which the shots were fired shortly after the assassination occurred (S_1).

S_1 Lee Harvey Oswald was seen in the book depository (from which the shots were fired) shortly after the assassination.
======================================
C   Lee Harvey Oswald shot President Kennedy.

Although this would offer *some* support for the conclusion that Oswald shot Kennedy, S_1 by itself is not very strong support for that proposition. Another argument could add to S_1 the fact that Oswald's palm print was on a rifle found near a window overlooking the site of the assassination (S_2).

S_1 Lee Harvey Oswald was seen in the book depository (from which the shots were fired) shortly after the assassination.
S_2 Oswald's palm print was on a rifle found near a window in the book depository overlooking the assassination.
======================================
C   Lee Harvey Oswald shot President Kennedy.

This would be a great deal stronger, but, as anyone who has read the Warren Commission Report knows, the case could be made stronger still. Suppose we add two more facts: that ballistics tests show the rifle could have fired the bullet that killed Kennedy, and that Oswald was identified in a police lineup by eyewitnesses as the man who fired a rifle from the window overlooking the assassination (S_3). This argument is very strong indeed:

S_1 Lee Harvey Oswald was seen in the book depository (from which the shots were fired) shortly after the assassination.
S_2 Oswald's palm print was on a rifle found near a window in the book depository overlooking the assassination.
S_3 Oswald was identified in a police lineup by an eyewitness; and ballistics tests show that the rifle (in S_2) could have fired the fatal shots.
======================================
C   Lee Harvey Oswald shot President Kennedy.

The support for C provided by S_1, S_2, and S_3 would appear overwhelming. But, in the actual case, even more support was gathered and there was still room for doubt.

Now, even the most deep-seated doubts would be removed if we could find some outlandishly perfect kind of evidence. Let us suppose—for the sake of argument—that we do find something literally unbelievable: small television cameras were installed throughout the book depository by a paranoid bureaucrat to monitor suspicious activity, and the entire episode is on videotape

(S_4). Allow that the light and camera vantage were so good that there can be no doubt of the activity or of Oswald's identity; if desirable, we can even suppose that the videotape contains unalterably reliable time and date marks. If we put S_1, S_2, S_3, and S_4 together as an argument for C, and ask the link question (Question II, if the support claims *were* true, how much support *would* they provide C?), the answer is: a truly colossal amount. This is about as strong as support ever gets: the case is practically airtight.

Of course it is still conceivable that Oswald did not do it, even if we suppose that S_1, S_2, S_3, and S_4 are true. A stupendously resourceful conspiracy could have built a precise replica of the book depository somewhere else, complete with TV cameras, staged a similar motorcade, had an Oswald look-alike do all the appropriate things, got it all down on tape, killed or bribed the participants, substituted the phony videotapes for the real ones, all without leaving any telltale traces or being observed. This would not, of course, be something anyone would take very seriously, but it is conceivable—as are many other bizarre stories, such as Martians monkeying with the local laws of nature.

It is possible to remove even this bare conceivability, however, if we are willing to pay the price. We can, by collecting the right support claims, tighten up the argument so completely that, given the support claims, there is no logically possible escape from the conclusion, no conceivable way it could be false. But in doing so we radically alter the nature of the argument. Up to this point the argument concerned the weight of *evidence;* in philosophic jargon it was an *inductive* argument. But as soon as we cross the line, as soon as the argument becomes absolutely tight, it loses its evidential character. For when this happens, the support claims become committed to the conclusion as a matter of language: implicitly or explicitly the conclusion is already contained within the support. Such an argument is called deductive. In most cases explicit containment is boring, but it does provide a clear illustration.

S_1 Lee Harvey Oswald was seen in the book depository just after the shooting.

S_2 His palm print was found on the rifle.

S_3 Oswald was identified in a police lineup by an eyewitness; and ballistics tests show that the rifle (in S_2) could have fired the fatal shots.

S_5 Lee Harvey Oswald shot President Kennedy.

C   Lee Harvey Oswald shot President Kennedy.

The conclusion here is explicitly contained within the support. Of course, nobody would ever offer such an argument except perhaps as an illustration, but it does make clear the way in which deductive arguments work, what their tightness consists in. It also allows us to see the sense in which deductive arguments are linguistic: if you assert the support claims and deny the conclusion, you contradict yourself. This is what it means to say that deductive arguments are a matter of logic, of semantics: once you accept the support claims you are already committed to accepting the conclusion, whether you know it or not.

In this case it is hard to imagine not knowing it; but there are more interesting cases in which the commitment (and the containment) is implicit. Consider the following syllogism, for instance.

S_1 President Kennedy was shot by Marina Oswald's husband.
S_2 Lee Harvey Oswald was Marina Oswald's (only) husband.

C   Lee Harvey Oswald shot President Kennedy.

In cases like this the support claims commit you to the conclusion just as inescapably as when it is explicitly written above the line. You still contradict yourself if you assert S_1 and S_2 but deny C. But understanding the commitment involves a slightly more subtle understanding of the statements involved. In still more complex cases, showing that the conclusion is already contained in the support will require a detailed sort of semantic unpacking of that support; it could even involve some calculation. The principle is the same at all levels of subtlety and complexity, however.*

A little more jargon will be helpful here. First, as you may have noticed, these last arguments are schematized in a slightly aberrant way: there is a single solid line separating conclusion from support. This will be the convention adopted for the rest of this book when an argument is, or is to be considered as, deductive. This last qualification is important because sometimes an argument is represented as deductive, but we find on examination that it is not tight enough to be deductive—even if the support claims are true there is still some possibility that the conclusion is false. To mark this sort of case it is convenient to say that such an argument is deductively *invalid*. It might still provide good evidence for C, it could still be a good inductive argument; that is another story. If it is represented as deductive (so that it would be schematized using a single solid line), but fails to meet the stringent criterion of deductiveness, we say it is deductively invalid. Just to keep the terminology symmetrical, arguments that do meet the criterion of deductiveness are called deductively valid.

So everything we said above may be rephrased in terms of validity. In a deductively valid argument, there is no consistent alternative to accepting the conclusion, *unless something in the support claims is given up.* Sometimes this fact will be disguised, difficult to see without logical or mathematical computation

---

*For an example of greater complexity see the last two illustrations on the right-hand side of the table on pp. 35–36.

(that is, without some unpacking). But sometimes it will be right on the surface, something any competent language user can recognize. And when it is, we can apply it as a test for deductive validity: merely ask, "Would the falsity of the conclusion simply *mean* there was something wrong among the support claims?" If so, the argument is deductively valid. This is how we recognize the validity of the Marina Oswald syllogism on page 22. Ingenuous use of the language demands that if Lee Harvey did not shoot President Kennedy, then either he was not Marina's only husband, or her husband was not the culprit. Something in the support would have to be given up.

Deductive validity, then, is wholly a matter of the *link,* the semantic connection between support and conclusion: it has nothing to do with whether the supporting statements are actually true—or even plausible. The link question (Question II) is in the subjunctive mood; it asks how much support the supporting statements *would* provide *were* they true. And for a valid deductive argument the answer is that the support would be conclusive: if the supporting statements were true, there would be absolutely no possibility that the conclusion was false. But this hypothetical claim may be made with equal certainty of

S₁   Bess Truman's husband shot President Kennedy.
S₂   Harry Truman was Bess Truman's (only) husband.

C   Harry Truman shot President Kennedy.

The link between support and conclusion here is just as strong as it is in the Marina Oswald syllogism above. So once it is determined that an argument is deductively valid, the entire burden of determining how much support C actually has is shifted to Question I, the truth question. As we shall see, this is sometimes helpful and sometimes not, depending on our interests.

For the sake of convenience, any argument that is not deductive will be referred to as inductive in this book. (This is not wholly arbitrary; there is some precedent in philosophy for marking the distinction in this way.) That is, anything that marshals support for a conclusion but that does not purport to meet the standards of deductive validity will be called an inductive argument. Whenever we are schematizing and wish to mark the fact that the argument in question is being considered as inductive, let us agree to use two solid lines to separate support from conclusion. We can thus usefully revert to our original picture, containing a pair of broken lines, either when we just do not know which the argument is supposed to be, or when we simply want to talk about arguments in general, irrespective of form (which is what we were doing in Chapter 1). So the three alternative schematizations would be

| | Deductive | Inductive | Uncertain or Unimportant |

$$S_1$$
$$S_2$$
$$S_3$$
————————
C

Deductive

$$S_1$$
$$S_2$$
$$S_3$$
════════
C

Inductive

$$S_1$$
$$S_2$$
$$S_3$$
= = = = = =
C

Uncertain or
Unimportant

The contrast between inductive and deductive arguments may best be captured in the sort of guarantees that good inductive arguments provide. Of course, a weak inductive argument (like the first Oswald example) will not provide a guarantee at all, just a bit of support. (There is no such thing as a weak deductive argument: it is either valid or invalid. No gradations are admitted or useful.) But a very strong inductive argument does provide a guarantee of one kind: a substantive guarantee, the guarantee of strong evidence. The guarantee that you will die if you are decapitated is this kind of guarantee. It is conceivable that you could keep everything going through the sudden intervention of an amazing surgeon or a spectacular machine. But you would be crazy to count on it. It is a pretty good guarantee. By contrast, a deductively valid argument provides a *logical* or *semantic* guarantee, which is a totally different sort of thing. If someone rolls a normal six-sided die, and you find out that the number that came up was even, this will *semantically* guarantee that the number was not three. You might call it a matter of definition. This is the kind of guarantee provided by a deductively valid argument; this is the sense in which you have already accepted the conclusion by accepting the supporting statements.

The peculiarly linguistic or definitional nature of deductive argument (sometimes called deductive inference) has allowed philosophers and mathematicians to build elaborate and elegant systems of deductive logic. These systems are capable of showing, for an enormous range of complicated and abstract arguments, whether they are deductively valid or not. The elegance of these systems sometimes tempts us to think that constructing them is all there is to reasoning. It will become clear very soon, however, that practical reasoning involves much that is not very elegant, and a great deal more than semantics. Deductive arguments will be employed in this text only when it seems helpful to do so.

But there is another extreme position that also must be resisted. Some philosophers have argued that inductive and deductive arguments are so radically different they should not be treated as the same kind of thing at all —perhaps should not both be called arguments (or inferences). And given our discussion in the first chapter, deductive arguments *are* rather peculiar arguments. The semantic or mathematical nature of the support they provide is radically different from the sort of support offered by what we usually call evidence. Nevertheless, as long as their systematic peculiarities are understood, there is no harm in treating valid deductions as arguments and schematizing them in the standard way. And doing so will turn out to be of great value to us in understanding certain aspects of our reasoning.

It is difficult to provide an introduction to the induction/deduction distinction without inadvertently encouraging one or the other of these opposite but equally mistaken temptations. Upon first encountering this distinction, some people are tempted to think of deductive arguments as intrinsically trivial semantic games, with no value for practical reasoning. Others are so taken by the tightness of the deductive link that they dismiss inductive arguments as poor substitutes for the real thing, to be avoided whenever possible. Although each is understandable, both temptations must be avoided. This section and the next are devoted to furthering our understanding of the distinction, aimed in part at removing those temptations.

The chart below provides a neat picture of the correlative features of induction and deduction.

RIVAL CONCLUSIONS

The last item of the chart introduces a new notion: *rival conclusions.* This notion allows us to turn the induction/deduction distinction into a useful tool

	INDUCTION	DEDUCTION
Schematic picture	S_1 S_2 S_3 ——— C	S_1 S_2 S_3 ——— C

Support relation (answer to Question II)	(In a good inductive argument)
	
	S_1, S_2, and S_3 provide evidence for C.
	
	If S_1, S_2, and S_3 are true, C will be one of a range of things:
	  –the best bet in the circumstances, but risky
	  –a good bet
	  –very likely true
	  –virtually certain
		(In a valid deductive argument)
		
		S_1, S_2, and S_3 provide a sematic guarantee of C.
		
		If S_1, S_2, and S_3 are true, C cannot possibly be false; we are already committed to the truth of C. (Accepting the truth of S_1, S_2, and S_3, yet denying C is self-contradictory.)

Other rival conclusions	Some always compatible with supporting statements, although sometimes only bizarre ones.	All semantically eliminated, even bizarre ones.

for argument analysis. Since it will dominate the next two chapters, it is important to be clear about it right from the start. Be sure this section is clear before going on to the rest of Part One.

When evaluating an argument, we may begin by asking why these particular supporting statements are being brought to bear on this particular conclusion. They might have been offered in support of all sorts of conclusions; why this one? Practical arguments usually have a purpose; they do not occur in a vacuum: they arise in a specific context and for a certain reason. And the reason can always be formulated as a *question* the argument is being used to *answer*. When we offer the argument

$$S_1$$
$$S_2$$
$$====$$
$$C$$

we are saying that S_1 and S_2 recommend C as the right answer to the question. It is this question that brings support and conclusion together.

The argument of the Warren Commission Report is trying to answer the question "Who shot President Kennedy?" The arithmetic argument at the end of the last chapter can be thought of as answering the question "What is the fourth power of 0.9?" We will normally be able to dig out of the context some question such as this, which an argument is being constructed to answer.* The conclusion, C, offered by the argument will then be one of the answers to that question. But there will of course be other, distinct answers to the question, and these may be thought of as C's *rivals:* the contrasting possibilities in that context. In choosing C from the list of possible answers, the argument may be taken to be urging the acceptance of C in preference to its rivals. This is what it means to say that the argument offers C as the *right* answer to the question, on the basis of the support in contains.

For the following analysis we will always need some question to fill this role. And a moment's reflection will reveal that we will always be able to formulate at least one appropriate question: "Is C true?" When the context is austere, and we know very little, we will sometimes be forced to this question as the ultimate fallback position. And occasionally this question will be good enough. But very often we can find a more helpful, more specific question than this; and when we can, it is in our interest to do so. For the fallback question ("Is C true?") has only two answers, "yes" and "no"; but "no" lumps together many different things it is often helpful to distinguish. That is, C can be false in many different *ways,* and these different ways are frequently of primary interest in the context of the argument. It might be false to say Oswald shot Kennedy, but in most contexts that automatically raises the question "Who did?" "Not-Oswald" lumps together everybody else.

---

*We will *always* be able to find *some* appropriate question; but sometimes it will be less than certain that it corresponds to the original intent of the argument.

We are now in a position to see the general strategy for argument analysis used in this book. To begin, we must understand the context in which the argument is offered well enough to determine the *implicit question* the argument (and in particular, its conclusion) is designed to answer. (A frequently useful device in this determination is to ask yourself what question the conclusion *sounds* as if it is answering in this context.) When we have the question, we are then able to form the list of possible conclusions—possible answers—from which the argument must choose. Sometimes both the forming and the choosing will be easy, but often enough one or the other will require some care. The next few pages are devoted to the issues that arise in forming the list; all the rest of Part One is devoted to choosing the best answer.

The list of distinct answers to the implicit question might best be described as the list of *mutually* rival conclusions—conclusions that rival each other, and from which the argument must select. The argument will normally choose one, which we have been calling C, as its conclusion; and then the list may be described as we did above: C plus its rivals, C's rivals simply constituting the remainder of the list when C is removed from it. Schematically:

$$\begin{array}{c} S_1 \\ S_2 \\ \text{Argument} \quad S_3 \\ \hline\hline \\ C \end{array}$$

Argument and Context ——————(yields)——————→ Implied Question, Q.

Q ——————(yields)——————→ List of distinct possible answers.

Equivalent Lists:

$$\begin{matrix} \text{List of distinct} \\ \text{possible answers} \end{matrix} \equiv \begin{matrix} \text{List of mutually} \\ \text{rival conclusions} \end{matrix} \equiv \begin{matrix} \text{C plus list of} \\ \text{C's rivals} \end{matrix}$$

$$\begin{Bmatrix} A_1 \\ A_2 \\ A_3 \\ A_4 \\ \cdot \\ \cdot \\ \cdot \\ A_n \end{Bmatrix} = \begin{Bmatrix} C_1 \\ C_2 \\ C_3 \\ C_4 \\ \cdot \\ \cdot \\ \cdot \\ C_n \end{Bmatrix} = \begin{matrix} C_3 \\ \begin{Bmatrix} C_1 \\ C_2 \\ C_4 \\ \cdot \\ \cdot \\ \cdot \\ C_n \end{Bmatrix} \end{matrix} \begin{matrix} = \quad C \\ \\ \\ = \quad \text{C's rivals} \end{matrix}$$

The most important formal property of the mutual rivals is that they are logically incompatible with each other. (C's rivals are incompatible with C and with each other too.) In other words, only one conclusion on the list can be true, only one answer can be right. If one turns out to be true, that logically rules out all the others. To assert two at once is self-contradictory. This is what it means to call them distinct answers, and this is what it means to call them rivals here.

For example, "What is the fourth power of 0.9?" has an infinite number of properly formed answers, namely all the numbers. The argument at the end of the last chapter picked 0.6561 out of all the numbers as the right answer. And by the nature of the case, if this is the right answer, all the other possible answers are *wrong* answers—another way of saying that the answers are incompatible: only one can be right. "Are the angles equal?" by contrast, has only two rival answers: "yes" and "no." They too are obviously incompatible; they cannot both be right. In a specific case we might formulate a geometrical argument that would support one answer, one rival conclusion, over the other.

Mathematical examples make nice illustrations because the rivals are neatly ordered and easy to state. They do not raise the worst complications. A further order of difficulty arises, however, when we consider arguments with substantive conclusions: rivals describing various aspects and happenings of our daily affairs. For descriptions of such things may always be given in more or less detail; different things may be lumped together or split apart depending on what we are concerned about. Even after we determine the implicit question, we still must decide how, and how finely, to chop up the list of answers. If we ask someone with a broken leg, "What happened?" a satisfactory reply might be "Skiing accident" even though that covers an enormous number of different things. We may not care about all the possible ways and places and times one could break a leg skiing, so discriminating this case from all the others like it, in great detail, would be boring and irrelevant. The list from which we wish to choose an answer would include 'fell down the stairs', 'shot myself while hunting', 'automobile accident', 'fell off my skateboard', and others like these. Each of these answers may be divided up almost indefinitely into further distinct answers, just like the first. If he fell down a flight of stairs, he did so at a specific time and place and in a certain way (trajectory and tumble); so each of the *other* possible ways and places and times he could have done it become other distinct—distinguishable—answers to the question. How much detail is appropriate, how finely to chop up the list, depends once again on practical features of the context—preeminently the purpose of the argument: why it was offered in the first place.

Let us exercise all this by applying it to the Kennedy assassination argument we have been examining. The question implicit in the Warren Commission's argument is "Who shot President Kennedy?" and the answer we have been considering—the conclusion the report offers—is "Oswald shot Kennedy." What are the rival conclusions for this argument (that is, what are the other, distinct answers to the implicit question which this one rules out)? The most complete list of mutually exclusive rivals would include all individuals, taken individually, and then all the possible group theories that could be constructed. In other words, following 'Oswald shot Kennedy', the first part of the list would be 'I shot Kennedy', 'Agent 3461 shot Kennedy', 'LBJ shot Kennedy', and so forth. The second part of the list would combine the individuals into groups, 'Oswald and I shot Kennedy', etc.*

Of course there is one further answer—another rival conclusion: 'nobody'. It is possible, despite appearances, that nobody shot President Kennedy. This would be so if what looked like bullet fragments were actually space debris; or, if they really were bullets, but ones accidentally or spontaneously discharged. So, after the individuals and the teams, a complete list would have to conclude with the catchall answer 'nobody'.

Now, this list obviously contains much more detail than would be relevant for most purposes. Looking at the list from the point of view of the original argument, C's rivals (the other conclusions on the list) simply give the different ways in which C might be wrong. But wrong is wrong, and sometimes we might not need to discriminate the rivals (ways) in such detail: we might wish to slice the pie into bigger pieces, lumping together whole ranges and categories of the original list.

For many purposes we would make a single division of the list, forming just two rival conclusions. We might, for example, be interested in a simple up or down on the original conclusion: Oswald did it acting alone, or no. So we would divide the list into just two mutual rivals, C and not-C, lumping all C's rivals on the original list into one super rival, not bothering to discriminate the different ways in which C might be mistaken. (This is recognizable as the ultimate fallback position of a few pages ago: it is sometimes just what we want.)

	Original List		*First Single Division*	
			(Warren Commission conclusion)	
	C_1		$C = C_3$	
	C_2			
	$C_3 (= C)$			C_1
	C_4			C_2
	C_5			C_4
	.			C_5
	.	not-C =	$\Bigg\{$	.
	.			.
	C_n			.
	Nobody			C_n
				Nobody

On the other hand, we might be interested in whether Oswald was involved in any way, alone or in complicity with others. This would naturally divide

*Bear in mind that the list must be constructed so that each entry is incompatible with every other entry in the manner discussed above. 'Oswald shot Kennedy' is on this list under the heading 'individuals', hence is to be understood, implicitly, as 'Oswald (alone) shot Kennedy'. It is thus incompatible with (its truth would rule out) 'Oswald and I shot Kennedy'.

the list in a slightly different way: into another conclusion C', lumping the original conclusion C, together with all the team theories including Oswald, as opposed simply to not-C, lumping together all the rest. An argument that Oswald was involved somehow or other would be an argument for C'.

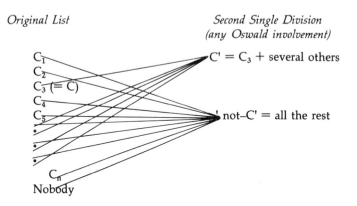

Original List   *Second Single Division*
                                   (any Oswald involvement)

C' = C_3 + several others

not–C' = all the rest

Other single divisions might be just as interesting. We might, for example, be interested in whether a federal agency was involved. So we would collect together all the items on the original list that include a federal agent. Make that C'', and see whether it could be supported over its rival not-C'', which of course would simply include what was left of the list after federal agents were removed.

Multiple divisions still lumping together whole ranges of the original list would be constructed in similar fashion, also in response to our interest and other contextual considerations. We might divide the list into four rivals: crazies of the left, crazies of the right, politically neutral crazies, and all the rest. But perhaps the most common multiple division would include a number of specific suspects, say Oswald and one or two other people, and then lump the rest of us together under the heading 'somebody else', and add 'nobody' as the final category.

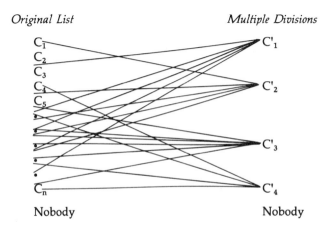

Original List   *Multiple Divisions*

Nobody   Nobody

One other feature of the list deserves comment. The final, catchall conclusion 'nobody' itself represents an indefinitely large collection of distinct states of affairs, lumped together because they in some sense provide the *same* answer to the implicit question. But it is actually a little strange to call "nobody" an answer to the question "Who shot President Kennedy?": it is more accurately a rejection of the question. Asking "Who shot the President?" presupposes somebody did. Answering "nobody" rejects that presupposition, and hence the question. This is not to suggest that "nobody" does not belong on the original list: since it is one of the possibilities, it is one of the rivals and hence an answer in the required sense. But if our argument does support this rival, if we do find reason to think nobody did it, that does challenge the context from which we retrieved the original question. When this happens it will usually be natural to *change* the question—the new context offers a slightly different implicit question. If nobody shot the President, then *just what did happen?*

Changing the implicit question always changes the argument somewhat, because different questions have different possible answers, and that affects the list of rivals. But in this case we are merely asking a more general question, so the effect on the list of rivals is subtle. The answers on the original list are still relevant, but so are many others: all the different possibilities under the heading 'nobody' now become distinct rivals, distinct answers to the new question. Space debris may be distinguished from spontaneous discharge and a host of others. Furthermore, each of the rivals on the original list may now be broken down into many distinct rivals: each different way in which Oswald could have shot the President is now a different answer to the new question. The simple statement "Oswald shot Kennedy" covers an enormous number of different answers to the more general question "What happened?" He could have done it from slightly different places, at slightly different times with a variety of weapons, each with the same result.

This new proliferation of rivals places an even greater burden on the practical context, but they can be handled just as before. Our interest, and other relevant considerations, can be used to collect the (now virtually infinite number of) rivals into groups we can handle. 'Space debris' is one such category: an indefinitely large number of different sources, velocities, angles, and substances is collected under that heading. For many purposes, lumping them all together under 'space debris' would be adequate; for others, it would be enough to say a little something about their source: 'probably part of a returning satellite'. A thorough investigation might wish to pursue the matter in elaborate detail, chopping up this rival into finer and finer pieces—talking about specific bits of particular satellites on exact trajectories, and the like. But in even the most thorough investigation we would not resolve these microrivals past our capacity to detect the difference. It would be silly to separate rivals by trajectory differences of a thousandth of an inch, or by exact rotational position of the individual pieces as they fall through the atmosphere. So even here practical considerations place an upper limit on the multiplication of rivals. But we go into this much detail only when it is useful to do so. Otherwise practical considerations require us to keep it uncomplicated. *We stop at the coarsest, least-refined level we can get away with.*

Original List	*New possible rivals opened up by new question*
C_1	$C_1a\ C_1b\ C_1c\ C_1d\ C_1e\ \ldots$
C_2	$C_2a\ C_2b\ C_2c\ C_2d\ C_2e\ \ldots$
C_3	$C_3a\ C_3b\ C_3c\ C_3d\ C_3e\ \ldots$ (all the different ways Oswald could have done it)
C_4	etc.
C_5	
•	
•	
•	
C_n	
Nobody	Space debris$_a$, space debris$_b$, $\ldots$ Spontaneous discharge$_a$, spont. disch.$_b$, $\ldots$ etc.

Example of coarse practical list under new question

C_3	Oswald did it, alone
C_A	Somebody else did it, alone or with help
C_B	Space debris
C_C	Something else happened

(Notice that this list contains all of the original rivals, simply lumped together into four categories: four super-rivals.)

We may now helpfully reformulate the induction/deduction distinction using our new understanding of rival conclusions. An argument consists of a collection of statements being offered in support of a conclusion.

$$
\begin{array}{c}
S_1 \\
S_2 \\
S_3 \\
==== \\
C
\end{array}
$$

And C is one of a list of mutually rival conclusions, determined by the argument's implicit question.

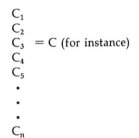

$$C_1$$
$$C_2$$
$$C_3 \quad = C \text{ (for instance)}$$
$$C_4$$
$$C_5$$
$$\cdot$$
$$\cdot$$
$$\cdot$$
$$C_n$$

Now the supporting statements, S_1, S_2, S_3, may themselves be logically incompatible with one or more of the conclusions on this list. That is, the support claims may, just by the way they are stated, semantically conflict with one or another of these rivals. If it were C_4, for example, then asserting S_1, S_2, S_3, and C_4 all together would be self-contradictory. The clearest illustration of this would again be almost trivial: suppose, for example, that S_3 simply *is* the denial of C_4, then the contradiction would be apparent.

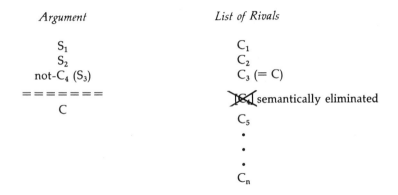

Argument	List of Rivals
S_1	C_1
S_2	C_2
not-C_4 (S_3)	C_3 (= C)
=======	~~C_4~~ semantically eliminated
C	C_5
	$\cdot$
	$\cdot$
	$\cdot$
	C_n

The conflict need not be so explicit, of course. In the Kennedy assassination case, we might discover that a certain Sally Smith was not in Dallas on the day of the assassination. This alone would not semantically conflict with saying Sally was the assassin, it would just make it a long shot. However, if we add to the support claims both that Sally was not in Dallas on that day *and* that whoever shot President Kennedy *was* in Dallas on that day, these two statements together would semantically conflict with the claim that Sally did it. These two statements together already say that Sally did *not* do it, and hence would contradict any rivals that say she did it, alone or together with anyone else.

In all such cases we can say that the rival or rivals in semantic conflict with the supporting statements are semantically eliminated by those statements. To declare the supporting statements true is automatically to declare the rivals in semantic conflict with them false. Their falsity is already contained in the support. So a deductively valid argument is very easy to characterize in these terms. It is an argument in which the supporting statements logically eliminate *all* the conclusions on the list except the one it takes as its own conclusion. Conversely, if so much as *one* of C's rivals is compatible with the support offered for C, then the argument for C is *not* deductively valid. This is standardly used as a test of validity—or proof of invalidity. If you can think of a rival that is compatible with the support, that shoots down the argument as deductive. If you cannot, that is some evidence that the argument is deductively valid.

What we have been calling 'inductive' arguments, then, are simply the arguments that do *not* eliminate all rivals to their conclusion by semantic means alone: arguments in which both C and one or more of its rivals are compatible with the supporting statements. (Again, not all such arguments will be interesting, but that is not important here: some will be.) The supporting statements of an inductive argument may—and typically will—eliminate some members of the list semantically, simply as a matter of how they are expressed. But inductive arguments are the ones in which there are some other members of the list left to choose among even after all linguistic considerations have been exhausted. Our preference for C in these cases will have to appeal to something further. Just what we appeal to is the subject of the following chapter. For now it is important only to understand the difference.

The following chart contains examples of the most typical inductive and deductive arguments you will encounter in a variety of contexts. They are meant to firm up your grasp of the points we have been discussing; so, as an exercise, try to state the 'implicit question' and some rival conclusions for each of these arguments. For each inductive argument be sure to formulate at least one rival that is compatible with the support claims: that is, one that could be true even if things are as the supporting statements claim. In the first inductive argument, for example, if we take the implicit question to be "What happened to the biscuit I dropped?" a rival to C would be that it fell through a cleverly concealed trapdoor which closed quietly and immediately after allowing the biscuit to tumble through. This would be compatible with the support claims as long as the biscuit by my foot could have gotten there in any other way. And since nothing in the support semantically eliminates the possibility that it was lying there all along, or that the waiter dropped it, compatibility is assured. The trapdoor rival is of course incredibly implausible —that will always be the case with strong inductive arguments. It is nevertheless not eliminated semantically. The skill required to distinguish deductive arguments from strong inductive ones is precisely the ability to discriminate the contradictory from the bizarre.

DEDUCTIVE SUPPORT AND THE QUESTION OF CERTAINTY

As remarked earlier, we may be tempted to think that because the deductive link is so tight we should always use deductive arguments instead of

(STRONG) INDUCTIVE ARGUMENTS	(VALID) DEDUCTIVE ARGUMENTS
(S$_1$) While eating dinner alone, I clumsily dropped a biscuit on the floor and it rolled under the table.	(S$_1$) All men are mortal.
	(S$_2$) Socrates is a man.
(S$_2$) I immediately looked under the table and saw a biscuit lying by my foot; nothing else appeared at all unusual.	(C) Socrates is mortal.
	(S$_1$) All cubes have twelve edges.
	(S$_2$) The planet Earth is a cube.
(C) The biscuit under the table was the one I dropped.	(C) The Earth has twelve edges.
	(S$_1$) I am not quite six feet tall.
(S$_1$) The PSA 727 and the Cessna 172 collided in midair.	(C) I am less than seven feet tall
(S$_2$) A short time later the PSA jet crashed in a nearby neighborhood.	(S$_1$) $X = 2Y$
(C) The collision caused the crash.	(C) $Y = 1/2X$
(S$_1$) Every winter since I've lived in Buzzard Gap we've established at least one, usually three or four, overnight low temperature records.	(S$_1$) Some criminal robbed the Russell mansion.
	(S$_2$) Whoever robbed the Russell mansion either had to break in or had an accomplice among the servants.
(C) This coming winter we will establish at least one overnight low temperature record.	(S$_3$) To break in one would have to either smash the door or pick the lock.
	(S$_4$) Only an expert locksmith could have picked the lock.
(S$_1$) The car was riding along just fine until Joe heard a muffled *pop*!	(S$_5$) Had anyone smashed the door he would have been heard.
(S$_2$) The car immediately became more difficult to control and the ride deteriorated badly, ending in a series of lurid wobbles as Joe slowed to a stop on the shoulder.	(S$_6$) Nobody was heard.
	(S$_7$) If the criminal who robbed the Russell mansion managed to fool the guard; he must have been a convincing actor.
(S$_3$) Examination reveals the right rear tire to be halfway off the rim, grotesquely shredded, and too hot to touch.	(S$_8$) No one could rob the Russell mansion unless he fooled the guard.
	(S$_9$) No criminal could be both an expert locksmith and a convincing actor.
(C) The *pop* was a blowout.	

(S_1) In a large and reasonably random sample of eligible voters, 64% say they are going to vote for Baker in next week's primary.

(C) Baker will win the primary.

(S_1) My mechanic says my motor needs to be rebuilt.

(S_2) He's always been extremely fair in his dealings with me and everybody I know.

(S_3) He's trained at the factory and all the work he has done for me has been satisfactory over the years.

(S_4) The clatter from my engine has been getting louder lately and oil consumption had been going up too.

C   My motor needs to be rebuilt.

(C) Some criminal had an accomplice among the servants.*

(S_1) $X - 2Y + 4 = 0$
(S_2) $2X - Y - 4 = 0$

(C) $Y = 4$

Although this last argument is deductively valid, that fact is not obvious to very many people. Like the arithmetic calculation at the end of Chapter 1 (which, incidentally, was also deductively valid), some steps must be interposed to show that the argument is valid—to show that Y does equal four. Steps most of us could reliably judge would be the following.

$X = 2Y - 4$ (S_1, adding $2Y - 4$ to each side)
$4Y - 8 - Y - 4 = 0$ (S_2, substituting the above expression for X)
$3Y = 12$ (Rearranging the above)
$Y = 4$

This is the sort of thing referred to above as 'semantic unpacking.'

*Example taken from I.M. Copi, *Introduction to Logic*, 2d ed. (New York: Macmillan, 1968), p. 334. This example is analyzed in Appendix A; but wait until you finish the following section before consulting that analysis.

inductive ones wherever possible. This is sometimes put by saying that deductive arguments make their conclusions certain, while inductive ones make their conclusions at best probable. But this is an important misunderstanding. The support an argument provides for its conclusion depends not merely on how tight the link is between support and conclusion; it depends as well on how plausible the supporting statements themselves are. How good an argument is depends on the answers to both Questions I (truth) and II (link), not II alone. Deductively valid arguments with implausible support claims provide practically no support for their conclusions (consider, for example, the twelve-edged Earth example in the last chart); while good inductive arguments from established support claims establish their conclusions as virtually certain (e.g., the PSA collision example).

In the practical matter of trying to provide support for some conclusion C, the idea is to get the best combined score on Questions I and II, with supporting statements that are readily available. Sometimes the supporting statements that naturally form inductive arguments are collectively so much better established than those required to make an argument for C deductively valid, that they easily compensate for the slightly looser link of a good induction. This is so in large measure because deductive arguments often require very general support claims to eliminate all conceivable rival conclusions semantically. And these very general statements are typically much more risky than the usual sort of evidence found in an inductive argument.

Consider, for instance, the following case. You get in your car one morning and attempt to start it; you can hear the starter cranking the engine, but the engine does not start. You then notice that the fuel gauge, which has been working properly, reads "empty." All this provides very strong support for the conclusion that the car is out of gas. But it is still *conceivable* that it is not out of gas. The data we have do not conflict semantically with the possibility that there is plenty of gas and the gauge is stuck on empty for some other reason: cars sometimes fail to start even when they have adequate fuel. The rivals here are long shots (which is just what it means to say the support for C is strong), but the mere fact that some are logically compatible with the support claims means that the argument you get by simply setting out the given data is inductive.

(S_1)   The starter turns the engine but the engine does not start.
(S_2)   The fuel gauge reads "empty."
(S_3)   The gauge has been working properly.

(C)   The car is out of gas.

This argument's implicit question is, obviously, "Why won't the car start?" And the list of distinct answers, rival conclusions, discriminated in a practical and orthodox way, would be something like the following.

C_1 Out of gas*
C_2 Wet ignition
C_3 Defective coil
C_4 Plugged fuel line
C_5 Faulty choke
C_6 Fouled spark plugs
C_7 Broken distributor cap
C_8 Starter won't work

*Bear in mind that since these are offered as rivals they must be constructed as incompatible: treated rather like the 'individual' candidates on the Kennedy assassination list. Combinations (choke and coil) would form separate rivals, neglected here because of implausibility.

Notice right away that C_8 *is* logically incompatible with the support claims. All it means for a starter to work is that it turns the engine over, and that much is explicitly stated in S_1. So C_8 is in semantic conflict with the support claims; it is semantically eliminated. Something in the support would have to be modified if we are to allow C_8 as a serious possibility. But this should not be surprising. The supporting statements of inductive arguments will often find themselves in semantic conflict with *some* answers to the implicit question. Some of the rivals will be semantically eliminated. Inductive arguments just do not eliminate them *all* semantically. And of course, C_1 through C_7 (and a long list of others not mentioned) are semantically compatible with the supporting statements: some are even live possibilities. So the argument is inductive.

Now we may construct a deductive argument in this case, and for this conclusion, simply by adding a fourth support claim that rules out all the remaining rival conclusions. The natural way to do this is to add the statement that whenever the three support claims listed above are true, the car is always out of gas. We would then have a deductively valid argument.

(S_1)   The starter turns the engine but the engine does not start.
(S_2)   The fuel gauge reads "empty."
(S_3)   The gauge has been working properly.
(S_4)   Whenever a car's engine cranks but will not start, and its fuel gauge, which has been functioning properly, reads "empty," then the car is *always* out of gas.

(C)   The car is out of gas.

But, of course, S_4 is certainly false: the rivals it conflicts with are long shots, but they certainly occur occasionally in cases like this. So the deductive argument provides C with no support at all—much less than the inductive one; it is just like the argument in the table on page 35 purporting to show that the Earth has twelve edges.

Though this last judgment may seem severe, it is important to see why it is proper. The deductive argument above contains within it the previous inductive one, and it is this inductive argument that is responsible for the residual support: the support that remains when the false S_4 is removed is no longer deductive *at all,* and that was the issue. The principle may be expressed as follows: If a deductively valid argument contains a false support claim, and the validity of the argument depends on that claim, then *as a deductive argument,* it provides no support for the conclusion. Its support claims may still be used in other arguments to provide support for the conclusion in question; but the original deductive argument is dead as an item of support. This is why the inductive argument in the last illustration provides C with so vastly much more support than the deductive one.

CASTING ARGUMENTS

The fuel gauge example provides a good illustration of another basic point as well: that arguments concerning substantive matters of fact may usually be cast either deductively or inductively depending on our whim or our interest. That is, if you are given some information relevant to a certain conclusion, and can appeal to general background knowledge, a little imagination will usually allow you to formulate several different arguments for the conclusion, some inductive and some deductive. Every argument on the left-hand side of the last chart may be 'turned into' a deductive one in a way much like the fuel gauge case. In the air crash example, one interesting way to eliminate all rival conclusions semantically, and hence make the argument deductively valid, would be as follows.

(S_1) The PSA 727 and the Cessna 172 collided in midair.
(S_2) A short time later the PSA jet crashed in a nearby neighborhood.
(S_3) The collision is a possible cause of the crash.
(S_4) The crash was caused by something.
(S_5) There were no other possible causes present.

(C) The collision caused the crash.

Although this reconstruction is interesting in a number of ways (about which more shortly), in tightening the link between C and the Ss we have once again resorted to a very general and hence very risky claim, namely S_5. In plane crash investigations there are usually a number of cause candidates present even though one may stand out as the overwhelming favorite. So in the collision example it is a very long shot to suppose the investigators will find no other possible causes. That means the deductive argument provides very weak support for C: a crucial support claim is very likely false. Furthermore, if it did turn out that S_5 actually was false, given the nature of the case, this might have no effect whatever on the support C gets from the inductively formulated version of the argument (the other possibilities might be long shots), while it would obviously destroy the deductive one. (For further discussion of this point see Appendix A.)

Just as the normal inductive argument may be converted into a deductive one by appropriate addition of supporting statements, the usual deductive argument, so long as it concerns questions of empirical fact of the sort inductive arguments deal with (as opposed, for example, to matters of logic, mathematics, or pure semantics), may be converted into an inductive argument for the same conclusion by *replacing* some support claims with others. In the most useful cases the general statements required for deductive validity may be replaced by the evidence we have for them.

(S₁)   All men are mortal.
(S₂)   Joe is a man.

(C)   Joe is mortal.

may be converted into

(Evidence for S₁)

> The oldest people today are about the same age as the oldest people of any period in recorded human history; there are no well-authenticated cases of people living over 114 years, and none even poorly authenticated over 138—this in spite of reasonably good records in many parts of the world for millennia.
>
> As well as the aging process is understood, it seems pretty clearly downhill after about age twenty for humans: parts gradually wear out and disease is increasingly difficult to overcome.
>
> Dramatic advances in medical technology have had little impact on normal longevity. As we overcome some problems, others take their place at an increased rate as we age.

(Evidence for S₂)   Joe appears in every way a normal human being: behavior, physiognomy, history.

(C)   Joe is mortal.

In this illustration both support claims have been converted, but the resulting argument would have been inductive had only one been replaced by its evidence. (Can you state why in a sentence or two?)

The importance of all this lies in the recognition that the substance of our reasoning does not come pre-cast into our argumentative forms and categories. How we characterize the material and how we cast the arguments depends on very practical aspects of the context, our interests and purposes not least of all. Inductive and deductive arguments have systematically different roles to play in our reasoning—their properties suit them for different functions. We have seen that in practical contexts deductive validity often requires very general statements that are themselves not well supported. So the uncomplicated, prototypical cases of evidence evaluation are virtually always best cast inductively. But as we will see in the following chapters, when the support picture becomes complicated, the logical and semantic relationships grounding deductive inference sometimes help structure the complicated picture. The support inevitably rests on inductive steps somewhere or other, but a deductive organization often shows how the evidence hangs together in support. Such hybrid arguments are usually a variation on—perhaps a com-pounding of—the following structure:

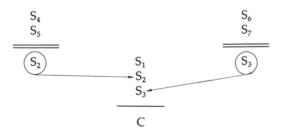

In this picture the immediate supporting argument is deductive; but it pro-vides support only because of evidence we have for S_2 and S_3. If you accept the deductive reconstruction of the San Diego air crash case, for example, it must be because you have some evidence for S_5.

In some contexts, this systematizing role of deduction can be of immense value: it can display interrelationships that clarify the support picture. In the abstract argument schematized above, for example, C rests ultimately on S_1, S_4, S_5, S_6, and S_7. But it might well be very puzzling to list simply these claims as C's support. That is, the argument

$$S_1$$
$$S_4$$
$$S_5$$
$$S_6$$
$$S_7$$
$$\overline{\overline{}}$$
$$C$$

might be confusing, or totally unclear: we might not be able to see *how* those five claims support C. In such a case, breaking the argument into several interrelated ones focused on a deductive central argument, as we did above, may be just what is required to make the support clear. Structuring the argument in this hybrid way, and interposing the intermediate support claims S_2 and S_3, is valuable if it achieves that end.

There is another important role for deductive argument in reasoning, one not directly related to supporting conclusions. It is often important to trace the *ramifications* of a certain position. You may be considering whether to accept a statement, or a collection of them, and be interested in investigating their commitments—their consequences. What follows from taking some position, what would I be committed to if I accepted it? For this purpose, you might be well advised to take the statement or statements in question, to-gether perhaps with others you already know to be true, and to deduce some interesting consequences. To this end you might use mathematics, if it is applicable, or some formal deductive mechanism the logicians have invented; or you might just use your common sense and native resourcefulness to eliminate rival conclusions semantically in a plausible way. In science it is relatively common to test a hypothesis by throwing it together with some plausible background assumptions to deduce some consequences (often with the help of mathematics), and then to check around to see if those consequences are true. If Hooke's Law holds of a certain wire, then doubling the weight hanging from the wire should stretch the wire so many millimeters. We can check the hypothesis that the law holds by checking the millimeters. The interest here is not in supporting any particular consequence, but rather in investigating the hypothesis. In the deductive argument the hypothesis is above the dividing line: it is part of the support.

The two properties of deductive arguments we have just examined—their systematicity and value in tracing ramifications—combine to suit them for yet another task: the structuring of investigations. The ability to relate statements to one another and derive consequences can be especially valuable in deciding what data to take. The deductive structuring of the air crash case does in a way reflect the structure of normal disaster investigations. The major questions concern just what the possible causes are and which ones were present. Such an argument may or may not structure the eventual results of such an investigation, but it can be helpful either way.

We will not treat deductive inference in any further detail in this book. The deductive steps required in practical reasoning are relatively straightforward semantic or arithmetic ones, and they will be clear enough in the contexts in which they are needed. The more exotic ones are studied in great detail in formal logic courses and you may wish to pursue that study. The point to remember is that the tightness of the deductive link is no shortcut to support strength. Determining the strength of support raises questions concerning the basic inductive procedure: the evaluation of evidence.

EXERCISES

A. Review Questions
1. Explain in a sentence or two why the truth of the supporting statements is irrelevant to the validity of a deductive argument.
2. Why are practical arguments in support of substantive conclusions most naturally cast inductively?
3. What happens when you assert the support claims of a valid deductive argument (that is, accept them as true) and at the same time deny its conclusion? In other words, what is the reliable consequence of such a joint assertion-and-denial that you would normally not wish to accept?

4. Even when we can support a conclusion with a deductive argument, there are two distinct reasons we might still be interested in inductive support for that conclusion. What are they?

5. Reread the inductive version of the gas gauge argument discussed on p. 37. Suppose we wish, for whatever reason, to take seriously the possibility that in spite of appearances the starter really is not working. What modest redescription of the supporting data will eliminate the semantic conflict between that rival and the support claims?

B. Arguments

1. For each of the arguments in the chart on pages 34–35 write down the most plausible implicit question: avoid the "ultimate fallback" question unless you cannot find a more helpful one. Then provide at least one *rival* conclusion; that is, give one answer to the implicit question other than the conclusion offered by the argument. For the deductive arguments explain as well as you can why the rival you wrote down is semantically incompatible with the support claims. You may appeal to direct semantic conflict, as well as the 'containment' and 'unpacking' metaphors, as long as what you say might help somebody understand it.) For the inductive arguments, explain why the rival you wrote down —or some other one—is semantically compatible with the support claims.

2. Consider the following passage:

On the evening of January 24, 1978, several residents of a barren area of the Northwest Territories reported a spectacular fireball over Baker Lake, a body of water just west of Hudson Bay. For several weeks U.S. tracking stations had been warning that a Soviet satellite, possibly containing a nuclear reactor, had dropped very low in its orbit and was likely soon to fall into the atmosphere. Its orbit would have taken it over northern Canada about the time the fireball was reported to have occurred. Later that same week the Russians admitted losing a nuclear-powered satellite, but added that the danger of nuclear contamination was remote. Shortly following this announcement, two geologists hiking down a river just east of Baker Lake discovered radioactive debris, of clearly human fabrication, poking out of a crater in the ice.

From all this, Canadian government officials concluded that the Soviet satellite had in fact returned to earth, burning up in the atmosphere in the vicinity of Baker Lake and showering that part of the Northwest Territories with radioactive debris.

This passage is inferentially complex, but we may extract from it the following argument:

(S₁)   The orbit of a nuclear-powered Soviet satellite was observed dropping dangerously close to the atmosphere.

(S₂)   The fireball observed over Baker Lake by local residents occurred at about the time its orbit would carry the satellite over that part of northern Canada.

(S₃)   Man-made radioactive debris was found the same week near Baker Lake, in a place the material could not have occupied for very long.

(C)   The fireball over Baker Lake was the returning Soviet satellite.

The natural question to take (C) to be answering in this context is "What was the fireball over Baker Lake?" So the argument is inductive, because there are many other answers to this question compatible with the support claims. (The argument is a rather good inductive argument too, but evaluative questions are left to the next chapter.) The fireball could have been merely a meteorite which came along at about the time the satellite passed over, and the satellite is still up there. The radioactive debris would then have to be from some other source: a hoax, perhaps, or something else coincidental. But these possibilities, though long shots, are not in semantic conflict with the support. All (S₃) says is the debris could not have been there very long; it could have come from anywhere. No *contradiction* is involved in saying it was dumped there by somebody trying to get rid of the results of a failed scientific experiment.

a. In arguments like this the implicit question may be thought of as a rival-story generator. For practice, provide some other uneliminated rivals (rival stories), describing them in enough detail to make it clear they are semantically compatible with the support given.

For the next three questions, suppose that there is a serious possibility that the fireball reports are themselves a cleverly orchestrated hoax designed to break the boredom of an arctic winter.

b. Why is the schematization offered above a bad one for allowing consideration of this possibility?

c. What simple change will remove this difficulty?

d. What rephrasing of the implicit question does this change require? (Note that answering this question is not mechanical: it requires some care and imagination).

3. (S₁)   For the past decade little Johnny has had difficulty breathing, tired easily, and was thought to be asthmatic.

(S₂)   Recently, physicians discovered a toy brick lodged in one of Johnny's lungs, apparently ingested years before.

(S₃)   When the brick was removed, Johnny's breathing difficulty vanished almost immediately.

================================

(C)   Johnny's breathing difficulty was due to the brick in his lung.

Taking this implicit question to be "What caused Johnny's breathing problem?":

a. State some rival conclusions.
b. Are any rivals (semantically) compatible with the support?
c. Is this argument inductive or deductive?
d. By altering or adding to the support, recast the argument as the other kind.
e. Is the new argument better than the first? Why or why not?

4. (S_1) All the important economic indicators are good.
   (S_2) When all the important economic indicators are good, the future of the economy will always be rosy, at least in the short run.

===================================

(C) The short-run future of the economy is rosy.

a. Is this argument inductive or deductive?
b. Cast it the other way as plausibly as you can.
c. Suppose that once, many years ago, all the important economic indicators were good just as the economy was plunging into a severe recession. Explain what difference there would be between the impact of this fact on the inductive version and its impact on the deductive version. That is, how would it affect the support provided for the conclusion in each case?

5. (S_1) Sally Robinson will be graduated from Millard Fillmore College next term, with a grade-point average just below 3.0.
   (S_2) Medical schools never have admitted a Millard Fillmore graduate whose grade-point average is below 3.5.

(C) Sally will not be admitted to medical school.

This argument is pretty obviously inductive (see if you can explain why in a sentence or two). It can be recast as a deductive argument simply by expanding (S_2) to read

(S_2') Medical schools never have and never will admit a Millard Fillmore graduate whose grade-point average is below 3.5.

a. Explain why the revised argument is deductively valid, by showing that denying (C) contradicts (S_1) and S_2').
b. In normal circumstances, which argument better captures the reason Sally might have for thinking she will not be admitted to medical school? Which argument would be stronger in these circumstances? Why?

6. As Steve hiked across the barren Nevada desert one cool autumn afternoon, he was increasingly impressed by the number of bleached and

weatherbeaten animal bones littering the trail he had been following since morning. To his anthropologically trained eye, they seemed to be the bones of large domestic mammals—horses and cows mostly. Farm animals! What could it be, he thought excitedly, but an ancient pioneer route to California? Thousands of families must have traveled this trail before railroads connected the coasts. Steve's heart raced as he squinted into the setting sun at the mountainous barrier ahead. What must it have been like for the first wagon through!

a. Schematize Steve's argument as efficiently as possible, omitting the peripheral padding.

b. What is this argument's implicit question?

c. Provide two rivals to Steve's conclusion (that is, two other answers to the question).

d. Is this argument inductive or deductive? Why?

7. In the six weeks immediately following an American Legion convention in Philadelphia, twenty-eight legionnaires who had attended died of remarkably similar illnesses. Yet in that time intensive investigation had failed to uncover any microbe or poison that could plausibly account for these deaths. It was therefore reasonable to conclude that this cluster of deaths was a statistical freak; that is to say, their occurrence all within a short period of time after the convention was mere coincidence.

a. Schematize this argument.

b. What is its implicit question?

c. Provide two rival conclusions that are compatible with the supporting statements.

3

Evidence

Our ability to evaluate deductive arguments depends on our *linguistic* skill: what we know about the meanings of words and the significance of sentences. Sometimes we can directly recognize a semantic guarantee, as we did in the simple syllogisms of the last chapter. But sometimes we detect such a guarantee indirectly, by semantically eliminating rival conclusions. In one way or another the test for deductive validity rests on our understanding the commitments of our words, the ramifications of what we say.

The skills we employ to evaluate inductive arguments are far more difficult to say anything useful about, however. Evaluating an inductive argument is a more complicated matter than judging the simple validity of a deduction, in part because choosing among the rivals raises questions of degree. Unlike deductive arguments, the link between support and conclusion in an inductive argument may vary in strength from relatively weak to very strong; and the argument can be useful anywhere in that range. In this chapter we undertake to say something helpful about the particular skills we employ to evaluate that link. Our task will be to say something that will usefully apply to the inductive arguments we encounter in practical contexts.

The strategy for accomplishing this task is straightforward. We will look carefully at some uncontroversial inductive inferences, cases in which the reasoning is clear, to see what principles are at work. These principles will then be used to build a technique for handling the more difficult cases, inferences about which we cannot so easily agree. This strategy is the strategy of practical argument sketched in Chapter 1: we progress by steps we are reasonably competent to handle. We resolve the tough cases into easy ones.

BACKGROUND

The evaluation of an inductive argument is always done against the background of our relevant knowledge: everything else we know about the matter being discussed is potentially relevant to evaluating the support being offered. If collisions with other aircraft actually made airplanes more air-worthy—like the weathering of raw recruits in actual combat*— the inductive inference in the PSA (jet crash) example would collapse. We judge that argument to be a good one in part because of what we know about airplanes and collisions. With a little imagination, the other inductive arguments may be used to make the same point.

Since background has as much impact on the strength of an argument as what is normally stated in the support claims, one might wonder why we do not explicitly include all the relevant background among the support claims. It turns out that there is very good reason to exclude most of our background knowledge from explicit mention: it is inexhaustibly boring. The distinction between support and background is a highly pragmatic one: it is largely a matter of convenience, emphasis, and other practical considerations. What we put down as support depends in part on what *needs* to be stated. It is completely proper simply to add some relevant detail of general knowledge to the support claims if our evaluation of an argument would be made easier by pointing it out. In some circumstances we might add to the fuel gauge example, as a fifth support claim, something we merely took for granted there: a car won't start if it is out of gas (S_5). This would be the inductive equivalent of interposing steps in a deductive argument: it would help us judge the strength of the argument without actually adding anything new.

The very practical nature of the distinction between (explicit) support and background should discourage us from trying to improve on our normal practice. Since we are perfectly free to add to the support claims anything we

---

*Staged collision might be part of the construction process having an effect analogous to the work-hardening of metal.

like, we should be careful to add only things that are important and helpful. A virtually inexhaustible supply of relevant detail may be added to nearly any inductive argument, most of it boring and not at all helpful in assessing the argument. Virtually everything we know about cars, engines, starters, gauges, gasoline, and perhaps even sounds is relevant to the fuel gauge case, even points of fine detail. If fuel gauges, rather like heaters, required that the engine be warm before they function properly, the inference would be demolished. They don't and that is relevant; but we need not mention that fact explicitly, nor myriad others just like it. They are all part of the presupposed background. It is important to avoid bogging down in the vast quagmire of relevant-but-uncontroversial detail, so we may have some hope of recognizing the significant factors for what they are. Explicit mention among the support claims is reserved primarily for *significant* matters, *helpful* considerations, *departures* from normal background assumptions.

Of course, what is background for somebody is not always background for everybody, and if an argument is intended to persuade others it must appeal only to *shared* background. Something one person might simply presuppose in reasoning for himself or herself might have to be explicitly mentioned among the support claims for someone else. The fuel gauge argument could be properly evaluated as it stands only among adults in automotive societies —and not even all of them. This is one way in which simple education helps us reason better: the more we know, the better able we are to judge support relations among statements. Conversely, the dependence of our reasoning on background also underlines the dangers of misinformation and miseducation: the ramifications of a faulty background are sometimes quite far-reaching. Whenever we admit something into our general body of knowledge too hastily, or without taking our biases into account, we open all relevant inferences to serious risk.

Another way of putting all this is that reasoning does not start from zero. Arguments increase our knowledge only by fashioning what we already know into support for something else. Like any other creative process, argument requires raw materials; it cannot create *ex nihilo* any more than an artist can create art without medium and materials.

In practical reasoning this is simply not a problem. In practice, inductive arguments occur in fairly well specified contexts, in which much of the background is clear, shared, and agreed upon. So, in the usual sort of controversy, establishing one side merely as firmly as the background which both sides share will effectively bring the controversy to an end. Supporting a conclusion only this well is doing very well indeed by the standards we all apply in leading our everyday lives. We will usually have done more than enough if we can establish that the car is out of gas as firmly as our general knowledge about cars, or if we can establish that Baker will win the primary as firmly as our general knowledge about elections and electorates. In this book we will never require more of an argument than this, and, it will turn out, an argument will often be of great value even if it falls far short of establishing its conclusion this well.

RIVAL CONCLUSIONS

Question II (the link question) asks how *much* support an argument provides for its conclusion. This is a quantitative question which is only very rarely answerable with any precision. Usually, if it can be answered at all, it will be on a very coarse scale of about five gradations: 'overwhelming', 'a lot', '50/50', 'a little', and 'almost none'. Even this limited precision will be valuable when it can be obtained, of course, and we will treat the quantitative aspect of Question II later in this chapter. But it is too difficult and uncertain a place to begin this discussion. It is better to start with an easier, nonquantitative question, which simply asks that we *compare* the conclusion at issue *with its rivals*. Various versions of this question will organize our entire discussion of evidence:

(R_1)   Do the support claims offered by the argument pick out *this* particular conclusion as the right answer to the implicit question?

In the last chapter we discussed the question that an argument 'implicitly' asks—e.g., "Who shot President Kennedy?" All the possible answers to this question were the rival conclusions of that argument. Now, part of what it means to offer a specific conclusion (C) as the conclusion of an argument is that its support claims do pick C out of all the rivals as the right answer to the argument's implicit question. So if the supporting statements actually back one of the others as a better answer than C, we would answer 'no' to R_1, and reject C as the conclusion. For this reason R_1 is actually more basic than the quantitative rendering of Question II, as well as easier to deal with. In this context, the quantitative question concerns how much better C is than the other answers to the implicit question. If C is actually not as good as some others, the quantitative question may be ignored.

So the most important thing to ask of an argument's support claims is that they provide some order among the argument's rival conclusions, especially concerning what is on top of the list. Finding Oswald's palm print on the rifle clearly elevated the answer 'Oswald shot Kennedy' to the top of the list of rival conclusions. It was not yet certain, but without further evidence, more complicated answers were clearly farther down the list. Accordingly, a more helpful way to ask the qualitative question (R_1) is

(R_2)   Given the supporting statements, which of the rival conclusions is best?

Answering this question will also answer R_1: if the answer to R_2 is 'C', then the answer to R_1 will be 'yes'; otherwise 'no'. For our purposes, R_2 is the single most important question to ask about an inductive argument. It yields an answer to the argument's implicit question; it can be answered even when the quantitative version of Question II cannot; and even when we can handle the quantitative question, R_2 is a necessary preliminary step. The answer to R_2 is often all we can know—and sometimes all we need to know. To mark the importance of R_1 and R_2, we will call an inductive argument *sound* if, for it, the answer to R_1 is 'yes'. That is, an inductive argument is sound if its conclusion is the *best of the rivals,* based on its support claims. How we show that is the subject of the next section.

DIAGNOSTIC SKILLS

Virtually everyone who has survived past infancy has a more or less well developed set of perceptual skills. These skills may be generally described as the ability to *tell what's going on* (sometimes) simply by seeing it (or hearing it or feeling it, or, to a lesser extent, smelling or tasting it). We can tell the door is open just by looking; we simply see that the oncoming car has crossed into our lane; we can tell what record is playing just by listening. The enormously rich experience we acquire simply in living our lives helps forge these perceptual skills into the far more general ability at the bottom of our empirical reasoning. This is the ability to tell what's going on—or what has gone on—even when we are not confronting it directly. We can often tell what has happened from the traces it leaves. We can tell there was a frost by the damaged trees; we know it has rained because the mountains are green; we can tell John had some trouble on the way home from the store by the rumpled fender and the broken headlight. We reconstruct the event from its telltale consequences. It is this diagnostic skill we exploit in the most basic sort of inductive arguments: it is the foundation of our ability to evaluate evidence.

The arguments that exploit this skill most directly are *diagnostic inductive arguments.* An argument is diagnostic if its implicit question is some version of "What's going on?" "What happened?" and "What caused this?" are versions of the general diagnostic question, so most of the inductive arguments we have looked at so far fall under this heading. "Who shot Kennedy?", "What was that *pop*?", and "What caused the crash?" are all diagnostic questions. Perhaps the most colloquial rendering of the question might be "What's the *story*?" (Why won't the car start?) This is a helpful way to put the question because in diagnostic arguments the rival conclusions may be thought of as abbreviations of rival stories: different stories about what happened, what's going on. Since these are the arguments that directly engage our basic diagnostic skills, it is natural to begin with these arguments in developing our understanding of induction. After we develop a systematic treatment of diagnostic inductive arguments, we will be able to extend that treatment to handle other inductive arguments.

A diagnostic problem always originates in some initial information, some data. Suppose Rocco the balloonist sets out from Nova Scotia in his hot-air balloon, planning to meet a friend on the Riviera. The next two days are stormy over the Atlantic, and when Rocco fails to show at his friend's villa, a search is organized. On the first day a coast guard cutter finds Rocco's gondola swamped and barely floating five hundred miles short of European landfall. In normal circumstances this would give us reason to think Rocco was dead: drowned in the North Atlantic. And our reason may be unpacked as a diagnostic induction.

The support claims can consist simply in laying out the data given concerning the trip, the weather, and the recovery of the gondola.

S_1 Rocco left Nova Scotia in a balloon.
S_2 The Atlantic was stormy.
S_3 His gondola was found a few days later, far at sea, swamped and empty.

The implicit question is simply "What happened to Rocco?", which is clearly diagnostic: just a specific version of the general diagnostic question "What is the story here?" And one of the answers is, obviously, "Rocco drowned." What are the other, distinct answers—the *rival* conclusions? They are the answers that *contrast with* this one, all the other things that could have happened to Rocco instead of drowning. Recall that the rivals are mutually incompatible: only one can be true. So although 'Rocco drowned' covers many things, there are lots of things it does not cover, and the rivals provide a list of those things. He might have fallen on the deck of a passing ship; set up a rendezvous with a Soviet submarine; been picked up by a flying saucer; swum to shore; teleported himself out of the galaxy; or he might still be out there somewhere, treading water.

On the relatively sketchy data we have, it would be natural to make the rivals fairly general, innocent of much detail. Although he could have fallen on the deck of a Liberian freighter, it would be silly at this stage to differentiate rivals into type of ship and country of registry when nothing in the data requires it. Even talking of falling on a ship, as opposed to near it and being hauled from the water, is best avoided. The appropriately general (super) rival that would include all such possibilities would be 'fortuitous rescue'. It is possible Rocco fell on a ship or some other inhabited thing out there, or near enough to one during calm enough weather to allow him to be hauled out of the water. All of this is best lumped together as the lucky-break rival. Similarly, rendezvous with a Soviet submarine is best lumped together with all such stories under some such heading as 'planned rendezvous.'

So all the reasonable possibilities, and a few unreasonable ones, would be included on the following list.

C_1 Rocco drowned at sea.
C_2 He was fortuitously rescued.
C_3 He accomplished a prearranged rendezvous.
C_4 He swam to shore.
C_5 He is still treading water.
C_6 He was teleported out of the galaxy.

Plausibility Ranking

The first component of our diagnostic skill can be seen in this list of rivals: sometimes, just given a bit of data, we are objectively able to rank a list of rival conclusions *in the order of their plausibility*. C_2 and C_3 are about equally plausible, and it could be argued that it is equally difficult to distinguish between C_4 and C_5. But given S_1, S_2, and S_3 (and assuming normal background knowledge), there is simply no question that C_1 is the best, the top of this list, and C_6 is the worst of these, and that the others fall somewhere in between. Diagrammatically,

Order
of
Plausibility

C_1
C_2 C_3
C_4 C_5
C_6

There is, of course, a practically unlimited number of rival answers at this level—that is, even without dividing these up more finely—many falling around C_3 or C_4 in plausibility. The reason to limit our attention to these six is simply to see how clearly we can judge relative plausibility in the easy cases, and that ordinary background knowledge is all that's required. Now, to complete the picture, to decide which of all the rival answers is best, requires an educated imagination. Once again this particular example makes it easy. We are all familiar enough with the subject matter and hence pretty good at cooking up stories like this; and the very best of the other rivals are in the C_2 to C_5 range in plausibility. Rocco could have landed in Europe undetected, put the gondola on an airplane, and had it dumped in the ocean. He might have died of a heart attack before hitting the water, and so on. But on the data we have, none of these is nearly as plausible as C_1. So making the reasonable assumption that we have thought of all the most plausible alternatives, we may confidently assert that the data we have supports C_1. In other words the argument we began to sketch above is *sound* when C_1 is chosen as its conclusion.

S_1	Rocco left Nova Scotia in a balloon.	Sound
S_2	The Atlantic was stormy.	Inductive
S_3	His gondola was found a few days later, far at sea, swamped and empty.	Argument

$$============================= d^*$$

C_1 Rocco drowned at sea.

This unpacks the earlier remark that, in normal circumstances, the data given here would be good reason to think Rocco dead.

Recall that a sound inductive argument does not have to be very strong. Saying an argument is sound only says that the conclusion is the best of the rivals, the most plausible answer to the implicit question. It could be only a very slight favorite and the support could be very light, in which case best would not be very good. The argument about Rocco is not one of these. The data offered not only support C_1, they support it very well. And we will eventually be able to say something about this quantitative judgment. But for now it is important to concentrate on the comparative questions R_1 and R_2, on the question of soundness. The Rocco argument would have been valuable had it merely been sound, and not very strong; it would have given reason to prefer one specific answer, one of the rival conclusions. That's what sound-ness is.

Before examining the second component of our diagnostic skill, two further aspects of this first component need brief discussion. We earlier saw that our background knowledge was crucial to our evaluation of inductive arguments. We can now see more clearly just how and why. For it should be clear that almost everything we know about balloons and storms and oceans and ships and espionage and even people is at least indirectly relevant to the plausibility ranking we gave various rival conclusions. If ship traffic on the Atlantic were as heavy as car traffic on the freeways out of Los Angeles on Friday night, C_2 would occur much higher in the rankings than it does, perhaps even challenging C_1 for the top spot. And greater general knowledge will increase our judgmental resolution, allowing us to decide finer differences in plausibil-ity. For example, studying the *Guinness Book of Records* and a little human physiology might well persuade us that C_4 and C_5 should be ranked closer to C_6 than C_3. In general the fact that we all share so much basic background allows us enormous agreement in plausibility ranking; this is what philoso-phers call "intersubjectivity": we can agree without prior consultation. This shared background, in other words, is why there are easy cases.

The next point emerges from this one. Arguments put forth in the public domain—in newspapers, handbills, on radio or TV, for example—if intended for public consumption, public evaluation, especially if intended for public

---

*For convenience a small 'd' will be inserted at the end of the double line to indicate that an inductive argument is diagnostic, when that fact is important or useful.

persuasion, may be legitimately taken to presume only generally shared background.* So we can use the first component of our diagnostic skill as a *test* for sound inductive arguments. As surprising as it sounds, inductive arguments that have never had R_1 or R_2 seriously asked about them are often put forth in public. Occasionally a very simple application of imagination will yield a conclusion as plausible as, or even more plausible than, the one offered. So the basic test of an inductive argument (at least one offered for public consumption) is to see if you can think of a rival conclusion that, on the support offered, is more plausible than the one given in the argument. The same test applies to exotic, technical arguments if you happen to have the relevant exotic, technical background. And of course, if a certain technical argument is very important to you, that would justify your making some effort to acquire the requisite background—to educate yourself—so that you could evaluate the argument.

An example of this test in action can be constructed on an argument offered by a traffic engineer of an unnamed Southern California city. This engineer observed that more pedestrians in his city were being killed at intersections that had crosswalks than at unmarked intersections. He inferred from this that crosswalks were hazardous, that their presence was causing pedestrian deaths, and went on to speculate that crosswalks must instill in pedestrians a false sense of security. But, on a moment's reflection, each of us is capable of constructing a rival conclusion—a rival answer to the question "Why are more pedestrians killed at marked intersections than unmarked ones?"—that is more plausible than the one offered by the engineer. Cities do not put crosswalks at intersections randomly. They systematically select the most heavily used intersections for the attention of their paint crews. So we should expect that there would be vastly more pedestrian traffic at marked intersections than at unmarked ones. That fact alone would account for the statistic offered by the engineer, even if crosswalks are far safer than unmarked intersections. Unmarked intersections could be substantially more hazardous than marked ones and still be the site of very few pedestrian fatalities simply because so few pedestrian crossings are made at unmarked intersections. As it stands, this conclusion is at the very least as plausible as the one originally offered, and hence the original argument is not sound.

If there is some peculiarity of the city in question that invalidates the test we have just applied, the traffic engineer has the responsibility to tell us about

---

*If an exotic background is required, an argument simply cannot be evaluated by people without that background—and offering it as though it can is at least unnecessarily confusing, and sometimes positively misleading. In more modest cases, a bit of exotic detail can be explicitly included among the support claims themselves, and this will allow those of us with ordinary backgrounds to evaluate an exotic argument. But since the arguer is our only source of this new background, we cannot simply presuppose it as we do normal background: it is just as important to ask Question I (the truth question) about it as about the other support claims.

it. If, for example, the city's lunatic traffic division paints crosswalks only on virtually unused intersections, that would radically alter the impact of the engineer's statistic. But it is also the sort of thing that is wholly unreasonable for us to suppose. Publishing the argument without mentioning such a bizarre fact would be simply malicious. Our evaluation must presume the author is being straight with us. What we really need to judge the relative safety of crosswalks is the ratio of deaths to pedestrian trips at the two types of intersections. Notice that if the two ratios were exactly the same—indicating no difference in hazardousness—the total number of deaths at each type of intersection would simply be proportional to the traffic. If there were, say, ten times as much pedestrian traffic at marked intersections, they could be one-fifth as hazardous (i.e., much safer) and still kill twice as many pedestrians as unmarked ones.

As a final point about the ranking of rival conclusions, it would be helpful here to review and extend the remarks in Chapter 2 concerning the divisibility of substantive rivals. We noted there that such conclusions may always be given in more detail, specified with greater precision. If Rocco drowned, he did so at a certain time and a specific spot on the surface of the earth. He had a certain relationship to the gondola and other ships on the Atlantic at the time. He was in a particular position and configuration, his vital signs deteriorated in a certain sequence, and his body began to decay in a certain way. The conclusion "Rocco drowned at sea" does not specify any of these things; it leaves them all open. And since every different specification along each of these dimensions represents a slightly different state of affairs, the general conclusion "Rocco drowned at sea" can be thought of as standing for not one, but a whole class of different conclusions. All the different ways and times and places of death, within a substantial range, are lumped together under the relatively general heading 'drowned at sea'.

Since there is usually an infinite amount of such detail which could be provided for any conclusion, we rely on practical considerations such as those we used in forming the original list to determine how much we need to supply—to determine how far we should go in distinguishing rival conclusions. One of the most important of these practical considerations is our *interest.* How specific a conclusion we need depends in large measure on what we wish to do with it—what we want it for. In Rocco's case, for his family, the bureau of vital statistics, or natural human curiosity, most of the detail beyond "drowned at sea" is unnecessary—certainly not worth the trouble to find out. There might be purposes for which we might need more information, but for the illustration here we will assume a relatively normal context. In general we must depend on pragmatic features of the context to determine the detail in which to provide the list of rivals—to determine how coarsely to lump them together or how finely to split them apart. For certain purposes, which we will examine in great detail later on, we will be interested only in a few broad categories of conclusions. That a particular conclusion falls in one or another of these categories will tell us all we want to know.*

Relevance

There are many circumstances in which we will not be satisfied simply to rank the rivals on the original data, pick the top one, and let it go at that. If the issue is very important to us, or if the argument, though sound, is not terribly strong, or if we are not confident in our ranking of the rivals, there is something we can do about it: collect more data. The second component of our diagnostic skill is our ability to gauge the *relevance* of further data to the plausibility ranking of our list of rivals.

Consider once again Rocco's adventure over the Atlantic. If Rocco's wife were to get a letter from Moscow in Rocco's handwriting containing the confession of a spy, details of a rendezvous with a submarine, and an apology for deceiving her, this would have a substantial effect on our ranking of the rivals. C_1 would not seem so clearly the best bet any longer. And if Rocco's wife were then to fly to Moscow and find someone there who looked and behaved just like Rocco and knew many things only she and Rocco could plausibly know, this would be enough to promote C_3 past C_1 to the top of our list of rival conclusions. If we were to add these two bits of data to our original support claims (as S_4 and S_5) we would have a new argument, one that would be in some obvious sense an improvement on the first one, but one that would be sound with C_3 as its conclusion.

S_1 Rocco left Nova Scotia in a balloon.
S_2 The Atlantic was stormy.
S_3 His gondola was found a few days later, far at sea, swamped and empty.
S_4 Rocco's wife received the letter from Moscow.
S_5 She went to Moscow and met someone who she was convinced was Rocco.
$$\rule{10cm}{0.4pt} = \text{d}$$
C_3 Rendezvous (which could now be made more specific if we like).

Similarly, we could change the ranking in favor of C_2 by adding (to the original data) that the skipper of a Norwegian freighter reported the discovery of a dazed man walking the deck of his ship during a storm, and giving enough information to identify Rocco (S_6). The point of discussing such cases in any detail is to show just what judgments we must make in evaluating inductive arguments, and to show just how clear and straightforward they are in practical contexts. What is relevant in such a case is often beyond dispute.

*In this case, for instance, if all we were interested in was whether Rocco was dead or alive, we could group all the possible descriptions of what happened into these two categories. There would then be only two rivals on the list: Rocco is dead (C), and Rocco is alive (not-C). These would include all those we considered in the original argument, just sorted into two huge groups, according to what they say about Rocco's life.

As too is irrelevance. The exact number of deaths per passenger mile on U.S. highways in 1967 would, by itself, have no effect on our ranking of the rivals in this case. Nor would the amount of change in my pocket or the weight of the Washington Monument. Somebody might be able to *show* their relevance, but it would certainly take some showing and we are right to be bored with those suggestions until such time.

An interesting variation would be to discover what might be called negative evidence. Suppose we found out that Rocco was a world-class water treader, prodigiously skilled at staying above water for long periods of time (S_7). This would drop C_1 but without elevating any other conclusion (even C_5) above it. S_7 would combine with the original data to yield a new argument (S_1, S_2, S_3, S_7 // C_1) for the original conclusion, which though sound would be (slightly) weaker than the original one.

Summary

Combining the points of the last few pages, it is best to think of diagnostic inductive arguments as stages in the dynamic procedure of investigation and discovery: a slice out of an ongoing process. A diagnostic problem is posed by some initial data; the expression of the problem yields our familiar 'implicit question', which determines what the rival conclusions are; and the initial data, together with our background knowledge, determine the plausibility ranking of the rivals. If one of the rivals is alone at the top of the list, we can construct a sound inductive argument by simply listing the initial data, drawing two lines, and writing that conclusion below. This is the first stage or slice—argument number one in a potential series. The technical jargon for the initial ranking of rivals is 'antecedent plausibility ranking'. 'Antecedent' here simply refers to the plausibilities before we begin looking for further data. The plausibility ranking that results from digging out further data will be called 'post hoc plausibility'—the newly ordered list. These terms have become relativized so that at *any* stage we can say that the antecedent plausibilities are those *before* the last datum was discovered, and the plausibilities resulting from that datum will be the post hoc ones for now. We generate our series of increasingly better informed arguments by adding the new data to the old and inferring whatever conclusion is on top of the list at that stage. We stop when we are as certain as we need to be for the practical task at hand, or when we can find no further data, whichever comes first.

So we choose among rival conclusions by two distinguishable steps:

1. Seeing how well they fit with the data we have—that is, determining their antecedent plausibility.
2. Looking for additional relevant data to determine increasingly informed post hoc plausibilities. This generates a series of different inductive arguments, in which we soundly infer whatever conclusion is concurrently at the top of the ever-changing plausibility order.

Inductive argument is as important as it is largely because we are *very* good at both steps in an enormous number of important contexts.

EXPLANATION

When we rank statements (here, conclusions) in the order of their plausibility, we are implicitly judging how well they fit in with everything we know. This is why background plays such a crucial role in our judgment. To assess this fit we must balance all the various competing considerations: some rivals fit better in some ways, others fit better in others. The one with the best combined "score" wins, but the score is a very complex combination of things.

At the center of this complex of judgments is the concept of explanation. When a rival fits better than all the rest it does so because it explains everything it has to explain better than the others. It fits into the network of things we know in the most coherent way. If a rival fits in less coherently, we say it leaves more things unexplained—it has some explaining to do. Our grasp of this 'network of things' is simply our understanding: our understanding of how things work, how the network hangs together. This is what we depend on to determine how any given rival fits with the relevant things we know. Our understanding forges our perceptual skill into a more general diagnostic ability. This is what allows us to tell what happened even when we were not there looking at the time.*

So the most useful characterization of what we are judging when we choose among rival conclusions is *explanatoriness.* The question implicit in diagnostic arguments is "What happened?" or, more generally, "What is the story?" The different answers to that question—the rival conclusions of the argument— are *rival explanations* of what happened. The rival conclusions in the balloonist example are rival explanations of what happened to Rocco. In the Warren Commission case, which is also a diagnostic argument, the rivals are rival explanations of how the President was killed. But in this case we know enough to ask a more specific question: we ask (for the explanation of) *who shot* Kennedy? But, as mentioned in that discussion, we could have discovered that no one did, and the implicit question then would have reverted to the more general one: what happened? In these cases, what we are looking for is the best account of the matter; and it is no accident that 'account' means both 'story' and 'explanation'. The sort of story we want is explanatory: if it doesn't answer the right questions it isn't the right story; we have yet to find out what's going on.

---

*It is important to resist the temptation to think of understanding as merely visceral, subjective, not worthy of a central role in reasoning. Like our ability to see things, our ability to comprehend complicated relationships is an objective feature of our lives. We can test our understanding just as we can test eyesight and hearing; intersubjectivity is the foundation of each. It is no accident that we use perceptual language (I see, I hear you) to talk of our comprehension: it is often as reliable as simple perception.

Explanatory Plausibility

Recall that the first component of our diagnostic skill is an ability to rank rival conclusions roughly in the order of their plausibility. It turns out that what we are skilled at ranking actually are explanations. On the original data, drowning explains Rocco's disappearance more easily than his being whisked to Moscow on a spy mission. This is all it means to say that drowning is the more plausible account of his disappearance. The data present selective hurdles for the rival conclusions. So when we 'see how well the rivals fit with the data we have'—the first step—we are determining how easy—or how difficult—it is for each conclusion to explain what happened—how easy it is for each to provide a story that can accommodate everything relevant we know. The hurdles are not as high for the explanations at the top of the list as they are for those farther down; they get gradually higher the farther down we go. But even though the difficulties facing explanations become greater only gradually, it is common to speak in absolute terms after a certain point. We say that a difficulty is *so* great—a hurdle is *so* high—that it *rules out* one of the explanations. As Ted drives along his car begins to make a loud knocking noise, which seems to slow down as the car slows down and speed up as the car accelerates. To see if it is an engine problem he puts the car in neutral and revs up the engine a bit. The knock does not speed up—it remains relatively constant as he coasts along. This, we would say, rules out the possibility that the knock is in the engine. And that is a perfectly legitimate way to put the point, so long as we understand what it means. It does not mean that an engine problem is impossible in any absolute sense; it is just that the little test of putting the car in neutral drops the possibility of the knock's being in the engine so far down in the plausibility ranking that it does not have to be taken seriously at this stage of the investigation. It still could be that ripples in the road where the test was run affected an engine malfunction in just such a way as to compensate for the increased engine speed during the test. But it would take some such freak coincidence to account for the steady knock. And being forced to include a freak coincidence presents an enormous barrier for the engine problem account to hurdle. The test effectively rules this account out, although we could be forced to reconsider it if there were equally serious difficulties raised for each of the rivals remaining above it in the ranking.

Whenever we rule out a rival account in this way—by showing it requires a freak coincidence to accommodate some piece of the data we already have—we say it is ruled out because it *can't explain* that piece of the data. The engine-problem theory can't explain the unvarying knock. The biscuit-is-now-in-the-cellar hypothesis can't explain the biscuit on the floor by your foot. This once again is absolute terminology signifying something that is actually a matter of degree—albeit enormous degree. These accounts could explain those troublesome bits of data, but only with great difficulty, wild coincidences. So we say they actually *can't* explain them. And again this is a perfectly legitimate way of talking, so long as we are clear about what it means. Things that are ruled out occasionally get ruled right back in; and things we can't explain sometimes get themselves explained after all. But the absolute terminology is helpful because it points to the fact that we can safely *ignore* certain rivals for the time being. There is danger only if we expunge them from the list entirely.

To avoid this, it is perhaps useful to look closely at the procedure in which we focus on a specific datum and contend a certain rival cannot explain it. Notice that this procedure may itself be represented as a complete diagnostic (sub)argument, within the larger argument. We merely extract from the larger amount (say, about what is causing the knocking noise) those parts (test results) that we think rule out the rival in question (engine problem), construct the list of rival explanations of those data, and note how far down in the plausibility ranking the allegedly ruled-out rival falls. Ruling it out is merely showing that it is very far down the list. That the knocking did not speed up when the engine was revved up is only part of the data relevant to the diagnostic problem, but it may be considered in isolation as the support claim for another argument (a subargument). The 'implicit question' in this argument is "Why didn't the knock speed up when the engine did?" Far and away the best answer is that the knock is not in the engine—it is somewhere else in the drivetrain or wheels. The other rivals that require one or another incredible coincidence are far below it on the list—rather like the rivals to drowning in the original version of the Rocco argument. This is the procedure underlying our legitimate claims that a rival account can't explain something in the data, that it has been ruled out.

Subargument construction is actually a very important aspect of diagnostic argument, and is not limited to ruling out unsupported coincidences. Very often investigations will be explicitly broken up into subinquiries, each attempting to account for various aspects of a large collection of data. Look again at Rocco and his balloon. In just the required sense the made-it-to-Europe hypothesis 'can't explain' the gondola in the Atlantic; not because it requires wild coincidences, but because what it requires is just as bizarre: somehow Rocco had to make it to land without the gondola, or the gondola had to get back from Europe against the prevailing winds, or some such thing. Nothing but incredible long shots. So if we put this subargument into our standard form, the 'implicit question' is "How did the gondola get there?" and the best answer (the most plausible account) is that the balloon went down in the storm. There are many others between this one and the made-it-to-Europe story, which in any case is so far down the list that it is effectively ruled out.

Notice that we may in this way 'rule out' rivals even when none of the remaining candidates is very good. That is, we can sometimes know what the story is *not* even when we cannot say what it *is*. As this is written, investigators are not sure what is causing the stratospheric booms heard over the eastern seaboard during recent autumns. But since these booms have a history going back hundreds of years, they can rule out methane from garbage dumped at sea, because dumping on a scale sufficient to produce much methane is a relatively recent institution.

Explanatory Relevance

In cases like this last one, it is natural to suggest that we look for further data—construct a different, better-informed argument to decide what is really going on. This is to appeal to the second component of our diagnostic skill: the ability to recognize what else would be relevant. This skill is also tied to explanatoriness. A fact is relevant to a certain case if its discovery would separate the rivals *explanatorily*—if it would be easier for some of the rivals to explain that it would be for others, for example. In Rocco's case, a letter from Moscow is clearly relevant because it would be easier for C_3 to explain than any of the others. The report of a man discovered walking dazedly on the deck of a Norwegian freighter in the middle of the storm would be relevant because it would distinguish C_2 from the others. So when we actively search for further data, what we set our sights on are things the occurrence or nonoccurrence of which would be easier to explain on some of the rivals than on others. We might ask residents of all the coastal villages of Scandinavia, Britain, France, Spain, and Portugal if they saw a huge red and yellow balloon drift past during the last few days. If some did, that would help the made-it-to-Europe story; if none did, that would hurt it a bit. Either way it is relevant.

Very simple applications of our ability to judge the relevance of new data can be forced into an impressive investigative device using the diagnostic argument picture sketched in this chapter. This can be seen most clearly when the matter being investigated is difficult or complex. Subarguments will structure branch investigations, which are then assembled into a giant, complex argument. In investigating the crash of a racing car, one of the more plausible accounts might appeal to a cut tire as the cause. So a branch investigation might usefully mount the deflated tires on unbroken rims and try to inflate them. If they hold air at all normally, that would rule out the cut-tire account. This case is especially interesting because it illustrates a very common asymmetry in evidence gathering. If the tires hold air, that virtually destroys the cut-tire hypothesis. But if they do *not* hold air, that fact does not help the cut-tire hypothesis very much—it is all too easy to cut a hole in a tire *during* a crash.

A more complex case will show just how powerful a tool we have in our simple ability to judge relevance. In November 1957, a Boeing 377 crashed in the Pacific on a flight from San Francisco to Honolulu. A week later some debris and the bodies of nineteen passengers were finally located, recovered, and subjected to detailed investigation. An excess of carbon monoxide in the bodies suggested there might have been a fire on board before the crash. All the floating debris was charred, but

> ... the fire damage on every scarred piece was on those portions that floated above the water. ... each piece had a definite water line below which there was no trace of charring.*

The in-flight fire theory would have a very hard time accommodating this datum. The investigators concluded this branch of the investigation with a negative. And we are all competent to join them in that conclusion.

Detailed Illustration

Our illustrations so far have been limited to aspects or branches of investigations; and the two real cases referred to actually remain unsolved. To pull together all the various points we have been discussing, and to illustrate the power of our normal diagnostic skills, it will be useful to show how they work together in a complete and successful investigation. The case we will examine is another air crash investigation, chosen not because of our general fascination with death and destruction, but because crash investigations are impressively challenging, pursued in enormous (and expensive) detail, and can usually be described in terms everyone can understand without special training. The investigation will be divided into four stages, each consisting in the acquisition of some new data and ending with a new argument to evaluate.

A McDonnell Douglas DC-10 jumbo jet departed Orly Airport, outside Paris, at 12:30 PM local time on March 3, 1974. This was Turkish Airlines flight 981 from Ankara to London, and it had been delayed half an hour to fill its empty seats with British Airways passengers stranded by a strike in London. Eleven minutes later, in a shallow dive, it slashed into a wooded area of rural France at a very high velocity. Trees were mowed down for about three-quarters of a mile, and the plane and its contents disintegrated so completely that there remained few pieces of anything larger than a suitcase. Several small fires broke out, and those first on the scene reported the heavy smell of kerosene throughout the area. Allow this much data to set the original argument, the first in a series of arguments attempting to answer the question, "What caused the crash?"

On its surface, this case is not just challenging, it seems hopeless. To anyone not familiar with the power of properly directed diagnostic skill, the completeness of the destruction seems an insuperable barrier to discovering what happened. Nevertheless, we already know enough to rule out some interesting rivals, provide a little order among the rest, and at least get the process started. The speed at impact and the smell of kerosene drop fuel-

*Robert J. Serling, *The Probable Cause* (New York: Doubleday, 1960).

exhaustion far down the list at the outset. Anything that would entail serious in-flight disintegration is also ruled out, since the aircraft came down rather solidly, all in one place. The investigation should begin, then, by focusing on the rival possibilities remaining near the top of the plausibility ranking. These (as usual) may be grouped in broad categories which may be broken into more specific ones when and if necessary.

C_1 Mechanical failure
$$\begin{cases} \text{engine} \\ \text{controls} \\ \text{air frame (probably ruled out)} \\ \text{other} \end{cases}$$

C_2 Pilot incapacitation
$$\begin{cases} \text{hijack} \\ \text{cockpit fire} \\ \text{other} \end{cases}$$

C_3 Collision
$$\begin{cases} \text{airplane} \\ \text{meteorite} \\ \text{space debris} \\ \text{other} \end{cases}$$

C_4 Bomb
C_5 Air turbulence
C_6 Pilot suicide

Given the original data, it is difficult to rank the first five of these; we cannot say that one is clearly better than the rest and hence cannot frame a sound inductive argument at this stage. We simply do not yet have any idea what happened.

I. S_1 High velocity impact, total destruction
     S_2 Smell of kerosene pervades crash site
     $$\overline{\rule{6cm}{0pt}} d$$
     ? $(C_1, C_2, C_3, C_4, \text{ or } C_5)$

The most efficient investigation would devote its attention to gathering further data which would differentiate explanatorily among the first five of these rivals: look for things that would be more difficult to explain on one hypothesis than the others.

The cockpit voice recorder was recovered and, as usual, provided useful detail.* About a minute and a quarter before the crash, just as the plane reached 12,500 feet (altitude), there was a loud bang audible on the recording, and the cockpit conversation indicated that the controls had given a jerk, then gone limp, and that the cabin depressurized immediately. The loss of cabin pressure suggested there was a hole in the airplane somewhere, and the

*Much of the following information was extracted from John Godson's *The Rise and Fall of the DC-10* (New York: David McKay, 1975).

cockpit conversation speculated that the bang might have been a collision, although no other aircraft had been observed. At about the time investigators were listening to this tape, Mme Dubois, a French farm wife, called to report six bodies and three sets of seats in her endive bed, which was directly under the DC-10's flight path and about ten miles from the crash site. This tended to confirm the view that there had been a hole in the plane at about the time the bang was heard. Further evidence compiled at this stage was the complete absence of weather normally associated with air turbulence and the absence of reported air traffic near the Turkish jet's position at the time of the bang.

So at this stage in the investigation, we can pretty well rule out incapacitation (C_2) and suicide (C_6) and drop both collision (C_3) and turbulence (C_5) below the remaining two. Of the latter, the bomb hypothesis seems a bit better because it would explain the bang and the loss of pressure very easily, and presumably could account for the problems with the controls if it had occurred in the right place. So the argument to construct at this stage would be

II. S_1 High velocity impact, total destruction
    S_2 Smell of kerosene
    S_3 Bang on reaching 12,500 ft., 1 ¼ min. before crash
    S_4 Immediate depressurization of cabin
    S_5 No air traffic observed or reported nearby
    S_6 Seats and bodies found 10 miles down flight path from crash site
    S_7 Absence of storm activity
$$========================= d$$
    C_4 A bomb exploded in flight (perhaps near an important part of the control system) causing the crash.

And since the plausibility ranking seems to be this

C_4
C_1
C_3
C_5
C_2
C_6

the above argument would be sound. But there is still great room for doubt: the argument though sound is not very strong. C_4 is not all that much better than C_1 (mechanical failure); further evidence could easily reverse the order.

At some stage we must explicitly add to our accumulating data some important background information. Certain design features of the DC-10 and their history as of March 1974 are clearly relevant to understanding what happened; and although any competent crash investigator would be intimately familiar with them, most readers of this book would not. The altitude at which jets fly dictates that their cabins be pressurized, and above 10,000 feet the difference in pressure between inside and outside is substantial. Given the enormous floor area in a DC-10, it was virtually impossible to build it strong enough to withstand the pressure if the cabin above it was pressurized and the baggage compartment below was not. Even at a few pounds per square inch, the total force on the floor would be hundreds of tons—in addition to passengers and seats. The obvious solution was to pressurize the baggage compartment (a solution adopted by all modern jets, by the way—not just the DC-10). But this raised another problem: the doors on the baggage compartment, which opened outward for convenience and space saving, must have very strong latches to prevent their being blown open by the tons of force on them at high altitudes.

McDonnell Douglas designed a very strong latching mechanism: massive hook-shaped grips that were driven into place around substantial bars on the doorsill by electric motors. Unfortunately, since the latching mechanism was inside the baggage compartment, the attendant in charge of latching the door could not see when the lock grips had been driven into place. So McDonnell Douglas incorporated a fail-safe into the latching mechanism to avoid any possibility that the plane could take off with the door not secured. It incorporated into the latch a series of lock pins that slid into grooves in the lock grips after they had been driven completely into place. These pins had two basic functions: they secured the grips and, more important, they could not slide into place until the grips were completely hooked around the bars on the doorsill. This last property was used to provide three separate signals when

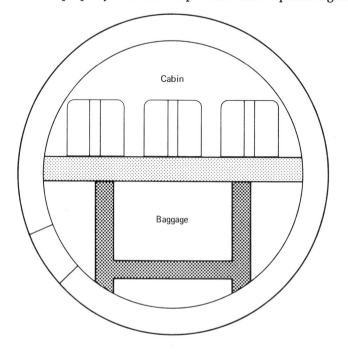

the door was not properly latched. First, the handle attached to the pins would not go into place if the pins did not: it would stick out from the side of the airplane in an obvious, noticeable way. Second, a large hole was opened in the door whenever the handle was in its unsecured position, so the plane could not be pressurized unless the door was properly latched: the hole was plugged by stowing the handle. And third, the whole mechanism was attached to a switch that turned off a light in the cockpit *only* when the handle was stowed (that is, in its secured or locked position).

Such ingenious redundancy sounds overdone, but it still turned out to be inadequate. Almost two years before the Turkish Airlines accident, on June 12, 1972, an American Airlines DC-10 took off from Wayne County Airport, outside Detroit, climbed to 11,500 feet, and experienced a loud bang accompanied by immediate depressurization. The pilot found he had no control over the rear engine and only partial control of the rear control surfaces. Some very delicate flying allowed a successful return to Detroit. Examination showed that the left rear cargo door had blown open in flight and the sudden depressurization had buckled the floor in the rear of the passenger cabin—part of the floor had actually fallen into the baggage compartment. Since the control lines and cables in the DC-10 run through the floor of the passenger cabin, many were severed or jammed when the floor buckled. It was estimated at the time that the only thing preventing the complete collapse of the floor, and the consequent total loss of control of the aircraft, was the light passenger load, and that nobody was sitting in the rear section of the cabin.

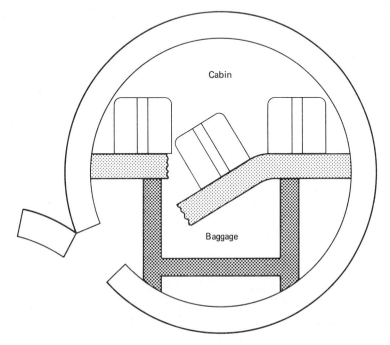

A baggage handler at Wayne County later admitted he had had to put his knee against the handle to stow it. Investigation revealed that if a force of about 120 pounds was put on the handle, it would stow even if the lock grips were not in place. This force would destroy the lock-pin linkage and plug the hole in the door. If the linkage broke in the right way, it would even activate the switch extinguishing the warning light in the cockpit.

This background, together with the previously ignored fact that the Turkish DC-10 was completely full, makes a fairly strong case for a specific mechanical failure, certainly reversing C_4 and C_1 from the previous list.

III. $S_1, S_2, S_3, S_4, S_5, S_6, S_7$
S_8 Plane fully loaded
S_9 Design data on door, floor, and control lines
S_{10} American Airlines incident

$$\rule{5in}{0.5pt} = d$$

C_1 Mechanical failure
(specifically: door blew off)

This argument is not just sound, it is particularly strong. Yet there were four more bits of data uncovered that strengthen the case even further.

After the American Airlines incident in Michigan, McDonnell Douglas redesigned the door-latching mechanism in three separate respects. Unfortunately, only one of these modifications was carried out on the Turkish Airlines DC-10. This one consisted in making a small inspection window in the bottom of the door for direct inspection of the locking mechanism, together with placing a number of notices on the door describing the basic latching procedure and warning attendants not to force the handle. On the Turkish plane these notices were written in both Turkish and English. Unfortunately, the attendant in charge of securing the rear baggage door at Orly Airport that Sunday was an Algerian who spoke (and could read) only French and Arabic. When questioned later he admitted having to hang on the handle to get it stowed (he weighed 220 pounds).

As if this were not enough, Turkish Airlines was able to identify the seats in Mme Dubois's garden as being from the very rear of the aircraft. Due to an unspecified difficulty, the original supplier could not provide enough seats for the entire plane, and those in the last few rows were from another manufacturer. One of the crew's jump seats, also from the rear of the plane, was found with the others. None of the seats, nor the bodies with them, showed any signs of blast or fire that might indicate a bomb had been responsible for their early departure from the plane.

The final piece of evidence fell into place about forty-eight hours after the crash. Some local residents brought in a piece of aluminum they found several miles farther from the crash site than Mme Dubois's farm, and right along the flight path. It was part of the left rear cargo door. There was no sign of blast damage on it either. With this the picture was practically complete; what had happened was fairly clear. It was a near duplication of the American Airlines incident, except that the weight of the passengers was so much greater that the rear cabin floor collapsed completely, severing all connection between cockpit and tail surfaces, and dooming the flight.

IV. $S_1, S_2, S_3, S_4, S_5, S_6, S_7, S_8, S_9, S_{10}$
 S_{11} Unmodified door
 S_{12} Language problem
 S_{13} Attendant hung on handle
 S_{14} Part of baggage door found further up flight path from seats and bodies
$$=\text{d}$$

C_1 Mechanical failure
 (specifically, door blew off)

The plausibility ranking at this (practically final) stage is

C_1
C_4
C_3
C_5
C_2
C_6

But C_1 is now so much better than C_4 the order is not likely to be reversed on any normal evidence; it would take something spectacular. This is part of what it means to say the argument is very strong.

This illustration fits the pieces of this chapter together in the following way. When a diagnostic investigation pauses to evaluate the evidence collected so far, that evaluation is a diagnostic inductive argument. The conclusion to be drawn at any stage is determined by answering R_2: namely, by determining which rival explanation is on top of the plausibility ranking at that stage. We can answer R_2 whenever the available data adequately complement the first component of our diagnostic skill, that is, whenever it is something we know enough about. The overall investigation, which links the individual inductive arguments together in a series, consists of a systematic application of the other component of our diagnostic skill: our ability to judge the relevance of new data. Later arguments in the series are always better informed than the earlier ones, because the later ones include all the data from the earlier ones, as well as what we have discovered since. But the later arguments are not always stronger. For we may discover negative evidence, hurting our best-looking conclusion without removing it from the top of the list. Discovering Rocco's water-treading prowess would be an example.

Traces

We may now add the final piece to our model of diagnostic induction by drawing a distinction between two kinds of evidence. The supporting statements of a diagnostic argument may relate to the rival explanations in two quite distinct ways. Some will themselves be explained by the rival explanations, some will not. Recall that the rival conclusions of a diagnostic argument are various answers to a question of the form "What happened?" In order to understand what this question is about in a specific case, we must know something about the context in which it arose. What led us to think anything happened? The answer is that we think something happened because something seems to have left some telltale traces. There was a fireball, or a gash in the woods, or a dead President in the back seat of the limousine. So although each of the relevant support claims has an impact on the plausibility ranking, some of them are special in this way: they bear an especially intimate relationship to the event or phenomenon the rivals are attempting to account for. These are the support claims that record the observations, the discoveries that led us to think something happened in the first place, and others that seem to confirm that suspicion. They actually give us *parts* or *aspects* or *consequences* of what happened (or of what led us to think something happened). They record plausible traces of something.

In the case we have just examined, the aircraft's disintegrating as it plowed through the woods is the most dramatic aspect of what happened. But it is reasonable to think that the part of the flight immediately preceding the terminal drama was also part of the happening under scrutiny. In explaining what happened the rivals will inevitably have to explain the plunge as well as the actual crash. So, in the sense relevant here, the bang, the depressurization, and the jerk of the controls are all part of what happened—or at least reasonably taken to be so at the outset. Likewise, the objects in Mme Dubois's garden are reasonably taken to be consequences of what happened. By contrast, the American Airlines incident in 1972, the baggage handler's language problem, and the design detail, though clearly relevant to the argument, are not part of what happened: they are not part of what the explanation of what happened would have to explain. These latter items will bear on the issue by filling in necessary background information, but they do not provide traces of the event.

This distinction closely parallels a relatively systematic distinction in the prepositions we use in talking about evidence. All of the support explicitly mentioned in a diagnostic argument can be described as evidence *for* the favored conclusion* (alternatively, evidence *that* it is the right explanation). But only data that are parts, aspects, or consequences of the event (or phe-

---

*Or 'against' in the case of negative evidence. This raises no special problem since both 'for' and 'against' contrast in the same way with 'of'.

nomenon) being inquired into are evidence *of* what happened. 'Evidence of' what happened is intimately connected to the happening itself, and means something like 'traces of' or 'traces left by' the thing itself. Evidence of a burglary might be a broken latch, missing valuables, and footprints: traces left by the burglar during the crime. Try it out yourself on other examples, like 'evidence of a wild party' or 'evidence of a hasty retreat'.

Accordingly, it will be convenient to call this special category of support *trace-data.* Trace-data are simply plausible traces of something: what are reasonably taken to be parts, aspects, or consequences of "what happened" —evidence *of* something.

Recall that the conclusion of a diagnostic argument is an explanation—it explains what happened. The rival conclusions are rival explanations of what happened. So, since the trace-data are parts (or aspects or consequences) of what happened, they are *part of what the conclusion must explain.* In explaining *what* happened, the conclusion explains *why* the traces were left. Discovering that the baggage door blew open explains what caused the Turkish DC-10 to crash. It also explains why the controls gave a jerk, why the cabin depressurized, why the bodies were in the endives, and why the door itself was found where it was.

This is the chief contrast between trace-data and the rest of the support; and it constitutes the major reason to draw the distinction. The rest of the evidence is *not* explained by the conclusion of a diagnostic inference. The door's blowing open does not explain the American Airlines incident in 1972,* nor the baggage handler's language problem, nor the absence of storms and other aircraft in the area. Of course, all this evidence is relevant—it is crucial to elevating C_1 to the top of the list. But in doing so it plays something like the same role as our general background knowledge. We have already noticed that it is occasionally helpful to include certain bits of ordinary background knowledge among the supporting statements of an argument. In a diagnostic argument these bits of background will normally be part of the 'rest of the evidence', not trace-data. Conversely, it is usually easy to think of contexts in which any given part of the nontrace evidence simply becomes background. For most professional air-crash investigators, the 1972 American Airlines incident did not need explicit mention in reconstructing the crash of the Turkish airliner. That was as well known as the impossibility of safe landing in a woods, and hence was simply presupposed. By contrast, the traces relate directly to the subject of the argument—they help specify the issue under scrutiny and determine the referent of the implicit question. So they can never fade into the background in quite the same way. It will usually be appropriate to mention them explicitly among the support claims, if only to specify what the argument is about and how it came to be raised in the form it did.

---

*A different door explains the American Airlines incident, of course.

Finally let us return to a proviso mentioned in passing a moment ago. Trace-data are those items that are reasonably taken to be traces of what happened. It could turn out that we were misled, our original supposition (though reasonable) was wrong. The "trace-data" are not all traces of the same thing, for instance. What then?

Actually, very little must be added to accommodate this complication. Different rivals will account for various bits of trace-data in different ways, of course. Only a few will account for the major items as traces of one single thing, even in the standard cases. Some will—in spite of appearances—account for them as traces of several different, unrelated things. The pilot-suicide story of the DC-10 crash, for example, might account for the noises on the cockpit recording and the objects in Mme Dubois's backyard by hypothesizing a wild party in the tourist section. The noises and bodies would be traces of something, just not traces of what we thought. This is why Mme Dubois's report raises an explanatory hurdle for the suicide rival: that rival must somehow account for the bodies in the endives. And there seems to be no antecedently plausible way to do this.

Because of their role in the argument, the noises and conversation on the tape, the bodies and seats and the location of the door will have to be explained—or explained away—by every rival, even dubious ones. So in general we can say that trace-data are all the things the conclusion might be expected to account for. We judge the various rivals by how well they do this; so one helpful way to express what it is that places C_1 at the top of the list of rival conclusions is that it provides the best account of the trace-data. Conversely, traces are evidence of whatever explains them best. For trace-data it is important to remember that the support or evidence relationship is just the reverse of the explanatory relationship. T is evidence of C if C explains T. Diagrammatically

$$\text{evidence} \left(\frac{T}{C} = d \right) \text{explanation}$$

For general background information and other non-trace-data the explanatory relationships are often very complicated, and can run the other way. But for traces, as that term is used here, the simple picture above holds.

Finally, we may now describe diagnostic induction in slightly different terms: a diagnostic inductive argument is one containing trace-data. Any argument offering data for the rival conclusions to explain in this direct fashion will be diagnostic. This characterization will sometimes be more helpful than the original one using the "What happened?" implicit question. But the two descriptions are equivalent for practical purposes. The implicit question of a diagnostic argument may always be put "What is the best explanation of this?", where 'this' refers to the trace-data that launched the argument. (Try this out on some of the examples we have used in this chapter.)

SCIENCE

Evidence evaluation in the sciences fits the pattern of diagnostic induction just as well as the less exotic examples we have been considering. Scientific investigations are directed and focused by an implicit question, and then are, of course, crucially dependent upon deciding just what evidence is relevant. The questions a scientific investigation attempts to answer, however, normally have a characteristic seldom found in those of accident investigations. They are in continuous present tense: they concern a *phenomenon,* not an *event.* Accident investigators want to know what happened—in a specific case; scientists wish to know what happens—in cases of a certain kind. Otherwise the two are quite parallel. What a scientific investigation attempts to provide evidence for *is* an explanation, in one form or another; and evaluating the evidence simply consists in determining which explanation is best, all things considered.

Sometimes the explanation is a theory in that word's most exalted sense: a very general account of some far-ranging collection of phenomena, such as Newtonian Theory, Quantum Theory, Relativity Theory, or the Kinetic Theory of Gases. Here the evidential picture is enormous and complex, but straighforwardly diagnostic in form. Support for a theory comes from all those phenomena for which it provides, collectively, the best accounts. The Kinetic Theory of Gases, for example, accounts for the various thermodynamic properties of gases; Newton offered an account of the motion of massive bodies, both celestial and terrestrial.

Also unlike accident investigations, in which a number of rivals could account for the data, the real task in general theorizing is finding *any* theory that will do a reasonable job. Very often, at this level, a theory is not merely the best explanation, it is the only one that comes even close to accounting adequately for the things it covers. So sometimes finding a theory that is roughly adequate in broad outline is automatically finding the best account we have. This is why scientists happily put up with flaws and oversimplifications in their basic theories. They are grateful to find something that looks like it can be developed, amended, and fine-tuned in the right way. But this also has a parallel in the cases we have already studied. In difficult investigations it is reasonable to look first for the general shape of the explanation, and then provide more detail as we are able to.

Other scientific inferences work the same way, but the data are a far more modest collection of things, and the conclusions are theories with a small *t.* Laboratory results might provide evidence for specific items: the existence of some entity, the property of a substance, the relationship between certain parameters. These are theories in the more mundane sense: the theory that a certain particle exists, or that crystals refract light in a certain way, or that air resistance is proportional to the square of velocity. Here too the data provide evidence for these theories only if they in turn provide the best account of that data.

Scientific examples very often depend on specially trained diagnostic skills, which limits their usefulness in a general-level text. It will nevertheless be useful to examine a specific case, both to observe the parallels with nonscientific cases, and to see what special perspective is required to judge such a case.

A typically complex example from the history of chemistry is the discovery of oxygen. At the end of the eighteenth century there was a great argument going on concerning what is happening when a substance undergoes what we would now call oxidation. In its most basic terms, the issue was whether, when a substance oxidized, something was given off or taken on by the substance. The theory accepted up until that time held that something was given up by the oxidizing substance: a substance called phlogiston. Although the word 'phlogiston' sounds vaguely amusing to the twentieth-century ear, it is important to avoid taking phlogiston theory too lightly. It was a remarkably fertile attempt to systematize chemistry and was able to account for a large number of chemical processes and reactions in a strikingly modern way.* Modern chemistry owes a great deal to phlogiston theory and actually incorporates many of its insights. (Phlogiston itself may be viewed as the essence of a reducing agent, and hence might be said to still play a metaphorical or heuristic role in oxidation and reduction explanations.) In any case,

---

*To gain some sense of the sophisticated theoretical role played by phlogiston in eighteenth-century chemistry, consider the following passage from E. J. Holmyard, *Makers of Modern Chemistry* (1931). "The phlogiston theory . . . offered a rational explanation of the formation of metallic calces and of the reduction of the latter to metals; but it did more. Like every scientific theory worthy of the name, it soon proved to be applicable to facts with which at first it seemed completely unconnected, and by bringing them all to a common denominator it achieved the earliest great synthesis of chemical philosophy. Thus the experimental facts (a) that when sulphur is burnt under suitable conditions it yields sulphuric acid, and (b) that by the action of charcoal upon sulphuric acid sulphur can be regenerated, were simply and consistently explained by assuming that sulphur is composed of sulphuric acid and phlogiston. Upon burning sulphur the phlogiston is lost and the acid remains, but when the acid is heated with charcoal—a substance rich in phlogiston—it once more combines with phlogiston to form sulphur. Again, if zinc is dissolved in dilute sulphuric acid a colorless inflammable gas (hydrogen) is evolved and a solution of white vitriol remains. The inflammable gas was regarded as practically pure phlogiston, and the reaction was explained by supposing that the acid split up the zinc into 'phlogiston' (which was evolved) and zinc calx, the latter dissolving in the acid to form the white vitriol. The logical deduction from this hypothesis was that if zinc were first burnt, so removing its phlogiston, the residual zinc calx should dissolve in dilute sulphuric acid, to yield a solution of white vitriol *without* evolution of the inflammable gas. Experiment shows that this deduction is correct, for the reaction takes place exactly as indicated.

Further, it follows from the phlogiston theory that if a metallic calx is heated in the above-mentioned inflammable gas, the metal ought to be regenerated . . . which once more is in perfect agreement with the experimentally established fact."

phlogiston theory explained oxidation as the giving off or releasing of phlogiston.

On the other side was the position advocated by Antoine Lavoisier, who was unrelatedly executed by the French revolutionaries in the middle of this controversy. Lavoisier claimed that what really happened in oxidation reactions was that something was taken from the air and combined with the original substance. The something taken from the air was, of course, oxygen, but we should not allow our familiarity with the term (or our hindsight knowledge of who won the fight) to influence our judgment here. The peculiar nature of scientific arguments may be appreciated in the following way. Lavoisier offered in support of his position a number of facts that were accepted by both sides; and these facts were just the kind that we, in everyday investigations, would take to rule out phlogiston theory. They would represent insuperable explanatory hurdles. But they did not have that impact simply because this case concerned the basic concepts of a scientific discipline.

One such fact was that, when done in the accepted way, the product of the oxidation (oxide) weighed more than the substance did before the reaction. This would seem, in mundane cases, to be impossible for the phlogiston interpretation to explain: if something (phlogiston) left the sample in the reaction, then the resulting product should weigh less, not more, than the original substance.

But the advocates of phlogiston theory had a powerful reply. Experiments like this are the way science discovers the properties of its basic concepts. Phlogiston was not any ordinary substance like water or air; it was a very abstract thing. So the result of this oxidation experiment can be taken as a discovery about phlogiston: it has negative weight. Once again, to the twentieth-century mind this sounds ludicrous. But negative weight is actually not as bizarre as the properties physicists have been recently attribut-

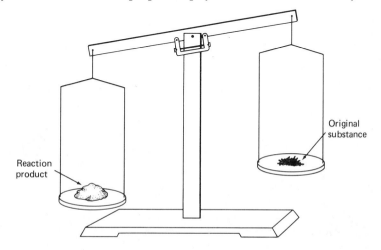

ing to the basic elements of matter. Negative weight would merely require that gravitational forces sometimes be repulsive, rather like magnetic and electrostatic forces. Two hundred years ago this was not nearly as radical a suggestion as it is now. The phlogiston theorists could not be refuted so easily.

Lavoisier (and oxygen) eventually did prevail in this dispute, but not because of any one experimental result, and not simply because oxygen was preferable to phlogiston as an explanation of oxidation. Phlogiston was taken to be a very basic substance, involved in all sorts of chemical reactions: it really did unify the chemistry of its time. Lavoisier and his successors abandoned phlogiston as a fundamental substance altogether, in all of these contexts. So there were a number of conflicts between the two camps, and Lavoisier's approach to chemistry was clearly superior to phlogiston theory only in some of those cases. In some the two were pretty well equivalent, and in still others phlogiston seemed to offer a better account of what was going on. But over a period of years it gradually became clear that Lavoisier's approach was pulling ahead in the competition; it seemed to handle the whole range of things a chemical theory was asked to handle in a simpler and more fertile way than phlogiston. It was really not any single episode, but the net force of its relative success in the entire field that won the day for the new theory.

This is typical of such arguments in science; and it explains why scientific arguments are often inaccessible to laymen—those of us with no special training in the field. Scientific arguments, and scientific investigation, do fall into the standard pattern of diagnostic induction, and require the application of our standard skills in plausibility ranking and relevance determination. But the background against which plausibility and relevance judgments are made is the entire body of knowledge constituting the area of science in question. The interpretation of every experiment, the evaluation of each piece of evidence, is conducted against that background. Even simple-looking questions like "Is something going in or coming out when a substance burns?" have far-reaching commitments to all the rest of our chemical knowledge. It is easy to be misled into thinking the question is easier to answer than it is, and we must guard against the temptation.

The preceding discussion of eighteenth-century chemistry involved primarily the first component of our diagnostic skill—ranking explanations in order of plausibility. The second component—judging the relevance of further data—is every bit as intimately connected to scientific investigation, however. The design of experiments is simply the exercise of this second component. If an experiment is to decide among competing accounts of some phenomenon, it should be designed so that whatever happens, some explanations will be able to handle the results more easily than others. This is just what it means for data to be relevant. An experiment is badly designed if all its possible results would be equally easy to explain on any of the (antecedently) most plausible hypotheses—if no matter how it came out, we would not change our plausibility ranking.

In fact, we can say a bit more than this. Most experiments will have an infinite number of different possible results: the apparatus can melt, explode, or talk to us in Hebrew, as well as what it is supposed to do. So it is reasonable to focus our attention on the (antecedently) most likely of these results. There will always be some bizarre possibilities that will be irrelevant, but this is of no great consequence if the antecedently likely ones are clearly relevant. So the practical principle is that an experiment is well designed if the most likely results are relevant to the rivals at the top of the list.

Clear examples of badly designed experiments are inclined to be slightly silly, but, for the sake of illustration, consider the following. The boss wants to know whether his secretary would mind letting him use her car for an errand. His experiment is simple: he asks her. The most likely results of the experiment are (a), the secretary says 'No', and (b), she says 'Yes, I do mind'. But normally, 'No' would be far more likely. In most circumstances, however, such a result is nearly uninformative: it is just as easy to explain on the hypothesis that she would mind as that she would not. She might say 'No' simply because she really doesn't mind; but she might say it out of normal human consideration, in spite of the fact that she does mind; and she might say it because she feels beholden or obligated as an employee, once again in spite of not really wanting to lend him the car. So the experiment is badly designed: the most likely outcome has essentially negligible impact on the antecedent plausibility ranking. The boss should try to find out some other way.

A classic example of a well-designed experiment was one carried out by the Eddington party in 1919. Albert Einstein's recently propounded gravitational equations strongly suggested that light rays would be deflected to a certain measurable extent by the gravitational field of our sun. In 1919 there happened to be a total solar eclipse visible in South Africa, at a time when a well-chartered star was directly behind the sun from the earth. If Einstein's relationships were correct, the star should be visible during the eclipse, due to the deflection of the light from the star in the sun's gravitational field. On the other hand, the competing gravitational theory (that of Newtonian, or classical, mechanics) would have an enormously difficult time explaining the star's being visible during the eclipse. Just why is itself difficult to explain, and is another illustration of the need for the proper scientific background in adjudicating scientific arguments. But this is a side issue. Accepting what the physicists tell us concerning explainability, the experiment was well designed simply by virtue of the fact that either of the two most likely results would have a clear impact on plausibility estimates. If the star was visible it would be hard for one theory to explain; if it was not, it would be hard for the other one to explain. The experiment was a model of a good design.

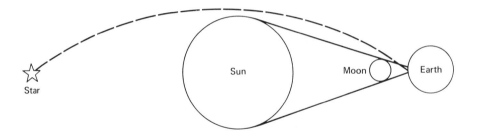

In testing diagnostic hypotheses (explanations) it sometimes turns out, however, that we must settle for a test that falls short of this ideal. Obviously there is no reason to run a test that would have no impact on the plausibility ranking no matter what result we got. But there are tests that fall between the two extremes, and one of the most striking features of such tests is what we earlier called their asymmetry. Some tests have the peculiar property that of, say, two possible results, one would be significant, but the other would be nearly irrelevant. A positive result, for example, might support a certain hypothesis, whereas a negative result would not hurt that hypothesis at all. You wish to determine whether the faint hiss you hear on the stereo is on the record, or in the system itself. As a test you change records. If the hiss disappears, that is significant: strong evidence that it was on the record. If the hiss does *not* disappear, the case is much less clear: it might be that it is just the normal record noise, but it could be in the system too. Recall that we called a piece of new data *relevant* in the context if it would have a detectable impact on the plausibility ranking. Accordingly, we can say for asymmetrical tests that some outcomes are relevant, and others not: whether they raise explanatory hurdles for any of the rivals depends on what results we get.

There are all sorts of good reasons to run asymmetrical tests in spite of the risk of getting an irrelevant result. Sometimes there are no perfectly ideal tests possible. In other cases the expense or effort required for an asymmetrical test is so low that little is lost in trying it, and there is a chance of discovering something nearly for free. We might check the mailbox to see if the mailman has come yet. We know beforehand that one of the likely outcomes (no mail) tells very little. But we check anyway because the other likely outcome (mail) is nearly conclusive, and it takes so little to run the test. (There are two relatively common circumstances that would invalidate this reasoning; can you think of them?) A third sort of circumstance that might justify an asymmetrical test would be that we already know that the chance of getting an irrelevant result is very low, so although there is some risk of wasting time and effort, the possibility is remote. In some respects all experiments are like this: awkward results are seldom completely ruled out. That is the significance of characterizing a well-designed experiment as one in which the *most likely* outcomes are relevant. In the Eddington gravitational experiment a long-shot possibility was that the star might appear in some bizarre place that neither theory could account for. This would suggest that the charts were wrong or that the equipment malfunctioned, and this sort of thing is always a possibility. But these possibilities were long shots, and that is what made the experiment a good one.

NONDIAGNOSTIC INDUCTION

The key to understanding diagnostic induction is the fundamental role played by the concept of explanation. The conclusion of a diagnostic induction is an explanation: it explains what happened. And since the 'happening' in question is specified in the supporting data, the conclusion will explain much of the support—sometimes all of it. There is a direct and intimate connection here between the concepts of evidence and explanation. The traces are evidence of whatever explains them best, and the rest of the evidence just helps determine which explanation tops the plausibility list.

But there remains the question of nonexplanatory conclusions, and explanatory ones that do not happen to explain any of the data. Obviously we can provide evidence for nondiagnostic statements (it will rain tomorrow), and even diagnostic ones for which we have no trace-data. But those conditions rule out the possibility that those statements are the conclusions of simple diagnostic arguments. So the question arises: what form does the supporting argument take? More specifically, if our ability to evaluate evidence depends on our diagnostic skills, how might these skills be brought to bear on nondiagnostic conclusions, or in a nondiagnostic way? The answer, although basically simple, raises some complicated issues.

A given collection of data may be used as evidence for many things besides the explanation of the traces it contains. The data we have might contain evidence that something happened, but we need to stop there. The mere fact that something happened will often tell us much else as well, and in this way the original evidence may be brought to bear on many other matters. We can infer from data *through* a best explanation, to the consequences of that explanation. In other words, explanations may themselves be used as support claims in further arguments, so the evidence for an explanation may become evidence for the inferential consequences of that explanation. In this way our diagnostic skills may be brought to bear on conclusions that are not simple explanations.

In drawing a consequence we will usually have to add further support claims, often simply *reasonable assumptions* on which there would be little trouble getting agreement. It is useful to distinguish these second echelon support claims (assumptions) by representing them with the letter A (A_1, A_2, A_3 ...) instead of the letter S, which we use for the first echelon support. The picture of overlapping arguments would therefore look like this:

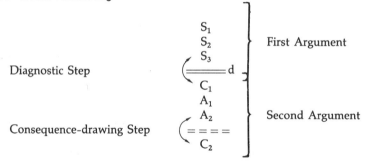

Here C_2 is our primary interest; and the argument directly bearing on C_2 is the second one, which takes C_1, A_1, and A_2 as its support claims. But since S_1, S_2, and S_3 provide evidence *directly* for C_1, through the previous diagnostic argument, they *indirectly* provide evidence for C_2 because of C_1's role in the consequence-drawing step.*

This second step is represented by a dotted double line because we have said nothing yet about what kind of step it is, inductive or deductive. What *is* clear is that it cannot be diagnostic. Our task here is to show how evidence may be brought to bear on nondiagnostic—even nonexplanatory—conclusions. So whatever the consequence-drawing step is, it cannot be diagnostic. For the moment, however, it will be best to say nothing further about the nature of this step—to leave it undetermined. We can very often recognize when a consequence is reasonably drawn and when it is not, without settling just what kind of argument it is. And since the exact nature of that step is slightly controversial, our first illustrations of nondiagnostic arguments will simply incorporate a consequence-drawing step of indeterminate form. Later in this section we will examine one view of what that form should be.

Perhaps the commonest nondiagnostic inductions are predictive: an argument providing evidence that something or other *will* happen. A meteorologist may provide evidence that it will rain tomorrow, a pollster may uncover evidence that Baker will win the upcoming primary election. Since the events predicted in such cases have not yet happened, they have left no traces to explain—there is no evidence *of* them yet, even though we have evidence *for* them. So the conclusions in each case do not explain any of our data; we are not inferrring directly to the best explanation of anything as we did in the diagnostic cases. But finding the best explanation of the data plays a crucial mediating role in these cases.

---

*When economy is more important than clarity, arguments like this may be schematized in one step, of course. Which of the following to prefer would depend on how obvious the As are.

$$
\begin{array}{ccc}
\begin{array}{c} S_1 \\ S_2 \\ S_3 \\ \hline \\ C_2 \end{array}
&
\begin{array}{c} S_1 \\ S_2 \\ S_3 \\ A_1 \\ \hline \\ C_2 \end{array}
&
\begin{array}{c} S_1 \\ S_2 \\ S_3 \\ A_1 \\ A_2 \\ \hline \\ C_2 \end{array}
\end{array}
$$

Consider the prediction of rain. Evidence for this prediction might be that it is raining across a broad area to the west, and the temperatures reported by various weather stations are dropping in a characteristic way. Suppose that the best explanation of these data is some standard meteorological phenomenon, say, that a storm front is moving in our direction. Suppose further that such frontal systems normally sweep unabated across our area within twenty-four hours of the time they reach their current location. We then can construct a second argument in which we take the best account of our weather data (storm front moving in) together with the supposition that it develops in the normal way, and from this pair of statements we can quite reasonably draw the consequence that it will rain tomorrow.

Nondiagnostic Induction

{
Diagnostic Induction
{
S_1 It is raining to the west.
S_2 Temperatures are falling in a characteristic way.
================================ d
C_1 A storm front is moving in our direction.

Consequence-drawing Step
{
A The storm will develop in the normal way.
========================
C_2 It will rain here during the next twenty-four hours.
}

This is typical of the way evidence is extended to nondiagnostic, nonexplanatory conclusions. The data do not include traces of the (nondiagnostic) conclusion, but they do include traces of something—in this case a weather system. And determining what those traces are traces of—the diagnostic step—plays a central role in this (overall) nondiagnostic inference. Typically, the diagnostic step in nondiagnostic induction will appeal to some *phenomenon* or *event* or *property* or *disposition* as the best account of the 'traces' part of the data; the nondiagnostic conclusion will then be a consequence of that phenomenon, event, property, or disposition. And usually some more or less reasonable assumptions will have to be added to the explanation in order to secure the required consequence.

The election example is also instructive. The survey was conducted according to reasonable guidelines, so we can call the sample of voters questioned reasonably random. Of that sample, 64.5% said they favored Baker. We wish to bring this evidence to bear on next Tuesday's primary. The first step is diagnostic: it is possible that the pollsters were systematically lied to, or that despite their precautions they ended up with an unrepresentative sample; but, given the little bit we know, we would have to say the best explanation of the survey data was that a large majority of the voters favor Baker. If we add to this diagnostic conclusion two further and rather standard assumptions, we can make the statistical evidence relevant to next Tuesday's results. Assumption number one is that nothing will happen between now and Tuesday to alter the electorate's preference for Baker; assumption two is that a reasonably representative selection of voters will actually vote in the primary. The picture once again looks like this.

$$
\text{Nondiagnostic Induction}
\begin{cases}
\text{Diagnostic Induction} & \begin{cases}
S_1 & \text{64.5\% of a reasonably random sample of voters favor Baker.} \\
\rule{6cm}{0.4pt}\qquad\qquad d \\
C_1 & \text{A substantial majority of the electorate favors Baker.}
\end{cases} \\
\\
\text{Consequence-drawing Step} & \begin{cases}
A_1 & \text{The sentiment of the electorate will not change much before Tuesday.} \\
A_2 & \text{A representative group of voters will cast ballots in the primary.} \\
\text{=========================} \\
C_2 & \text{Baker will win the primary.}
\end{cases}
\end{cases}
$$

The plausibility of the assumptions in the consequence-drawing step may derive from any source that will provide it, of course. Nevertheless, we will often be able to provide further independent evidence for them; that is, we may construct inductive arguments (either diagnostic or nondiagnostic) with those assumptions as their conclusions. The picture would look like this.

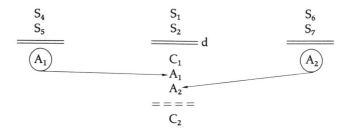

In defending C_2 in this way, we spread the support over six different support claims (S_1, S_2, S_3, S_4, S_5, and S_6) and at least four separate steps. The primary election case just discussed would normally be filled out in this way. If pressed, we would provide evidence for A_1 by examining the normal behavior of similar electorates and (in the specific case) pointing out the absence of reason to expect any dramatic revelations between poll and election. Similarly for A_2.* (Predictive assumptions like A_1 and A_2 are often amenable to a particular kind of support, however, which will be examined at the end of this section.)

---

*Obviously, we may insist on further evidence for the new support claims as well. Where we stop asking for further support is a practical matter and depends on what we are confident of in the particular context. In the next section, on strength, we will discuss our reliable perceptions as one sort of natural stopping point.

Predictive inference is only one (very large) class of nondiagnostic induction. Statements about the past and present may also be the subject of a nondiagnostic argument. The fact that Jane's entire family is myopic—nearsighted—will in some circumstances provide evidence that Jane too is myopic. And it would be most plausible to reconstruct this inference nondiagnostically. The best account of the data would not refer directly to Jane: it would explain the widespread myopia as due to a genetic trait typical of the family. Then, making the reasonable assumption that Jane shared the trait, we, in a second step, draw the consequence that she too is myopic.

S_1 Although we have no direct data on Jane herself, all the other members of her family are myopic.

_____ d

C_1 Jane's family harbors a genetic trait responsible for myopic eyes.
A_1 Jane shares that trait.

==

C_2 Jane is myopic.

Notice that in this case the conclusion could have been the object of a diagnostic argument (Jane might be constantly falling over things and running into doors, and myopia might be the best explanation of that). But since the data we have contain nothing that could be construed as a *trace* of her myopia, the argument could not be diagnostic in form. The traces were of something else—a genetic mechanism, perhaps—and Jane's myopia would be a *consequence* of that. So the argument's form is nondiagnostic.

In a sense, therefore, nondiagnostic arguments are the more general. Any conclusion, explanatory or not, may be the conclusion of a nondiagnostic argument, whereas a diagnostic argument requires an explanation as its conclusion. Nevertheless, it is important to understand diagnostic arguments first, because they play such a central role in nondiagnostic ones. And, of course, they do often stand on their own.

The following passage from Roger Angell's *Five Seasons** contains a nondiagnostic argument illustrating another kind of typical nondiagnostic step. The second conclusion is neither a diagnosis nor a prediction, but a *recommendation.*

For two decades, the central affliction of big-league baseball has been its sagging batting averages. Last year, the cumulative National League average stood at .248, and the American League at .239. These are figures to be taken seriously by any baseball fan or baseball magnate not just because they indicate that the game is declining in pleasure and energy but because they suggest that today's big-league stars are less capable than their famous predecessors. It is this unspoken belief that has the most serious effect upon the game's national popu-

*New York: Simon & Schuster, 1977, p. 86.

larity, and yet it is probably false. In every sport where comparable performances can be fairly measured—track and swimming come to mind—the modern athlete regularly and overwhelmingly exceeds the best marks recorded twenty or thirty years ago. There is no reason to assume that the strength and capabilities of contemporary baseball players are an exception. The hitting drought, then, is almost certainly due to a number of technical alterations in the game—night baseball, bigger ball parks, bigger infielders' gloves, the slider, the size and strength of today's pitchers, and the vastly increased and more effective use of relief pitchers. The redress should be minimal and precise—a further alteration of the strike zone, a livelier baseball, a more visible baseball, a shaving of the dimensions of the plate. By some means, baseball must bring back its long-lost hero, the .350 hitter—who is, in all likelihood, the same deserving young slugger now struggling so earnestly to maintain himself at .275.

The argument may be schematized in the standard way.

(S_1)   Major league batting averages have decreased in recent years.
(S_2)   The capability of athletes in general seems clearly *not* to have declined.
(S_3)   Many recent technical alterations in the game have been tough on hitters.
═══ d
(C_1)   The decline in major league batting averages is due to technical alterations of the game (things like night games, the advent of the slider, and the increased use of relief pitching).
(A_1)   Raising batting averages would be good for the sport.
(A_2)   Compensatory technical alterations in the game would do it.
═══
(C_2)   Baseball should institute some changes to raise batting averages (for instance, change the strike zone, or the ball itself).

The rendering here is comfortably idiomatic. Perhaps it would be clearer to change the phrasing of the conclusion to match A_1 more exactly ("It would be good for baseball to institute . . . "). The point is the same either way. To get a recommendation as a consequence, some principle such as A_1 will be appealed to, explicitly or implicitly, in the consequence-drawing step.

Another nondiagnostic example will bring us back to the question of providing a form for the consequence-drawing step. The inductive version of the 'Joe is mortal' argument in Chapter 2 (see p. 40) is best construed nondiagnostically.

(S_1)   The oldest people today are about the same age as the oldest people of any period in recorded human history; there are no well-authenticated cases of people living more than 114 years, and none even poorly authenticated more than 138. This in spite of reasonably good records in many parts of the world for millennia.
(S_2)   As well as the aging process is understood, it seems pretty clearly downhill after about age twenty for humans: parts gradually wear out, and disease is increasingly difficult to overcome.

(S₃)   Dramatic advances in medical technology have had little impact on normal longevity. As we overcome some problems, others take their place at an increasing rate as we age.

$$== d$$

(C₁)   Humans are constructed in such a way that nothing can keep us going more than a century or two.*

(A₁)   Joe is a human.

_____

(C₂)   Joe is mortal.

This second conclusion is a simple consequence of the original explanation (C₁) when taken together with a reasonable assumption. That Joe is mortal does not account for anything in the original evidence, but it is a consequence of the best account of that evidence.

Perhaps the most interesting feature of this illustration is that the consequence-drawing part is a deductive argument. In fact it is merely a colloquial version of the syllogism we were discussing in Chapter 2. In the usual context, and for any practical purposes, C₁ may simply be taken to say 'all men are mortal'; and A₁ captures precisely what was intended by 'Joe is a man'. So the consequence-drawing stage is

(C₁)   All men are mortal.

(A₁)   Joe is a man.

_____

(C₂)   Joe is mortal.

This suggests a promising way to proceed when there is a *question* about the consequence-drawing step. We have been assuming that the consequences to be drawn from a diagnostic conclusion may be made clear enough to secure agreement among reasonable people, without dealing with the exact form the consequence-drawing must take. But sometimes this will not be possible. We will then have to provide some inferential detail to establish whether a controversial consequence can actually be drawn—that is, to settle the matter. A plausible and helpful way to do this is to cast the consequence-drawing step as a deductive argument.

We saw in Chapter 2 that this can always be done: any argument may be cast deductively. And since the consequence-drawing step cannot be diagnostic, deduction is the natural alternative. For deduction is the only other kind of inferential step that we know clearly employs actual human skills.

---

*This may sound like a funny thing to call an explanation, but it is explanatory in a very important respect. That is, it locates the limitation in the way we are constructed: traces it to our makeup. The particular way our makeup places this limitation is not particularly relevant to the consequence-drawing step, so we need go no further in specification. Nondiagnostic arguments can employ such sketchy, skeletal explanations to bring evidence to bear on conclusions of great practical value.

Any competent language user has, or can readily develop, the ability to eliminate rival conclusions semantically; more generally, we can come to recognize when two statements contradict each other. So if there is a disagreement about what consequence may be drawn, a wise strategy would be to cast the consequence-drawing step as a deduction: to see if enough can be dug out of the context to make that step logically tight.

Remember that none of this is relevant if the consequence under discussion is clear and uncontentious. We make a fuss about the form of step two only when the consequence being drawn is problematic. But when it is, deduction is ideally suited to the task. We wish to know what follows, what are the ramifications of a given explanation; and this is what deduction does best.

Making step two deductive means including enough in the support to semantically eliminate all rivals to the conclusion (consequence) of choice. And this will usually require making explicit some things we would commonly take for granted. We could cast step two of the weather forecast deductively merely by specifying normal development.

C_1	A storm front is moving in our direction.
A	The storm will develop in the normal way.
E*	Storms like this normally sweep unabated across our area within 24 hours.

C_2	It will rain here within the next 24 hours.

Recall the general test for a valid deduction: if the conclusion is false, that simply means something is false among the support claims. This argument passes the test. For unless C_1 is false, if it doesn't rain here tomorrow, then that simply means the storm failed to develop in the normal way (given the gloss of 'normal' in E). In other words, no rivals are compatible with the supporting statements: if anything besides C_2 occurs that requires some revision of the support.

Part of the practical payoff of constructing step two in this way is that in making explicit what we have been presupposing we often uncover the source of disagreement. To make step two of the myopia argument deductive, we might add, in explication of what we take a genetic trait to be, that everybody having the genetic trait responsible for myopia is myopic.

C_1	Jane's family harbors a genetic trait responsible for myopic eyes.
A_1	Jane shares that trait.
E	Everybody with that trait is myopic.

C_2	Jane is myopic.

*E stands for 'explication': a statement making explicit what was implicit—taken for granted—in the context of the argument. More generally, E is intended to cover anything you have to dig out of the context to make the step deductive.

This argument is clearly deductive, in a way rather parallel to the 'Joe is mortal' syllogism. But no matter how generously we characterize 'genetic trait', E is too general to be true. For people with the myopic trait could lose their sight altogether in an accident, for instance, and would not be accurately described as myopic. Furthermore, there might be surgical procedures, traumas, or old compensatory genetic deformations that would change the shape of the eyeball to eliminate myopia in some people with this trait.

So to make a plausible deduction we would have to back off and appeal once again to plausible presumptions of normalcy.

C_1 Jane's family harbors a genetic trait responsible for myopic eyes.
A_1 Jane shares the trait.
E' People with that trait normally are myopic.
A_2 Jane is one of the normal ones.

C_2 Jane is myopic.

Here A_2 (together with E') preserves the deductiveness of this step without including something clearly false. But it also shows how the argument might be challenged by further data.

This sort of case naturally raises the complex possibility of collisions between diagnostic and nondiagnostic arguments. As mentioned earlier, C_2 might be the conclusion of a diagnostic argument too. In which case the two arguments would augment each other. On the other hand, one of C_2's rivals (e.g., Jane has eyes like a hawk) might be supported by a diagnostic argument, in which case it would be pulling against the above nondiagnostic one. Care and common sense are required to adjudicate such conflicts. Sometimes the two arguments will simply neutralize each other, but sometimes one or the other will be so strong that we reasonably accept its conclusion in spite of the competition. A nondiagnostic argument can overwhelm a diagnostic one —and vice versa. If we discover that Jane does not wear glasses, that changes things only slightly: she might be vain and she could wear contacts. But if we know her well enough to know she does not wear contact lenses, and she is a superb marksman, then we have direct evidence overwhelming the nondiagnostic argument above. The diagnostic argument

S_1 Jane is a superb marksman.
S_2 Jane does not wear glasses.
S_3 Jane does not wear contact lenses.
$$=========================== d$$
C_3 Jane has eyes like a hawk.

for one of C_2's rivals is stronger than the indirect evidence we have for C_2. So in this case we would accept the rival.

To return to the basic point, when it is necessary to provide some formal detail for the consequence-drawing step of a nondiagnostic induction, it is useful to cast that step deductively. So the picture would be this:

$$
\text{Nondiagnostic Induction}
\begin{cases}
\text{Diagnostic Step} & \begin{cases} S_1 \\ S_2 \\ \overline{} = d \\ C_1 \end{cases} \\[2em]
\text{Deductive Consequence} & \begin{cases} A_1 \\ A_2 \\ \overline{} \\ C_2 \end{cases}
\end{cases}
$$

It is necessary to go this far, however, only when the consequence to be drawn is controversial.

This is the general picture. There is, however, one specific form of assumption support, and one specific kind of assumption, that is important enough to justify more detailed attention. The possibility of prediction—that is, predictive inference—depends on the fact that some properties of physical systems are relatively stable. We can predict roughly where a baseball is going when we throw it, in large part because, within broad limits, the properties of the baseball, the air through which it passes, the earth, and the thrower are relatively stable. If any of these vary capriciously (hurricane force gusts, for example) that makes the prediction that much less secure.* The evidence for these stable properties is simply the vast array of data we have on each of these topics. Everything we know about baseballs (and other small solid objects), air, gravity, and throwing testifies to these properties.

The most interesting feature of these properties is that our evidence for them may be cast into diagnostic form: their existence is the best explanation of the data we have on the subject. The best account of our ability to make a baseball go roughly where we want it to is that there is a set of properties affecting where it goes *on which we can rely* in normal circumstances. That is to say they are stable: they do not normally change abruptly or without cause. Some stable properties, like the acceleration of gravity, may not change at all, ever.

Particular stable properties are valuable to us insofar as we can recognize when something *has* them, and when conditions are normal. Just walking around without running into things requires an immense competence at these two recognitions, and this in turn provides a background for many more exotic predictions. It is the stability of certain properties that connects past

---

*At another level, the capricious variations may themselves depend on other stable properties, of course. If we have access to data at that level, prediction will once again be within reach. As a practical matter, in the baseball example we do not have access to data allowing us to predict wind gusts. That is why predictive ability deteriorates so badly in that case. Prediction requires stable properties *at the level at which we have data.*

data to future occurrences and connects diagnostic induction to predictive inference. For their stability is what we have direct, diagnostic evidence of.

The prediction that Baker will win the primary election took advantage of the presumption of stability: that voters in general (and/or this voting population in particular) change their opinions very little in the course of a week, unless there is some startling occurrence. This property does have a truly colossal amount of support: its existence is the best account of an immense amount of election data at our disposal. By contrast, the weather prediction is less secure precisely because the coarse meteorological properties we must appeal to in such forecasts are not very stable: influences beyond our antecedent grasp too often divert the flow of events.

To be sure, various scientific disciplines are always looking for further explanations of these surface regularities. Investigation can sometimes determine the causes, conditions, and limits of the stability. The underlying explanation will appeal to a different set of regularities and further stable properties, and consequently will often provide another way of making the predictive inference. But it is important to understand that the original predictive inference, using the old surface properties, is still every bit as good as before. In fact, we usually strengthen the first by discovering the second.

Consider sunrise. Long before they knew much about the solar system and planetary dynamics, the ancients had very good evidence that the sun would rise the next morning. The evidence was roughly the same as that possessed by primitive tribes and astronomically unsophisticated people today— namely, that the world they live in has a complex but stable property: it hangs together in such a way that light follows dark in a systematic but annually variable pattern—a pattern related directly to the diurnal appearance and disappearance of the sun.* The best explanation of the pattern was that such a property existed, and it was natural to appeal to that property in the (nondiagnostic) inference to tomorrow's sunrise. In fact, the property was sufficiently stable to allow fairly accurate calculation of the time of the event.

We have in recent centuries come to understand the dynamic roots of the stable disposition of light to follow dark in the familiar pattern. We can now use our knowledge of the earth's rotational velocity, tilt of axis, and orbital motion to make the same computation. We would rightly argue that the planetary dynamics provide the best explanation of the historical data, and go on to appeal to the specific dynamic phenomena to calculate sunrise.

But their uncertain grasp of celestial motions does not undermine the ancient Babylonians' computation of tomorrow's sunrise. Their computations were very nearly as reliable as ours are today (the major advantage our

---

*Once again, the fact that this explanation—diagnosis—is sketchy and cosmologically unexciting is irrelevant to the issue. The skeletal diagnosis is just what we need here: it says just enough to underwrite the desired consequence, but so little that it is strongly supported by the evidence available. The more it says the riskier it is.

increased sophistication provides would be in compensating for changes in the pattern resulting from anticipatable celestial phenomena) and provide accuracy adequate for most practical purposes. Our planetary sophistication may be viewed as merely providing the detail underlying the very property the ancients appealed to in making their calculation. In an important sense, our predictions appeal to the same property they did; we just understand it better. The ancients understood *that* things hang together in such a way as to produce the well-known pattern; we understand just *how* they hang together to produce it. But *that* they hang together is all we need for predictive inference, and the ancients had overwhelming evidence for that.

Predictive inference is the most common kind of nondiagnostic induction, but there are many others.* Any inductive argument with a nonexplanatory conclusion counts as nondiagnostic. To use our diagnostic skills in their evaluation we structure them as two-step arguments: first find the diagnostic step, and then see what assumptions are required to secure the desired consequence. Evidence *for* something normally contains evidence *of* something too. In diagnostic cases the two 'somethings' are the same; in nondiagnostic ones they are not.

Since they are structurally more complex than diagnostic arguments, the nondiagnostic arguments we have been examining may go awry in more ways. We may of course make a slip in the diagnostic phase and get the wrong explanation on top of the list; but even if we get that part right, we can still add an unreasonable assumption, or simply draw an improper consequence in the second step. Every substantive item in an argument is always open to challenge, and hence subject to further argument. Where we stop is always a practical matter: we must decide when we are satisfied with what we've got. Arguments employing only diagnostic and deductive steps may ramify in patterns such as the following:

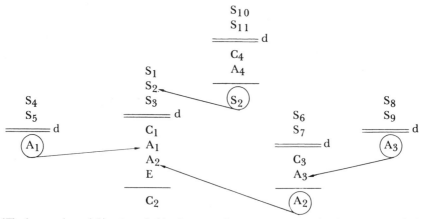

*The largest class of these is probably the normative ones: arguments having recommendations as their conclusions. Investigation of their peculiarities as a class is a fascinating possibility, but unfortunately that is beyond the scope of this text.

STRENGTH

It is difficult to say anything perfectly general about our ability to determine the strength of an inductive argument, but a few summary observations will be useful. The most important thing to notice is that, as always, there are easy cases: we are all pretty good at recognizing strength (and weakness) in the right cirumstances. We have already seen cases in which the argument is not just sound, but clearly very strong (the first version of the Rocco case, the final version of the DC-10 crash argument); and we have seen others in which the argument, although sound, was clearly not very strong (intermediate versions of the DC-10 case). Sometimes the best explanation is not terribly good, although clearly better than its rivals: sometimes there are too many unanswered (sub)questions to be confident. Of course, weaker and weaker arguments trail off into relationships nobody would seriously take to be offering evidence at all.

At the other end of the spectrum, stronger and stronger arguments merge with perception. Our perceptions make use of the fact that, in some circumstances, we are *very* good at telling what is going on simply by being there with our eyes and ears open. What we see and hear makes us think something in particular is happening; and in some cases (where we are perceptually competent), that fact alone provides overwhelming evidence that what we think is happening *is* what is happening. I look out the window and see it raining. The mere fact that what I see makes me think it is raining is overwhelming evidence that it is raining: I am very good at that diagnosis. Nevertheless, I could (barely) be wrong; my perceptions are fallible. So the inferential reconstruction of my perception would be in standard diagnostic form: 'it's raining' would be far and away the best explanation of my thinking it's raining, with the next best so far down the scale it may safely be ignored. Further data could drop 'raining' below some other account, but in most cases —cases that do not strain my competence: a teeming deluge, say, not an inchoate sprinkle—it would have to be a spectacular bit of data. It would have to account for the fact that someone so good at spotting rain was fooled.

This is not to say that perception involves an explicit inductive inference, as some philosophers seem to urge. When we see the rain falling, hear a clever dissonance resolution, or feel the warmth of the fire, we do not perceive one thing and infer something else; we simply see (or hear or feel) what's going on. This is true even of explicitly diagnostic perceptions: we simply see the brick smash the TV tube for instance; we do not observe a coincidence of events (brick arrives at screen just as the latter goes to pieces) and infer a causal relationship. Nevertheless, these perceptions all may be reconstructed inferentially: their warrant lies in our diagnostic skill.

Illusions take advantage of our competence. By introducing a subtle novelty we can be deceived into thinking we are perceiving something when we are not. But even the deception depends crucially on our skill: if we were not right most of the time we simply could not make the connection the illusion depends upon. If an illusion becomes common it destroys the perception, and hence itself. After a few encounters with them nobody is deceived by the puddle mirages on highways in the summer: what we see simply does not make us think there is water there anymore. Our basic perceptions are self-correcting in this way, which is why they are our basic perceptions.

This is also why strong inductive arguments merge with perception: the strongest of them simply are reformulated perceptions. I say the brick smashed the TV tube, although I realize what I witnessed *could* (barely) be accounted for by something else shattering the screen just as the brick got there. But without something to raise a difficulty with the straightforward (normal) account, the bizarre one may be safely ignored. The argument might be rendered,

S_1 The tube broke just as the brick got there.
S_2 I noticed nothing untoward.
—————————————————————————— d
C   The brick broke the tube.

We could perhaps improve on this argument by providing further detail, but there is no need to for our purposes.* The point is merely that, in our perceptions, we constantly exercise and constantly test our diagnostic skills. Our mistakes sometimes quite literally hit us in the face. These contexts provide the foundation of our evidence-evaluating ability and the clearest instances of its application. The extension of that ability to cases which are less directly perceptual is what inductive argument—and this chapter—is all about.

The inductive underpinning of perception also completes the picture we sketched at the end of Chapter 2. Even when the support for a substantive conclusion is cast as a simple deductive argument it will inevitably contain perceptual statements, the substance of someone's perceptions. So if the warrant of reliable perception is basically inductive, substantive support will always rest on inductive steps. This fact is disguised when the inductive steps merely represent uncontroversial perceptions that nobody feels the need to write down. Their strength is what makes them difficult to see.

Calculated Risks and Plausibility Gaps

Curiously, the closest we can get to a helpful generalization about firmness of support concerns the middle range of strength: arguments neither conclusively strong nor contemptibly weak. The generalization is as follows:

---

*Further detail, and the general form of such arguments, is provided in section two of the next chapter.

Arguments in which the best rivals (two or more) are close together in the plausibility ranking are always relatively weak.

To show why this is so will require that we impose a coarse quantitative structure on our rough plausibility ranking. As we have employed it, the ranking goes from certainly false at the bottom to certainly true at the top, with various degrees of comparative plausibility in the middle. The common way to impose numbers on this ranking is to call the bottom zero and the top 100.

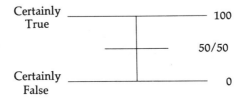

A statement falling near the top of this scale is far more likely to be true than to be false. One near the bottom is more likely to be false than true. So we may locate an important midpoint on our scale as that point at which a statement just as likely to be true as false would fall. Call that the 50/50 level.

We may now introduce the helpful metaphor 'plausibility gap' to refer to the distance along this scale between our rough plausibility estimates. We could use this metaphor without a full-blown scale, of course. It is natural to speak of a large plausibility gap between a plausible rival and a bizarre one, for instance, whether or not you have the above scale in mind. But we could represent their respective plausibilities on that scale and display the gap graphically.

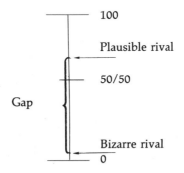

The gap is small between two rivals if they are hard to distinguish in the ranking. We may prefer one, but not by much. In some sound arguments, for example, one rival is clearly best, but the next best rival is not far behind. The plausibility gap between them is small. These arguments are the subject of the generalization above. It may thus be rephrased:

Arguments in which the plausibility gap is small between the best rival and the next best (one or more) are always relatively weak.

'Relatively weak' may be made more specific now too.

When the gap is small the best rival will never be far above the 50/50 level. Usually it will be more likely false than true.

This point is easier to understand if we first look at the case in which the gap is zero: two rivals actually tied at the top of the ranking, indistinguishable on the data given. When this happens, then as a matter of logic neither one can be above the 50/50 level, which may be shown as follows.

Consider the simplest sort of case in which we divide the list of rivals into just two (super) rivals, C_1 and not-C_1. If these are tied in the plausibility ranking they are automatically tied at the top. There are no others. One way to express the fact that C_1 and not-C_1 are tied in the plausibility ranking is to say the probability C_1 is true is the same as the probability not-C_1 is true. But since 'not-C_1 is true' simply means 'C_1 is false', it follows that the probability that C_1 is true is the same as the probability C_1 is false. C_1 is just as likely true as false: and that is the significance of the 50/50 level on our rough scale. In such a case both rivals are at the 50/50 level.

Now, if we have divided the list into more than two rivals, and still find two tied at the top, the odds on the top two drop below 50/50. For if there is any chance at all of one of the other rivals farther down the list being true, the chance that either of the top ones is true is reduced. So the very best that can be expected from tied rivals is 50/50; it could be much worse. An analogous argument may be constructed when three, four, five, or any number of rivals tie at the top of the ranking. In these cases the residual chance would simply be divided by three, four, five, etc. instead of two.

The reason we are examining this argument is for the illumination it will shed on rankings in which the top two rivals are not quite tied, but have a very small gap between them. Although one rival is clearly better than all the others, it is not very much better. All things considered, we would have to choose C_1, but C_2 is not that far behind; a very minor change in the picture could reverse the order. Stage II of the DC-10 crash investigation is such an argument. Such cases do not depart by very much from the situation in which two rivals are tied at the top of this list. Consequently, when C_1 beats C_2 by very little, C_1 cannot be much better than 50/50 on the data so far. And if there are other rivals not yet completely ruled out, C_1, although still the best account, would be below 50/50—perhaps substantially below: because C_1 and C_2 would then not even be dividing up the whole pie between them. (Stage II of the DC-10 investigation fits here as well.) This is what was intended by the earlier comment that sometimes the best account is not very good: although strong arguments must be sound,* sound arguments need not be very strong.

---

*This of course follows from the above arithmetic as well: if one rival is better than 50/50 no others can be, and hence none can be better than the one that is.

There is still a legitimate question about sound inductive arguments that do not support their conclusion beyond the 50/50 level. Since their conclusions are more likely to be false than true, why be interested in them? Such arguments are useful in at least three distinct ways, one of which we have been examining in this chapter. Determining the best account at any stage of an investigation tends to focus the inquiry; and this is so even when the best is not very good. At one stage in the DC-10 inquiry, we were hanging between an explosion, a collision, and some other structural failure, with a slight edge going to the first of these. Clearly, the efficient procedure at that stage was to look for further evidence of these three phenomena, especially an explosion, although none of them was individually very likely on the data available. Even very early in the process we need to know the most plausible accounts in order to know how best to spend our time. The general notion of a 'clue' is at home here for just this reason. When we "haven't a clue," we just don't know where to start looking; when we find a clue, that suggests other things to do: data to take, checks to run. But a clue is a weak argument. It is suggestive but inconclusive evidence: just a beginning. A clue is useful precisely because it elevates one of the rivals to the top of the list, even though the top is not very high just yet.

Recall that in our discussion of experimental design, the sign of a well-designed experiment was taken to be that the most likely outcomes had some clear impact on the plausibility ranking. We usually cannot create tests in which all possible results will be useful, so we allow those in which the most likely ones will be. Efficient scientific investigation requires that we use everything we already know about the rival accounts to determine what further data is worth taking. The antecedent plausibility ranking is crucial when the absolute values are low.

The other two places in which weak inductive arguments are useful depend more heavily on the soundness of those arguments: despite the inconclusiveness of the evidence, the conclusion is nevertheless the best account of the matter. Even though it is more likely false than true, the conclusion of a sound-but-weak argument is still more likely true than any of the other rival accounts.* So, for example, if we must act or make a decision on inconclusive evidence, it is often prudent to act on the best bet even when that bet is not

---

*It is important to emphasize this because we may be tempted to think we can automatically formulate a better account by disjoining all the other rivals. I might say, "Well, C_1 may be better than C_2, C_3, C_4, or C_5 taken alone, but it is not better than my special account, which is the compound conclusion, C_2 or C_3 or C_4 or C_5. Assuming these are all the significant rivals, then since C_1 is more likely false than true, my disjunctive account is more likely true than false—and hence more likely than C_1." But my fancy, compound conclusion simply does not count as an account—a rival—in this context. Recall that the argument's implicit question, together with the circumstances in which the argument is offered, determines the list of rivals. This is done before we do any ranking, and can be done before we have much in the way of evidence. So if the list of rivals is C_1, C_2, C_3, C_4, and C_5, saying C_1 is the best account simply means the best of these. Given this question, and these circumstances, C_2 or C_3 (or any other compound) simply is not an account, a rival: it is the disjunction of two.

very good. Suppose you have a job offer from three companies, B, G, and L, but it is crucial to you that you work for the company that gets the upcoming government defense contract. Only B, G, and L have bid on the contract, and you must decide which job to take before the contract is awarded. So you sniff around for evidence that the Defense Department favors one of these companies, and finally come up with something, but not much—just a clue. Whatever you have discovered pushes G slightly ahead of the other two, but not even close to the 50/50 level. If this is the way things stand when your day of decision arrives, it would be wise to accept the position at G: G would be the best bet.

This case is somewhat idealized to make the point clear. Actual cases will usually be more complicated, evaluatively messier. Other differences among three jobs will nearly always figure in the calculation. And when alternatives become interrelated, decisions must appeal to principles of game theory too elaborate to treat in this text. But real cases often approximate our idealization, and to that extent weak evidence is relevant to action in a perfectly straightforward way: act as though the best bet is true.

Games of chance offer a helpful analogy here. In rolling a pair of fair dice, if you must bet on one particular number (the sum of the spots on the two faces showing), it is prudent to bet on seven. This in spite of the fact that the chance seven will *not* show is much greater than the chance it will. It is wise to bet on seven because it has the *best* chance (one in six) of any single number. Every other sum is less likely than seven even though seven falls far short of 50/50. When choices have this sort of structure, sound-but-weak inductive arguments are very valuable indeed—sometimes the best that can be hoped for.

The third useful application of weak inductive argument is simply in our holding reasonable opinions on difficult matters. It is reasonable and normal to hold tentative, revisable views on many topics of general interest about which we have only sketchy evidence. The nature of extraterrestrial life, the quantity of our usable petroleum reserves, the effect of fluorocarbons on the atmosphere, the accounts of the most reliable UFO observations, and the social roots of crime, are all topics on which best bets are not very good. Nevertheless some views of these matters are far more plausible than others; while we do not *know for sure* what is going on, we do have *some* idea. In these circumstances it is reasonable to adopt the most plausible story in each case, if there is one alone at the top of the ranking. As long as we realize that what we have here is a tentative best bet, very likely in need of some revision, there is no harm in this; and it displays a commendable sensitivity to evidence.

Larger Gaps

Something like the converse of the small-gap criterion holds too, although it is far less helpful in our practical evaluations. If the gap between the top of the list and the next best is large enough, that guarantees the argument is a strong one. But to say just *how* large and *how* strong would require that we place our plausibility judgments on a rather precise numerical scale. And nothing in our experience with the run of these judgments will allow us to place them on such a scale with enough precision to make the numbers meaningful.* We will sometimes say, as we did at the end of the DC-10 investigation, that the argument is strong because it would take something truly incredible to drop the best bet below any of the other formerly serious rivals. This relates strength to a large plausibility gap. But it is not at all clear whether we judge strength by appeal to gap size or gap size by appeal to strength. All we may say with certainty is that sometimes we recognize a strong argument when we see one. If our judgment of strength is controversial, the best thing to do in general is to make a stronger argument: dig out some background, or dig up some trace-data.

SUMMARY: PRACTICAL EPISTEMOLOGY

Evidence evaluation involves a hunt for explanations. Whenever supporting data include traces, whenever an inference depends on our understanding what those traces are evidence *of,* the inference will crucially depend on finding the best explanation of those data. To determine the best explanation requires application of our two basic diagnostic skills: the ability to form a plausibility ranking on the present data, and to judge what further data would be relevant. The soundness of our diagnostic judgment is in turn largely determined by how much we know about the matter in question. Education and experience are the major requisites of competent evidence evaluation; the more we know the better we can do. It is for this reason that inductive argument—unlike deductive argument—is very importantly a matter of content as well as form.

It is also partly for this reason that philosophers are impatient with inductive argument. For tying it to our knowledge and judgment seems to defy the natural philosophical urge to provide induction with a pure logical "foundation." And perhaps it does, but that is irrelevant to our purpose here. The modest task of this chapter has been to show what skills are at work in the clearest cases of inductive argument, and to develop them into a technique for handling such arguments more generally, and in tougher cases. At their best, our judgments of plausibility and relevance are as clear and objective as anything ever gets in such contexts, as good as our best perceptions. Philosophers may still raise abstract questions of deception and hallucination and ask for further justification of our skill; but in our practical endeavor we

---

*In certain rare but important circumstances we can quantify our plausibility judgments with some precision, of course: this is what makes statistics so valuable in some fields of endeavor. We touch briefly on these circumstances in Chapter 4.

may safely ignore this request. Using the procedure developed in this chapter, the best arguments we can produce are the ones showing that the collision caused the crash, the brick broke the picture tube, or the sun will rise tomorrow. These are as strong as anyone could hope for or care about in practical applications. As standards for practical evidence evaluation, these are actually very high; judging evidence by comparison with these is appropriate in nearly every case. We should resist the temptation to apologize for not doing more.

EXERCISES

Review Questions

1. How can an inductive argument be sound but not very strong? Think up a novel illustration. Why is the converse (strong but not sound) not possible?
2. What is a diagnostic inductive argument (give two characterizations if you can)?
3. How can a nondiagnostic induction make important use of a diagnostic one?
4. When is an inductive argument for an explanatory (that is, potentially diagnostic) conclusion nondiagnostic?
5. In what way does the implicit question of a diagnostic argument directly involve that argument's trace-data?
6. Why is it usually better to describe new data as relevant to an investigation than to a particular argument? What does an argument have in common with an investigation which would make it part of that investigation?
7. What is it about new information that decides its relevance to a diagnostic investigation?
8. What is an explanatory hurdle?
9. How do gaps in the plausibility ranking relate to the strength of an argument?
10. When is a weak inductive argument nevertheless useful?
11. What principle of experimental design derives directly from the second component of our diagnostic skill?
12. What is an asymmetrical test?
13. What is antecedent plausibility?
14. In the inductive version of the gas-gauge argument in Chapter 22 (pp. 37–38) both a broken starter and a dead battery are ruled out by the support provided, but in different ways. Explain the difference.
15. Give an example of background information that is clearly relevant to the DC-10 investigation, but which is reasonably omitted from the supporting statements because it is so generally well known.

Arguments

1. Suppose that, before they learned anything else about the matter, those who witnessed the fireball over Baker Lake (see argument 2 in the exercises for Chapter 2) thought it was a meteorite. This may be represented as thinking that the following diagnostic induction is sound.

$$\frac{(S_1)\quad \text{Fireball}}{(C)\quad \text{Meteorite}}=d$$

That is, they are offering a meteorite as the best account of the fireball, on what they know. Allow this to be the starting point of an investigation into the cause of the fireball. The argument's implicit question (and hence that of the investigation) is simply "What was that?"—what produced that flash in the sky over Baker Lake? So the list of mutually rival conclusions will look something like this.

C_1 Meteorite ($= C$)
C_2 ICBM test
C_3 Failed rocket launch
C_4 Exploding aircraft
C_5 Falling satellite
C_6 Atmospheric phenomenon (aurora, St. Elmo's fire, etc.)
C_7 Exploding swamp gas
C_8 UFO from another civilization

a. Extend this list as far as you think it profitable, and then, just for practice, arrange the list in order of plausibility on the single bit of information provided in S_1.

b. What *general background information*—that is, information not specifically about this case—would change the ranking you provided? How would it change? (Hint: for example, if you knew that not a single national or international airline route went anywhere near Baker Lake, that might drop C_4 lower in the ranking.)

As the investigation proceeds it uncovers the information presented in last chapter's exercise, and a bit more. So the next stage in the investigation yields the following argument:

(S_1) Fireball (over Baker Lake).

(S_2) For the previous week tracking stations had reported a Soviet satellite dropping dangerously low in its orbit.

(S_3) Radio contact with that satellite had been lost the evening of the fireball.

(S_4) The satellite was due to pass over northern Canada at about the time the fireball was sighted.

(S_5) Fireballs are typical of falling satellites.

(S_6) The fireball traveled west-to-east, comporting with the Soviet satellite's orbit.

(S$_7$)   Radioactive debris of plausibly human fabrication was found poking out of a crater in the ice of a frozen river just to the east of Baker Lake.

(S$_8$)   The Soviets reported that the satellite in question was powered by a nuclear reactor.

$$===d$$

(C$_5$)   The fireball was a falling satellite.

  c.   Which support claims contain trace-data? Briefly state why in each case.

  d.   Briefly explain why the others do not contain traces.

  e.   What are the major explanatory hurdles for the meteorite account in this argument?

  f.   What further information would clearly promote the meteorite account back to the top of the list? (How would it get past the hurdles)?

  g.   Suppose that, a week after the fireball, the satellite mentioned in S$_2$ begins transmitting a signal once again, from about the same orbit.

    i.   Explain in a sentence or two why this would meet the criterion of relevance offered in this chapter.

    ii.   Why would this statement, if made part of the support, *not* semantically eliminate C$_5$?

    iii.   Why would it not *semantically* eliminate even the conclusion that the fireball was the satellite in S$_2$ falling back to earth?

    iv.   In what way would this new information dramatically affect our view of the trace-data in the argument above? (Hint: what would it suggest about what the traces are traces *of*?)

2.   Exercise 2a. of Chapter 1l (p. 14) offers an argument about a midair collision.

  a.   Provide some modestly plausible rivals to the conclusion stated in that exercise.

  b.   What are the crucial trace-data these rivals must accommodate? How do they do it? (You may ignore this question if the phrasing of a rival makes the answer obvious.)

  c.   What new information would *clearly* elevate one of your rivals past the one offered in the exercise?

3.   Rank the rival conclusions you provided for argument 3 in the exercises for Chapter 2 (p. 44) in the order of their plausibility on the data given. Provide some new data that would have a clear and substantial impact on that ranking. Briefly describe the impact you think the data would have, and explain why you think so.

4.   Late one night on a fog-shrouded stretch of rural interstate highway, a chain-reaction collision involving several trucks and dozens of cars touched off a spectacular blaze that eventually engulfed nearly all of the vehicles. In the investigation the following day, police were at first unable to locate the driver of one of the cars. She was later found at the

bottom of a very steep embankment bordering the crash site, dead apparently of injuries suffered in the fall. Police theorized that the woman, distraught over wrecking her brand-new car, committed suicide by hurling herself over the guardrail against which her car had come to rest.

a. What conclusion do the police draw about the woman's death?

b. State two rival conclusions (explanations), one of which is clearly more plausible than the one given and the other clearly less plausible, on the data provided in the paragraph.

c. Assuming that this paragraph contains all the information the police had relevant to the woman's death, what does your response to *b* tell you about their inference?

5. In 1963 Sweden introduced nationwide automobile inspection. At that time the average life of an automobile in Sweden was just over ten years. During the first eleven years of the inspection program, the average life of an automobile increased to over fourteen years. Swedish government officials have inferred from this that the inspection program has increased vehicle life.

a. Is this inference sound? Why?

b. Describe some new data that would affect your evaluation of this inference. What effect would it have and why?

6. Through a rain of embers and fly ash from a nearby brush fire, Herman scrambled up a ladder onto his roof, carrying a hose.

a. Accept this as the sole support claim in an argument answering the question "Why is Herman doing that?" What conclusion may be soundly inferred (that is, what is the best explanation)?

b. State two rival conclusions.

c. Give some data that is *not* trace-data which would (if discovered) clearly elevate one of these two rivals to the top of the plausibility ranking.

d. Give some trace-data that would now (that is, including *c*) elevate the other rival to the top of the list.

7. During a series of operations on the surface of Mars, the scoop arm on Viking I stopped responding to commands. When the Viking simulator on earth (a near twin to the mechanism on Mars) was subjected to the same series of operations, a pin malfunctioned and jammed the arm. Subsequently, a simple operation on the simulator caused the pin in question to fall out, freeing the arm. Delighted with this turn of events, the scientists in charge of Viking I on Mars commanded it to perform the same operation. When they did, the Viking I arm once again functioned normally. A television camera on board Viking I was then trained on the ground directly beneath the scoop arm; a pin just like the one that had jammed the simulator arm was observed lying in the Martian dust.

Take this to be an argument for the conclusion that the scoop arm of Viking I had been jammed by a malfunctioning pin.

a. By the rival-conclusions test, show that this is an inductive argument.

b. Provide some new information that, when added to that given above, would yield a *weaker* argument for the same conclusion. That is, think of something that would not remove the pin hypothesis from the top of the ranking, but would move its competition closer to it.

8. Schematize the diagnostic inductive argument offered in the following newspaper story.

New Theory Offered on Death of Dinosaurs
Robert Strand

A team of scientists is proposing that dinosaurs were wiped out 65 million years ago by a spectacular collision of Earth with an asteroid that cast the globe into several years of dust-choked semi-darkness.

This new hypothesis would explain why 75 percent of all living species disappeared at the same time. The idea was advanced Friday at the annual meeting of the American Association for the Advancement of Science.

The most common explanation for the global catastrophe has been that water retreating from the continental shelves caused climatic changes to which the dinosaurs could not adjust.

A recent theory suggests that the climatic changes were caused by a massive invasion into the oceans of fresh water from the Arctic Basin.

But Dale A. Russell, a Canadian paleontologist, told a symposium that no physical evidence exists to support the notion of sharp temperature declines.

The new hypothesis was explained by Luiz W. Alvarez, a Nobel laureate physicist at the University of California. His team has been pondering mysterious deposits of a rare element, iridium, at sites in Denmark, Italy and Spain.

The iridium was laid down in limestone at the exact time of the dinosaurs' demise, and the iridium concentration was 160 times what might have been expected.

Iridium is a thousand times more abundant in meteorites than in the Earth's crust, a fact that suggests the deposits came from an extraterrestrial source.

Alvarez proposed that Earth was struck by an asteroid six miles in diameter that blasted a crater 100 miles wide with the force of 100 million hydrogen bombs.

Such an explosion would have thrown an enormous quantity of dust into the stratosphere where, according to the hypothesis, it remained for several years casting Earth into semidarkness.

Lack of sunlight would have killed plankton in the ocean and plants on land, thus depriving fish and animals of food. Russell concluded from evidence in fossils that 75 percent of all living species, including the dinosaurs, the most intelligent creatures of the time, became extinct.

a. What rivals to the newly proposed account are offered in the story? (How might they naturally be lumped together into one, more general rival?)

b. What trace-data recommends the proposed account over those rivals?

c. What rather precise measurement does this superiority depend on?

d. Think up another rival.

e. What new data would clearly benefit your rival at the expense of the others mentioned? (The new data does not have to promote it past them, however.)

9. Write down the evidence Officer McLain offers in the following story for his contention that it was not his motorcycle's microphone that transmitted the recording in question.

Officer Retracts Evidence on JFK Shots Recording

A Dallas policeman says his microphone could not have transmitted the recording that prompted the House Assassinations Committee to conclude a conspiracy existed in the slaying of President Kennedy.

After listening to the recording yesterday, Officer H. B. McLain said it could not have come from the microphone on his motorcycle.

He previously had told the House Assassinations Committee his microphone could have been the one that picked up the sound of four shots —but that was before he heard the tape.

The tape supplied new acoustical evidence committee members said "establishes a high probability that two gunmen fired at President Kennedy."

The committee determined the tape recording was made during Kennedy's assassination in Dallas, and that the tape was recorded from a stuck transmitter on McLain's motorcycle.

The House Committee said the officer's new statement would have no effect on its findings despite its apparent challenge to the validity of the evidence and its interpretation by experts.

"That wasn't my motorcycle," McLain said. "There would have been a siren on that Channel 1 all the way to the hospital. Everybody had their sirens on . . . you would have heard it on Channel 1."

Motorcycles assigned to the presidential motorcade were supposed to be transmitting on Channel 2. The recording was made at police headquarters of a transmission over Channel 1.

Photos of McLain's motorcycle parked at Dallas' Parkland Memorial Hospital show the radio was tuned to Channel 1. But McClain said the radio was probably switched by a passerby.

Kennedy was taken to Parkland Memorial after the shooting 15 years ago in Dallas' Dealey Plaza.

McLain said he now remembers hearing then-Dallas Police Chief Jesse Curry tell patrolmen to accompany the motorcade to the hospital. That order was only sent on Channel 2.

"If I had been on Channel 1, from the time he said, 'let's go to the hospital,' you would have had a siren screaming three times as loud as you hear on the tape," McLain said.

"There was about six or eight of 'em (sirens) that was going at the same time. . . . They was just screaming," he said.

McLain was escorting the Kennedy motorcade at the time of the president's assassination.

At one point on the recording, sirens sound as if they are heading toward a stationary point and then are heard going away from it. The sirens are heard less than a minute but the actual trip from Dealey Plaza to Parkland Memorial Hospital took several minutes.

Acoustical experts testifying before the House Assassinations Committee last week said the sounds were of the motorcade just before, during and after the shooting. They say the sounds came through McLain's microphone, which was accidentally stuck open, and were routinely recorded at police headquarters.

Dallas police theorize the microphone stuck open was not on a motorcycle in the motorcade but actually was at the Dallas Trade Mart, more than two miles from Dealey Plaza. They said if the motorcycle was at the Trade Mart, which was on the route from the plaza to the hospital, it would account for the sound of the approaching, then fading sirens.

McLain said as soon as Kennedy was hit, officers in the motorcade were radioed to escort the Kennedy car at high speed to Parkland hospital.

"As soon as we got the word I got on it (the siren)," he said. "All the sirens were on. I couldn't distinguish one from another, but I know mine was going."

McLain said he stayed close to the motorcade the entire trip to Parkland and the sounds of sirens should have been fairly constant, instead of increasing and then receding.

a. What does the list of rival conclusions look like?
b. How does this help explain the utility of having such emphatically negative evidence?
c. What subdivision of Officer McLain's conclusion is suggested by the Dallas police?
d. Presuming that McLain is not lying, which of his contentions represents the greatest explanatory hurdle for the acoustical expert's theory?
e. What new discovery would effectively eliminate that hurdle?
f. What would it take to get around all the hurdles in Officer McLain's testimony (that is, what is the *most* plausible story contra-McLain)?

10. Eleanor Langen paused briefly on her walk from the bus stop to gaze sadly at the majestic shade trees she had known since her youth—or what was left of them. Soon none would remain to shade her walk on hot summer days or cast stark silhouettes against a gray winter sky. Six or eight had died each summer for the past few years, and now nearly half of the original stand was gone. Eleanor was convinced the mysterious disease could be stopped if the city would just take the problem seriously. But she was sure it wouldn't: she had already wasted hundreds of hours chasing through the municipal bureaucracy, trying to find a responsive agency.

a. What evidence does Eleanor have that the shade trees will all soon be gone?

b. Schematize the argument for this conclusion in two-step, nondiagnostic form.

c. State one or two important assumptions required in the consequence-drawing step.

d. Provide a rival for the diagnostic conclusion, which, if true, would undermine the consequence-drawing step.

e. What new information would make the rival you provided more plausible than Eleanor's diagnosis?

11. In the middle of a writing exercise with her fifth grade class, Mrs. Lippencott heard a strange roar and the windows began to rattle. Ever since coming to California she had worried about how she would react when this happened; now she would get the chance to find out. "It's an earthquake, children," she said with only a touch of panic. "We all had better get under our desks until it is over."

a. Schematize Mrs. Lippencott's argument as a two-step, nondiagnostic argument.

b. Identify the trace-data in the diagnostic step. Why is it trace-data?

c. State a rival to the diagnostic conclusion that would undermine the consequence-drawing step.

d. Provide some new information that would elevate the rival you provided to the top of the plausibility ranking.

e. Is the information you provided trace-data or not? Why?

12. Southern California has not had a very large earthquake (in the neighborhood of eight on the Richter scale) in more than a century. It is therefore likely that that area will have such an earthquake in the relatively near future.

a. Structure this predictive inference as a two-step, nondiagnostic induction.

b. How does this structure help you explain why a similar prediction cannot be drawn from the observation that South Dakota also has not had a very large earthquake in over a century?

4

Applications

The picture of evidence evaluation developed in the last chapter can shed light on many different kinds of argument and many different aspects of reasoning. Some puzzles about how we reason—or how we *can* reason in certain ways—may be resolved by noticing how our diagnostic skills are brought to bear in different contexts and on various topics. These topics naturally group themselves under an even half-dozen headings. The first covers basic *conversational reasoning,* the second focuses specifically on *testimony* as evidence, the third concerns the logic of *sampling,* the fourth inference to *causes,* the fifth *circumstantial evidence,* and the sixth treats induction by *enumeration.* Under these headings we will get some practice identifying diagnostic induction in its natural habitat and learn how to recognize its various guises. Our central aim will be to cultivate the habit of picking out the trace-data offered by an argument and automatically asking of it, "What's the best explanation of this?" Simply raising the question is often enough to organize our thinking in a helpful way.

BASIC CONVERSATIONAL REASONING

JOE: What's up, neighbor?

NEIGHBOR: My electric bill, Joe. I tell ya, the kid's gone crazy over the tube. Soon as school was out, she sat down in front of it and hasn't got up except occasionally to eat or sleep. Cartoons, game shows, soap operas, situation comedies, old movies, new movies, cops and robbers, documentaries, talk shows—she's completely indiscriminate: if it's on she'll watch it. I'm going broke. You should see the bill; we'll have to take out a loan.

JOE: Seems to me you've got two problems, not one. I guess I'd worry about what's driving the kid to watch so much T.V., but that's probably not adding much to your utility bill. Recent solid-state sets like yours don't use much electricity. I'd bet your bill is high because of that muggy weather last month. If your air conditioner ran all night like mine did during that spell, you'd really notice that.

This conversation illustrates diagnostic induction at work. Joe's neighbor begins with a bit of trace-data: his dramatically increased electric bill. And he offers his daughter's recent TV mania as the best explanation of it. Joe disagrees, suggesting that TV mania is not a particularly plausible explanation, given the low wattage of modern sets. He then offers what he takes to be a more plausible account, appealing to likely use of the air conditioner during last month's muggy nights.

As we noticed early in Chapter 3, the soundness and strength of an inductive argument depend on much that is not stated in the support claims. An immense amount of background is required and presupposed when we evaluate evidence. So when two people, approaching the same data, have backgrounds that differ in a relevant way, we can usually expect that their plausibility rankings will not be the same. They will sometimes even disagree on which rival tops the list, on which conclusion may be soundly inferred from the data in question. In this way simple conversation can have a substantial impact on our inferences. Conversation often consists in the ingenuous exchange of mundane information, which modifies and supplements our background in more or less subtle ways. In the course of time we simply change our minds about certain things: we have learned some new things, and unlearned some others, and hence changed the inferences we draw from the same collection of data.

The considerations raised by Joe in disputing his neighbor's diagnosis both have the effect of background differences, although one fits that description more comfortably than the other. His neighbor might well have not known or cared much about wattage, nor the reductions that resulted when the television industry changed to transistors. So Joe's pointing it out, or his checking the set, can easily be taken as filling in a bit of relevant background. We cannot as plausibly suppose, however, that the neighbor did not know about last month's muggy weather, or that the air conditioner probably ran much of the night during that spell. These are things he doubtless knew, but just did not think of when formulating his argument. But not thinking of relevant facts—ignoring them—has the same effect on our evaluative judgment as not knowing them in the first place. Each jeopardizes our plausibility ranking in the same way. It is important to remember that both can have this effect, and that they may be treated in something like the same way. So for our purposes a 'background problem' will concern relevant facts that are either unknown or ignored in arriving at a plausibility judgment.

Background problems, in this very broad sense, are at the heart of much human disagreement. This is the kind of disagreement we were addressing in Chapter 1 when we discussed digging out assumptions. If a disagreement can be traced to a difference in background, we can often formulate that difference as an assumption (or several) that one person makes and the other does not. This will at least locate the disagreement, and it will sometimes provide the key to eliminating it. The assumption may be easy to check, like the wattage of a TV set.

Assumption digging is often associated exclusively with deductive argument: digging up enough to eliminate all rival conclusions semantically. And the assumptions dug out in the nondiagnostic arguments of the last chapter did naturally provide deductive connections. But assumption digging is possible for diagnostic induction too. In evaluating evidence, relevant background assumptions will be those having an impact on our plausibility ranking. As usual, there will be an inexhaustibly large collection of them lurking just out of sight. The only sensible strategy is to concentrate on those that are not shared, or which are otherwise likely to be questioned. In our little dialogue the most interesting relevant assumptions are these:

JOE	NEIGHBOR
1. His neighbor's TV set is a modern, low-wattage model.	1. His TV set draws a high current.
2. The electric bill in question covered the period of last month's muggy weather.	

These are the issues on which Joe and his neighbor should focus their attention if they wish to settle their dispute. All of these are relatively easy to check; and if they can agree on these, they very likely can agree on the cause of the surprising utility bill.

As suggested above, tracing a disagreement to an unshared presupposition will sometimes serve only to locate the problem. Whether it also solves the problem will depend on whether the presupposition thus isolated is easily checked or otherwise agreed upon. This in turn will often rest on the nature and quality of our perceptions. In tracing the reasons we believe something, we eventually come to statements we simply feel are true. We can say very little about why we think they are true; they just seem, on reflection, to be pretty clearly true. In a broad, literary sense, these are our perceptions: our basic, unarticulated judgments. They determine the shape of our view of life, and of the world itself; and they constitute the basic stock of presuppositions on which our inferences rest.

Our reliability in making basic judgments will vary from area to area, topic to topic. Our basic perceptions of ordinary physical phenomena are highly reliable, almost perfectly intersubjective (which is to say, shared). We seldom go far wrong in identifying trees and cars, people and dinner plates. Nor an open door, a threatening storm, piano music, the taste of salt, or the color of the sky. For these perceptions figure so importantly and frequently in our day-to-day lives that we are constantly exercising them, constantly testing them; we simply cannot afford to ignore serious unreliability in them. If a person cannot distinguish open doors from closed ones he very soon embarrasses (or hurts) himself. It is not surprising we all more or less agree. Less ordinary perceptions, especially those concerning complex, abstract matters, have none of these attributes. They are tested relatively infrequently, the consequences of error are not so harsh or immediate, and there is broad disagreement about them. We can easily harbor a mistaken picture of international relations, federal economics, or the limits of cultural diversity, without much detriment to our daily lives.

Much of our casual conversation concerns matters like this, on which our basic, unarticulated perceptions are not very reliable and (hence) not broadly shared. This is why disagreement is so common and so intractable. The basic presuppositions of an argument on such a topic will themselves often lead to other arguments; these may require entire investigations dwarfing the original argument, and wholly beyond our immediate competence to carry out. On another occasion our two neighbors were haggling over the absurd cost of housing. Joe maintained it was due to a loose conspiracy among realtors and other speculators to create an artificial buyers' panic. His neighbor thought it was due rather to the scarcity and high cost of building materials. Joe's argument clearly presupposed that a speculators' conspiracy was competent to maintain inflation in the housing industry over a period of time. His neighbor disputed this, holding that normal market forces would prevent speculators from maintaining artificially high prices.

This is not the sort of dispute that can easily be settled over the backyard fence. But since it arose in idle conversation, Joe and his neighbor are hardly prepared to launch a research project on it. So if the exchange becomes a bit testy, as it often does, the reasonable course would be to drop the subject— agree to disagree, as they say. But we do not gladly suffer assault on our basic perceptions. It is too close to an attack on our character. We usually will not let the matter drop. It is the nature of perception* to seem straightforward; so in cases of simple perceptual disagreement we tend to see the matter as an attack on our basic judgmental competence by someone whose own judgment we cannot respect. This is responsible for much of the heat generated by social and political disputes.

One of the more difficult things in life is recognizing the limits of our personal perceptions. But clear disagreement with thoughtful people of similar background provides valuable data for us in this important endeavor. It is a simple diagnostic task: finding the best explanation of the disagreement. Sometimes it will be that the other guy is deluded, incompetent, or malicious. But it will often be tough to justify any of these smug diagnoses. And when it is, we will have gained some evidence that our perceptual competence has run out.

EVALUATING TESTIMONY: AUTHORITY AND OTHER GENETIC ARGUMENTS

It is worth repeating that, unlike our complex social and political judgments, our basic perceptions concerning the mundane matters of day-to-day living are often impressively reliable. We are so good at recognizing, characterizing, and appropriately reacting to our everyday environment that our competence seldom draws our attention. We only notice it when it surprises us in failing: when we read the clock wrong, trip over an unnoticed doorsill, or fail to recognize a friend on sight, for example. This is why perception claims can function in such strong arguments in the last chapter. Given the right context, our word, our authority can provide the strongest possible support for a position. But it is always a matter of the right context. For our testimony is sometimes uncertain, and occasionally worthless.

Testimony as Evidence

Evaluating a statement as testimony is a branch of evidence evaluation. In some circumstances, the mere utterance of a statement—the fact that somebody said it—counts as evidence for its truth. And the circumstances here will naturally include the character and competence of the person making the statement. This is why arguments evaluating testimony are called 'genetic' arguments: they ask us to "consider the source."

Genetic arguments fall neatly into the diagnostic pattern sketched in the last chapter. Explaining why a certain statement was made (by a particular person, in specific circumstances) provides the framework needed to evaluate the statement as testimony. Sometimes a statement is made simply because

*It is important to bear in mind that our perceptions here are merely how things *seem* to us, that 'perception' here means merely 'unarticulated judgment or commitment,' and nothing more. In some contexts 'perception' carries more weight than this, and it is possible to be misled when it is pressed into its more belletristic service in this context.

it is true. Other times the explanation is more complex, appealing to motivation, perception, or access to the data. So the question to ask about any statement offered as testimony—as support for itself—is "Why did he [or she] say that?" What is the best account of that person's making that statement in those circumstances? In the easy cases the answer is so obvious that the question itself is rude. "I wonder why she said it is quarter past ten?" "Perhaps because it is quarter past ten." Or, "I said it was raining because it *was* raining. There was nothing ulterior in it."

Now this is a peculiar kind of explanation, but it is singularly appropriate to evaluating testimony. Because in forming the list of rival explanations we will want to lump them together into groups specifically according to *how they bear on the truth of the statement* in question. So all those explanations that must appeal to the truth of the statement in explaining its utterance are reasonably lumped together here as the (super) rival 'said it because true' (C_1). Shortly it will be useful to divide this group into more specific rivals for some purposes; but for now it is best to consider it as a single aggregate. The major contrasting rival will then be one covering all those explanations not appealing to the truth of the statement to explain its utterance, those in which its truth is irrelevant (C_2). If the best explanations of the utterance are bad judgment, illusion, hope, fear, pity, or simply mistake, that would undermine it as testimony. The best explanation of someone's saying it's quarter past ten is, in some circumstances, that her watch has stopped. In these circumstances the statement would of course *not* be reliable testimony; the mere fact that the statement was made would not be evidence for its truth. (It still could be true, of course; we would just have to have some other reason to think so.)

There is one remaining (super) rival: the statement was made because it is false (C_3). But this category is relatively unimportant. For even when somebody lies, they seldom say what they say because it is false, but rather in spite of its being false. Explaining the lie usually requires some motivational factor from the previous category. In other words, the falsity of the statement fails to stop the liar from making it, but it usually does not explain why he did. Nevertheless, on rare occasions someone will say something in part because it is false, and then it will be important to remember this third rival account.

So as a helpful first step we can set out the preliminary form of a genetic argument in a simple one-step diagnostic induction. The data would be that the *statement* in question was made, in a specific set of *circumstances,* by someone of a certain *character* and *competence.* And the conclusion would be

S_1 Statement
S_2 Circumstances
S_3 Relevant biographical remarks
————————————————————— = d
C (best account)

one of the three rivals discussed above: 'said it because true' (C_1), 'said for reasons not related to truth' (C_2), 'said it because false' (C_3). In other words, the utterance of the statement (in the circumstances) can provide evidence for it (C_1), or against it (C_3), and it can fail to engage the issue (C_2). But remember that although it sounds nice and neutral, C_2 totally destroys the statement as testimony: it shows the utterance to be irrelevant to its truth. C_2 says, roughly, "that may be true, but your saying so gives me no reason to think so."

Let us illustrate this in an easy case. You meet Sarah on your way across campus and ask what time it is. She looks at her watch and says "Just about 10:15." Suppose you know her well enough to know she is usually punctual and ingenuous, and has no special reason to be deceptive or 'cute.' In normal conditions this would generate a sound diagnostic argument for the claim that it is just about 10:15.

S_1 Sarah says it is just about 10:15.
S_2 Normal campus encounter, no special reason to be deceptive.
S_3 Sarah is normally punctual and ingenuous.

===d

C   It is just about 10:15.

A change in S_3 would have a substantial impact on the argument. If Sarah was not punctual, but rather never on time for anything, and this was due to a watch that ran fitfully—sometimes fast, sometimes slow, sometimes not at all —and which seemed to bother her not at all, her testimony would be of little value. The best account of her statement would appeal to the unreliable watch (a version of C_2) and not to the actual time. It *might* be 10:15, but do not count on it.

This is the simple picture, and it will work in many simple cases. But there is a more revealing—if more complex—way to schematize genetic arguments. Notice that criticism of genetic arguments can take either of two systematically different forms. On the one hand, testimony might be undermined by questioning the honesty or the *sincerity* of the testifier: his motivation might be suspect. On the other hand, he might be quite sincere in his belief that he speaks the truth, but yet be undermined by criticism of his judgment or *competence.* Conversely, if testimony can pass both the sincerity and competence tests, it will have done about as much as we could expect of it.

It turns out to be helpful to expand the above argument schema into two stages, to reflect the different impact of honesty and competence considerations on genetic arguments. In the first stage we consider whether the utterance can be accounted for *directly* by appeal to (sincere) beliefs: specifically, a confidence that the statement uttered is true. If it can, we then go to the second stage and try to account for that confidence in terms of perceptions and other judgments. In most cases this expansion is not just more revealing, it is more plausible. Instead of "He said it because it is true," it is often more natural to say, "He said it because he believed it, and he believed it because he saw it happen." Instead of offering its truth directly as the best account of an utterance, we break the explanation, and hence the argument in two. The best account of someone's making a statement is (sometimes) that he is confident that it is true; and the best account of his confidence is (frequently) a reliable perception. Schematically:

First Stage S_1 Statement (utterance)
          S_2 Circumstances
          S_3 Relevant biographical remarks
              (bearing on sincerity)
          $\overline{\phantom{S_3 \quad \text{Relevant biographical remarks}}}$ d
          C   (Best account of the utterance)

If the best account at this stage involves misrepresentation, deception, joke, or the like, then the argument need go no further: the testimony can be rejected. We proceed to the second stage only if the best account here is that whoever authored the statement did so because he believed it to be true.

Second Stage S_4 Confidence (that the statement is true)
          S_5 More circumstances
          S_6 More relevant biographical remarks (bearing on
              competence)
          $\overline{\phantom{S_6 \quad \text{More relevant biographical remarks (bearing on}}}$ d
          C'   (Best account of the confidence)

Several things needs to be said about these schemata. First, in both stages 'biographical remarks' may be lumped together with circumstances whenever it is convenient to do so. They are explicitly separated here to emphasize the characteristic genetic nature of these arguments, and to make it easier to raise some issues later on. Second, the relevant circumstances—and the relevant biographical data too, of course—may be the same in both stages; but they need not be the same, so it is worth using different subscripts for the two stages. Third, unlike the nondiagnostic arguments of the last chapter, these two-step arguments may be collapsed into a single diagnostic induction, because both steps are themselves diagnostic inductions. With some loss of useful detail, most arguments of this sort may be handled in the (one-step) 'said it because true' form with which we began, and need not be cracked in two over beliefs as we have done here. Expanding a genetic argument into two stages is valuable only to the extent that it aids clarity, which it will most of the time.

As an illustration let us fill out these two schematized stages using the case of my reporting rain, making all the orthodox presumptions we would in the normal, unproblematic case. This is the easiest sort of case, one we are best equipped to handle.

First Stage S_1 I say that it is raining.

S_2 I was just looking out the window, I made the statement in a usual, matter-of-fact way, with no untoward gestures or facial expressions. The context was the normal social one and called for nothing unusual.

S_3 I am a rather normal human, have no history of compulsive practical joking or psychopathic dishonesty.

$========================= d$

C_1 I sincerely believe it is raining. (Best account of my saying so in the circumstances.)

Second Stage S_4 I am confident that it is raining.

S_5 The window I was just facing is a normal, outside window.

S_6 I am a normal competent observer with no great personal stake in having it rain.

$========================= d$

C_1 It is raining. (Best account of my confidence)

The precise features included under 'circumstances' and 'biography' will obviously depend on details of the specific case. Those included in this illustration are typical. But it is worth drawing attention to the fact that 'circumstances' include both background and trace-data. And the circumstances relevant to the first stage will include some of the subtlest trace-data we will ever detect: facial expression, inflection of voice, and general manner and deportment. Much of our communication relies on data at this level. Sometimes its impact will be absolutely clear: occasionally a lie is absolutely transparent. But even when the impact of this special kind of data is not so clear, it represents something the conclusion you reach must account for. "Why did he say it like that? And what was the wry smile all about?" Such observations might raise real doubts about the best account of the utterance; and it could be the consideration that tips the scales against the testimony.

In general, criticism of these genetic arguments—of testimony—will attempt to show either that the statement in question did not result from sincere belief, or, if it did, that its truth is not the best account of its author's confidence: that there is a better rival explanation at one stage or the other. First-stage rivals will be exclusively motivational. The major reasons we have for saying things we do not believe fall into the categories of deception and joke: we wish somebody to believe something we do not, if only for a moment. In such cases, looking at the circumstances and at our biographies will sometimes reveal the motivation. When it does it will undermine our testimony. If the best explanation of my saying something is that I was making a joke, or attempting deceit, that ruins it as testimony: we need not even look at stage two.

Criticizing the second stage raises more complex and interesting issues: the rivals will concern perceptual reliability and self-deception. We are most likely to believe something false when we fail to recognize the limits of our perceptual (or judgmental) competence, or when we have a great personal stake in the substance of that belief. The latter is again a matter of motivation, but usually the motivational issues in stage two are not the same as those involved in stage one. Still, the immediate circumstances and the personal history of the author often contain enough detail for a reasoned judgment. A mother on the witness stand sincerely may believe her son could not have killed all those people. But her enormous emotional stake in the issue raises an immense obstacle to accepting its truth as the best account of her confidence.

Mothers-on-witness-stands also raise the nonmotivational issues peculiar to stage-two evaluation and criticism. None of us—mothers included—is well acquainted with the characteristic antecedents of psychopathic killing sprees. These are relatively infrequent events, which quite typically come as a complete shock to everybody who knows the perpetrator; they are almost always totally out of character. But even knowing this it is difficult for normal human beings to believe that someone they knew well—the quiet, unassuming clerk, the neighbor who always said "hello"—actually killed all those people, or even anybody at all. Here we once again encounter the limits of our perception—of our unreflective judgment—and the trouble they cause us. In the easy cases, the contexts in which our competence is enormous and demonstrable, how confident we are in a judgment—how comfortable we feel about it—is a good guide to its security. We are conditioned by our failures to feel uneasy when tempted to make a mistake rather like ones we have suffered for in the past. Unless a judgment concerns something easy, clear, and uncontroversial, however, our feeling of confidence is an unreliable guide: our comfort may be due simply to a lack of any feedback whatever. And, as pointed out earlier, we are often not very good at recognizing when we have crossed the line—left an area of competence and ventured into uncharted waters.

So the second-stage rivals of the two-step schematization will be close relatives of the rivals (C_1, C_2, and C_3) we isolated for the one-step version. The rival that *underwrites* the testimony as evidence, the new C_1', accounts for the author's confidence (instead of the statement itself) in terms of the statement's truth: the author's confidence is due to its truth. The rivals that *undermine* the testimony, the new C_2's, would explain the confidence as the product of bad judgment, illusion, hope, fear, and the rest. Sometimes the best explanation of your confidence that you were going only fifty-five miles per hour (in spite of what the officer says) is that you misread the speedometer. Sometimes the best account of my (mistaken) confidence that the rattling windows signal an earthquake is that I am just not very good at distinguishing mild earthquakes from sonic booms. And it is important to recognize that these "misplaced confidence" rivals undermine testimony—discredit it as evidence—even when it turns out to be true. Anybody can make a lucky guess. The rattling windows might actually *be* an earthquake; but my saying so provides no reason to believe it if I am simply incompetent to judge. That is, if I am confident simply because I fail to grasp my perceptual limitations, then my confidence is worthless as evidence.

In short, when evaluating testimony—genetic arguments as schematized above—the important rival accounts at stage one will be motivational, those at stage two will concern perceptual or judgmental reliability. But since our judgment is sometimes distorted by our motives, it is helpful to further divide the second-stage rivals into (further) motivational ones and others. Finally, it will as a practical matter be helpful to divide 'others' into questions of simple reliability and questions of access to the relevant data. Nonmotivational criticism of confidence as an indicator of truth may be accomplished either by showing that the subject did not have access to adequate data, *or* by showing that he is not competent to judge even if adequate data were present.* So the picture looks like this:

TESTIMONY CHECKLIST

First-Stage Explanations (rival accounts)

C_1	Statement made because of author's confidence in it.	(go on to stage two)
C_2	Statement made in spite of author's lack of confidence in it (major rival categories: deception, joke).	(no point in going on to stage two)

Second-Stage Explanations

C_1'	Confidence due to truth (justified confidence rival).	(underwrites testimony)

C_2'	Confidence due to something else (misplaced confidence rivals).
	a. Self-deception (motivational)
	b. Misjudgment (others)
	    i. Perceptual incompetence (reliability)
	    ii. Inadequate information (access)
		(undermines testimony)

If no serious rivals can be generated under C_2 at either stage, the testimony in question is very likely worthy of *our* confidence.

---

*This distinction is only made by appeal to the typical observer: we would take successful diagnosis by an extraordinary observer to indicate the presence of adequate data no matter how little that was.

Application of this checklist to the rain example provides a useful illustration. A C_2-rival to the first conclusion would be that I said it was raining not because it was raining, but rather to distract two antagonists from their heated exchange and thereby prevent what looked to be a certain breach of civility. On the data provided this is a very long shot, because so much unstated detail would be required to make it plausible. But if we discovered that there *had* been a dangerous-looking argument, which *did* break up after my remark, because of the predictable panic about the party all set up on the lawn, and I *am* a good enough actor to pull it off convincingly, then we would have gone a long way toward making this rival the best bet.

An undermining rival account for the second stage, still compatible with the support provided, could be generated under C_2', b, ii. Perhaps the yard into which I was looking when I thought I saw rain contained a sophisticated overhead watering system, which looked a lot like ordinary rain when it ran. This too is a long shot, which is part of what it means to say the argument offered is a strong one. But if we did discover such an irrigation system, it would tend to undermine my testimony.

One final point on lay testimony. There is a special, Latin name for genetic arguments that specifically attack someone's testimony by appeal to what we have called 'biographical remarks'. These are the famous *ad hominem* arguments: attacks on the man. In philosophical contexts the term has been normally intended as pejorative, the presumption being that ad hominem arguments are bad arguments. This is because ad hominem arguments are often directed not against mere testimony, which must be backed by personal considerations, but against other arguments, which are good or bad quite independent of who offers them. When an ad hominem remark is made in response to a full-blown argument, it is nearly always wholly inappropriate and should be dismissed out of hand. But when it is directed as *testimony,* it might provide precisely the consideration needed for proper evaluation. If someone is colorblind, nearsighted, a notorious liar, or in love with a protagonist, his testimony might be suspect for just that reason. Whether it is or is not may be determined by plugging it into our genetic-argument schema, to see if the personal consideration has an objective impact on the best account of the statement in question. Colorblindness is clearly irrelevant to some kinds of testimony, as, too, sometimes is love.

Authority

Against this background we may easily display the structure of what is traditionally called argument from authority, appeal to authority, or *expert* testimony. These are the cases in which someone is appealed to as an authority. They fit easily into the testimony schemata simply by allowing our checklist to range over extraordinary reliability (due to training), extraordinary access (due, perhaps, to research and study), and even in some cases extraordinary motivation. The motivational considerations primarily concern professional reputation or visibility and work both ways: they might count for or against testimony, depending on the circumstances. The other two (extraordinary access and reliability) require mostly a word of caution. We have the same trouble estimating the limits of others' competence that we have with our own. It is important to know just what specific competence the expert has and whether the testimony falls squarely within it. This requires effort on our part if our evaluation is to be any good—sometimes more effort than we are prepared to exert.

In general there is an important difference between sincerely claimed expertise and reliable testimony about a specific subject matter. We must have reason to think the expertise reliably yields the information we require. This unfortunately means that we as evaluators must sometimes acquire at least modest familiarity with the field in question—and even with experts in general. For the limits of specially trained perception and judgment are every bit as hard to detect as those of ordinary ones, and perhaps even less likely to arouse our suspicion. We are all quite understandably impressed with the learning and dedication of people who become authorities in their field. We are almost universally inclined to let our immense respect cloud our judgment of what they say. As an antidote, it is probably good policy to be slightly skeptical all the time. *Make doubly sure* the authority's competence is in the appropriate area; *ask* whether there is general agreement in that area on the matter in question; try to *determine* if it is the sort of thing experts are wrong about all the time. If testimony can clearly pass these tests, we can be sure we have some pretty good information.

The first two of these tests are fairly straightforward. In general we should not uncritically accept what even very good physicists tell us about the history of science. And if a matter is in hot dispute among authorities in a field, we should not accept whatever position is held by the one we happen to have. The third test, however, is tricky. Just as our judgment is sometimes dangerously uncritical because of our respect, it is sometimes dangerously contemptuous as the result of celebrated mistakes and oversimplifications. Our evidence tends to be anecdotal: "I once knew an expert who said X, but it turned out to be Y." Everybody has stories like this. But for an expert to be any good, for his testimony to be reliable, for his information to be of value to you does not require infallibility. It merely requires that he be substantially better than you are without help. So we should try to find out what we can about experts in our field of interest. Sometimes it will be obvious that the expertise is valuable: weather forecasters are not *very* good, but they are usually far better than we could be, left to our own resources. On the other hand, for years the recommendations of stockbrokers have generally performed only about as well as the market itself. So the investor would have done as well to select stocks to buy *randomly* as he would have (randomly) taking the advice of brokers. In general, either extreme position is untenable. *In general,* all we can say is that we sometimes do know enough to feel secure in expert judgment. These last three headings provide a useful guide in determining when that is.

If the matter in question is sufficiently important, however, there is something further we can do to guide our judgment: we can examine an expert's track record. Of course one need not be a certified expert or authority to have a track record, so let us refer to him or her—the author of the testimony we are interested in—as our 'informant'. Examining an informant's actual performance will often yield all the data we need to answer the crucial question: is he (or she) able to answer reliably the kinds of questions we are interested in? The 'performance' here may be actual past testimony under similar conditions, or it could be responses to a test we administer. Either way, if the reliability may be captured in a success ratio (e.g., six right out of ten), we can make our determination simply by examining our own interest. Interest here has two components: subject matter and difficulty. An informant is valuable to us only if he can maintain a *high* success ratio on *difficult* questions about the *subject matter* we are concerned with.

The subject matter restriction is, obviously, the same old one: if we want information about the stock market we should not rely too heavily on someone whose successes have been exclusively in predicting earthquakes. Once again, drawing boundaries between disciplines raises difficult questions, but we know enough that it must be done—skills do not transfer well from one area to another. We can rely on information only in those cases in which we *can* reliably draw those lines: it is required to determine the relevance of an informant's record to our need. The other two considerations—success ratio and difficulty—go hand in hand. The question is, Can our informant do better than we could without his help—enough better to justify his cost to us? In other words, a bare success ratio is of no value to us; if we could do as well, why hassle with an expert? Only if he can do well on tough questions—ones we could not do well on—is he worth the trouble. Correctly predicting clear skies in Palm Springs 80% of the time is boring: we could easily do as well. But a fat man predicting productive oil wells in the swamps of New Jersey only 40% of the time is worth his weight in gold. Once again, an informant is valuable if he can provide a high percentage of right answers to tough questions in the right field. In complicated or borderline cases, whether he would be good enough to justify using him (i.e., to compensate for all costs and risks) would depend on expectation computations beyond the scope of this text. There are enough easy, nonborderline applications, however, to make the principle constantly useful.

For example, we are sometimes struck by particularly accurate predictions and diagnoses found on the newspaper's horoscope page. As a result, we sometimes speak as though we have found on that page a worthy, reliable informant. For most such pages, this inference is seriously flawed in a way characterizable in terms of the above principle. A preliminary flaw is that we virtually never keep tabs on the column adequate to form an explicit success ratio. This, because we are understandably more impressed with success than failure here, allows us to deceive ourselves by selectively ignoring the failures. But even if the actual success ratio were very high indeed, it is not at all clear we could infer that we had found a good informant. For the claims typically made on such pages are precisely the easy, high-base-rate ones we should all be bored with: you seek to improve yourself, you are impatient with hypocrites, you will have some good fortune. Who won't (or isn't)? (Many things on that page are not really claims that may be evaluated as true or false. Sometimes they have the form of general advice: avoid risky entanglements; face life with cheer and optimism despite adversity. To the extent that these may be evaluated, say, as wise or unwise, they have the same trouble as the others; they are rather low-level advice anybody could give.) Philosophers, politicians, advertising executives, and con men are intimately familiar with the principle: If you make a claim sufficiently vague and general, it will be true under so many circumstances you almost can't go wrong; yet you still give the appearance of having said something.

A typical horoscope's apparent impressiveness is best explained by selective perception and low-risk statements. Usually there is no evidence of a reliable informant. But if such a column—or any other informant—*can* pass the tests described above, that provides the best sort of reason to value the information it contains or produces.

Summary

The utterance of a statement is in some circumstances evidence for its truth. Estimating the strength of the evidence is a standard diagnostic problem: finding the best explanation of the utterance and seeing how closely connected it is to truth. For general testimony the rival explanation checklist is

Motivation
Access
Judgment (Perception)

These provide the categories within which other rival accounts will fall, as well as a list of checks on the truth-related account. If we use a two-stage schema, which is most natural in many cases, the motivation category will (usually) contain two separate considerations that it is important to keep distinct.

Expert testimony is handled in the same way, although the checklist categories contain a few special items. Central among these are three in the 'judgment/perception' category. We must make sure the expert's expertise is in the right field, that experts are in general agreement about the topic in question, and that expertise in the field is not itself suspect.

This latter point leads naturally to concern with testing an informant's judgment. We can *directly* test an informant if we find some adequately *tough* questions, in the *relevant* field, to which we know (or can find) the answers. (This is easy if the answers are simple predictions.) If the informant's success ratio is better than we could do, the information is of some value to us. How much value depends on *how much* better it is than we could do.

SAMPLES, POPULATIONS, AND STATISTICAL INFERENCE

In testing an informant we are doing what a statistician would call sampling a population. It is sometimes helpful to think of what we were doing there as inferring *from* a sample *to* a population it was presumed to represent. The sample consists of the responses by the informant we are testing to our test questions, and the population is the complete collection of that informant's responses to similar questions, actual and possible. Of course, the term 'population' comes originally from actual groups of people, the collective properties of which are always of some interest to somebody. But as the term is used in this context, it can refer to *any* collection: anything that can be counted —ships and shoes and jelly beans, but also marriages, meter readings, and responses to questions. In each case we use the sample, which is available, to learn about the population, which is what we are really interested in.

If we wish to find out about a population by studying a sample taken from it, the sample must *faithfully represent* the population in all important respects. When a sample has a certain property, P, we may infer that the population has that property only if we have good reason to think the sample is representative (of the population) in that respect: it must look like the population in that respect at least. So making a statistical inference (inferring from P in a sample to P in a population) involves *discovering evidence* for a sample's representativeness.

This is done, once again, by appeal to our diagnostic principle of Chapter 3. Suppose we are interested in a specific property of a population, and our sample has that property. To decide whether we may soundly infer that the *population* has that property, we must ask, "What is the best explanation of the sample's having that property?" We are primarily interested in the various rival explanations only insofar as they tell us something about representativeness. So the rival explanation of major interest is C_1: the sample has property P *because* the population has property P. If this account is best, we have evidence that the sample is representative. If not, not. So this will be one context in which a *single* division of the list will be appropriate: all the remaining rivals are best lumped together as not-C_1. They will for the most part be various ways of explaining how a sample with property P came to be drawn from a population that does not have that property.

C_1: The sample has P *because* the population has P.

not-C_1: The sample has P, but *not because* the population has P.

Within this latter category (not-C_1) it is common and useful to distinguish two subrivals. There are two systematically different *ways* to explain how we got an unrepresentative sample. First, the sample might have property P not because the population has it, but rather because of some *distorting feature of the selection procedure*—the procedure used to select the sample. Call this C_2. C_2 will include all the explanations holding that a sample with P was drawn from a population not having P due to something in the *way* it was drawn. The second way to explain an unrepresentative sample is just chance (C_3). Sometimes we will draw a sample with P from a population without it, just by chance. Sometimes luck will be the best explanation of a sample's having property P. For investigative purposes it is best to deal with C_2 and C_3 separately. But *both* C_2 and C_3 characterize a sample as an unreliable guide to its population. So their weight must be added together in the final argument:

$$not\text{-}C_1 \cong C_2 + C_3$$

And it is against this sum that C_1 must compete. Let's illustrate all this with a simpleminded example.

Suppose you have taken a half-dozen cookies from the jar in the kitchen, and they all turned out to be the same kind: chocolate-chip fudge. The composition of this sample might be explainable in any of the above three ways, and we would favor one or the other depending on the circumstances. The sample might have turned out that way (case 1) simply *because* all the cookies in the jar were chocolate-chip judge. That certainly would explain it, in the right circumstances. On the other hand, it might be that most of the cookies in the jar are oatmeal raisin, just the top few layers being chocolate-chip fudge. In that case, the unrepresentative uniformity of your sample might be explained (case 2) by the way you selected the sample: simply reaching in and taking the cookies on top. That would explain it, if that is what happened. But suppose you took only one or two off the top. For the rest you groped around further down, boorishly reaching all the way to the bottom for at least one. In this case, if it turned out that most of the cookies were indeed oatmeal raisin, we would attribute your (now bizarre) sample (case 3) to the luck of the draw: sometimes unlikely things do occur. In this complex story, the first sample is the only representative one—one that would allow an inference to the nature of the population in question. This of course is a product of the way the illustration was set up: the other two kinds of explanations are merely ways of explaining why the sample you got was not representative.

But how does this help? To choose the appropriate explanation here we relied on knowing the nature of the population. When we need to infer from a sample property to a population property this is precisely what we do not know. The whole point of the inference is to discover something about the population that we do not already know. Can we settle the explanatory question without already knowing what we are trying to find out?

Yes, of course, and it is interesting to see how. In practice, the procedure for establishing the strength of a statistical inference is the very one we used in our diagnostic investigations of Chapter 3. To assure ourselves that a sample property is best explained by a population property we show that rival explanations of the other two kinds are ruled out. And we do this by combining antecedent plausibility considerations with the raising and lowering of explanatory hurdles. If the resulting plausibility of not-C_1 (i.e., C_2 + C_3) is *not clearly lower* than C_1, then the inference to the population property is not sound. We need a new argument, a new sample, under different conditions: we must collect more data, just as in the investigations of the last chapter.

Cookies make a good illustration of all this too. Suppose we do not know anything very specific about the kinds of cookies in the jar. Assume a normal, typical familiar set of circumstances: an ordinary ceramic (nontransparent) cookie jar, in a normal sort of kitchen, nearly filled with cookies of the usual shape and size. But we haven't looked in, were not there when it was being filled, and in general have not cheated on the presupposition of ignorance. Given all this, if we now select a sample of cookies, we can say something about which category of explanation its properties have, simply by noting its size and the way it was selected. We can occasionally, if things are right, extract information about the population without knowing it beforehand. But in any case, some clear distinctions may be drawn.

If the sample consists of one sugar cookie taken off the top, it tells precious little about what else is in the jar. This is because it is about equally well (or badly) explainable as having been drawn from a variety of different populations. It could be one of two or three plain sugar cookies in a varied assortment—the top cookie had to be *something,* after all. A layer explanation works well here too, as does the 100% sugar cookie account. But just as good as any of these is one that suggests that the population is *mostly* sugar cookies, not in layers, just evenly distributed but predominant in number. None of these is clearly much better than any of the rest, which is just what it means to say the sample does not tell us much.

Using the rival categories distinguished above, the analysis would read as follows. The sample is 100% sugar cookies; so C_1 would say the population *also* was 100% sugar cookies: it would explain the sample as just what we would expect to draw from a jar full of sugar cookies. C_2 would include primarily the layer account (although with some imagination you might think of others). This rival would explain the sample as coming from a layer of sugar cookies on top of other kinds. C_3 would include the rest: we might just by *chance* get a sugar cookie out of a varied assortment; and there would be a *good* chance of getting a sugar cookie if the jar contained mostly sugar cookies, but not all. So the rival picture would look like this:

$C_1 = 100\%$ sugar cookies
$C_2 =$ layers
$C_3 =$ chance draw from a $\left.\begin{array}{l}\\\\\\\end{array}\right\} = $ not-C_1
    variety of populations

At this stage we would have to say that not-C_1 (i.e., $C_2 + C_3$) is a better bet than C_1: the sample is unlikely to be representative.

(S_1)   Sample property: 100% sugar cookies.
(S_2)   Sample consists of one cookie taken off the top.
$$\overline{\hspace{7cm}} = d$$
(not-C_1) Sample property not due to population property.

If we augment the sample by taking five more cookies off the top, and they turn out also to be sugar cookies, that places an enormous hurdle in front of the 'variety' account, but leaves the others pretty much intact. This would increase the odds on representativeness, but probably not enough to make it the best bet: C_1 still has too much competition.

Without increasing the size of our sample we could rule out the 'layer' hypothesis by reaching around in the jar, taking cookies from various layers. If the sample still comes up uniformly sugar cookies, the only plausible explanations remaining are the last two: all or most of the cookies in the jar match those in the sample. Notice that it is still *possible* that, for example, we just by chance got all the sugar cookies by reaching around in the jar, trying for a representative sample. But that explanation is a very long shot at this stage. Any population that includes just six—or even seven or eight—sugar cookies is practically ruled out. And this rules out virtually anything we would describe as a varied assortment. So at this stage the argument would run:

(S_1)   Sample property 100% sugar cookies.
(S_2)   Sample consists of six cookies selected at random throughout the jar.
$$\overline{\hspace{7cm}} = d$$
    ?

The two remaining plausible rivals would be

$C_1 = 100\%$ sugar cookies

      chance draw from a
$C_3 =$ population of mostly $=$ (roughly) not-C_1
      sugar cookies

It is not clear which would be the better bet at this stage. But recall that in such circumstances (two top rivals nearly indistinguishable in plausibility) the best bet is not terribly good. So it is still very far from certain that the sample is representative.

Distinguishing between the remaining two explanations (i.e., populations) is actually very difficult. Even if we sampled half the cookies in the jar, the chance that we missed one or two left over from an earlier batch is still pretty high. It might be that they are all sugar cookies, but there could easily be a chocolate-chip fudge lurking in there somewhere. Given a few plausible assumptions, it is easy to see that if we sampled half the jar and there was one aberrant cookie, the odds of missing it would be just 50/50.

It is important to bear in mind that what we are doing here is a direct extension of our diagnostic-argument procedure of Chapter 3: we are trying to determine the best account of different collections of data. Just as in Chapter 3, our substantive background is of central importance to our judgment. Part of the reason we can be relatively confident about our inferences in these illustrations is that we know a great deal about the physical properties of cookies, and about the institutions surrounding kitchens and cookie jars. We take the layer hypothesis seriously because we know something of the way cookies go into and come out of cookie jars. If they were rather like jelly beans, we would not have to take layers so seriously. All of which serves to underline a central point. As in any inductive inference, everything we know about the sample and the population in question is potentially relevant to our inference. The best explanation is best only given what we know.

Nevertheless, there are a few general characteristics of sample-population inferences that it is helpful to point out. Let us consider just any sample selected from a specific population.* We can examine the individuals in the sample, but not the other members of the population. The individuals in the sample have a certain property, P (e.g., all chocolate chip), and we wish to know what this tells us about the population. The systematic peculiarity of sample-population inferences, the feature accounting for both their value and their danger, arises at this point. For the individuals making it into the sample manage to do *this* also because of some property or properties they have. The cookies *on the top* made it into my sample in one case: they got in *because* they had that property. If I conduct a street corner survey, only the people who pass that corner while I am there will be part of the sample. The part of the population not having that property is excluded. So the members of the sample are always distinguishable from the population in general in at least one respect, which is to say they are atypical: *unrepresentative* in this respect at least. And if this unrepresentativeness is relevant to the property we are interested in, P, it will undermine our inference.

---

*It is of course possible that we mistakenly sample the wrong population. We intend to sample dentists' receptionists, but get our hands on the wrong list of telephone numbers. For this discussion we will assume we have always sampled the intended population. This is something else to watch out for in tricky cases.

It is important to understand that any sample can be characterized in this way, no matter how plausibly drawn. If I reach all around in the cookie jar, the ones I pick will still have a distinguishing characteristic: they were the ones in my grasp when I finally decided to take one. If I conduct my survey by throwing darts at a city map and interviewing people at the addresses nearest the holes, those addresses, and hence those people, have the distinction of being at the end of those trajectories. Accordingly, to select samples from which inferences may confidently be drawn, the inevitable unrepresentativeness due to the selection procedure must be *irrelevant* to the property of interest. If there is no connection, no correlation between the property used to select the sample and the property we wish to use in our inference (P), then the sample's inevitable atypicality is innocuous.

Showing that it is innocuous is what we earlier called raising obstacles to explanations from category two. If the selection procedure is what gave the sample property P, then the atypicality is not innocuous, it ruins the inference. If, on the other hand, the procedure does not explain the sample's having property P, then the unrepresentativeness due to the procedure is innocuous for inferences concerning P. The reason we prefer one method of sampling the cookie jar over another is that we already know a great deal about the connections among sample properties: what's likely to explain what. And if we are interested in what kind of cookies are in the jar, we know we are better off to sample by groping around in the jar than by taking cookies off the top. Layer explanations are too plausible in the latter case. This of course raises once again the issue of background knowledge: the more you know about the property in question the better sample you can select. Conversely, the less you know the more difficult it is to select intelligently. But this is merely a reflection of the fact that sample-population inferences are ordinary inductive arguments; plausiblity ranking cannot take place in an informational vacuum.

When we have assured ourselves that all explanatory connection has been broken between P and the sampling procedure, we call the selection unbiased. An unbiased sample is one in which no unrepresentativeness can be traced to the selection procedure; all explanations from category C_2 have been ruled out as implausible. If a selection procedure *is* responsible for unrepresentativeness in the sample, the sample is biased: biased by the selection procedure. Perhaps the most celebrated case of a biased selection procedure is the 1936 presidential election poll conducted by the *Literary Digest*. The *Digest* randomly selected names from telephone books all over the country, telephoned the selected individuals, and compiled the results. On the basis of their sample they confidently predicted a landslide win for Alf Landon, the Republican nominee. But Landon's opponent, Franklin Roosevelt, was the one who won by a landslide, severely embarrassing the *Digest*'s editors, and contributing to the magazine's demise. The unrepresentativeness of the *Digest*'s sample is easily traceable to the selection procedures. For in 1936 the vast majority of the nation's poor and lower-middle-class voters could not afford a telephone. The telephone was a relative luxury at the time, and the whole world was just then struggling out of the worst depression in history. So by limiting its sample to those voters listed in telephone directories, the *Literary Digest* inadvertently biased its sample heavily in favor of the relatively affluent. In 1936 even more than today, our relatively affluent citizens tended overwhelmingly to be Republicans, and to favor Landon to a much greater extent than the population as a whole.

This case illustrates the degree to which sample-population inferences fall into the pattern of diagnostic induction, especially in criticism. For the best explanation of the *Digest*'s sample having the property in question (overwhelmingly favoring Landon) *is* the selection procedure itself (i.e., C_2), not the population's preference. The best account of that sample's overwhelming preference for Landon was that it contained atypically wealthy voters, not that voters in general preferred Landon. And once again, the importance of a trained and exercised imagination is underscored: unless the list of rival explanations contains all the plausible ones, the ranking and hence the inference will be jeopardized.

It is important to notice that a given selection may be unbiased for one property yet not for another. Selection procedures will naturally be connected with some properties and not others, so a selection procedure that is quite adequate for inferences about one property may well be inadequate for others. A sample's inevitable atypicality will be innocuous for some and not others. It might well turn out, for example, that there is no connection between eye color and wealth; so the *Literary Digest* sample might be perfectly adequate to estimate the eye-color distribution in the population, even though it failed miserably to represent political preference. Once again, *all* samples are atypical in some respect or other; which ones we can use for what inferences depends on what we know about the connections among their properties. Fortunately, we often do know a great deal, more than enough to proceed.

Finally, some mention must be made of the relation between bias and randomness. The notion of random selection has already been appealed to several times, and the idiom is sufficiently clear to be unproblematic in normal contexts. But to avoid confusion it is worth pointing out that unbiased samples are frequently not random samples. Random samples are by their nature unbiased, but they are a particular *sort* of unbiased sample; not all unbiased samples qualify.

Statisticians will often describe a random sampling procedure as one in which *every member* of the population has an *equal chance* of being selected. This would, for example, rule out street corner surveys even if they were notoriously reliable for the property in question, because some members of the population are much more likely to make it into the sample than others. Some people are, by the nature of their lives, unlikely to pass by your selected street corner today, or perhaps ever. To give every member an equal shot at making it into the sample requires not only that there be no connection between the selection procedure and P, it requires that there be no connection between the procedure and any statistical property of the sample. This ideal is seldom achievable, of course (perhaps only by procedures that make selection dependent upon the outcome of some quantum mechanical phenomenon): if we look hard enough we will usually find *some* characteristic of the sample linked to the selection procedure. But even though we can seldom actually produce one, the *concept* of a random sample is still important in our practical reasoning.

Our interest in random samples stems largely from the limits of what we know: specifically from our ignorance of the connections among properties. We are often unsure which connections between P and the sampling procedure might bias the sample and which would be innocuous. In uncertainty, we understandably wish to break all connection—every tie between procedure and sample—just to be sure to have broken all the important ones. And this would be to pursue the absolutely random sample we could probably never achieve. But the idea is still helpful. Unachievable ideals like this are sometimes valuable because we can learn how to approximate the ideal more or less closely, as required for some purpose. And of course our ignorance is virtually never complete. We usually know something about P, often a great deal about the procedure: enough to ignore some connections as irrelevant. In such circumstances, a procedure is effectively random if there is no explanatory connection between the procedure and any statistical property of the sample *that is at all likely to correlate with P.* Drawing names from a hat will be effectively random in this sense. Certain properties of the paper slips on which the names are written—size, shape, thickness, weight, wrinkledness, or edge condition—may well affect the selection. But since there is unlikely to be any connection between these properties and the names themselves, the selection is "random enough" for most purposes.

So the value of a random, or effectively random, sample is that it is often our only route to unbiasedness; and this is increasingly the case the less we know about the property in question. An unbiased sample requires that there be no explanatory connection between the selection procedure and P. And the less we know about P, the less clear we can be about specifically what connections we must break. We thus turn to breaking as many as we can—ideally all of them—but in any case all that might have some influence, no matter how indirect. As we learn more and more about P, the less and less indiscriminate our connection breaking has to be. If we know a great deal about P and the effects of a selection procedure, we may rely on an emphatically nonrandom sample with confidence that it is nevertheless unbiased. Even street corner surveys are adequate for inferences about some properties.

Unbiased selection of the sample is only half the battle, however. Even a random sample may not be representative: there is still the matter of bad luck to deal with. We might do all the right things, get a complete list of the population, use a table of random numbers, employ redundant safeguards, and nevertheless end up with all fat ones or all Democrats or all chocolate-chip fudge, purely by chance (C_3). It just happens that way sometimes. And although nothing will ever eliminate this possibility altogether, we may do things to reduce its likelihood. In fact, we can reduce the odds on such a freak to any level we like—make it vanishingly small—merely by increasing the size of our sample. The only limits are practical considerations of time, effort, and, of course, money. In our simple case, if we make the sample larger and still get the same property—all sugar cookies—the odds that the jar actually contains mostly something else get smaller and smaller. Concomitantly, the odds get higher that it contains virtually all sugar cookies. Statisticians, however, can be far more precise than this.

In the simple cases we are examining, the most helpful way to characterize P, the property we are interested in, is as a certain fraction or proportion. So far we have limited consideration to qualitative characterizations (landslides) or extreme cases in which the individuals in the sample are *all* of one kind (e.g., sugar cookies). But in general P will be a *percentage*. P percent of the sample will be of kind K. Half or three-quarters or 19% of the sample will be sugar cookies. Furthermore, since the sample will typically have far fewer members than the population, and usually some weird fraction as well, the percentage of Ks in the sample usually cannot be exactly the same as in the population for reasons of simple arithmetic.* So the question we ask must be modified to: "*How close* is the percentage of Ks in the population to that in the sample?"

If the sample is random we may put confidence limits on the answer to this question that depend only on the size of the sample. We may say something about just how confident we can be in that answer. If the sample is small we cannot be very confident that the percentage of Ks in the population is close to that in the sample—pure chance is too large a possibility. As the size of the sample increases, so can our confidence that the proportion of Ks in the sample mirrors that in the population. The odds on pure chance get progressively longer. We decide when to stop increasing sample size for the same sort of reasons we decide to stop taking data in any diagnostic investigation: when we are certain enough for the practical purposes at hand, or when the cost of taking further data exceeds the likely benefit in increased certainty.

To see this in some detail, consider a population of 1000 red and white jelly beans from which we randomly select 10. The sample contains 6 red, 4 white. On the basis of this sample we should say, if we had to choose a number, that the best estimate was that 600 of the jelly beans are red and 400 white. But because the sample is so small, that bet is not much better than its neighbors: it's just about as likely that the ratio is 500/500, or 550/450. In fact, we can say quite precisely that the chances are just 50/50 that the

---

*Say 618 of a population of 1000 are fat. Suppose the sample has seven members. The closest it could get to 61.8% is 52.1% on one side or 71.4% on the other (4/7 and 5/7 respectively). This problem obviously does not arise for the extreme cases.

number of red jelly beans lies between 491 and 682. If we need to be more certain, we must expand the limits somewhat. The chances are 9 in 10 that the number (of reds) lies between 351 and 800; 99 in 100 that it lies between 235 and 885. These are known as confidence limits, and the last of them is the famous 99% confidence limit used in much of estimation and error theory.

Just what these confidence limits mean can be understood as follows. Before sampling, we know only that the jar contains 1000 jelly beans, each either red or white. It could contain 1000 red and no white, 500 of each, 1000 white and no red, or anything in between. Each of the 1000 different possibilities is equally likely. So as an aid to understanding, we may think of there actually being 1001 jars to choose from, containing all the various possibilities. Jar #1 is all white, jar #2 contains one red jelly bean and 999 white, #3 contains 2r/998w, #501 contains 500r/500w, #800 contains 799r/201w and so on. We may now think of what we did as equivalent to thoroughly mixing up the jars and randomly taking a sample of 10 from one of them; and we note that it contains 6r/4w.

It is important to notice that for any given population (i.e., jar) there is a determinable number of ways in which any particular sample can be drawn from it. The population (jar) may be thought of as *containing* a specific number of different samples of that size and makeup. For a simple illustration, consider a very small population consisting of just four jelly beans, two red and two white (r_1, r_2, w_1, w_2). This population contains two different samples consisting of a single red jelly bean: r_1 is one, r_2 is the other. A sample of *two* red can be arrived at in just one way: (r_1, r_2). A sample of one red and one white can be drawn in four different ways, however: (r_1, w_1), (r_1, w_2), (r_2, w_1), (r_2, w_2). This is to say that the population in question contains four distinct samples made up of one red and one white jelly bean. Notice that if our population of four had contained one red and three white there would only be *three* samples possible containing one red and one white: (r_1, w_1), (r_1, w_2), (r_1, w_3). So in general how many distinct samples of a certain size and makeup can be drawn from a population will depend on the makeup of the population: this is why we are able to infer something about the makeup of the population from examing the makeup of the sample. As the population size increases, the number of possible samples like these increases dramatically, but it is always determinable.

Returning to our 1001 jars, we may now ask some precise questions and generate some interesting numbers. The question, "Given that we drew a sample of 6r/4w, what is the most likely percentage of red jelly beans in the population we sampled?" translates into, "Which of our 1001 jars did we most likely sample?" or "Which jar did the sample most likely come from?" And this question is easy to answer: the one containing the most samples of that size and makeup. We may even say *how* likely any population (jar) is, given that sample. If a jar contains twice as many samples like that one as any other jar, then it is twice as likely to be the jar we sampled as it is to be any other jar in our collection. If one jar contains half of all the possible samples—that is, as many as all the other jars combined—then it is just as likely to be that jar we sampled as all the 1000 others combined.

For the particular case we are examining, the numbers are staggering, but revealing nonetheless. Jar #601 (containing 600r/400w) contains slightly under 66.402 sextillion* possible 6r/4w samples. And this is in fact more than any other single jar, but not by much. Its neighbors on either side (600 and 602) contain just over 66.400 sextillion such samples, differing by just 2 quintillion (2×10^{18}), or a tiny fraction of 1%. Because the sample is so small all the jars within thirty or so of #601 contain nearly the same number of possible 6r/4w samples: 65 or 66 sextillion. In fact, we have to add the samples in all the jars from 492 to 682 before we reach half. This gives us what might be called the 50% range: it is just as likely that the sample came from within that range as outside it. If we add the possible 6r/4w samples in the jars from #236 to #885, we get 23.5 septillion (2.35×10^{25}) or 99% of all the possible samples. This is the famous 99% range: the chances are 99 to 1 that the sample came from one of these jars. In other words, it is overwhelmingly likely that the population we have sampled falls between 235 and 885 red.

Of course, there are fewer than 6 red in jars #1–6 and fewer than 4 white in jars #998–1001, so *no* 6r/4w samples can be found in those jars: the chances of having drawn our sample from them is zero. All this may be found on the following graph. Details of the calculation, as well as the table of complete results, may be found in Appendix A.

As we should expect from our sample, the distribution peaks at 600r/400w. This means that (on our sample) the best bet is that the population is divided 600r/400w. But since the neighboring populations contain nearly as many 6r/4w samples, the best bet in this case is not very good. The 600r/400w population contains only 0.28% (about a quarter of one percent) of the 6r/4w samples to be found in the populations on the graph; so the odds are only about 1 in 400 that the population is split exactly as the sample. However, some very good bets, which may be read on the graph, allow us to see the importance and value of sampling—and statistics—for practical matters.

First of all, there is practically no chance at all (1 in 200) that there are fewer than 235 red in the jar; and it is just as unlikely that the number of reds exceeds 885. Sometimes this is enormously valuable to know (e.g., if we need 200 reds for some purpose), and we have discovered it from a relatively tiny sample. If we are willing to allow slightly greater risk, we can say that there is very little chance (1 in 20) that there are fewer than 351 red, or more than 800. These would be more than just best bets, they would be very good indeed.

We can improve every aspect of this picture simply by increasing the sample. If we double it to 20 (12r/8w), the odds that the population is split

*6.6402×10^{22} or 66,402,000,000,000,000,000,000.

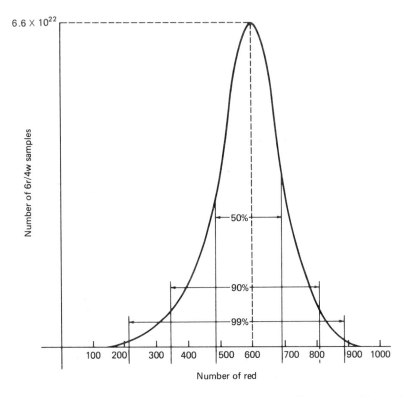

exactly 600r/400w rise to 0.38%, which is of course still a very bad bet. More impressive, the 99% range drops from 650 to 502: the odds are 99 in 100 that the population falls between 325 and 827 red. The table below displays the changes in these parameters as sample size increases.

The point of this exercise is this. If the sample property we are concerned with is an exact percentage, we will usually not be able to infer reasonably that the population has that same property exactly. We can often do the next best thing, however. Depending on sample size (and assuming that everything from C_2 has been ruled out), we can say *how close* to the distribution in the sample the distribution in the population is likely to fall. But the more confidence we require, the broader the range must be. We could very easily

SAMPLE SIZE	PROBABILITY THAT POPU- LATION IS EXACTLY 600/400	50% RANGE	90% RANGE	99% RANGE
10 (6r/4W)	0.28% (1 in 800)	489–682	351–800	235–884
20 (12r/8w)	0.38% (1 in 300)	522–663	419–754	326–827
40 (24r/16w)	0.54% (1 in 200)	546–646	472–714	402–772
50 (30r/20w)	0.60% (1 in 150)	552–641	486–703	423–756

get a 6r/4w sample from a 500r/500w population just by chance (C_3). It would be far more difficult to get this sample from a population split 200r/800w. In fact, it would be nearly impossible unless we distorted the selection procedure (C_2).

Accordingly, it is common to express C_1 in such cases as a *range* of populations, or, rather, as populations with a *range* of properties.

C_1 =   The sample has P (that is, P% of Xs) because the population has P $\pm$ Δ (that is, P $\pm$ Δ % of Xs).

And we make the range (Δ) as broad as we can afford to (for our practical purposes) in order to elevate our confidence level: to make the bet as good as we can.

To illustrate the practical value of this procedure, consider an election poll. If 64.5% of the voters sampled express a preference for Baker, and the sample was taken in such a way as to rule out explanations from C_2, the confidence limits allow us to say the following: If the lower limit of the 99% confidence range is above 50% (say Δ is 10, so $P_{99} = 64.5 \pm 10$), then it is virtually certain that a majority of voters would admit to a preference for Baker. And since a majority will elect him, this is a very useful thing to determine.

To sum up our discussion, if the statistical properties of a population are accurately reflected (represented) in a sample, then we may of course infer the properties of the population from those of the sample. We call such an ideal sample *representative.* The central issue in this section has been to see how we might discover that a sample was representative—at least roughly and relevantly—without first knowing what we wanted to infer. The way we do this is to treat everything we know about the sample and the way it was selected as data in a diagnostic inductive argument. The implicit question in this argument is "Why does the sample have the property (or properties) we are interested in?" The rival explanations fall into three usefully distinct categories: appeal to population properties, appeal to selection procedure, chance. Explanations in the first category license the inference: the sample has property P *because* the population has property P. And sometimes the only way to elevate first category accounts to the top of the list is explicitly to eliminate accounts from the other two categories. So, in the standard manner, we can get *evidence for representativeness:* evidence that the sample accurately represents the population, at least in its possession of P.

CAUSES AND CORRELATIONS

Many of the questions we dealt with in the foregoing section are actually *causal* questions. The connections between selection procedure and the resulting sample are *causal* connections. A selection procedure may *cause* the sample to have some of its characteristics, and be thus unrepresentative of the population from which it was drawn. It should not be surprising, therefore, to find some strong parallels between sample-population inferences and certain causal inferences.

The inferences of interest here are those that begin with a correlation between two things, A and B. A might be working around asbestos and B might be contracting emphysema. There is a correlation between these two things if, for example, a greater percentage of those working around asbestos develop emphysema than those who do not. Such a correlation may be treated as trace-data in an inductive argument, which focuses our attention on the question "What is the best explanation of the correlation between A and B?"

Actually, we could use a slightly broader term here. 'Correlation' suggests a long run of similar cases, while our diagnostic technique is quite capable of handling unique events. The mere co-occurrence of a collision and a crash, for instance, is enough to launch a diagnostic argument. But since there is no term that comfortably covers everything we would like, 'correlation' will be pressed into this more general service. In addition to its more usual use, the term 'correlation' will be used in this section to stand for co-occurrences of unique events and any other systematic relationship between two things that might be explained by a causal connection.

When we ask, "What is the best explanation of a correlation between A and B (or of a co-occurrence of A and B, etc.)?" it is useful to distinguish two different *kinds* of answers:

1. The correlation is explained by some causal connection between A and B.
2. The correlation is due to chance or coincidence (and hence there is no causal connection between A and B).

The correlation between asbestos and emphysema almost certainly falls in the first group: working around asbestos leads naturally to breathing it into the lungs, which in turn eventually results in the physiological condition known as emphysema. Similarly, the co-occurrence on the same evening of an earthquake and a collapsed garage is plausibly traced to a causal link between the two. On the other hand, even though the correlation between sunspot activity and the fortunes of the stock market was very impressive for several decades, it is fairly certain that the correlation was merely a dramatic coincidence of cosmic and economic forces. The structure of causal inferences may be helpfully displayed under these two headings.

Causal Connections

Like any diagnostic argument, assessing the soundness of a causal inference requires sorting through the list of rival explanations to see which is most plausible on the data available. But if the explanation takes the form of a causal link between two parts of a correlation, we may helpfully group these rivals into three categories:

1. A causes (or caused) B. [A→B]
2. B causes (or caused) A. [B→A]
3. A and B are (were) both brought about independently by some third factor (called a common cause). $[C{\nwarrow^A_B}]$

These three categories capture the essential variations in what might be called the direction of causal influence. Given that A and B are causally connected, there are still three distinct forms that connection might take, which would dramatically affect the sort of explanation to be given. Learning to distinguish among these forms constitutes about half of what is important in the study of causal inference.

In the run of normal, easy cases, the questions of this section practically answer themselves. It is clear not only that A and B are causally connected, it is also clear which way the influence runs. In our previous examples the impact of the brick caused the tube to break, the collision caused the planes to crash. As those cases were described there can be little room for doubt about any aspect of the description. But what strikes most people initially is how thunderously implausible would be any confusion between the first and second categories. The possibility that we have simply *reversed* the causal order seems incoherent. How could the breaking of the tube *cause* the impact of the brick? Preposterous. But the fact that there are cases in which it is outlandish to confuse the two categories makes it even more important to examine cases in which this is a serious possibility.

We are in the greatest danger of simply reversing the causal order when the *temporal* order of a single A/B pair is unrecorded or difficult to detect. Our racing car crash from the last chapter provides a clear illustration. After we drag all the broken bits and pieces back to the shop, study reveals that one of the rear tires is cut all the way through. Given just this much, it is often hard to say whether the crash caused the cut or the cut caused the crash. But such cases are seldom intractable. The way to decide what caused what is simply another application of our standard diagnostic procedure. There will usually be something about the nature of the cut, the disposition of the pieces, testimony of observers, or marks left by the doomed vehicle that an imaginative investigator can marshal in support of one of the alternatives: it is the familiar appeal to explanatory hurdles once again. If a suspension rod was found jammed into the tire through the cut, this counts heavily against the cut as the cause of the crash. It might be that, during the crash, the rod fortuitously went through a hole that was already there, but it is not very likely. A far better bet would be that the rod cut the tire during the crash. On the other hand, if, at the point the car left the track, there are only three of the typical black marks left by hard braking, and where the fourth should be there are signs of metallic scraping and gouging, that would count heavily in favor of the cut as the cause of the crash. The specific point is this: the best account of the crash is the account that can most easily explain not just the crash itself, but circumstances surrounding the event as well. Different causes operate in different ways and leave distinct traces.

This fact—that different causes operate in different ways—provides the key to many causal investigations. It is so important that the characteristic way in which a cause operates is given a Latin name: *modus operandi* (literally, method of operation). The term is used primarily in criminal investigations, referring to the characteristic technique of a particular extortionist or burglar or rapist, for example. A specific modus operandi will often leave characteristic traces, which can be used to uncover the perpetrator. Since our discussion here concerns detective work to uncover causes, we may think of the modus operandi in this more general context as simply an expanded version of the criminal one. The modus operandi of a cause will refer to the way it typically works: the path it takes and the things it does along the way. As with criminals, a causal modus operandi will frequently leave traces on the surrounding circumstances: traces that may be used to single out the perpetrator —the cause. Explaining the traces provides evidence of guilt.

In the racing car crash we were, of course, looking for the cause of a single event. But the first two forms of causal connections may also be difficult to decide between as accounts of *literal* correlations; and they may be handled in something like the same way. An apologist for the tobacco companies might wish to argue that the correlation between smoking and lung cancer is explained by the fact that contracting lung cancer causes people to smoke, rather than the other way around. He might contend, for example, that the very early stages of lung cancer induce a craving for smoky air, which craving is satisfied by lighting up a cigarette. This possibility is worth raising not because it should be taken seriously (it shouldn't), but to show just how we might be mistaken about the direction of causal influence in a case like this, and what evidence we could adduce pro and con. The current debate does not take this rival seriously precisely because it must overcome such enormous and well-known hurdles. For one thing, there is simply no reason to think we are so seriously mistaken about the onset of the disease as this hypothesis would require. Most smokers take up the habit early in life, when their lungs are quite healthy. And lung cancer victims die much later in life from a form of cancer which develops and spreads with notorious speed. There is always the bare possibility that we have missed something subtle in our investigations, but there are an infinite number of bare possibilities just like this. To take the reversed-cause thesis seriously, we should at least have some data it was needed to explain; so far there has been none.

A second hurdle for the cancer-causes-smoking hypothesis is the stature of its competition. If there were no natural explanation for the smoking/cancer correlation we would be forced to take seriously relatively outlandish theories even when they conflict with our body of medical knowledge. But the orthodox account of the correlation has no such difficulties. Tobacco combustion products contain an established carcinogen: it reliably produces tumors on certain animal tissues. So smoking introduces a documented carcinogen directly into the lungs. This makes the usual story overwhelmingly plausible: given this we should be slightly surprised if there were no correlation between smoking and cancer.

In this case we do not have to delve very deeply into what we called the causal modus operandi to determine which way the influence flows. Rather coarse, general features of the case provide enough selective hurdles to do the job. If the alternative were more serious, however, we might have to look in some detail at the actual physiological process involved, like returning to the scene of the accident. This would be the sort of 'surrounding circumstances' that would be decisive in such a case. The direction of causation would be determined by seeing which account of the circumstances was most plausible.

Although we must be alert to the possibility of simply reversing the causal order, a far more frequent mistake is ignoring the possibility of a *common* cause. Since it is the correlation (or co-occurrence) of A and B that has attracted our attention, it is natural to think that, if there *is* a causal connection, it takes the form either of A→B or B→A. But it is important to bear in mind that a more complex causal relationship, in which A and B are independently brought about by some third agency C, would also account for the correlation as something other than mere coincidence. For example, eclipses do not *cause* high tides, but there is a nearly perfect correlation between those two phenomena. The cause of the high tides is the alignment of the sun's and moon's gravitational fields, a consequence of the alignment of the bodies themselves, which in turn produces the eclipse. Similarly, there was at one time an alarming correlation between certain skin lesions and death from the disease known as smallpox. But the skin lesions were virtually never the cause of death. Death usually resulted from lesions on the heart and nervous system, which were in turn traceable to the same virus that produced the skin eruptions. Our evidence for the common cause picture in these cases consists of standard modus operandi considerations: we know enough about light and shadow patterns to know they cannot hump up the seas, and realize superficial pockmarks are unlikely to be fatal. But there is another sort of procedure we can use in some cases to check out the possibility of a common cause.

To see this, consider a slightly more plausible defense of the tobacco companies than the one we entertained above. It would appeal to some environmental or physiological common cause: something that *independently* inclines certain people to *both* lung cancer and smoking. Since there are more urban than rural smokers, we might try city life as the culprit. Perhaps the hassles and pace of city life drive people to smoke, while the polluted air is what produces the carcinoma. Very strong evidence for or against this account of the correlation could be found simply by selectively eliminating city dwellers from the data, by focusing our attention on rural smokers and nonsmokers alone. If rural smokers had the same incidence of lung cancer as rural nonsmokers, that would support the common cause thesis. But if we found the familiar smoking/cancer correlation among nonurbanites, it would be difficult to keep that particular common-cause thesis on our list of plausible explanations of the correlation. We would have raised a great hurdle in the path of that rival. The same hurdle would be raised by discovering the familiar cancer/smoking correlation among urbanites too, of course. If we restricted our attention *to* city dwellers, and found that urban smokers contracted lung cancer at the familiar elevated rate—above urban nonsmokers—that would demolish the common-cause thesis too.

In sum, evidence for claims about the direction of causal influence fit squarely into the diagnostic mold. Considerations of causal modus operandi will often differentiate explanatorily among the competing rivals. One will be able to account for the surrounding detail more easily than another, some will be practically ruled out. And when the allegation is that there is a common cause, a further step is possible. Since the claim is that C causes both A and B, we should try to examine—or arrange for—just those cases in which C is constantly absent (or, alternatively, constantly present) and check whether the correlation still holds in those cases. If it does, that will hurt the common-cause thesis: a direct causal connection will better account for this much at least.

Determining the direction of causal influence is often of first importance because it profoundly affects our actions and expectations. If B→A we should not expect to bring about B *by* bringing about A, or to eliminate B *by* eliminating A. Whereas if A→B each of those manipulations might be expected in some circumstances. Similarly, if $C{\nearrow^A_B}$, our manipulation of B should concern C, not A; even though B *correlates* with A.

For example, there is a well-known correlation between infection in a human body and a high white cell count in its bloodstream. But attempting to combat the infection (B) by directly lowering the white cell count (A) would be not just ineffective, but foolish and dangerous as well. We know enough about the direction of causal influence to know that killing off the white cells would make things worse. We might reasonably pause, therefore, in the face of the avalanche of statistical correlations pouring from our social and medical institutions, to consider alternatives to the causal pictures which immediately suggest themselves. Sometimes alternative flowcharts will be too plausible to ignore. This is the sort of thing that makes causal inference so tricky, and at the same time so important.

Chance

Contrasting with all the various cause-based explanations of a correlation is always the possibility that it is a mere coincidence. A and B might have occurred together through a freak of good or bad luck. In the terminology of experimental design, the hypothesis that a correlation is due to mere chance is known as the null hypothesis. It is the hypothesis that, in a certain sense, there is nothing to learn from this particular correlation.

That a correlation between A and B is due to chance or coincidence does not, of course, mean that A and B were not themselves caused by anything. It just means that their causes are *independent.* A did not cause B; B did not cause A; and no third thing caused them both. More generally, their underlying explanations are not related in any interesting or helpful way. To say it is just a coincidence that all recent wars have started on a Wednesday is to say there is nothing about midweek to help us understand why the wars began when they did. If there turns out to be something about Wednesdays that does help us understand the onset of hostilities, then we must give up the null hypothesis. It would then be no accident they started on Wednesday.

Evidence that a correlation is due to chance, that it has no causal account, is of exactly the same kind as for a positive causal explanation. As before, it is best to look first at relative antecedent plausibilities and then at finding the best account of the surrounding circumstances. And once again the various possibilities fall naturally under three headings.

Low Antecedent Plausibility.   We are sometimes struck by an impressive

or dramatic correlation between two items that we would normally take to be wholly independent. Because the correlation is so striking, however, we entertain the possibility that, as bizarre as it sounds, the two things are actually causally related. The remarkable correlation between sunspot activity and the fortunes of the stock exchange is an instance of this type, as was the telephone's ringing just as we sat down to dinner three nights running. We have seen what is required to establish a causal relation in such cases; to show that they are a matter of chance is roughly the reverse. Two cases are worth distinguishing.

In some cases it is sufficient to look through the surrounding circumstances and note that *nothing* in them *requires a causal connection* for its explanation. If such a connection is already implausible, and we can find no traces of its modus operandi, then the mere fact that we are struck by the correlation is often inadequate to save the hypothesis. I might establish a causal link between dinnertime and the phone calls by uncovering a well-intentioned conspiracy among my friends to prevent my overeating. Or I could discover some common causal relationship relating both to another aspect of my life and schedule. But if I cannot, and, further, the calls are from different time zones and even include a wrong number, coincidence becomes overwhelmingly the best bet. Any causal-connection hypothesis must overcome too many explanatory hurdles to be taken seriously.

Occasionally A and B are of such a nature that we can explicitly discover an account of one which so clearly *bypasses* the other that any causal link between them seems ruled out. And if such a link is antecedently implausible to begin with, finding such a bypassing account will be practically conclusive.

Co-occurrences of unique events are particularly susceptible to this move. While shopping in the supermarket I sneeze and immediately all the lights in the store go out. It could be that the store was staging a publicity stunt and had somebody stationed at the main switch with instructions to kill the lights the first time she heard a sneeze. But any such connection is quite unlikely antecedently. And if subsequent investigation reveals that an errant tractor-trailer rig knocked down a utility pole, cutting electricity to the entire neighborhood at just about the time I sneezed, that eliminates all question. The remarkable coincidence of sneeze and darkness was just that: a matter of chance.

High Antecedent Plausibility. The major difference between these cases and those treated under the previous heading is that the burden of proof is shifted. In the cases above if we could find no particular aspect of the circumstances that required a causal link for its explanation, then we opted for chance. Here, by contrast, the circumstances must make a rather strong negative case if we are to deny a causal link.

The standard trick is once again to examine the surrounding circumstances for traces of a relevant modus operandi, and to see if a better case can be constructed for a bypassing account. Suppose it rains on election day (A) and Jones is narrowly defeated (B) in a light turnout of voters. Jones blames his defeat on the weather (A→B), reasoning that since he pitched his campaign at the poor and the aged, the weather was more of an obstacle to his supporters than to those of his opponent. This is a plausible account on its face. But if it were found that identifiably poor precincts, and those containing concentrations of senior citizens, produced comparatively high voter turnouts, that would shake Jones's story pretty badly. If, in addition, postelection interviews with some poor and aged voters who did not make it to the polls revealed a slight preference for Jones's opponent, it would begin to appear that the weather had nothing whatever to do with Jones's defeat. The surrounding circumstances raise substantial hurdles for Jones's thesis. At this stage the null hypothesis would be a pretty good bet.

In addition to rather normal cases such as Jones's defeat, this heading covers some strange but interesting cases of causal *overdetermination.* An event (B) is causally overdetermined when there are two or more factors in the circumstances (A_1, A_2, A_3, ... etc.) that would bring it about, given the chance. Standard examples are firing squads (overdetermining death) and the various elements (e.g., overdetermining the deterioration of housepaint). The overdetermination in these examples is sometimes called simultaneous, since all the causal agents are working away on the effect pretty much at the same time, none precluding any other. But the cases of interest to us here are the ones in which only one of the several agents is actually involved in bringing about the effect in question. They are not simultaneous (they are sometimes called sequential) and one of them gets the job done before others have the chance. Since more than one possible cause is present and active and leaving traces of its modus operandi, discriminating the actual cause, the right explanation, requires an extra measure of care and attention to subtlety.

Seconds before the bombs from the airplanes above reach the bridge, a demolition crew blows the supports and drops it into the riverbed below. Even if nobody was watching, it is often possible to tell which of the overdetermining causes actually did the deed, by examining the array of bits in the riverbed. The pattern of explosion marks and the way in which the pieces are broken will usually reveal much about where those pieces were when the various explosions took place. But because of the overlapping and intermingling of the two sequences of events, disentangling them requires time, care, and expertise, rather like air crash investigations. The importance of including such cases in this discussion is to point out one more way in which causally unrelated events might correlate in a plausible and suggestive way. Sorting out what happened once again involves raising selective explanatory hurdles, as in any diagnostic investigation.

Determinism. This is not the place to deal with the tissue of conceptual issues surrounding the notion of cause; but one philosophical shibboleth does seem to require explicit treatment. This is the slogan or thesis "Every event has a cause." A number of scholars have maintained that a mere examination of the concepts involved in the thesis shows it to be true: that there can be no uncaused events, that every event must be caused by something or other. This in turn has been used to establish or defend a number of philosophical doctrines.

Now, it is possible that the intended application of that slogan is so far removed from ordinary diagnostic inference that nobody should think it relevant to our present discussion. But its irrelevance is not obvious to everyone, so it is worth a precautionary notice: Whatever it means, the slogan cannot be taken at face value in this context. For one way to discover that A and B are causally independent is to discover that the subsequent one of them (say B) was *not brought about by anything* at all, that it was a wholly random event. At a certain stage in an investigation that might be the best account of all the relevant data. And if it is, then we have reason to think A and B causally unrelated.

To be sure, none of the usual events of our lives is wholly random in this way; therefore we would have to be driven very hard to accept such an account. And we would be right to resist the suggestion in most cases. But certain kinds of events—namely some of the basic microphysical phenomena studied in subatomic physics—we *do* have very good reason to think are wholly random in the required sense. Far and away the best account of them is that they are not caused by anything. So there is nothing in principle to keep such a hypothesis off the list of rival explanations for any sort of event, although it would usually be far down the ranking.

More important, we can, by artificial contrivance, connect the large-scale events of our lives to the random events of microphysics: scintillation counters can trigger bombs, or be used to make selections in randomization experiments. This device can be of enormous value in causal or correlational studies, because it breaks all of the normal causal links to past events, and hence isolates the events being studied in a nearly ideal way. In other words we can arrange things so that the best account of some event (B) is that it is the direct result of a wholly random process, and thus unrelated to any other antecedent event (A) we happen to be concerned with. Furthermore, if we can *arrange* for this to be so, then it is also the sort of thing that *might* occur naturally. We could *discover* that such a connection already existed in nature.

Noncorrelational Inference

The issues raised in this section are of primary concern only in cases in which we know that both correlates (A and B) have occurred and merely have to assure ourselves of the causal connection between them. But of course we do sometimes look for the cause of an event (say, B) even when we do not have a recognized correlate (A) to raise the difficulties discussed here. In such a case, the evidence we have for a causal connection between A and B is *also* evidence that A occurred. When the Turkish DC-10 crashed we had no independent evidence that the rear cabin floor collapsed, snapping the control lines to the rear of the plane. But the evidence we have overwhelmingly supports the view that the floor's collapse was directly responsible for the plane's diving to the ground out of control. By inferring that the collapse caused the dive, we indirectly infer that the collapse itself occurred. The existence of the cause is, in a way, part of the conclusion. Such arguments are standard diagnostic inductions and do not explicitly raise correlational issues.

Summary

When any two things, A and B, bear a striking, regular, or otherwise systematic relation to one another (e.g., occur together), that fact may be used to focus a diagnostic investigation into the surrounding circumstances. And it, together with some of those circumstances, will naturally form the support claims of a diagnostic inductive argument for one or another explanation of the relation between A and B. For convenience and suggestiveness here we have referred to this relation as a correlation between A and B, even though that is an important oversimplification.

S_1 "Correlation" between A and B
S_2 Relevant features of the surrounding circumstances
$$\overline{} d$$
C   (Best account from among the following categories)

To organize our thinking it is helpful to divide possible accounts of correlations into two categories: causal and chance coincidence. Causal accounts may be further divided into three basic kinds: simple cause [A→B], reversed cause [B→A], and common cause [$C{\nwarrow^A_B}$]. The major burden of this section has been to sort through the kinds of explanatory hurdles that might discriminate among the different kinds of causal account, and to examine others that would elevate chance (the null hypothesis) to the top of the explanatory list.

CIRCUMSTANTIAL EVIDENCE

In the previous section we often appealed to the surrounding circumstances for evidence of a causal connection. Sometimes the circumstances are crucial to determining what really happened; without them we would be lost. Furthermore, this evidence is often very strong, even overwhelming. The cause of the DC-10 crash examined in Chapter 3 was dug out of the surrounding circumstances, yet the evidence was virtually conclusive.

Nevertheless, the expression 'circumstantial evidence' is often a term of derision, as though it stood for an especially weak form of evidence. "Since the case was merely circumstantial, the jury refused to convict the defendant." But it is obvious from the many examples we have already examined that not all evidence from surrounding circumstances is weak. So it is important to see just what invidious contrast is being drawn here, and how it might be abused.

When somebody calls evidence *merely* circumstantial, that evidence is being contrasted with direct observation: the *direct* evidence of the senses. A defense attorney might argue that a case is merely circumstantial if no witness can be found who actually saw his client do it (whatever he is accused of). And there are instances in which this is a perfectly legitimate point to make. But these are very special cases in which very special direct observations are being compared with a particular kind of circumstance.

Nobody (still living) actually saw the defendant kill the service station attendant. But several witnesses have testified that a car of the same make and color as the defendant's was in the vicinity of the service station in question just before the murder. Furthermore, the suspect has no alibi whatever, and was, later that evening, observed throwing a lot of money around at a bar in a neighboring community (the murder was committed during a robbery).

Here it is quite clear both that the case for a murder conviction is rather weak, and that the weakness is in large part due to the absence of direct identification of the defendant himself at or near the scene of the crime. The direct observation of the crime by a reliable witness who recognizes the suspect is an ideal kind of evidence in this context. *This* is the sort of contrast usually intended when evidence is called merely circumstantial. The indirect evidence from the circumstances is of a typical and relatively weak kind. And the direct observation—the identification—is the sort of thing that can be very strong evidence. Our ability to recognize people, to discriminate among other human beings, is one of our subtlest and most well-developed perceptual skills. In the right circumstances, personal recognition is among our most reliable perceptions. It can be of enormous value as an item of data in an inductive inference. So as long as 'circumstantial evidence' is restricted to tenuous, distant items like car descriptions, and the issue in question involves the recognition of a person under relatively normal conditions, the contrast is clear: circumstantial evidence in this sense will almost always be substantially inferior to some easily conceivable direct observation.

But the lesson to be learned from this is a narrow, pragmatic one, not a general, logical one. For as soon as we break the constraints we have imposed on the two kinds of evidence the contrast vanishes. Even in a murder, other, more elaborate evidence from the surrounding circumstances can make an overwhelming case. Suppose we discover that the suspect's fresh fingerprints were found on the steel cash drawer of the service station's cash register; that the bullet taken from the attendant's body was fired from the defendant's gun, which he was notorious for never letting out of his sight; and that the bills in the cash register at the service station were marked in anticipation of a robbery, and some of those were the ones spent by the suspect at the bar later that evening. Furthermore, two days after the robbery he was suddenly able to pay off the people who had been threatening to break both his legs; and it has proven strangely difficult to trace the inheritance he claims was the source of his remarkable ability to mollify his malefactors. Such a case would be circumstantial, but not merely circumstantial: it would be easily as strong as any isolated eyewitness account.

In fact, at a certain point, indirect evidence becomes so strong that we quite properly doubt—even reject—eyewitness accounts conflicting with it. Spectators testify that the victim was standing when the shot was fired, but the path of the bullet through the body makes that inconceivable. We reject the eyewitness testimony as deluded or dishonest. It is here that the notion of 'explaining away' has an important role to play. It is easier to explain away the direct observations* than the path of the bullet. This means, in the locations we have been using, that the bullet path raises a greater explanatory hurdle for the account offered by the eyewitnesses than vice versa. Used in this manner, explaining away is not only legitimate, it is a crucial part of inductive inference.

The best way to capture the pragmatic point of calling a case 'merely' circumstantial is simply that sometimes common appeals to circumstances are rather easy to explain away: too easy if anything important is at stake. But

---

*Perhaps it is important to point out that to make the contrast between direct observation and indirect evidence we must always have a single object, which we have direct observations *of* and indirect evidence *for*. Indirect evidence of X (prone victim) is always direct observation of something else (bullet path).

we must recognize that there is nothing absolute about the testimony of our senses. Direct observations may be undermined in all sorts of ways, and in some circumstances they are virtually worthless. They frequently conflict, for example: equally reliable eyewitnesses testify to different, incompatible things. One might say that the victim was standing, another that he was already on the ground. Such cases are very common, especially when there is much excitement or emotional involvement. If guns are going off and a lot of angry, violent things are happening and we are scared out of our wits, our perceptual reliability often suffers. Similarly, if we have a deep commitment to someone or something in the action, we often let our wishes guide our eyes, and see what we want to have happened, rather than what did. Conflict among direct observations undermines them all here, and we will then let the indirect evidence tell us which eyewitness to believe rather than the other way around.

These same considerations (terror, distraction, emotional involvement) undermine direct observation reports even when there is no conflict, of course. Even our best direct observations may occasionally be undermined by some indirect feature of the case: the existence of an identical twin can demolish even a very competent personal identification. So the general rule is (once again) to back up and look at the total picture. Put down all the relevant data, direct and indirect, and find the best account of it all. Sometimes the eyewitness testimony can be discounted, sometimes it will be impossible to explain away.

INDUCTION BY ENUMERATION

This final section has a more philosophical cast than the others. Induction by enumeration raises issues of interest primarily to those of a slightly philosophical turn of mind. It is included here in part because we are in a position to make some interesting points about those issues, and also because they do sometimes seem to have an impact on our practical reasoning.

Consider:

Crow number 1 is black
Crow number 2 is black
Crow number 3 is black
Crow number 4 is black
Crow number 5 is black

.

.

.

Crow number 276 is black

———————————————

All crows are black

We are sometimes tempted to think that there is something in the simple, unvarnished counting of cases—instances—that allows us to make inductive inferences without getting caught up in the elaborate apparatus of diagnostic induction. Some philosophers have actually argued that simple enumeration is the basic inductive concept, the basic move underpinning the more elaborate arguments we have been examining. This is a nice thought, but attempts to show how such an underpinning might work have not met with any success. And the reason is that even the purest cases of induction by enumeration seem to presuppose all the things we uncovered in Chapter 3: they are diagnostic inductions in disguise. There seem to be no unvarnished cases.

The lesson in all this for practical argument is simply an extension of the observations we made about samples and populations.* For any actual case in which we are tempted to infer from a simple list of cases to a generalization about them, we must always ask whether or not the generalization represents the best account of the list. There are usually a number of interesting rivals. And just having to ask the question brings in all the apparatus we were trying to exclude.

None of this is to say that induction by enumeration never works. Sometimes it clearly makes a sound argument: the crow example we began with may well be a case in point. But when it works it does so for the same reasons as any other diagnostic induction: because of all the things we know about the case, and how the instances were selected. Just because it has snowed in Zanesville the first week of March for the past eighteen years, we do not even rate it a good bet that it always has or always will snow there during the first week of March. Freaky weather is too much a part of our lives to make such an inference: we know too much to be taken in by the string of instances.

Even more striking are cases in which we know enough about a series of instances to know they are leading inexorably to a refutation of the very generalization simple enumeration would require. Every day on which Southern California goes without a major earthquake would further secure the generalization that there will *never* be a major quake in that geologically benighted region.

Day 1, no earthquake
Day 2, no earthquake
    etc.

But geologists tell us that a far better explanation of the long string of relatively quiet days is that the subterranean forces are building up for a big

---

*Induction by enumeration may, of course, be viewed as a relatively simple sample-population inference, subject to all the points raised in the section on statistical inference. The different perspective of this section supports a separate treatment, however, because it makes the methodological issues easier to display.

rumble; and the longer the string, the larger the eventual shake is likely to be. Similarly, the evidence of our daily lives would, by enumeration, yield immortality:

Day 1, I did not die
Day 2, I did not die
    etc.

But we know full well that with each passing day death is closer, not more remote.

Accordingly, if the fact that all the crows I have ever seen are black *does* support the generalization that all crows are black, it does so because of what I know about ornithology, animal pigmentation, and the range of habitats I have examined. It might be that the best account of all *those* crows being black is that all crows everywhere are black, but it is not a matter of mere counting.

A usefully different way to make this same point is to notice what is required to distinguish among the instances we count. For the generalization 'all crows are black' we naturally counted individual crows (crow 1, crow 2, etc.). But since crows could conceivably change color from day to day, the fact that a crow continues to be black day after day also confirms the generalization. We could, in other words, count the same crow over again every day, if it stays black. And since different crows would still count, the basic instance would be crow-days, not simply crows.

Crow 1 is black on day 1
Crow 1 is black on day 2
Crow 1 is black on day 3
    •
    •
    •
Crow 2 is black on day 1
Crow 2 is black on day 2
    •
    •
    •
Crow 3 is black on day 1
    •
    •
    •

The unit of a day is arbitrary, of course. We could count crow-minutes—or any other unit of time—instead, and get an endless proliferation of instances.

But we know enough about birds and pigments to know that such proliferation is a waste of time, and possibly misleading in the bargain: 500 bird-minutes spread out over 500 birds is far more impressive evidence than 500 bird-minutes on the same one. Some instances are so much less important than others that it is misleading to call them instances of the same thing. So we ignore bird-minutes and bird-days and count only individuals. And quite properly. But this shows how profoundly our background knowledge is presupposed by enumeration: in ignorance we simply do not know what counts. Enumerative induction is another instance of diagnostic induction.

EXERCISES

Review Questions

1. What evidence do we have for the reliability of our simplest, everyday perceptions? How does this suggest a way to detect the limits of our perceptual competence?
2. Rival conclusions appealing to an author's motivation are appropriate in each stage of the expanded, two-step schema for evaluating testimony. What is the major difference between them (that is, what distinguishes the motivational considerations relevant to the two stages)?
3. Why is a high success ratio not always impressive?
4. For the sake of simplicity, in the following questions take representativeness and bias always to concern a specific property (or properties) of interest.
   a. Can a representative sample be biased? Why or why not?
   b. Can a random sample be biased? Why or why not?
   c. Can a random sample be unrepresentative? Why or why not?
   d. Can a representative sample be nonrandom? Why or why not?
5. In a causal investigation, what is a bypassing account?
6. How do modus operandi considerations provide trace-data in a causal investigation?
7. Explain what causal overdetermination is. Describe an example of overdetermination (preferably one not mentioned in this text).
8. What new data would make the direction of causal influence clear in the Ivan Potter example (argument 2b in the exercises for Chapter 1).
9. The evidence that a pin had jammed the scoop arm of Viking I (argument 7 in the exercises for Chapter 3) was all circumstantial: it consisted primarily in several indications that the scoop had freed itself following a sequence of commands, together with a television picture of a pin lying on the Martian surface. We had no direct observations of the pin jamming the arm.
   a. Explain why this is not a serious challenge to the strength of the evidence.
   b. Describe some of the difficulties we might have in getting a direct, eyewitness report reliable enough to challenge the indirect evidence in this case.
10. In general, how do we decide between indirect, circumstantial evidence

and eyewitness reports, when they conflict—that is, when these two
kinds of evidence are on opposite sides of an issue, which do we choose
and how?

11.

Study Rules Out Genetic Link in Smoking Deaths

The theory that smokers die younger than nonsmokers because of some
environmental or genetic difference—not the cigarettes they use—is disputed
by an 11-year study published Thursday.

The argument, voiced by tobacco industry spokesmen, among others, was
tested in a review of the habits of 4,004 smokers and nonsmokers in
California. The researchers, paid by a tobacco industry-backed group,
concluded they could find no evidence to support the idea.

They kept track of 4,004 middle-aged men and women for 11 years and
found that the death rate among the smokers was 2.6 times higher than
among nonsmokers.

"I think this adds more evidence that smoking is indeed a causal factor
leading to death," said Gary D. Friedman, who directed the study.

A report on the research, conducted at the Kaiser-Permanente Medical
Care Program in Oakland, Calif., was published in Thursday's New England
Journal of Medicine.

In Washington, a spokesman for the Tobacco Institute declined comment
on the findings. The study was paid for by the Council for Tobacco
Research-U.S.A., an organization financed by tobacco companies.

The researchers took into consideration 48 characteristics of the persons'
jobs, health and personalities that might have contributed to a difference in
death rates. Among them were alcohol consumption, blood pressure,
occupational exposure to chemicals, use of sleeping pills and complaints of
insomnia and depression.

"None of them explained away the smoking-mortality relationship,"
Friedman said in an interview.

For example, if the smokers had emotional disturbances, their death rate
was 2.8 times higher than nonsmokers with similar problems. If they did not,
the rate was 2.5 times higher than emotionally stable nonsmokers.

If the smokers were exposed to industrial hazards, their death rate was 2.9
times higher; if not, it was 2.4 times higher.

Characterize the results of this study in terms of the test for common
causes in the section on causal connections. That is, explicitly state the
general type of thesis for which this study raises an explanatory hurdle,
and explain why it is a hurdle.

Arguments

1. MRS. HASKELL: I've got to stop by Joe's this afternoon to have new points
   and plugs put in the Mercedes.

   TONY (*her son*): The car's running fine, why waste money on it?

   MRS. HASKELL: Look, Joe says it needs points and plugs, and he is as
   honest as the day is long. He'd never try to rip us off.

TONY: Yeah, Joe's honest alright, but he doesn't know anything about servicing a Mercedes. He should stick to Toyotas, something he understands.

   a. Schematize Tony's argument (about Joe's recommendation) as a two-step evaluation of testimony.

   b. Where does Tony's second conclusion fit on the testimony checklist (p. 116)?

   c. State one rival to Tony's first-stage conclusion.

   d. State one rival to Tony's second-stage conclusion.

   e. Provide some new information that would, if discovered, clearly elevate the underwriting rival to the top of the plausibility ranking.

2. Consider the following statement by an oil company executive, testifying before a Senate subcommittee:

> If the government will decontrol our industry and allow our prices to seek their natural level in an open market, that will enable us to locate and extract vast quantities of petroleum, which are currently unavailable.

   a. Consulting the testimony checklist, under what headings might the senators raise the most serious difficulties with this testimony? Describe the most plausible difficulty (rival) for each stage.

   b. Why are the other aspects of the checklist more secure in this case? (That is, why are rivals under the other headings less plausible?)

   c. What data could the executive supply that would allay the kind of difficulties you mentioned?

3. Suppose I have a medium-sized cardboard box, into which I can neither see nor reach my hand. I would like to know something about its contents, so I tie a small magnet on a string, drop it into the box, and examine the things clinging to it when I pull it back up. I drop the magnet in several times and each time several small pieces of metal cling to it— never anything else. I infer from my accumulated sample that the box contains only small pieces of metal.

   a. Why does the way the sample was selected undermine the inference? That is, why does the connection between the selection procedure and the sample property explain that property better than an appeal to the population's having that property?

   b. What sort of property might the sample have that we could more securely infer in the population? That is, what else might I notice about the little pieces of metal that would be better explained as a property of the population than by the selection procedure?

   c. Think of a selection procedure (within the restrictions mentioned) that, if it yielded the *same* sample, would allow me to infer that the box probably contained nothing but small pieces of metal

4. In the past ten years, just over four thousand students have taken Professor Ogden's introductory course. The grade for the course is determined

by three quizzes given during the term, and a final paper due the last day of class. Over this span of ten years, 284 students have come to see Professor Ogden during the last week to discuss some matter pertaining to the course. Of these conversations, 279 were prompted by the student's conviction that his or her quizzes had been graded too severely. This statistic provides strong support for the view that the overwhelming majority of Professor Ogden's students in this course think their quiz scores underrepresent their performance.

Treat this as a simple diagnostic inference from a sample to a population. The property of the sample, which is being inferred to exist in the population as a whole, is a general dissatisfaction with the quiz scores.

  a. What is the most plausible C_2-category rival you can think of? That is, describe the connection between the way the sample was selected and the sample property (general dissatisfaction) that would most plausibly explain the sample's having that property even if the population did not.
  b. How plausible is this rival?
  c. How would you select a sample in this case that would essentially rule out this rival as a significant possibility?

5. Policemen occasionally become deeply pessimistic about the human condition: they come to think badly of the general level of civility, motivation, and self-control in the community. Analyze this pessimistic perception as a misguided sample-to-population inference. In other words, treating a policeman's experience in the community as his sample, explain why this sample might be unrepresentative. (Use your imagination: there are several things worth mentioning.)

6. In the American population there is a clear but modest correlation between coffee drinking and heart attacks: if you drink a great deal of coffee you are more likely to be the victim of a heart attack than if you drink little or no coffee. Treat this as correlational trace-data for a causal inference.
  a. Clearly state the correlates A and B.
  b. Provide a rival explanation of this correlation under each of the following four headings (N.B.: each rival should be an explanatory story):
      i.   A causes B
      ii. B causes A
      iii. Common cause
      iv. Chance
  c. Provide some additional information that, if discovered, would clearly elevate your rival under ii to the top of the plausibility ranking. Do the same for your rival under the other headings.

7. As Peter Revson rounded Barbecue Bend on the Kyalami track, his Formula One race car darted off the track into the guardrail, demolishing

itself and killing Revson. In the subsequent investigation a main suspension component was found to be broken in such a way as to lead investigators to suspect that it caused the crash.

   a. Taking the broken part to be A and the crash to be B, schematize this passage as a standard diagnostic inference from correlation to cause, taking the investigator's suspicion as its conclusion.

   b. Provide rival conclusions (stories) under each of the following headings.

      i. B caused A

      ii. Common cause

      iii. Chance

   c. What additional information would make the argument schematized in *a.* clearly sound?

8. Consider the following article as a standard diagnostic inference from correlation to cause:

Music Hath Charms, Maybe Even Longevity for Its Lifelong Devotees

Harold M. Schmeck

NEW YORK—Music may have charms little considered even by the poets who write so much about it or the musicians who create it. Under the right circumstances, a life devoted to music may be a prescription for longevity.

This is the conclusion of an associate professor of medicine at the University of California at San Diego who is also a lifelong symphony devotee and amateur musician. Struck by the fact that Leopold Stokowski died in his 96th year, the professor, Dr. Donald H. Atlas, did a little epidemiological research on the longevity of symphony conductors. He published the results in *Forum on Medicine,* a publication of the American College of Physicians.

The doctor noted that Arturo Toscanini lived an active life to the age of 90; Bruno Walter to 85; Ernest Ansermet to 86 and Walter Damrosch to 88. . . .

But is this evident longevity of gifted musicians a myth based on a few famous examples, or is it real?

"The death of Stokowski prompted me to examine statistically the life span of members of this distinguished profession," Atlas said.

From several source books and his own experience, Atlas compiled a list of 35 deceased major symphony leaders and found their mean length of life to be 73.4 years. The life expectancy of American men in general is 68.5 years, he said, and the difference is statistically significant.

"I am aware that a comparison of the current survival expectancy of American men to that of European-born conductors from the last century may be open to question," Atlas said. "Nevertheless, since I have not been able to find a single death in this group at an age younger than 58, I firmly believe that these men were protected by some undetermined factors from the modern scourge of early fatal ischemic vascular disease," disease of the heart and circulatory system.

a. Carefully describe the two correlates (A and B) between which Dr. Atlas claims to have found a correlation.

b. What explanation does Dr. Atlas offer of this correlation?

c. Granting Dr. Atlas' figures, describe what you take to be the most plausible rival to Dr. Atlas' explanation of it.

d. Which of these is more plausible on the information given?

d. What new information would, if discovered, clearly promote the less plausible of these to the top of the plausibility ranking? (If you ranked them equal, promote either one.)

9. Suppose it were found that couples who lived together before they got married had a higher divorce rate than those who did not. This might reasonably be taken to be evidence for a direct causal link between the correlates: namely that living together before getting married damages a couple's chances for a successful marriage.

a. What common-cause account would you want to rule out before accepting the above inference to a direct causal link?

b. What further data would, if discovered, substantially lower the plausibility of the common-cause account?

c. What further data would clearly raise the common-cause account to the top of the plausibility ranking?

5

Characterizational Fallacies

We have so far concerned ourselves with the substance of argument, presuming that the terms in which the support and conclusion are expressed are themselves satisfactory. It is time now to relax that presumption and take a brief look at the semantics of argument (as opposed to semantic arguments, which are the subject of Part Two). This will serve as a transition to the more profound linguistic issues treated later.

Many of the difficulties we encounter in practical argument are characterizational: they concern simply how we *describe* the matter at issue. Sometimes our choice of words—our very natural choice of words—misleads us; it can trick us into thinking we have seen more than we have, or into thinking we composed a better argument than we did. The limits of our linguistic skill can sneak up on us just as the limits of our perceptual skill can. It is difficult to see where special care is required in simply describing things. So we find ourselves beating on straw men, trapped in phantom dilemmas, squinting uncertainly through a grammatical fog we ourselves have helped to create. In this chapter we examine a few of the most typical and tempting of these missteps; you will likely be able to find others on your own.

NO EVIDENCE

We have dubbed a diagnostic inductive argument 'sound' if, on the evidence presented, one rival account is clearly better than the rest and that one is offered as the argument's conclusion. The conclusion of a sound diagnostic argument will be the preferable account of the trace-data, and those data will raise hurdles for other accounts. This is so even if the best account is far from established, possibly not even very good.

The concept of soundness is reflected in our common talk about evidence in the following way. Normally, if we can produce a sound argument, we capture this fact by saying *we have some evidence for C*, the soundly inferred conclusion. Put another way, when we say we have some evidence for C, frequently what we mean is that we have some data that are best accounted for by C. It may not be a *lot* of evidence—which is to say the account may not be very *good*. But if it is the best account of something, then we have some evidence for it.

If we know that a satellite's orbit is sinking dangerously close to the atmosphere and that it is due over northern Canada tonight, then this evening's widespread reports of a fireball over Baker Lake constitute evidence that the satellite has fallen back to earth. The evidence is far from conclusive, of course; at this stage the fireball still could be a meteorite or, perhaps, some other satellite. But the best bet is that it is the satellite everybody is so concerned about. And that is why we call the fireball evidence of the satellite rather than of something else. In the absence of our special background information it would quite reasonably be taken to be (evidence of) a meteorite. *That* would be the best account of it. But as things stand the streak in the sky is evidence of a falling satellite—and a specific one at that.

The semantics of 'evidence' is important because it is common to ignore it in some circumstances, to the detriment of public discourse. The problem arises most frequently in the pronouncements of public officials, especially those designed to avert responsibility or allay public fears. During the swine-flu vaccination program, for example, there was a well-publicized incident in which three elderly patients died shortly after being vaccinated at one clinic in Pennsylvania. This raised some general fears about the safety of the program, which the officials involved were anxious to quell. But what they said was that there was *no evidence* that the deaths were linked to the vaccination program. Given the important feature of evidence-talk sketched above, this is a confusing—nearly incomprehensible—thing to say in the context. The whole reason for the announcement, the cause of the fears, was the publication of something reasonably taken to be evidence of that causal connection. Given what we know about the human body's reaction to vaccination, it would not be surprising if frail, older people were sometimes not able to survive it. Against normal background, the best account of the striking correlation between vaccinations and death in this incident seems clearly to be some causal connection. In short, the published correlation simply is (some) evidence of a causal link between the two.

The most charitable reading of what the officials meant by their statement is that they knew something that was not common knowledge, and which promoted some other account (some form of the null hypothesis) above the naturally suspected one. But if this *is* what they were trying to say, they did it in a spectacularly inept and misleading way. To avoid the appearance of foolishness—or deceit—they should have at least told us that they were privy to something we did not suspect and which would certainly change our plausibility estimate. The best thing—or at least the clearest thing—they could have done was to reveal their little secret: to tell us what they knew and what account of the correlation it recommended. As it stands they should forgive us if we suspect they were trying to get away with something—to divert attention using the famous mindboggling-obfuscation ploy, hoping the whole thing would blow over before anybody caught on.

Other examples of this same kind of pronouncement are even more clearly public relations gambits, and should be treated in the same way. When tobacco company spokesmen say there is no evidence that cigarette smoking causes cancer, they have the responsibility to show why some other account of the correlation is better. It might be that we have the direction of causal influence wrong, or that pure chance is a better bet than we think. But, again, given normal background, these other hypotheses have substantial difficulties to overcome: the orthodox view is a far better account. In the context, the cancer/smoking correlation simply *is* (some) evidence for the thesis that smoking causes cancer.

PROOF

In practical contexts it always seems possible to raise a question about whether we have *proved* something, no matter how well we have established it. In mathematical or formal logical arguments there are relatively clear and settled criteria for accomplishing a proof. And this fact sometimes encourages us to insist that we should adopt the formal criteria everywhere, including practical evidence evaluation. But, of course, the formal criteria are unmeetable—even incoherent—in practice, which leads to the view that, in practical matters, we can never prove anything.

All this is unfortunate. The notion of proof originated in the informal circumstances of our everyday lives, and it has a clear and useful role to play there. When people say "That doesn't prove anything," or "You can't prove it," they are not uttering empty words, they are making a specific kind of point. A proof is of course a very strong kind of argument; so when they say "You can't prove it," they are alleging that you cannot produce that kind of argument. To see what kind of argument that is, we have to see what would rebut the challenge in practice. When would we have done enough?

The notion that captures the usual distinction between having proved something and not is the *reasonability* of doubt. If the evidence is so strong that doubt about an issue is unreasonable, it is proved: the demand for further evidence, more support, is unreasonable. In other words, our criterion for proof is the satisfaction of an ideal "reasonable man": if a reasonable person would still have some doubt, then the issue is not proved. On the other hand, if the evidence is so strong that doubt would itself be evidence of unreasonability, then the proof is adequate.

Take, for example, the claim by a student at school A that A's football team is better than school B's. And suppose he offered as proof a ten-pound average weight advantage in both the offensive and defensive lines. A booster of school B might reasonably reply, "That doesn't prove anything," and go on to point out that avoirdupois is no substitute for skill, training, and coaching, and that quality of backfield is impossible to ignore in the calculation. In short, doubt is not just reasonable at this stage, it is almost obligatory. Now, had the two schools already played each other twice, and A had won each time, by a touchdown or so, the boasts of A boosters would have more substance. But there would still be room for doubt. That would not prove it, although the argument is stronger. Now, if A had won the first game 40–0, in spite of the team's being decimated by flu, and won the second 42–14 playing their reserves for most of the second half, and B had been at full strength each time, that would pretty well establish the A boosters' case. If there was nothing otherwise unusual about the contests, doubting the superiority of A would then be unreasonable. As a practical matter, what more proof could you want?

A further complication is worth mentioning, however. In many circumstances, the reasonability of doubt will depend not only on the weight of the evidence, but on what is at stake as well. Sometimes the consequences of a mistaken judgment are so stark that it is not unreasonable to hold out for greater than normal assurance. Accordingly, in such cases standards for proof will be higher. For example, if I balanced my checkbook using two quite different methods and got the same result, we would normally say I had adequate proof of the balance. If, however, something enormous hung on it —an eccentric relative has tied my inheritance to my having a certain exact balance on a certain day—then it would be reasonable to check it more elaborately and more carefully. I might even want to call in expert help, just to make sure. And since it takes a stronger case to make doubt unreasonable, it is correspondingly more difficult to provide what we would call proof. To this extent, then, the concept of proof is tied not only to the strength of the evidence, but also to the purposes of the argument. What is adequate proof for some purposes is not for others.

In practical contexts we prove things by showing that doubt is unreasonable, not that it is impossible in any very strong sense. And this is a perfectly adequate criterion for practical purposes: it takes into account both what we know and what is at stake. It is important to resist the temptation to impose more formal criteria, which are insensitive to our practical concerns.

STRAW MEN

In Chapter 1 we invoked a principle of charity (Charity I), which cautioned against wasting time criticizing artificially weak arguments. The straw man fallacy is simply a specific way of violating the charity rule. It is worth special attention only because our temptation to dereliction here is so strong.

'Straw man' is a metaphor for the weak opponent we construct just so that we have something easy to knock down. By misrepresenting the argument, we essentially *substitute a different and weaker argument for the original* and criticize the substitute. And if our aim is to impress the gullible with our demonstration, this stratagem may be just the ticket. But, as before, if we are really interested in the subject matter—in the argument—we are wasting our time and energy. What is worse, we sometimes deceive ourselves; our own facility in dispatching a straw man may impress *us* so much that we end up taking it seriously and misunderstanding the whole matter.

We find the temptation to construct straw men most irresistible when we are outraged. When we find a position or an argument deeply offensive, the urge to say something nasty sometimes blinds us to the subtlety or complexity of the issue. We blurt out the caricature of a rebuttal, which is easily ignored or set aside as missing the point.

> Dear Editor,
>
> In keeping with the logic of (State Senator) John Briggs who proposes a repeal of the 55 mph speed limit because of widespread disregard of this law, I suggest the following: Because of widespread disregard for the laws against rape and child abuse, let us also repeal these statutes.
>
> Indeed, what better way to put an end to the increasing lawlessness of our civilization than to simply eliminate all those laws which certain individuals feel they have a right to ignore? . . .

This is perhaps the most common form of straw man attack. Somebody offers an argument on a narrow, specific topic, but is criticized as though the argument were sweeping and general. Sweeping, general arguments are easier to attack, of course, and so they make straw men. Here Senator Briggs is offering a specific argument for changing a specific law, but is criticized as though he were giving a *general* argument for changing *any* law whatever. The straw man is further weakened by some sleight of hand with the word "widespread" until we have something so silly nobody would take it seriously.

Any significant violation of any law is reason to get rid of the law.

Even if this accurately captured what Senator Briggs was arguing, it would be a mistake to dwell on it in criticism. For a stronger, less sweeping, less vulnerable argument is so easy to construct here that shooting at an easy target is a waste of time. But it is preposterous to suppose the senator intended anything so sweeping (and silly). Specific cases demand specific arguments, and legislation is no exception. Choosing an exact velocity to impose on highway traffic involves a kind of arbitrariness quite foreign to writing statutes outlawing rape, murder, theft, and arson. What weighs in favor of one speed rather than another is a very loose and uncertain collection of things: convenience, safety, noise, energy consumption, and the like. When we strike a balance among all these things, a difference of five or ten mph is difficult to justify. The speed limit is in this way importantly distinct from the run of entries in the criminal code. Furthermore, in unrestricted areas, one venerable way to set speed limits has been simply to check the speed drivers naturally travel on the stretch in question, and set the limit directly by appeal to that figure—for example, the limit might be set so that only 15% of the drivers would be in violation of it. So the Briggs argument is relevant to *this* law in a way it is not to laws in general.

Moreover, the "widespread disregard" of the traffic laws involves a substantial percentage of the population, whereas the "widespread disregard" of the rape statutes involves only a tiny fraction of that number. The cases are simply not comparable in any helpful way: the argument falls of its own weight. And it is a pity too. Because there are important issues of cost and benefit which might helpfully be brought to bear on the question of highway speed limits. And these matters tend to be obscured and neglected in the smoke of burning straw.

This case is actually a slightly complex variation on the normal conversational context within which straw men find a natural home. When someone disagrees with us in a way we find annoying or outrageous, we usually do not carefully distinguish, in our reply, between making an argument and merely expressing our outrage. When we express outrage (or annoyance or impatience) it is natural to exaggerate, to offer a caricature of the offensive position, heaping ridicule on the error, simply assuming it is an error.

So you think public education in Southern California should be bilingual, do you? How should we do it: put every other word in Spanish, or every other sentence?

Although hyperbolic ridicule like this is uncivil, and may invite a fight, it is not directly harmful to reasoning unless it is mistaken for an argument. And this particular example is so silly nobody is likely to make that mistake. But we do not get far from the silly cases before we find ourselves tempted to think of ridicule as argument. It usually makes a ridiculous argument—like the speed limit letter above.

A related danger of straw man arguments is that they are sometimes so fatuous that it is not clear how to respond to them. The mind boggles, it is difficult to think of anything to say. So the perpetrator thinks he has made a good point and begins to think of his silly remark as an argument.

> I don't see any point in studying history: it's all about dead people. I'm interested in the living.

It is tough to treat a remark like this seriously. But it can be taken seriously, and sometimes it is worth the effort. If the author of this "argument" is actually taken in by it, we can point out that understanding many aspects of the lives of living people is far easier—sometimes only possible—with a historical perspective. Current hostilities often derive from ancient antipathies; complicated political boundaries are comprehensible only as the resolution of old conflicts; institutions are shaped by historical forces: to understand their rationale it helps to know how they arose. All pretty obvious things, but that is precisely what straw man arguments deny.

To get out of the straw man habit, it is good practice to put yourself in your opponent's shoes occasionally. When you feel yourself smugly comfortable in a reply or an objection to somebody else's view on a matter, try to imagine yourself taking the opposing view and defending it soberly. It may be difficult at first, but it becomes easier with practice. And it is one of the first skills to develop if you want to have any claim to being more than just normally reasonable.

FALSE DILEMMAS

In the last section we saw how mischaracterizing a position could make it seem weaker and less defensible than it really is. In this section we will examine cases in which the very opposite is true: a position appears stronger than it is because it is misdescribed, oversimplified in a particular way. These cases are worth a special section because the oversimplifications that create false dilemmas are so tempting, so deceptive, and sometimes so persuasive.

Consider the following hypothetical diatribe delivered from the floor of the academic senate of a large university.

> Are we going to offer a solid, traditional education, or are we going to run slavishly after every curricular fad that comes along.

This is an easy case, but that makes it a good place to start. The author of this diatribe offers us a choice between two distinct alternatives: traditional education and a faddish one. But we clearly are not limited to these two choices. For, first of all, we could have any number of different mixtures of fad with tradition, some of which might even be serious educational possibilities. Moreover, many alternatives cannot be reasonably called either fads or part of the tradition. Nothing rules out the possibility of serious, nonfaddish innovation.

To be sure, in saying all this we have not raised any substantive educational considerations at all. The point is that there is, to begin with, a far greater range of alternatives for educational considerations to choose among than the speaker seems to allow. The speaker's characterization excludes the very consideration of whole ranges of possibilities—and from what is left the choice seems obvious. This is typical of the false dilemma as a rhetorical device. The range of choices is artfully oversimplified to make it appear that there are just some small number of alternatives, among which one is clearly to be preferred.

The antidote is a little imagination. Whenever alternatives seem drawn with suspicious boldness and clarity, it is good practice to ask, "Is this an accurate representation of the possibilities?" And one way in which a representation may fail is simply in not including them all, as in the academic speech above. But there is another kind of inaccuracy that, while equally dangerous, is even more subtle: sometimes the alternatives offered are not really distinct—or at least not in the way or degree alleged.

Conservative economists are fond of saying things like, "Do you realize that you work each week until Tuesday afternoon or Wednesday morning just to pay your taxes: it is that far into the week before you start working for yourself." Their point is that the amount of taxes we pay is a certain percentage of our income—the exact percentage depending on the size of our income. And if we simply transfer this percentage to the time we spend at work, the time spent is around two days—plus or minus a bit depending on the case. And everyone knows what these economists are talking about; nobody particularly loves paying taxes. But to cast the distinction the way they do is indefensibly misleading. For it clearly implies that the taxes we pay —and hence the time we spend working to pay them—are *not* for ourselves: that they do not benefit the taxpayer. And that is simply and generally false.

We may not approve of all the things government does with our money —in a democracy it would be truly remarkable if everyone agreed on any-thing—but most of us are happy to have the order and protection afforded by tax-supported government agencies and institutions. It would be difficult to have the sort of fire and police protection we have outside governmental structure, not to mention general national defense. Police protection includes the elaborate judiciary and penal institutions as well, and there are innumerable other aspects of our lives that are benefited in one way or another by the existence of tax-supported structures. In our impatience with what we do not like, and our frustration in not being able to change it very much, we some-times talk as though it would be good to scrap all of government and all of taxes. But this is virtually always an intemperate exaggeration, which one can get away with simply because it is so far from a live possibility. The point simply is this. The time we spend working to pay our taxes is not just thrown away, of no benefit to ourselves. Computing the optimum amount of govern-ment—and hence taxes—is a complex, difficult question which cannot be reduced to a simple contrast between what I get and what I waste on taxes. Enflaming our passions with a bit of cheap hyperbole, as workweek rhetoric does here, tends to make us less able to reason objectively about the matter.

So once again we have a false dilemma: clear-cut alternatives that are not so clear-cut. Boldly drawn divisions inevitably ignore many subtle things, and frequently this is harmless enough. But sometimes the damaged subtlety is crucial to the issue in question; it is *just* what cannot be ignored. Spotting false dilemmas is just one more skill that requires a well-exercised imagina-tion.

BEGGING THE QUESTION

This is perhaps the most difficult to grasp of the characterizational fallacies, but it is worth a shot to try. The traditional way to state the fallacy is as follows: You have begged the question if you simply *presuppose* the conclusion you are trying to support, if you just assume it is true as part of the argument. This captures the spirit of the fallacy, but it is not an accurate guide. It is hard to fit many standard question-begging cases under this description, and at the same time it includes some perfectly legitimate arguments. So it is important to set out some real examples and develop a subtler, more accurate characteri-zation.

The clearest cases of question begging occur in what must be millions of letters to the nation's editors each year, which read something like this:

Dear Editor,

. . . Mr. Trowbridge states religion deserves absolutely no respect and that it is "a rather disgusting plague" from which he ought to be free. I wonder what he will say to his Creator when he faces Him on judgment day.

But of course the question of consequences on judgment day does not even arise for Trowbridge: that is certainly part of what he has discarded along with what he takes to be the plague of religion. So if we take this reply to be directed at Trowbridge it is an unhelpful waste of time: it simply *assumes* as true *part of what is at issue.*

This is already a better way to put it: it is not so much some specific conclusion we must not presume, it is any part of "what's at issue." But determining what is at issue is frequently a trickly business, taking in the whole argumentative context. Even all cases similar to the letter above cannot be ruled out, for sometimes simply drawing attention to some aspect or consequence of a position will be just what is required to get its backer to give it up.

A: I can make it from here to Nashville in fifteen minutes on my new bike.
B: Not a chance. The frost heaves through Wolf's Hollow will put you right in the stream bed if you even approach the speed limit through there. You'd be lucky to be out of Green County in fifteen minutes.
A: Yeah, you're right. I forgot about that bad stretch of road.

So it all depends on the case, the context. It is essential to be sensitive to what our opponent is likely to know, to be thinking of, and what he is likely to be forgetting. The letter to the editor begs Mr. Trowbridge's question only because it is stupendously implausible to suppose that, in his deprecation of religion, Trowbridge simply overlooked his inevitable confrontation with the Creator. If it were plausible to suppose that Trowbridge might respond to this letter by saying, "Oh, of course, silly of me to forget that. I guess religion is important after all," then the letter would not beg the question. But it is not plausible. And *this* is the judgment we must make in asserting that a question has been begged.

Accordingly, it is fallacious to presuppose a conclusion, or something else that is at issue, *only* if the conclusion—or premise, or whatever is at issue— is in a form that the opposing party would reject. To understand whether a question has been begged requires knowing not only something about the issue, but a good deal about the likely concerns and perspectives of the protagonists. Begging the question is at bottom a conversational notion. Where there are no real opponents, we can talk about begging the question *only* by supposing what a real opponent *would* know or think or reject.

All this helps explain how deductive arguments can escape the charge of begging the question. In a valid deduction the conclusion is semantically contained in the support: presupposed in a very strong sense. If it is presupposed in a way that is not obvious, then showing that a conclusion follows deductively from some support claims can be very helpful indeed. Somebody could presuppose P without knowing it, without being aware of it. So the argument

$$S_1$$
$$S_2$$
$$S_3$$
$$\overline{}$$
$$P$$

can be perfectly legitimate, informative, helpful—that is to say, *not* question begging—so long as S_1, S_2, and S_3 contain P in a way not obvious to an opponent who denies P. This may well depend on the opponent, of course.

But sometimes we can be pretty sure that a deduction begs the question for *anybody*. For example, in the first deductive argument we produced in Chapter 2 (pp. 20–21), 'Oswald killed Kennedy' is the conclusion, and it is also—in just that form—included as one of the support claims. It is a valid deductive argument all right, but it begs the question in almost any context. context.

The Marina Oswald syllogism is less clear. It might be informative—not question begging—in some contexts; but it would be unhelpful in most. The arithmetic and algebraic examples, however, provide the clearest illustrations of deductive arguments that are quite generally not question begging. Even if we know (S_1) $X - 2Y + 4 = 0$ and (S_2) $2X - Y - 4 = 0$, most of us cannot immediately tell that $Y = 4$. Showing that $Y = 4$ is already contained in S_1 and S_2 is informative, helpful. So using S_1 and S_2 as an argument for the conclusion that $Y = 4$ would not beg the question for most of us in most contexts.

EVALUATIVE CHARACTERIZATIONS

One common, nearly irresistible temptation to beg questions arises in our use of evaluative characterizations. We sometimes include in the very description of an issue a judgment about it wholly unacceptable to our opponent. The description seems reasonable enough to us, because it captures our settled assessment of the matter, but since that assessment is precisely what is at issue, an argument simply cannot begin there.

Suppose A and B are disputing the relative merits of trains and trucks for the long-distance transport of goods. A favors trains, B favors trucks. If A insists on characterizing the use of trucks as "the irresponsible squandering of our precious natural resources," that is pretty much the end of it. To be sure, the phrase "irresponsible squandering" does have some uncontentious descriptive content: using up quantities of petroleum, for example. But its main impact of this context is to say that, whatever is used, it is definitely *not a good thing.* Accordingly, a truck proponent would certainly want to argue that the use of trucks is a perfectly responsible use of the nation's resources. If that possibility is excluded from the outset, a useful exchange cannot even get started. Only by allowing the characterization "irresponsible squandering" to become part of the issue under discussion can productive debate hope to continue. The best way to assure this is to back off the loaded characterization and not beg that question at the outset. (One way to put the efficiency point that would not beg the question would be simply to point out that rail transport takes only a fraction of the energy of highway transport per ton-mile. This would allow other cost-benefit considerations to bear on the responsibility issue, which really is quite complex.)

There is a nearly inexhaustible list of other characterizations that have this same question-begging property in many of their applications, especially in political rhetoric—"blackmail," "terrorism," "confiscatory taxation," "demagogy," "vandalism," "mutilation," "honest work," "isolationism," "surrender," "welfare loafer," "aggression," "reprisal raid," and "rip off," to mention just a few. Each of these terms has some descriptive content, just as "irresponsible squandering" does. But each will frequently also be dominated by its (good or bad) evaluative component. That is, the term will usually not just describe the thing in question, but recommend up or down on the matter as well. To call something naked aggression is not just to suggest tanks rolling neutrally through the countryside. It carries a denunciation along with the description. That is why the "aggressors" seldom accept the characterization themselves. The evaluative component of the characterization is part of what is at issue, not yet settled: a question begged by the application of the term.

When someone relies on the weight of a loaded description to make a contentious point, he or she is guilty of what might be called argument by characterization. And as with so many rhetorical tricks, argument by characterization disguises something that *needs* an argument as something else—in this case as a simple description, a mere perception of what is going on. Sometimes loaded phrases do sound like simple descriptions—straightforward, objective, something open to inspection. But if there is at the outset disagreement about the evaluation imported by the phrase—whether the thing in question is good or bad—then simply hauling out the characterization begs the question. The argument must turn its attention to the characterization itself. Is this the right way to represent the matter? Was the aggression wholly unprovoked? Our antecedent sympathies can blind us to the complex and subtle considerations bearing on such a diagnosis. It is quite common for each of two hostile nations to refer to the other's raids as "terrorist," while its own are always "reprisals." We must be constantly on our guard.

None of this is to suggest that we can never objectively make evaluative characterizations stick. The point is only that, if there is a disagreement, it takes an argument to make it stick. Sometimes there is not even any disagreement. The blackmailer frequently will concede the point; less commonly so will the terrorist. But when there is a disagreement, argument can be successful. We can challenge the alleged aggressor to point out the provocation that justified his action. If even he cannot provide plausible rationale, the burden of proof, at least, is shifted.

Nevertheless, in real cases—especially social or political cases—matters are often so complex that most easy descriptions are flawed in one way or another—there is always something to make the label not quite fit. In long-standing antipathies there is always something to point to as provocation justifying either side's attack on the other.

EXERCISES

Review Questions

1. What determines whether our doubt about some matter is reasonable, besides the strength of the evidence we have?
2. Give two reasons to avoid constructing straw man arguments.
3. When an argument sets out a few clear alternatives among which the choice seems obvious, what twin dangers do we have to watch out for (that is, what two questions should we automatically ask ourselves about those alternatives)?
4. What is the point in describing question begging as a basically conversational notion?
5. Suppose San Francisco is flattened by a terrific shaking of the ground that residents all describe as a great earthquake. Comment on each of the following statements made by local geologists the following day.
   a. There was no evidence of seismic activity in the San Francisco area yesterday.
   b. We have no evidence that the earthquake involved the San Andreas fault system (the major fault system running through the area, and site of the 1906 earthquake).
   c. There is no evidence that San Francisco has split off from the rest of California.

Arguments

The following gambits represent potential characterizational fallacies. For each one, give the fallacy it naturally falls under (more than one if you can); briefly state why it fits under that heading; and explain why it might be important to mention the fallacy in an actual argumentative exchange.

1. The biggest enemy of our national wellbeing is the environmentalist who would gladly throw people out of work for the sake of an inedible fish and a few weeds nobody ever heard of.
2. The criminal justice pendulum has swung too far in the direction of protecting the criminal and away from protecting the victims of crime.
3. It is one thing for the municipal police to go on strike for higher pay; it is quite another for them to mug a city into submission.

TWO

LANGUAGE

6

Linguistic Skills

One aim of a book on reasoning is to encourage reflection and reflectiveness generally. But as with any human activity, we easily get out of our depth if we are not careful. And when our ruminations stray very far from our familiar everyday concerns they become deceptively difficult and hazardous. Unless done with great sensitivity to our familiarities and limitations, reflection can do more harm than good. This is especially true when reflection becomes *abstract:* when it concerns semantics, the nature of concepts, what words mean. For here we come face to face with the immense complexity of natural languages, and the skills we have developed to handle them. It is something our mundane, everyday reasoning scarcely prepares us for.

So it is important to set out some guidelines to aid our reflection when it finds itself tangled in semantic or linguistic issues. In Part Two, we examine some of the basic properties of language and our ability to use it, and the implications of all this for our more abstract reasoning. The most treacherous hazards we uncover will appear more than once, often in different chapters. In this way we get to view them from different perspectives, against different backgrounds, thus gaining the kind of three-dimensional familiarity we need to recognize them when the example and the circumstances change.

By its very nature, this discussion will appeal primarily to those who find themselves naturally drawn to abstract reasoning: to semantics, language, the nature of concepts. In this sense Part Two has a more "philosophical" cast than Part One. But the discussion of language in the next three chapters is continuous with, dependent upon, even parasitic on some major points developed in Part One. Understanding and use of language depend on an ability to evaluate a very complex and subtle kind of evidence. Recognizing the significance of words is in one way just like the recognition of anything else: it may be reconstructed as an empirical inference . Written shapes and spoken sounds may be viewed as trace-data in a diagnostic argument. So our investigation of language in Part Two will benefit greatly from the background provided in Part One. Much of what we do here will be further examination of our diagnostic skills at work. The strategy of this investigation will be the same as the strategy in our discussion of argument analysis. We will examine easy cases, cases in which our grasp of language is clear, to see what skills and principles are at work, and what features are important. We will then use what we have learned to make some progress in handling tougher cases.

UNDERSTANDING OUR SKILLS

Natural languages (English, German, Swahili, and Urdu are examples; we will be concerned here almost exclusively with English) are primarily and preeminently practical tools for the human activity of communication. Their characteristics, and our skill in using them, have developed almost exclusively to aid in that activity. It is nearly impossible to understand them in any other way. For both language and our linguistic skills are marvelously subtle and, in their way, staggeringly complex. Yet we clearly succeed in using them, succeed in communicating our practical, everyday interests, and sometimes much more than that. How is this possible? Why does the complexity and subtlety not defeat us? Because language develops its character—its complex structure—precisely to engage those skills we have (or can develop) to handle it. Much of a language's systematic detail develops simply because it works: it allows real people with normal skills to succeed in communicating. Keeping this in mind will allow us to understand the most important aspects of language as it is involved in our reasoning.

Two Skills

It is best to think of our linguistic skills as being of basically two different kinds: recognition and performance. The first (recognition) is involved when we *understand* what someone else has said; the second (performance) involves our actually *producing* a bit of language that can be understood by others. Although these two skills are clearly related, their distinctness becomes apparent, for example, when we try to learn a foreign language. We are usually able to read German before we can write it, and to understand it before we can speak it. The more passive recognition skill is generally easier to master than the more active performance skill.

The reason to distinguish these two skills is that we may gain some insight into our linguistic skills by examining our general ability to recognize things and to perform complex tasks. We recognize lots of things besides bits of language; and we are capable of many skillful performances besides talking and writing. We recognize colors and people, textures, tastes, and sounds; and we can walk, whistle, sing, swing a bat, and play musical instruments. A few observations about these activities will give us some perspective on our capacity to use language.

An interesting feature of all recognition and performance skills is that our competence usually far outstrips our ability to describe it. Important features of what we do, and how we do it, routinely escape our notice. We have all had the frustrating experience of trying to describe someone we know well. A friend volunteers to save me the trouble of meeting my brother at the airport. I try to describe him so that he will be reconizable to a stranger, but he is rather too ordinary-looking: no helpful distinguishing features. Yet I would recognize him in an instant. I finally resort to his height, hair color, and whether he wears glasses. But these are not crucial to my own recognition: I would know him on stilts, wearing a hat. I cannot *say* just how I recognize him.

More basic recognitions find us even less articulate. Most of us can easily recognize the color red, a musical dissonance, the smell of baking bread, and the feel of a light mist blowing in our face. But saying anything helpful about *how* we manage these recognitions—just what we appeal to in making them —would range from difficult to hopeless. Moreover, our inarticulateness does not detract one whit from our skill. Nothing can be clearer than our skill in these cases—the evidence that we can recognize such things as brothers, colors, and aromas is overwhelming.

Performance skills illustrate this same point even more impressively. Most people who can snap their fingers are wholly unaware of the importance of the fourth finger to the snap. And anyone who has ever tried to explain how to whistle to someone who cannot realizes how little we know about what makes the noise come out. It is not just blowing through a pucker.

More complicated performances are even more clearly relevant. I can play a certain piece on the piano from memory—I have done it many times. And this consists (in part) in putting certain fingers on certain notes in a certain order. Yet I could not begin to write down either the notes or the fingering from memory. In fact, if I wanted to write down the notes—or the fingering —one thing I might do is to play the piece and observe what I do, stopping long enough to write bits of it down before proceeding. In other words, I can use my established competence in a performance to *generate* a description of it.

A similar point can be made about recognition. If somebody wished to discover just what it is I appeal to in recognizing something, they might change it in various ways to see what has a significant effect on my reliability in making the identification. They might, for instance, try various selective disguises on my brother to determine the conditions under which I could no longer pick him out of a crowd. They could change first his complexion, then his hairline, head shape, teeth, height, and so on, combining the changes in various ways. Some things would have no effect, others would matter only in certain combinations, some might have great impact individually. After a while we could develop a pretty good profile of this particular recognition, detailing the degree of its dependence on various characteristics.

The point is that for either kind of skill, our initial attempts to say just what we are doing and how we do it may well be inaccurate. What we know is that we can *do* it; details of just *what* and *how* can easily go unnoticed. So descriptions of the skill—descriptions of what we do and how we do it—must be checked against the skill itself at work. Sometimes they can be generated only by careful observation of the performance or recognition, observation from the point of view of a spectator.

Sadly, our skills often suffer from such reflection: when we concentrate too much on noticing just what we are doing—as opposed to concentrating on *doing* it—our competence may abandon us. This is the final observation to make about our general skillfulness. Complicated performances are sometimes best done unreflectively. When I think too hard about just how the fingers should go, I forget how the piece goes. This is called the centipede effect, after the legendary myriapod who was asked how he managed to coordinate all his legs in such a precise and orderly fashion. After puzzling about it for a while he was flabbergasted at the magnitude of the task: he could not imagine how he was able to do it. So boggled was his mind that he never recovered the skill which had been so effortless, and he suffered a terminal paralysis. None of this is to suggest that we should not reflect on our complicated skills. It is merely to emphasize a danger in doing so. Like the surgeon operating on himself, we may disable ourselves in the process. We should separate the performance from its observation as much as possible: have someone else do the observing or use a videotape. When we cannot do this we must be constantly aware that the reflection may distort the skill, and try to compensate as best we can. Only in this way is our reflection likely to help our reasoning; only in this way is the good likely to outweigh the harm.

Linguistic Performance and Recognition

Each of the points made in the preceding section has important application to our specifically linguistic skills. We learn language by applying words and fashioning sentences in very specific, practical contexts. We master our native tongue long before we ever see a definition or a grammatical rule. It should come as no surprise, therefore, that the skill underpinning our use of language —what we are good at—is simply choosing and recognizing the right word in the right context: understanding and being understood when we make simple statements. We are *not* very good at writing dictionaries and grammar books. Since our skill is in the application, we can and do succeed in communicating without noticing much that is subtle and systematic in our use of words. Describing just what we do and how we do it is a difficult and uncertain process. We must be guided by actual—successful—application, and we must be wary of damaging our skill in the observation. Examining these points in some detail will provide valuable insight into the linguistic issues of reasoning.

It will serve our purposes best to focus on words. Words do all kinds of different jobs in communication. Some, like 'Nixon', may refer to specific things (e.g., an individual); some, like 'table', may stand for certain *kinds* of things; others represent more abstract properties and relationships, such as 'blue', 'underneath', and 'nuclear'; but some, like 'if', 'of', 'might', 'yes', 'would', and 'never' do not properly stand for or refer to anything at all: they just play certain important roles in our sentences. Some words, such as 'I', 'you', 'us', and 'me', depend on who says them; others, like 'this' and 'that', sometimes depend on gestures and the position of the speaker. More important, the same word can do one job in one context and a completely different one in another. The word 'table' does three different jobs in 'dinner table', 'table the motion', and 'table of contents'.

Learning a language requires learning the different jobs words can do. *Using* a language involves matching up words and contexts to make the jobs clear. In reflecting on the operation of language, it is easy to misunderstand—to underrate—the role played by context. For context is what engages our basic perceptual skills and enables us to communicate with such facility and reliability. Conversely, misunderstanding the context is nearly always fatal to communication.

Although familiar, the notion of context is so basic to this discussion as to be worth a few clarifying remarks. 'Context' here refers to the entire environment in which a word occurs: anything that might help us understand its job. To know what a word means—what job it is doing—requires that we know a great deal about its surroundings: where it occurs in a sentence (if it is in a sentence) and where that sentence itself occurs. The former might be labeled syntactic context, the latter substantive context. Syntactic context is clearly crucial: a word's relation to others in a sentence frequently determines what part of speech it is, and this dramatically affects the jobs it may have. The word 'lead' does radically different jobs in the following two sentences, a fact that is clear from its relationship to the other words.

We let John lead the group back to civilization.

Refineries are exploring ways to raise the octane of gasoline without using lead.

This is a particularly dramatic illustration because, out of context, we would not even know how to pronounce 'lead'.

Substantive context will be of far greater concern to us here, however. 'Substantive context' simply covers everything else about the environment in which the word occurs that may be relevant to understanding its job. Commonly, the most important aspect of substantive context is the *subject matter:* what we are talking about. If the word occurs in a conversation, the substance of that conversation will provide much of the context; similarly if it occurs in a textbook, an article, or a newspaper story. Knowing the topic under discussion will usually be helpful, sometimes crucial, to understanding the point of a sentence and the sense of its words. But other, more formal considerations help too. Wedding announcements, bank statements, Christmas cards, service manuals, advertising promotions, and dial-a-prayer all create special contexts. Even physical location matters: it helps to know whether a word is on a political wall poster, in a newspaper headline, emblazoned on the facade of a movie theater, or spelled out in lights on the Goodyear blimp. Anything that might help us understand what is being said is included in context.

The record is in the bag

means one thing walking out of Musicland, and quite another talking to space scientists about the bored astronauts circling endlessly overhead in their cramped and lonely laboratory. When we talk of context here it will refer to all these things, both syntactic and substantive; but substantive issues will concern us most.

THE ROLES OF CONTEXT

The degree to which our linguistic skill depends on recognizing key features of a word's environment—especially the substantive context—is enormous. It is one aspect of our skill that often escapes our notice. The most prominent function of context is the one we have made appeal to in the previous section: the resolution of potential ambiguity.

Ambiguity

A large number of common words* in English—and every other natural language—routinely perform several distinct jobs. Some will be related, like the two jobs of 'table' in 'dinner table' and 'table the motion'. But some will be wholly unrelated: the 'can' in 'can of chicken soup' bears no plausible relation to that word in 'can I go now?' In each of these cases the different jobs are in different parts of speech, but that is not always the case for a word's different jobs. The word 'pen', for instance, is a noun in both 'fountain pen' and 'pig pen'.

A casual look through any competent dictionary reveals that a surprising percentage—perhaps a majority—of the words in our common vocabulary require two or more entries. The different entries nearly always indicate different jobs: sometimes only slightly distinct, but often quite unrelated. Occasionally the proliferation of entries will astonish us—even though we are competent to handle them all. The most striking example is the word 'take'. My small dictionary lists thirty distinct entries under 'take', with as many as seven subheadings under the numbered entries. A look down the list reveals very few exotic jobs; most of them are quite familiar. Yet most of us are surprised to find such a common word doing so many distinct jobs.

We are surprised for the same reason that it is unproblematic: the potential ambiguity is effortlessly resolved by the context in most normal cases. Both in performance and in recognition we are very skillful at selecting the right job for the context. We are so good at it that it never occurs to us to list all the problems that would arise if we were not. In most normal contexts there is simply no question of what job 'pen' does in

The pig is in the pen.

Nobody would confuse it with the job normally done by 'pen' in

The ink is in the pen.

Talking about pigs on the one hand and ink on the other supplies enough substantive context to resolve the question effortlessly.

*'Word' here may be either written shape or spoken sound, and the same points may be made about the spoken or written language. 'Lead' is ambiguous between the heavy metal and the present tense of the verb *only* in writing. In speech, the metal would be confused with the past tense of the verb (namely 'led').

Notice that we could, by supplying an unorthodox context, reverse the jobs done by 'pen' in those two sentences. Being less orthodox, however, the case requires more elaborate description. Suppose Pete and Charlie are entering a pig-decorating contest tomorrow, and one of the ways they plan to decorate old Greased Lightning is with indelible ink pinstriping. Pete shows up late, after Charlie has everything set up in G.L.'s pen, and asks Charlie what he did with the indelible ink. Charlie, of course, says

The ink is in the pen

and, presto, 'pen' has changed jobs.

Ambiguity is not always resolved so completely or easily, of course. Sometimes the context is unclear, or not well specified, and then we may fail to understand, or actually *mis*understand, the job of a crucial word. We will shortly discuss how we can identify such occasions. When we do identify them, the remedy is usually explicitly to provide a bit of context. The point of this section is to draw attention to how frequent such misunderstanding might be were it not for our sensitivity to and sophisticated use of context.

Exercise: Before going on, describe a context that would swap jobs for the word 'pen' in the other sentence ('The pig is in the pen').

Nuance

In the last section the different jobs held by a single word were quite distinct: the word meant something completely different in the various contexts. But the significance of a word can vary from context to context in very subtle ways too. The differences may be important but small: just a nuance, a shade. What we referred to as a single job in the previous section will, when examined more closely, often turn out to be a tight cluster of related jobs. This too is largely unproblematic in practice, because familiar or well-developed contexts will support very fine distinctions. And these fine distinctions reveal a further range of commonly unnoticed features of our linguistic skill.

Suppose a story read:

The speaker paused briefly for a sip of water, cleared his throat, and continued in somewhat better voice.

The context makes it quite clear that the speaker is a human being. But the word 'speaker' does a closely related job in the following sentence, though it refers to an inorganic object.

The coffee on the dashboard spilled directly into the radio speaker.

It is important to recognize that these two jobs are far less distinct than the different jobs attributed to 'table', 'can', and 'pen' in the last section. 'Speaker' is doing something closer to the same kind of job in these two cases. Still, the distinction is clear and unproblematic for nearly everybody. In fact, it is not very subtle at all.

Increasingly subtle shades may be found in the following examples. Consider the job of 'light' in

a light-green dress
take it out into the light so we can see it

or the job of 'take' in

take your seat
take a rest
take it away

or the job of 'bench' in

park bench
piano bench
work bench

The communicative significance of these words—and most others as well —changes more or less subtly from context to context. But since we learn how to use (and understand) these words in the very contexts in which these distinctions are drawn, we have no difficulty handling the subtlety. Our skill *is* in the application, and these are the applications. With a little effort we could extend almost indefinitely this list of words with context-dependent nuance.

▶ *Exercise:* Write at least three sentences in which the verb 'to play' is doing distinct but closely related jobs. Do the same for the verb 'to pass' and the preposition 'on'. (An arrow preceding an exercise indicates that an answer or answers for it are provided in the back of the book.)

Contrast

The significance of some words varies in a relatively systematic way from context to context. This is so, for instance, when part of a word's job is to draw a certain kind of contrast. When the word 'red' is used to designate a color, the actual hue properly called 'red' will vary from case to case, depending on what it is contrasted with. Consider

Red Georgia clay.
The little girl with the red hair.
Red sky at morning (sailors take warning).

The actual hues referred to by 'red' in these cases are quite distinct; and none of them would be labeled 'red' in a paint catalog or ordinary color chart.

Nevertheless the chromatic significance of 'red' is perfectly clear in each case, primarily due to the contrast implicit in the context. Red clay is typically a kind of purplish-brown. But when set next to the whites, grays, blues, and tans of other clays, the ruddy contrast is clear. 'Red' is quite unambiguous given the limited possibilities. A few years ago, when Yamaha first imported motorcycles into this country, they offered three colors: red, white, and blue. In a paint catalog, the red they offered would be described as a kind of metallic burgundy. Nevertheless, in the context 'red' was perfectly appropriate. If you asked the salesman for a red one and he said they didn't make a red one, he probably deserved to lose the sale.

Similarly with red hair and red skies: there is a sense in which the color would be better described as brown or orange or vermilion, or any number of things other than red. But in the context the contrast is clear. Only Charlie Brown would try to explain to the little red-haired girl that her hair was not really red, but rather a kind of burnt orange.

An observation of something like the same kind can be made about 'open' in 'the door is open'. In some contexts the contrast is with shut: "Johnny, did you close the door when you left the house?" "No, Mom, I thought you wanted to air the place out after the breakfast disaster." But when someone knocks on a closed door, we commonly say "Come on in, the door's open." Here the contrast is with locked, not with shut.

Exercise: Suppose someone complained that a "talking computer"—or other machine—does not really talk, it just selects among prerecorded messages: it just gives the *appearance* of talking. Defend the label 'talking computer' by appeal to a clear and useful contrast it might draw in normal contexts. Do the same for the protest that a book of stamps is not really a book.

Comparison

Closely related to contrast is the relatively systematic contextual variation of comparative terms. The primary job of one entire class of terms is to specify a relative degree or magnitude of something. The relativity of the comparison entails that these terms lean rather heavily on the substantive context for much of their significance. Such terms usually come in pairs: 'large', 'small', 'expensive', 'cheap', 'tall', 'short', 'heavy', 'light', 'near', 'far', 'bright', 'dim', even 'good', and 'bad'.

What is expensive for a meal is cheap for a car; and what is expensive for a car is cheap for a house. Furthermore, what is cheap for a house in some suburbs of Washington, D.C., might be outrageously expensive, even for a house, in a small town in eastern Oregon. So, even when we know the price of something, to know whether it is expensive we must know the appropriate comparison. And sometimes the comparisons are quite specific.

In general, appropriate comparisons include not only the kind of thing in question, but many other features of the substantive context as well. A very tall man may nevertheless be a very short forward in the National Basketball Association. And that same man might have been a tall forward in the NBA twenty years ago. Comparative terms like 'tall' have a built-in contextual place-holder: a variable component that must be filled in by contextual detail before the term is applicable.

▶ *Exercise:* Display the comparative nature of the adjective 'firm' by exercising it in two or three contexts in which the variation in what counts as firm is clear. Do the same for 'exactly'.

Metaphor

One of the most valuable aspects of our linguistic skill is our ability to use and appreciate metaphor. Words and phrases that have developed their standard jobs in one context, in one set of applications, will sometimes be of great value when simply transferred into a novel context and directed to an unusual subject. (When we talk of character assassination, for instance.) By dragging their old, familiar associations—and perhaps some conceptual apparatus—with them into the new context, metaphorical expressions frequently organize our perception of the new subject in a helpful way. Communication is made easier.

Sometimes the message is simple. Geologists say the moon is geologically *dead;* we talk of a *shower* of shooting stars, *green* recruits, throwing some *light* on a topic, and a *photographic* memory. Driving instructors speak of traffic lights as *fresh* or *stale,* depending on how long they have been green. In each of these cases the value of the metaphorical expression is modest but clear. And the clarity is, once again, traceable to our grasp of the substantive context. For when we drag a term and all its associations into a novel context, some of the old associations will not transfer. Part of the old, standard job is normally not appropriate to the new subject. But in the easy cases above, the context makes the inappropriate aspects of the old job *so* clear that confusion is nearly impossible. Nobody expects to get wet standing under a shower of shooting stars, nor a dead moon to decay; and anyone caught testing a traffic light to see if it is stale would be joking—or deranged. A clear context will rule out these gaffes just as naturally as it will rule out the wrong job for 'pen' in the expression 'fountain pen'.

These same considerations allow the development of more ambitious metaphors, which are sometimes stunning in their ability to capture economically a complex perception or a subtle insight.

In September the National League East was a crowded and dangerous tenement.*
The men with the cans tried to pour out the oil in splashes like water out of a bucket, but the narrow openings only squirted derisive little jets.†

*Roger Angell, *Five Seasons* (New York: Simon & Schuster, 1977).
†André Malraux, *Man's Fate* (New York: Random House, Modern Library Edition, 1934), p. 99.

> Writing is, for most, laborious and slow. The mind travels faster than the pen; consequently, writing becomes a question of learning to make occasional wing shots, bringing down the bird of thought as it flashes by.*

Similarly, characterizing the sky as sullen or a relationship as stormy may capture the desired mood better, more clearly than any less metaphorical description.

Our ability to make this sort of transfer, to use a word's job in one context to help organize our understanding in another, is part of what makes language rich and dynamic. The organic development of language occurs in part through the death of metaphors. A metaphor may be so useful, become so common, that it ceases to be a metaphor: the word simply gains a new (i.e., literal) job. We may even forget the original connection. The verb 'to jack-knife'—referring to what a semi-trailer rig will occasionally do when the driver loses control of it—doubtless originated as a metaphor. When the rig 'jackknifes', it folds the way a jackknife does. But the term's popularity ruined it as a metaphor. Jackknifing simply *became* what a semi-trailer rig does when it folds up in a skid. People who have never seen a jackknife commonly know what the verb means.

Thus languages evolve. Something like the same thing has happened to many other terms. 'Guinea pig', 'sitting duck', 'butterfly stroke', 'insulation', 'bucket seat', and 'high' (as in intoxicated) are all dead metaphors: dead as a result of their usefulness. Only the good die young.

Exercise: Write a sentence using the word 'key' in a metaphorical way. Do the same for 'shadow', 'fog', and 'teeth'.

ARTICULATION

Our skill in using context to help determine a word's job—including subtle shades and contrasts—is a large part of what makes language the rich and valuable tool it is. But it is easy to overlook the context dependency of our skill, and hence to misunderstand the subtlety to which it gives rise. This can damage our reasoning. The most important damage is reflected in the over-worked and often misguided demand that we "define our terms." We are sometimes tempted to think we do not *know* what a word means unless we can *say* what it means. But this is simply a mistake, a misapprehension of our skills. We can almost never give more than a very rough description on the spur of the moment, and sometimes we can say nothing at all. What we are good at, once again, is the application: actual communication in practical contexts. It is generally very difficult to characterize accurately the work a word does in communication, even if we limit our attention to just one of its

*E. B. White, *The Elements of Style,* 3d ed. (New York: Macmillan, 1979).

jobs. The variations in nuance from context to context, the natural contrasts and comparisons, and the metaphorical overtones are things we normally do not dwell upon, and they can be reconstructed only through a patient study of the various relevant applications. Our inarticulateness about our linguistic skills is simply one aspect of our inarticulateness about skills in general: it is just what we should expect of a complicated skill that we master on the job, by trial and error.

The most striking illustrations of all this may be found in our basic vocabulary. We all know perfectly well what 'if' means, for example, but would have a hard time trying to say anything at all helpful about what it means. Similarly for 'the', 'and', 'of', 'to', and a host of others. Our ability to handle these words in their usual jobs is so clear that the question never arises. It is not even clear what sort of description somebody would want. So it is quite possible to be wholly inarticulate about the job of a word we are thoroughly familiar with.

About less basic vocabulary, by contrast, we are usually not completely speechless: we can usually say something or other about a word's job. But what we come up with on the spur of the moment is usually very rough: suggestive, perhaps, but not an accurate characterization of the job. And it is here that one great danger can arise. If we take these hip-shot descriptions too seriously we may try to force our usage to conform to the description rather than the other way around. We thus risk crippling our language by misunderstanding our skills. For our hip-shot descriptions will virtually always overlook some subtlety, and will occasionally fail to record some absolutely central feature of the context, on which the job in question crucially depends. This is a consequence of the fact that our skill hinges on simple recognition of appropriate contexts—recognition that, like the familiar physiognomy of a friend, defies casual articulation.

An interesting illustration of this is contained in a famous story told by the philosopher William James:

> Some years ago, being with a camping party in the mountains, I returned from a solitary ramble to find everyone engaged in a ferocious metaphysical dispute. The *corpus* of the dispute was a squirrel—a live squirrel supposed to be clinging to one side of a tree-trunk; while over against the tree's opposite side a human being was imagined to stand. The human witness tries to get sight of the squirrel by moving rapidly round the tree, but no matter how fast he goes, the squirrel moves as fast in the opposite direction, and always keeps the tree between himself and the man, so that never a glimpse of him is caught. The resultant metaphysical problem is this: *Does the man go round the squirrel or not?* He goes round the tree, sure enough, and the squirrel is on the tree; but does he go round the squirrel? In the unlimited leisure of the wilderness, discussion had been worn threadbare. Everyone had taken sides, and was obstinate; and the numbers on both sides were even. Each side, when I appeared, therefore appealed to me to make it a majority. Mindful of the scholastic adage that whenever you meet a

contradiction you must make a distinction, I immediately sought and found one, as follows: "Which party is right," I said, "depends on what you *practically mean* by 'going round' the squirrel. If you mean passing from the north of him to the east, then to the south, then to the west, and then to the north of him again, obviously the man does go round him, for he occupies these successive positions. But if on the contrary you mean being first in front of him, then on the right of him, then behind him, then on his left, and finally in front again, it is quite obvious that the man fails to go round him, for by the compensating movements the squirrel makes, he keeps his belly turned towards the man all the time, and his back turned away. Make the distinction, and there is no occasion for any further dispute. You are both right and both wrong according as you conceive the verb 'go round' in one practical fashion or the other."*

Unfortunately, this anecdote has been used for years to illustrate the value of "definitions" in resolving semantic disputes. But, whether or not James's gambit settled the actual dispute, the picture it provides of language and our skill with it is fundamentally mistaken and dangerously insensitive to important detail. Although James uses the British spelling for the crucial verb, this discussion will assume the story would be unchanged by using the Americanized 'go around'. In these terms the difficulty with James's "solution" is easy to state. He suggests that the verb 'go around' is ambiguous here, that there are two distinct jobs it might have, and that the disagreement arises from the disputants' failure to recognize that they are using the term in different ways. However, this diagnosis depends on job descriptions so crude as to be worthless in this argument. As they stand, neither even remotely describes a job 'go around' has in this context or any other. Neither suggestion plausibly captures what anybody thinks it is to go around something.

To see this all we have to do is exercise the suggested jobs a little. If to 'go around' something is simply ". . . passing from the north of him to the east, then to the south, then to the west, and then to the north of him again . . ." then not only does the hunter go around the squirrel, the squirrel goes around the hunter as well. For the squirrel moves successively into these positions relative to the hunter, just as surely as the reverse. So this cannot capture what anybody would seriously take 'go around' to mean.

What about the other suggestion? It is just as bad. If, as the hunter and squirrel perform their little dance about the tree, a third person stands motionless, observing the proceedings from a discreet distance, then that third person goes around the squirrel (and the hunter!) in James's second "sense" of 'go around'. For that spectator is "first in front of him, then on the right of him, then behind him, then on his left, and finally in front again . . ." as the squirrel moves around the tree. But this is absurd; and it is absurd to think anyone in the hunting party would want to give 'go around' this job either.

*William James, *Pragmatism* (New York: Longmans, Green, 1907).

Although James's analysis contains a grain of insight, it is mistaken in suggesting that the verb 'go around' is importantly ambiguous in this context. The difficulty in characterizing the hunter as 'going around' the squirrel is actually rather subtle and hard to state accurately. We may begin to see what has gone wrong by noticing that this case dramatically and systematically lacks one feature of the cases in which 'go around' gets its normal job, a feature so clear and obvious it is easy to overlook. In the normal context in which 'A goes around B' has its clearest application, B is stationary, fixed in the appropriate frame of reference. The hunter goes around the tree, I go around the block, we all go around the mulberry bush; the tree, the block, and the bush do not move. When Magellan went around the world, what he went around constitutes the frame of reference, and hence is fixed in the most global sense. The squirrel raises a problem because it moves around on the tree.

There is further subtlety to consider, however: the requirement that B be stationary is not absolute—the central body may move, even in the contextually presumed reference frame, as long as that motion is negligible. It is interesting to notice what is negligible and what is not. In astronomy it is wholly unproblematic to say that a satellite (A) goes around a larger body (B) even though B is moving rotationally, revolving on an axis. The earth goes around the sun, the moon and thousands of other satellites go around the earth, even though the sun and earth are themselves moving rotationally in the respective frames of reference. So that motion is (generally) negligible. But not always. If the motion of a satellite is systematically related to the rotation of the central body in one particular way, it is no longer negligible: it will defeat the claim that A goes around B. This occurs when the motion of the satellite is so synchronized with the rotation of the central body that it remains poised above one spot on its surface. The earth has a number of these stationary satellites (mostly for television rebroadcasting), and they do *not* go around the earth, precisely because their motion is synchronized with the earth's daily rotation.

Celestial satellites illustrate yet another kind of interesting central body motion that is sometimes negligible. As the moon goes around the earth its gravitational attraction causes the earth to wobble a bit. (The more precise characterization is that both bodies move smoothly around a point inside the body of the earth representing the mass-center of the earth-moon system.) But since the earth is so much bigger than the moon, the wobble is so small we can neglect it for the purpose of practical characterization. It is quite sensible to say the moon goes around the earth in spite of the systematic wobble in the process. If the moon were gradually to acquire greater and greater mass, however, the wobble induced in the earth would become gradually more pronounced. It would eventually reach a point at which it could no longer be neglected: the earth-moon system would no longer resemble the standard context enough to allow 'go around' to do its standard descriptive job.* In the extreme case, when the two bodies are of equal mass, the natural way to describe their relative motion is to say they each orbit a point halfway between them: neither goes around the other. Binary stars are rather like this: in any such system in which the bodies are even close to equal, the systematic mutual wobble will make any simple application of 'A goes around B' inapplicable. For A to go around B in a gravitational two-body system, B must be much bigger (i.e., more massive) than A.

Now we are in a position to say something more precise about what went wrong in Professor James's example. The squirrel's rotation is synchronized with the motion of the hunter in just the manner of a stationary satellite; and its motion around the tree is very similar to the wobble of the smaller of two binary stars. In short, 'go around' cannot do anything like its normal job here, because the squirrel fails in two separate ways to provide a suitably stable central reference point. It quite spectacularly violates the negligible-movement requirement.

This is a fairly typical case: the point is subtle, something that does not normally attract our explicit attention, and which requires care and reflection to bring out. Such is the nature of our linguistic skill and the problems to which it gives rise. We become skillful in boringly normal contexts trying to express mundane, practical sentiments. So when the context departs from normal, and the issue is no longer practical, we can easily lose our bearing: we do not know what to say, and we are not sure what has gone wrong. It is here that misunderstanding our skills is likely to do the most damage. We settle for guesses about what is important in the job a word does and formulate hip-shot descriptions that are embarrassingly wide of the mark. We risk abandoning a job—firing a word from a perfectly good job—just because we cannot *describe* the job as effortlessly as we can *handle* it. This is the temptation to resist here.

Notice that diagnosing what has gone wrong in the hunting story does not require anything like an actual description of the job 'go around' does in that context, just attention to one specific detail. And that is fortunate indeed. An adequate description, one that would address each important or interesting feature of the job, would require even greater time and effort, far beyond anything anybody would want to invest. It should say something about the nature of reference frames and the conditions under which they may be presupposed, what variations in the motion of A are allowable, and the various kinds of things that can count as A and B. In addition, this particular job of 'go around' would have to be located in the overlapping cluster of jobs it does in related contexts. For this simple phrase illustrates much of the context-dependent subtlety and contrasts discussed earlier. For instance, in some cases neither A nor B moves when A goes around B: a road going around

---

*Exactly what we *could* say in such contexts is a very tricky issue, which will be treated in great detail later when we discuss semantic indeterminacy.

a mountain, say, or a fence around a barnyard. More interesting, 'around' often contrasts with 'through', and will then not entail any kind of encircling at all. "We have two alternatives: we can go through the city on surface streets, or around it on the freeway. I suggest we go around it and avoid the traffic." And so on.

In general, when we are unclear whether a familiar word fits a certain case —whether it does the right job in that context—it is usually hopeless to try to settle the matter by explicit appeal to a description of the relevant job. An adequately rich description will commonly be beyond our resources and patience. The only other recourse is to direct comparison with standard cases: just what we did for the squirrel and the hunter. This too requires care and sensitivity to detail, but, as we have seen, it is sometimes a plausible endeavor when a full-blown description is out of the question.

As a final remark on this topic, it is worth mentioning that the above uncertainty can arise in two separate ways. Two different difficulties can cause us to become confused about the applicability of a familiar term, and they require slightly different treatments. In the first we, like the hunters, try to apply the term in genuinely unusual—nonstandard—circumstances. They are close enough to the standard cases to have a kind of surface plausibility, but distinct enough to raise doubts. Here all we can do is what we did for the squirrel: examine standard cases to see if we can detect any crucial missing elements. The result of our examination will normally fall into one of four categories: no crucial elements missing; crucial elements missing, but that is okay (metaphor); crucial elements missing, which rules out applicability; too tough to call. Only the first of these licenses the literal application of the term. The third rules it out, and the second salvages application at the expense of conceding that the term is not doing its standard job anymore. The fourth will be discussed in great detail in Chapter 7.

The other reason we become uncertain about the application of a familiar term is a relative of the centipede effect: the case we are puzzled about actually *is* a standard case, but something has undermined our skill and we no longer recognize it. Sometimes—especially when we worry a lot about language—a beguiling picture of how language works, or should work, will capture our minds and disrupt the fragile tissue of performance and recognition skills we have built into our communicative competence. The foundation of that competence will then begin to erode: we begin to lose some of our ability to recognize the jobs familiar words do in standard contexts. Our perception becomes distorted and unreliable. Somebody might come to think the word 'thoughtful' must mean something like 'heavily cerebral', 'involving a great deal of careful thinking'—that is, '*full* of thought'. As a result he might object to a grateful old man's thanking a youngster for being so thoughtful in offering him her seat on a crowded bus. "That doesn't take any thought, an idiot could have done it. She probably did it out of mere habit anyway." But of course, the job the old man gave 'thoughtful' simply *is* its standard one in the context. 'Thoughtful' does not require a lot of thinking, just thinking of someone else.

Attacks of this malaise are occasionally intractable, but the remedy suggested above sometimes works here too: looking for independent, external identification of standard cases. Victims must try to gain something like a spectator's vantage on language, watching others do what they used to be able to do themselves. Reading and passively observing conversation is perhaps best. Actual participation in conversation risks spreading the affliction, although sometimes the risk is worth taking. With some care the patient can avoid poisoning the conversation and ruining the evidence.

The task is analogous to a baseball player's trying to work his way out of a batting slump. Sometimes the more he thinks about it the worse it gets. Trying to do it without thinking sometimes works, but once the slump has progressed far enough more drastic measures are usually required. These might consist nowadays in the batter's studying videotapes of his own swing before, when he was hitting .326, and now, to see if any visible changes had occurred. But the aim is only secondarily to understand what has gone wrong. First and foremost it is to regain the competence: to do it right *naturally.* Similarly for our use of language (and for the centipede's walking): recovering the skill is of central importance. Talking about it is interesting only if (and because) we can *do* it.

Nevertheless, talking about certain versions of this affliction is sometimes valuable, even therapeutic. Certain understandable but crippling pictures of how language must or should work may be avoided by coming to understand them and what drives us to them. These will be our major concerns in the next two chapters.

▶ *Exercise:* Comment on the following exchange:

> DISSATISFIED STUDENT: What does "explanation" mean, anyway?
> TEACHING ASSISTANT: Well, this is the sort of thing I mean: the explanation of your being here is your dissatisfaction with your grade.
> DISSATISFIED STUDENT: No, give me a definition.
> TEACHING ASSISTANT: Oh, that would be very difficult. I don't know of a decent one offhand.
> DISSATISFIED STUDENT: Then you don't really know what the word means, do you?

LINGUISTIC KNOWLEDGE: EVIDENCE OF UNDERSTANDING

If adequate job descriptions are so difficult to give, what then should we say when someone asks what we mean by a word? "What do you mean by

'X'?" Normally, such a request is prompted by a specific confusion and does not require a recounting of all the contextual detail, contrasts, and the like found in a general description. An adequate reply will treat the specific problem that gave rise to the question, ignoring clearly unproblematic parts of the job. We may almost always presuppose *some* understanding of the job in question.

> A: "You have two days to respond after the notice has been posted."
> B: "What do you mean by 'posted'?"
> A: "I mean on the bulletin board outside my office."

This reply treats only one small aspect of the job done by 'posted' here. To understand the reply the questioner must already know a good deal about what 'posted' means and have an intimate familiarity with the context. But he certainly would: the question is not likely to arise in this form unless he met these conditions. The reply is just what is required.

This issue is part of the larger and more important question of knowing when we understand what has been said, and, conversely, of knowing when we have been properly understood ourselves. How do we tell? Sometimes it is very easy, and looking at the easy cases is, once again, revealing.

Because language is a practical tool, it naturally lends itself to practical tests. If we wish to know whether a preschooler knows what 'blue' means (in its normal, chromatic sense), we know how to go about finding out. If the kid reliably produces the blue object out of a multicolored selection, and reliably points to the blue patch on different pages of a book, we can be pretty sure he has a rudimentary command of the color. Other, more sophisticated tests are easily generable on this model. If he uses the single word 'soap' with an interrogative inflection, while pointing to a bar of soap, and then is delighted when presented with the bar, we have good reason to think he not only knows what 'soap' means, but has some grasp of the function of inflection in speech as well.

Tests of young children are the most difficult of the easy cases, however, because we can presume only a very slight grasp of the substantive context. For more mature, well-developed language users—especially those immersed in the same substantive context—evidence of understanding is richer, more immediate and more persuasive. I am helping a neighbor work on her car, and I ask, "Would you hand me the 3/8-drive ratchet handle with a 5/8 socket on it?" If she successfully carries out the instruction, that alone constitutes strong evidence for her command of a substantial amount of language. If she failed to understand any of the important words in that sentence, it is unlikely she would respond properly. In conversation we are constantly giving and receiving evidence of linguistic competence and understanding. Gestures, facial expression, and tone of voice provide an immense amount of relevant data. Serious misunderstandings show up almost immediately in puzzling or bizarre responses ("I don't even know how to drive a ratchet"). While the remedy may be difficult, detecting a misunderstanding is often quite straight-forward. In normal conversation, evidence of understanding is commonly overwhelming.

Of course, the rich possibilities afforded by conversation encourage an-other kind of test as well. Instead of indirect tests appealing to simple tasks and responses, we can sometimes demonstrate our understanding by direct attention to the language itself. To discover if someone understands a certain sentence we can ask him to reformulate it: say the same thing in different words. If he can do it, that counts as evidence he understood the first. To discover whether he understands what job a word is doing in a cer-tain sentence, we can ask him to say the same thing without using the word.

This last kind of test sometimes leads us to think we must be able to describe a word's job to show that we know it. But it should be clear by now that *saying* what a word means (or does) is only one thing we can do among many to show we *know* what it means. Furthermore, in this endeavor, what counts as saying what a word means can fall far short of a detailed job description. Sometimes giving a very rough synonym will do, other times a bit of allegory or onomatopoeia.

> "Do you know what a ratchet is?"
> "Yes, it's that mechanism at the end of the rather fat handle that makes a clicking sound and allows the handle to free-wheel in one direction."

This is a rough-and-ready description of what 'ratchet' refers to in the con-text, but perfectly adequate as evidence of understanding.

The brief exchange about 'posted' at the beginning of this section, then, should be understood in something like this way. The question "What do you mean by 'posted'?" expresses some unclarity about the job 'posted' is doing in the previous sentence. The reply is adequate in the circumstances because it supplies just enough data to deal with that specific unclarity: evidence of what specific point the speaker is attempting to make.

The evidence we exchange in conversation—and in test situations too—may all be cast in the forms we explored in Chapter 3. The most interesting and most constantly useful are simple diagnostic arguments. A person's re-sponse—in conversation and test alike—is a trace of her understanding. We get evidence of understanding when the best explanation of the response is that she understood what was said. Everything else counts too: gestures, facial expression, tone of voice. The best explanation is the one that accounts best for all of it. Everything must fit. We begin to get evidence that we have been *mis*understood when the responses become inappropriate. Some-thing about the words or the tone or the expression raises suspicion, plants a hurdle in the way of the everything's-okay explanation. Wisdom usually requires that we then keep an eye out for further relevant evidence of misunderstanding, which will provide a guide to what (if anything) has gone wrong.

Even more interesting is the evidence we gather from the other side of the exchange. When we are the passive member—the reader or listener—trying to understand what has been said, the procedure is once again basically diagnostic. In understanding language, we are constantly trying to find the most plausible interpretation to put on the words we hear or read. When there is a question about what a word means, we ask, "Why would the author have used that word?"—what is the best explanation of it? The study of old texts is a diagnostic inquiry very much of a piece with accident investigations. If we cannot find a best account, the text remains unclear; if we can, that settles the matter—for now, at least.

In normal reading and conversation our diagnosis is instantaneous, effortless, and automatic. In specific contexts, spotting the plausible interpretation is the trick we are so very good at, the human skill that makes language the rich and valuable tool it is. We see immediately that, in this context, the best account of 'pen' is agricultural—there is simply no question about it; the next best bet is so implausible as to be effectively ruled out. In this respect, our diagnostic prowess here is *perceptual.* As in our simple perceptions, we do not explicitly formulate an argument for each linguistic diagnosis. But the process may be unpacked diagnostically: its warrant is diagnostic. When we understand, what we do—automatically—is simply select the most plausible of the rival interpretations: the one that best explains the choice of words. Only when the interpretation is unclear does an explicit diagnostic interpretation become necessary.

This explains why substantive context is so thunderously important to communication. For context provides the background against which plausibility is judged, as well as myriad perceptual cues that function as additional trace-data. Inflection, facial expression, gestures, and other histrionics are all part of it. Language is crucially geared to context because the context provides the data required to make language work: what human beings require to understand each other.

The inductive underpinning of our linguistic diagnoses strongly parallel Stage I of the testimony arguments we examined in Chapter 4. There we appealed to contextual cues to help us explain a statement (already interpreted) in terms of its author's beliefs. Here we appeal to some of the same cues to help us understand what statement is being made by the words: to explain the words in terms of an interpretation. So our linguistic skill involves our diagnostic skill: crucially depends on it to make communication work. That is why the examination of inductive argument comes before the treatment of language in this text.

Exercise: Consider the following conversation:

SMITH: Barlow, do you know what "yes" means?

BARLOW: Well, roughly, it means "I agree."

SMITH: That doesn't really cover all the cases, does it? For instance, suppose you ask me if I'm going to the store, and I say "yes," that would make perfectly good sense. But if I had said "I agree," that would have been incoherent, wouldn't it? There's nothing to agree *to.*

BARLOW (testily): Of course I can't give you a perfect dictionary definition on the spot.

SMITH: Then you don't really know what the word means, do you?

Does Barlow know what 'yes' means? Explain why you think so or think not.

A SECOND PRINCIPLE OF CHARITY

Nearly any sentence you can construct will be unclear when deprived of all substantive context. Most will be hopelessly ambiguous, or entirely pointless. All common words have a variety of jobs to do, differing by a lot, a little, or just a shade. The burden of determining the proper interpretation, the right job, falls most importantly on the substantive context.

The record is in the bag.

It accomplishes this by providing background and trace-data that allow us to estimate the relative plausibility of various interpretations. The proper interpretation is clear when it stands out in the context as much better than the rest. Our linguistic skill consists partly in picking out the most plausible interpretation automatically, instantaneously in the usual run of cases. This quasi-perceptual skill is at the bottom of successful communication. Conversation—and most other linguistic endeavors—would be impossible without it.

So our understanding of language is dominated by a charity principle: *always give the words their most plausible interpretation in the context.* Let us call this principle Charity II. The fact that we adhere to this principle automatically when we read or listen is a large part of what makes rich, rapid communication possible. Intimate familiarity with the context allows us to digest linguistic trace-data at an enormous rate in accord with this diagnostic principle. Sometimes we know so well where the conversation is leading that we need only hints from the words themselves. We easily compensate for mispronunciation (or misspellings in print), slips of the tongue, bad grammar, even illiteracy if what is being said is simple enough. The plausible interpretation usually jumps right out at us. But Charity II is also the diagnostic principle we appeal to explicitly when the going gets rough, when no interpretation jumps out at all. It is the rule we follow in deciding what interpretation to place on something puzzling or obscure.

For our purposes, the most important application of this principle is in determining the *implications* of what someone says. This represents one of the direct connections between language and our reasoning. For in practical communication, placing an interpretation on words typically requires us to fill in features of the context that are merely implicit, not stated explicitly. These features will be more or less strongly required depending on how essential they are to making plausible sense of the words. Something indispensable to making plausible sense of them we may say is *presupposed.* Such things are the strongest, most inescapable implications the words have in that context.

One reason that linguistic performance (speaking, writing) is more difficult than recognition (understanding what is said or written) is that creating intelligible language requires an author constantly to see things from the perspective of his audience. The task of expressing a specific proposition is to string words together in such a way that their most plausible interpretation in the context will be the proposition he wishes to express. Becoming competent at speaking and writing simply consists in becoming good at judging what interpretation will naturally be given to our words by other people.

We do become competent, of course. On normal, everyday matters there is seldom any question at all; we know perfectly well how our words will be taken: what the best-looking account of them requires, what implications they have. We can often hold people responsible for understanding the natural interpretation of their words. If I say I cannot come to your party because my mother died, I know perfectly well you will think my mother *just* died, and I cannot come because of circumstances immediately following a death in the family. I am either too grieved to be sociable or am needed at home to pull things together, or support the rest of the family, or some such thing. If it turns out that my mother died years ago, but made my inheritance dependent upon never going to a party thrown by any relation of your aunt Emma's, whom she hated, then I can be accused of deliberately misleading you. I have abused the language. Specifically, I have used your natural tendency to put the charitable interpretation on my words to trick you into believing something false.

Nor can I avoid the charge by pleading that what I said was "strictly" true. For in the context what I clearly and knowingly implied is clearly false. I used the wrong words to express myself—I said the wrong thing. The accurate thing to have said is that I could not come because of a stipulation in my late mother's will, that I would lose my inheritance if my being there were discovered. Which, of course, is monumentally different from what I did say. So if there is a sense in which what I said was "strictly" true, then this sort of "strict" truth is as reprehensible as falsehood. It was a shabby thing to say.

Perhaps the most fundamental and pervasive application of Charity II concerns the purpose, the practical or communicative significance of the words we use. One reason context helps us understand a bit of language is that it allows us to understand the *motivation* behind an utterance. We understand the words in part because we understand why somebody would want to say or ask such a thing, express such a sentiment then and there. "Hand me the 3/8-drive ratchet," "Is it raining?" "The pig is in the pen." To understand these sentences we naturally place them in (skeletal) contexts in which they have some human significance. If we cannot do this we have trouble understanding what has been said.

Hand me the floor, please.

Even if we are familiar with the words we often will not understand what has been said until we understand why it was a significant thing to say.

So a substantial component of our automatic charity consists in viewing others' statements as significant. If we cannot find a significant interpretation we conclude something has gone wrong. Either we do not fully grasp the context, or the author has made a slip of the tongue, or does not understand the language, or, perhaps, is babbling incoherently.

Unfortunately, sometimes the best explanation is deception. Politicians and advertisers will sometimes resort to statements that have clearly false implications when interpreted as significant remarks—as they naturally will be—but which may be defended by appeal to the shabby notion of "strict" truth we used above. That is, their statements can be construed as true only if stripped of the natural significance every competent language user would charitably give them.

A few years ago an advertising agency was exercising the venerable formula of listing all the attributes its client's product shared with similar products costing much more when it ran gaudily afoul of the significance requirement. The flattering-comparison technique is always dangerous in this way, but the case in point provides a useful illustration nevertheless. The product was a medium-priced family sedan, so we were to be impressed with the fact that it shared certain characteristics with far more expensive cars: it had some of the same interior dimensions as the Rolls Royce, for instance, and front-wheel drive "like the Cadillac Eldorado." Such claims were skating on exceptionally thin ice already, but the formula collapsed altogether when it reached "the $16,000 Aston Martin." The trait it shared with this expensive sports car (this was back when $16,000 was a great deal of money) was independent front suspension. "Independent front suspension, like the $16,000 Aston Martin."

The difficulty with this is that virtually all cars, for years, have had independent front suspension. It is as common as door handles and headlights. But since most people do not know much about how the wheels are hung on their cars, they naturally inclined to take the comparison with the Aston Martin as significant. Even the naturally skeptical would have a hard time believing that anyone would say something as fatuous as

It has left and right headlights like the $16,000 Aston Martin.

But the comparison of suspension systems is just as silly. So the advertising ploy openly offended the presumption of significance. The only reason to mention the similarity in this context was that it was flattering to the less expensive car. This implication is certainly why it was part of the ad. And it is grotesquely implausible to suppose the advertisers did not know it was false. In short, the ad was dishonest.

Once again, the claim may be defended by appeal to the reprehensible notion of "strict" truth. The sedan in question did have independent front suspension, and in that respect did resemble the expensive sports car. There is no need to review the emptiness of this defense. The common appeal to such defenses in advertising and in politics goes a long way toward establishing the radical claim of some social critics that the institutions surrounding those activities undermine and subvert language itself. The presumption of significance is an important part of what makes language work.

Exercise
▶ 1. Characterize each of the roles of context discussed above (pp. 174–180) in terms of the second principle of charity. That is, explain how each of those five headings involves Charity II at work.
  2. How does Charity II help us understand what somebody intends in answering a question with "Well, yes and no." What interpretation does it practically rule out?

EQUIVOCATION

Our effortless ability to adjust the jobs words do from context to context, though crucial to our use of language, can sometimes get us into trouble. Like any skill, it will let us down if we overestimate it, or are cavalier in its use. A talented violinist who does not practice, a skilled surgeon who does not take due care, an expert marksman who is not terribly circumspect, may make serious, even tragic mistakes that someone less skilled but more careful would avoid. Trouble arises from our effortless linguistic skill when we fail to notice that a crucial word has changed from one job to another in a way that undermines our reasoning. This is called equivocation.

Blatant equivocation is usually easy to spot, and hence not much of a problem.

Since apple trees produce apples, then shoe trees must produce shoes.

The job the word 'tree' does in the expression 'shoe trees' is radically different from the one it does in 'apple tree', so the reasoning collapses. The significance of 'tree' in the two clauses is so different, in fact, that no competent language user would take the first to be even relevant to the second, much less provide support for it. Blatant equivocation like this is at the bottom of many jokes—especially puns—and they are funny (*if* they are funny) because the confusion is so absurd.

> When the Roman Empire fell it must have been from quite an altitude because so much stuff got broken.

We are unlikely to be confused by so transparent a pun.

Subtler cases do represent a real threat to reasoning, however. An officer of an unnamed board of education, embroiled in a heated controversy, concealed a tape recorder in her purse and secretly taped the proceedings of a closed meeting. The meeting had been closed to the public in order to permit candid discussion of a sensitive issue at the center of the controversy. When the tape recording was revealed, those who had voted to close the meeting protested that the officer had surreptitiously frustrated the will of the board's majority: the recording of a closed meeting violates the spirit and the purpose of closure. But the officer protested that since she was officially the board's recording secretary, what she had done was fully within the responsibilities of her office.

This of course is a pun too; but since somebody seems to have taken it seriously, to have been misled by it, it deserves the heavy title 'equivocation' as well. For what a recording secretary is responsible for are just the minutes: a skeletal, stylized, usually discrete record of a meeting's business. The job done by the term 'recording' in the expression 'recording secretary' does not automatically license the *tape* recording of anything, let alone a closed meeting. This defense involves the confusion—or perhaps the intentional conflation—of two distinct but related jobs of the word 'recording'.

Just what makes one job shift a transparent pun and another a captious threat to reasoning is difficult to say. It doubtless has something to do with the intimacy or subtlety of the relationship between the two jobs. But it is also bound up with our perceptions, our motivation, and our preconceptions about the language, all of which make it difficult to anticipate trouble and even to articulate what has gone wrong when it occurs. This is perhaps why equivocation can play such a persuasive role in public relations gambits, and why ambiguity is so enormously attractive in desperate times. In the following example we can see something of the attraction, as well as the subtle distinctions to which we must sometimes be sensitive.

Reacting to the government's antismoking campaign, a tobacco company spokesman once said:

> Since we have not yet *discovered* the cause of cancer, how can anyone say that *smoking* causes cancer?

The question is rhetorical,* naturally: the implication is that nobody can. If we had discovered that smoking causes cancer, then it would appear mistaken to say the cause of cancer remains undiscovered. But the appearance is deceptive. For the job done by 'cause' when used with the definite article ('the') in this context is subtly but crucially distinct from the job it does in the simple, relational statement "x causes y". When scientists inquire into *the* cause of cancer (especially in the singular) they are looking for something very general, for some physiological account of malignancy in animal tissue. They want to understand the organic, chemical, possibly molecular sequence of events that leads to the strange cell behavior we know as cancer. They want to understand this sequence of events independent of the particular physical event triggering it, and perhaps even independent of its location in the body.

By contrast, when we say that smoking (or too much sun, or ingesting cyclamates and nitrosamines) causes cancer, we are talking about the triggers, not the physiology. The point has been covered elaborately in Chapters 3 and 4: we have a correlation between smoking and lung cancer that requires a causal connection between the two to explain. We know enough to rule out reversed-cause accounts as implausible, leaving us with 'smoking causes cancer' as the best of the rivals. We can discover all this without understanding anything at all about *how* smoking causes cancer. And this is just what we have done. We have learned a great deal about cancer's triggers, while remaining largely in the dark about the underlying physiology.

So the spokesman's gambit involves an equivocation. His first clause is true only of the underlying physiology: that is what we have not yet discovered. But he wants to trick us by using the same word ('cause') into thinking he has rebutted the claim that smoking can trigger malignant cell growth, which he has not. The case is rather like complaining to the disease-plagued builders of the Panama Canal earlier in this century:

> Since we have not yet *discovered* the cause of malaria, how can you say that *mosquito bites* cause malaria?

Easily, really, once you see the equivocation.

▶ *Exercise:* Explain the equivocation in the famous bumper sticker "If guns are outlawed only outlaws will have guns."

---

*Rhetorical questions deserve a passing remark. When prosecuting a serious argument on a difficult issue it is not bad policy to avoid them altogether. They are sometimes good for humor when clear, but more often they are only clever devices for distracting attention from important complexities. The opposing side will almost always deny their implication, or its relevance.

ARROGANCE

Our discussion has made constant reference to the immense linguistic competence we all share. But it is important to keep all this in proper perspective. Our competence is primarily in expressing mundane (although sometimes very important) sentiments in familiar, practical contexts. This is the major role of language in our lives and constitutes its major value to us. It also yields some insight into the nature and limits of our linguistic skill. The familiar contexts of human concern provide simultaneously the rich background against which human perception and diagnosis are most reliable, nearly immediate feedback when our understanding fails us, and the most extensive (and sometimes riveting) exercise of all our related skills and capacities. So it should not be surprising that we have developed a useful level of linguistic competence in such contexts. But the limited scope of these ideal circumstances should serve as a warning: the further we stray from practical matters and familiar circumstances, the greater the risk we will exceed the limits of our competence.

It is often easy for linguistic competence, like any other largely unreflective skill, to fail us without drawing our notice. Because they tax us more, our performance skills normally run out before our recognition skills do, but both gradually deteriorate as we cross unfamiliar terrain. In the United States today, the erosion of speaking and writing skills is epidemic. Very little explicit training occurs in public education, facility in expression is not a generally held value, dictionaries have fallen into disuse, good habits never develop. Although we can often recognize them in a context, we do not trouble to master the sometimes elaborate subtlety in the jobs familiar words do. The man in the street, a microphone suddenly thrust in his face, finds himself reduced to embarrassed grunts and gestures trying to create what he can only recognize. "See, well it's like this, man, y'know, I think its the pits, man. You know what I mean?" Unfortunately, we seldom do.

This is relevant here because in many respects language is a fragile tool. Lazy, cavalier, careless, or arrogant performance can damage it. Especially in an era of easy mass communication, insensitive bastardizations can crush subtlety, blur valuable distinctions, make useful things difficult to say. The language simply *is* what is written and spoken. Recognition is in this way parasitic on performance. So the erosion of performance skills—in general, but especially among journalists—results directly in the erosion of the language itself. When headlines repeatedly use 'refute' to mean a particularly spunky denial, it blurs the worthwhile distinction between refutation and denial. When 'parameters' is used as an exotic-sounding synonym for 'limits' it robs us of the more subtle job 'parameters' was formerly commissioned to do in nearly identical contexts. We end up with two words for the same job and make it increasingly difficult for 'parameters' ever to do its earlier, distinctive job.

The richness and value of a natural language in communication depend on the stability of its major components. For the subtlety and precision with which we can speak to each other is limited by our grasp of the linguistic devices and institutions required to do so. And the only plausible way to improve the general level of competence in this regard—even in a relatively small linguistic community—is by mastering the currently available institutions, which have survived a tough evolutionary winnowing, and by building on them where required. It is hopeless to try to rebuild basic linguistic institutions from the ground up every generation or every season or every conversation. Whenever we blunder into a discipline of even slightly unfamiliar jargon, we feel vaguely lost. It is difficult to understand anything but the broad outline of what is being said. Time and familiarity are required before the finer points may be grasped. At every level, linguistic patterns take time to develop and more time to sink in; and the more refined they are the longer they take.

Rapid linguistic turnover does not just limit communication among different age groups. It limits the capacity of the language itself. The parts that are late to develop or hard to learn simply never disseminate. It is accordingly in the interest of all members of a linguistic community to nurture and refine their performance skills, to become familiar with the rich panoply of existing linguistic institutions—not just because it gives them greater access to a valuable tool, although it does that too, but because it is required to maintain the tool itself. The best advice is to get a good dictionary (*not* just any dictionary) and to use it up. It helps to develop some curiosity about the institutions surrounding familiar words and constructions: which words go naturally with what prepositions, for instance, or the subtle differences between transitive and intransitive application of the same verb. If your dictionary lasts more than just a few years, you are probably not using it enough.

SUMMARY

Perhaps the most important observation in this chapter is that our linguistic skills are parasitic on our diagnostic skills. Our ability to communicate depends crucially on our perception of the substantive context, and our (related) ability to place the most plausible interpretation on words, once the context is recognized. Normally, this is all done automatically, instantaneously, unreflectively, much like diagnostic perception. The fact that we are good at these diagnoses is what makes language the valuable tool it is, and what makes it worth our time to investigate its impact on our reasoning.

Our reasoning is sometimes damaged by our failure to understand just what skills we have and which we do not, and by our failure to grasp when we have exceeded the limits of the skills we do have. Often great distances separate the abstract, unfamiliar contexts in which we try to use language from those concrete, familiar ones in which we have mastered our skill. We may avoid many language-based reasoning difficulties simply by reminding ourselves that our principal linguistic skill lies in specific applications in practical contexts. More abstract use of language requires far more care than we customarily allow it: we are far less skilled at abstract characterization than we commonly tend to think. This is especially true of abstractions about the jobs common words do.

7

Word Games:
Our Worst Temptations

Misunderstanding language can wreak havoc with our more abstract reasoning. If we ignore the observations of the last chapter our abstract, philosophical reflection can easily lead us to confusing, misleading, even outrageous formulations of important sentiments. Perhaps the most general hazard, the most frequent culprit when our ruminations go awry, is our temptation to hasty and ill-considered revision of the language. We are quick to think that clear thought or trenchant expression of insight requires linguistic reform, so we begin campaigning words in and out of certain jobs. In these moods we do considerably more firing than hiring, but there is some of each, much of it ill advised. To be sure, words do occasionally find themselves used in befuddling or otherwise objectionable ways, and sometimes the cure is to purge the language itself of an institution or two; but this is appropriate far less often than we are inclined to think. And when it is, the rationale is far more modest (and even vain) than we like to believe. Usually, our temptation to savage the language proceeds from one of a small number of stubborn myths about our linguistic skills, or about how the language should operate —myths we are now in a position to dispel.

ETYMOLOGY

Studying the historical development of a word (its etymology), or noticing that it is composed of certain component parts, can sometimes help us understand how that word came to have some of its jobs. It can even help us understand those jobs better. Knowing what an accordion is helps us understand what an accordion pleat is; knowing that 'tweet' is used to refer to the high-pitched sound of common songbirds makes it easier to understand the job 'tweeter' is given in stereo systems; and understanding that *fenestra* is the Latin word for window might help us understand how 'defenestration' could be a form of homicide.

Struck by the value of this useful device, we are sometimes tempted to turn it into a pedantic rule: a rule determining what job a word should have and, more destructive, which ones it should not. Unfortunately, language does not work this way: many of the jobs words would be given using this "rule" are ones they do *not* have, and many that they do have are ones they would not get on this "rule." We are occasionally inclined to press ahead nevertheless, determined to reshape the language the way it "should" be according to our "rule": firing words from their established jobs, and rehiring them for others. Wielding a self-righteous sword, we campaign for a more rational etymology, a more "logical" language.

But all this neglects both the essentially practical foundation of language in human communication, and the fragile complexity of our linguistic skills. Once a word has established itself in an important, useful job, it is almost never wise to try uprooting it and replacing it with something else. (There are cases we will shortly touch on in which this advice may be ignored.) The best thing is usually to thank our lucky stars that some word has the job we need, learn it, and use our estimable skill with contexts to make the subtle points we must. Our ability to handle specific jobs in well-specified contexts allows us to grasp what has been said without concern for weird components or incoherent etymology. These esoteric, academic matters are sometimes worth mentioning as curiosities, but they should not obtrude very far on our talking with each other.

A striking illustration of this may be found in music. When a part (or an instrument) is referred to using the word 'obbligato', it means that the part (or instrument) is mere accompaniment, and may be omitted if desired. This is so in spite of the fact that *obbligato* is an Italian word meaning obligatory —that is, it sounds as if it should mean just the opposite of what it does.

Music dictionaries admit that the evolution of the word into its current paradoxical use is confusing and most likely involves a simple mistake somewhere along the line; but this is just an explanation, not an objection. The term has been accepted among composers and performers, and it does the job satisfactorily. If the paradoxical history is mentioned at all, it is mentioned only as a curiosity.

Consider an easier case. The blackboard in my office is green. That fact has encouraged some to argue that it should not be *called* a blackboard. Blackboards, they say, should be black. It might be mentioned in passing that the color of most things the protestants would allow to be blackboards is slate gray, not black. But this is not the crucial point here. The crucial point is that in offices, classrooms, and the like, 'blackboard' unproblematically refers to all kinds of different writing surfaces, suitable for use with chalk. Within a substantial range, the color does not matter much. The job of 'blackboard' in "the blackboard in my office is green" is perfectly clear in the context for normal English speakers. And that is all we can ask of words and their jobs. The fact that all blackboards used to be black—or at least gray—is an interesting historical curiosity; but it is not a good reason to take away one of the jobs 'blackboard' currently does quite satisfactorily in a range of useful contexts.

So, once again, breaking up a word into components, like studying its historical roots, although sometimes useful, does not provide a reliable guide to the jobs that word has. It is important to resist the temptation to scrap great chunks of a language and rework it in the hope of making this procedure more helpful and more reliable. The way in which a language evolves and words get their jobs is very complex and subtle: it is shaped by our entire network of perceptual and linguistic skills. Hence what jobs a word gets is only partly controlled by any one consideration, such as ancient roots or simple composition. The primary task of language is clear communication of mundane human concerns in practical contexts. Our sense of elegance and concern for transparent etymology is of secondary importance. What matters for practical, human communication is primarily that a word's jobs be clear and useful in specific contexts. And the job of 'blackboard' in classrooms and 'obbligato' in music—and many others with strange or paradoxical histories—is perfectly satisfactory from that point of view.

Exercise

1. Suppose somebody insisted that 'fireplace' meant (had to mean) any place there was a fire. How would you (sympathetically) try to talk them out of it?

▶ 2. Do the same for someone who thinks 'valuable' means 'able to be valued' —that is, anything anyone ever managed to value was therefore valuable.

SCIENCE

The demand for an elegant etymology is only one source of misguided revision of the language. Another, which is sometimes even more powerfully tempting, derives from our respect for science. Occasionally, because a word (or form of a word) has a particular job in science or technology, we may be tempted to think that other jobs this word has are inferior, *un*scientific, even illegitimate. For instance, in elementary thermodynamics it is common to distinguish three modes of heat transfer, three ways in which heat may be transferred from one thing to another: conduction, convection, and radiation. Conduction occurs when a warm body (or substance) is placed in contact with a cold one; convection occurs when a liquid or gas passes over a substance of different temperature, warming or cooling it, and radiation is the transfer of heat from a warm body to colder surroundings (or vice versa) through electromagnetic waves—commonly infrared radiation. Considering this technical terminology, some people (often, high school science teachers) have argued that it is silly, or even mistaken, for us to use the word 'radiator' to refer to the radiator of a car. This is so, they argue, because the heat transfer provided by a car's radiator is almost entirely accomplished by conduction and convection, an insignificant fraction of it being due to radiation.

But once again this involves a misunderstanding of language and its many practical tasks. Knowledge of the three modes of heat transfer, and even their application to automotive cooling systems, is very interesting and useful in some important contexts. But this does not remotely recommend that we fire the word 'radiator' from its established job in other (nonthermodynamic) contexts. The nontechnical use of 'radiator' is both clear and practically valuable in these contexts; and its practical value is enough to grant it job security. That the automotive job of the word 'radiator' ignores a technical distinction is irrelevant. "I need a new radiator cap." "Would you flush the radiator while the car's being serviced?" "The mess on the garage floor is due to my leaky radiator." The job of 'radiator' is clear in each of these sentences; none would be improved by carping about conduction and convection.

Furthermore, as we should expect, our skill in grasping substantive context will easily allow the word 'radiator' to do different jobs here without confusion. Those familiar with thermodynamics have no trouble getting their car's cooling system fixed. And when a physicist reads "An ideal black-body is the optimum radiator of heat," he (or she) does not think of fins, pipes, and ethylene glycol.

Exercise: Suppose somebody insisted that the President's limousine was not (really) black because it reflects some of the light falling on it (it's shiny), unlike *really* black things, such as black holes and ideal black bodies, which do not. In the spirit of this section, explain what confusion about the jobs done by 'black' might be responsible for this insistence.

IN GENERAL

When we find ourselves in a reformist mood, enthusiastically firing words from their jobs, we must try to keep a grip on a central observation of the last chapter. Common words do many different jobs in different contexts, some dramatically distinct, some closely related, others only shades apart. And all this variety is both useful and completely within our normal competence. Only when we misunderstand our skills, especially our appreciation of substantive context, do we begin to feel uneasy with the normal range of jobs words do. Insecurity then drives us to think words should be restricted to etymologically transparent jobs, or, perhaps, to their most important jobs in science. This is the *myth of one proper use,* one of the most prevalent and damaging of our myths about language. Much of this chapter will be devoted to reducing its appeal.

In general, the fact that a word has an established job in a certain context creates an enormous presumption in favor of keeping that job. The job will nearly always have arisen because we have found it useful, and our understanding of the context will normally allow us to distinguish this particular job from others the word might have. In some contexts 'thoughtful' *does* mean something like 'full of thought' or 'heavily cerebral'—not unexpected from simply putting 'thought' together with 'ful'. But, as we noticed in the last chapter, 'thoughtful' frequently registers a kind of considerateness largely unrelated to the intensity of thought involved. Just why we find this a useful job for 'thoughtful' to have is difficult to articulate, as is so much of our handling of language. But we do find it useful, and it is wholly unproblematic in the appropriate contexts. There is no reason to fire the word from either job. It does them both quite well.

What, then, would justify firing a word from an established job? Are not some jobs inherently damaging to communication or thought? It is interesting to notice how modest even the best-looking cases are. We are so good at using context to make subtle distinctions, and so adept at finding the best interpretation of someone's words, that even the most offensive barbarisms seldom deceive us more than momentarily. Consider, for example, the journalistic abuse of 'refute', mentioned in the last chapter. Suppose a headline reads, "GM Chairman Refutes Union Charges." The union has charged that GM is an immensely wealthy organization that can easily afford the new contract proposed by union negotiators. Very often in such a case, what the GM executive will have said will be something like this:

The union spokesman fails to understand our predicament. Because of the gasoline shortage, this has been an extremely slow sales year, our profit margin is very small compared to past years. We simply cannot afford the union's lavish demands: they would be out of line in a good year, this year they are just impossible.

In normal circumstances (which we will assume), this statement falls embarrassingly short of being a refutation of the union's charges. The GM chairman has *denied* the charges—emphatically—and has sketched the outlines of an argument for his denial; but he has *not conclusively established* his position. He has said the union charges are false, he has argued that they are false, but he has not shown them to be false, he has not refuted them. There is an enormous difference between saying and showing here.

Now this much is so obvious that the attentive reader immediately realizes that the headline writer has misused the word 'refute'—given it a job that is not (yet, at least) in the dictionary. It is terribly implausible to suppose the writer actually thought that what the GM executive said was conclusive, did provide a refutation. So we automatically adopt the more plausible interpretation: he is giving 'refute' a nonstandard job. Perhaps he thinks it means an emphatic denial, or a plausible denial, or some support for a denial, but he simply cannot realize it means a conclusive denial, a knock-down argument. That is staggeringly implausible on its face. So even here, when a word is given a job it does not even have yet, and one fraught with dangerous and misleading possibilities, we are capable of understanding an author's confusion and compensating for it—enough, at least, to understand what was said. We can rewrite the headline ourselves. "Oh, what he meant to say was 'GM Chairman Emphatically Denies Union Charges' or, perhaps 'GM Chairman Argues Union Charges Unfounded'."

The point of all this is not to license barbaric bastardizations that find their way into print. It is to show how careful we must be in saying why we wish to deny a job to a certain word. The above case is one of the clearest possible. There is all the reason in the world to fight the sloppy handling of 'refute' by journalists. There is all the reason in the world to resist letting 'refute' do the job given to it by the headline writer, and even to fire it if it gets that job; we discussed it all in the last chapter. But the reason is *not* that we cannot tell the jobs apart in practice, or that we usually misunderstand what was said. Our skills are too good, too resilient, too difficult to trick for that. All we can offer is some modest but reasonable speculation about the future of our valuable linguistic institutions—something we are not very good at, and which will not support grand generalizations. Something like the following

Look, giving 'refute' two closely related but incompatible jobs in very similar contexts is asking for trouble. It will doubtless make talking about such things more difficult than it is already, and increase the possibility of confusion. And since we already have words or phrases that do exactly what the headline writer above wanted 'refute' to do, it seems reasonable to stick with the current array of jobs these words do.

This is about as strong as such an argument can get; and given that the journalistic abuse has not yet found wide acceptance, it is a very strong argument indeed. Once a job is deeply ingrained in linguistic practice, however, the case is much more difficult to make. Innocence is hard to recover.

There are other reasons to fire words from certain jobs—or at least to resist using them. But these are largely personal or social reasons, and have next to nothing to do with our ability to communicate clearly. Some words we might not want to use simply because they are signs of illiteracy. 'Ain't' and 'irregardless' are perfectly clear in application, for example, but are usually avoided in literate contexts. We might want to argue that 'irregardless' should be fired from its job because it is just an embarrassing conflation of 'irrespective' with 'regardless'. But embarrassment is all we can plead here; it is not a matter of obfuscation. We usually know what people mean when they use it.

Similar objections may be raised against clichés and hackneyed phrases. For a whole variety of social and personal reasons they are likely to be offensive, and sometimes that is a very good reason to avoid them. We often wish what we say (and write) to be not just clear, but pleasant, and this requires as much effort as does mere clarity. But as important as they are, these considerations are beyond the scope of the present discussion. Trying to understand what allows an expression to be clear and valuable in a certain job is enough to occupy us here.

DETAILED ILLUSTRATIONS: RESISTING THE MYTH

This chapter is devoted to uncovering bad (though tempting) reasons for firing words from their established jobs: temptations that are usually understandable, but ones we must try to resist. Most of them proceed from misunderstandings about how language works, and may be treated by close attention to some basic aspects of our linguistic skills.

Each of the cases discussed thus far illustrates one or another aspect of what we have called the myth of one proper use: the myth that we can figure out the proper job for a word by looking at something like science or etymology, neglecting the details of established linguistic practice. But as we noticed in Chapter 6, words have many different jobs to do, all proper in their respective contexts. And in those contexts nearly all of them are perfectly clear, perfectly good English, and wholly inoffensive to normal language users. To avoid the temptations we must come to see how silly the demands for scientific purity and etymological transparency are in our normal use of words. To this end we will examine four more interesting examples, each sufficiently tempting to have had some currency on college campuses during the past decade.

Sunrise

Among the misplaced demands for scientific purity, one of the most persistent is the view that we should stop saying that the sun rises in the morning, because of what modern astronomy tells us about the relative motion of the bodies in our solar system.

A: I got started so early this morning that I watched the sun rise while waiting for the bus.

B: Don't you know the sun doesn't actually rise? The sun stands rather still at the center of the planetary system; what appears to be the sun's rising is actually the earth's own rotation, gradually bringing us out into the sun's light.

Because of the understandable respect accorded to science in our society, A will often respond apologetically to this attack on his idiom. He may even rework what he said in astronautic jargon to avoid the phrase B despises:

A: Oh, I'm sorry, what I meant to say was that the morning terminator crossed my bus stop while I waited there this morning.

But now we begin to see the damage to practical communication that can result from the affliction we are examining, for this revised version is a very strange way to express A's original sentiment. If A walked into a roomful of normal English speakers and tried to tell us how early he had gotten up by talking about the morning terminator, he would be in real trouble. Most of us would not understand him at all. And those who did would wonder why he put it that way instead of talking in normal English. In other words, A's strange idiom would raise Charity II problems: it would raise difficulties in our finding a plausible interpretation for his words. We would be at a loss to explain his strange choice. "If all he's trying to say is he got up before sunrise, why didn't he just say so?"

The point is that all the astronomy is simply irrelevant—irrelevant both to the point A is making and to the job 'rise' has in its normal talk about dawn. When we speak of the sun's rising in normal, mundane contexts, that is simply our institutionalized way of referring to the sun's first coming into view in the morning. The underlying cosmological explanation of the phenomenon is beside the point—boring. It could be that the earth stands still and the sun circles around it; it could be that the sun stands still and the earth rotates before it; it could be anything in between. If all we are trying to say is how early we got up, or how pretty dawn looked or any one of an endless number of normal, human concerns, it simply does not matter which astronomical picture is right, or which one we believe. The job we give 'rise' in those contexts is clear and uncontroversial. There is no need to apologize for it, and certainly no need to fire it.

Once again, the reason we find 'rise' the right word to give the crucial job at dawn is hard to articulate. Some argue that it is in fact an anachronistic leftover from old, discredited geostatic cosmology. This is a nasty-sounding thing to say about it, but we must remind ourselves that a tawdry history is only a curiosity, not an objection to idiom. We all allow 'lunatic' to be a convenient synonym for 'insane person', untroubled by ancient theories on the effects of the moon.

A much more plausible explanation of our finding 'rise' a natural way to characterize the parting of sun and horizon in the morning is that for practical purposes it is incredibly convenient to take the earth as the frame of reference: to treat it as though it were absolutely stationary. We simply take it to be fixed for the purpose of describing motion, just as we take the cabin of an airplane to be fixed to describe, say, the dealing of cards during a flight. And for most purposes this is wholly unproblematic. We must occasionally remind ourselves of the spinning when we use spring balances or when Coriolis effects are large; just as the card players must remind themselves that they are flying through the air when weather gets rough or the pilot changes direction. But for most practical purposes there is nothing to be gained from adopting an astronomically exotic frame of reference, and everything to be gained from using mother earth. To refer everything first to a nonrotating reference frame and then explicitly compensate for the earth's spin would add gratuitous complexity to simple problems, and push already complex ones beyond our normal grasp. In the exotic (nonrotating) reference frame we do not, for example, go from New York to San Francisco; instead we stop keeping up with the rotation of the earth so completely, allowing San Francisco to come to us. And the trip, in a jet, would be a few miles to the east rather than a few thousand west (going the other direction could be a much longer trip). For most practical purposes this perspective is not just absurd, it is counterproductive. We have no difficulty "keeping up with" the earth's rotation; we do not have to try. What requires effort and concern is the 3,000 miles west, not the few miles east. What reasonably occupies our attention is overcoming impediments to our moving around on (i.e., with respect to) the face of this planet. Our normal interest in sunrise concerns the time, the ambient illumination, or the beauty of dawn: nothing astronomical. So in describing it there is no reason to jettison the orthodox perspective and adopt an exotic one. The sun really rises just as we really do go from New York to San Francisco. Both 'rises' and 'go' take the earth as their reference frame; and this is not merely reasonable, it is usually required for successful communication. It is sensible to ignore extraneous complications when their impact on our concerns is negligible. This is one of the things practical language does best.

To be perfectly clear: in some obvious contexts the astronomical perspective is appropriate, helpful, even necessary. The task is to be clear about when it is and when it is not. And for most practical purposes it is not. Forcing the exotic perspective on mundane conversation damages our communication, our thought, and even our behavior. In short, the job speaker A gave to 'rise' at the start of this section is perfectly clear and wholly unproblematic. It neither affirms nor denies any particular cosmological theory. On the other hand to use exotic astronomical expressions in this context would be obscure and potentially misleading to nearly everybody. Listeners would wonder why A did not say it in the normal way; and this would raise explanatory hurdles in the path of the interpretation A wished them to place on his words. Communication would become less clear, less certain, all at the expense of greater effort.

Fruit

Although the preceding case does illustrate a misplaced insistence on the perspective of science, it does not specifically involve the technical use of a word. The dispute concerns the use of 'rise' in a relatively pedestrian sense. In fact, one reason to trouble ourselves over the semantics of sunrise is to see that cases like this do not always involve a technical term. It is time now to return to the kind of case we discussed earlier, and exercise our discrimination of a word's technical and non-technical jobs. To do this it will be interesting to consider a statement sometimes made by beginning botany students:

Did you realize that a tomato is a fruit, not a vegetable?

The confusion displayed here is a version of the myth of one proper use: the insistence that the word 'fruit' do its technical, scientific job in an especially inappropriate context.

Perhaps the best way to see this is to hark back to the notion of contrast we discussed early in Chapter 6. Sometimes a central feature of a word's job will be the contrast it draws, and that contrast can change from one context to another. Ignoring (or misunderstanding) the contextual variability of contrast is a major source of reformist misadventure, and is neatly illustrated in this case.

In the sense in which a tomato is a fruit, it is a structural part of a plant, the part containing seeds and hence playing a role in reproducing tomato plants. In this sense 'fruit' contrasts with 'stem', 'leaf', and 'root', for example, but it does not contrast with 'vegetable'. 'Vegetable' is not on the list of structural parts of a plant. A tomato is 'the fruit *of* the tomato plant', as opposed to the leaf, stem, or root of that plant. But there is no 'vegetable *of* the tomato plant'. So in the sense in which tomato is a fruit, it is not a fruit as opposed to a vegetable.

When 'fruit' does contrast with 'vegetable', it is performing its nontechnical, nontaxonomic job. This is the one it commonly gets at mealtime, in kitchens, and at produce counters. Here 'fruit' has something to do with taste, and hence what kind of salad it goes into or whether it is right for dessert. And in this sense a tomato is not a fruit, it is a vegetable. Tomatoes do not go into fruit salads, but rather the other kind. Tomato juice is not a fruit juice. Tomatoes are one of the eight vegetables in V8. All sorts of things that are fruits in structural taxonomy are vegetables in grocery stores: squash, cucumbers, eggplants, and beans, to name only a few. Furthermore, some things that are not structural fruits, such as rhubarb, count as fruit in that word's other job.

None of this should be surprising now. Words do many different jobs, and the context is generally up to the task of sorting the right one from the wrong ones. Usually we do this effortlessly. Only when we misapprehend our skills —or are in the grip of the centipede effect—do problems arise in normal contexts. Then the task is to regain the skill, not spread the affliction. If you ask for fruit juice and the waiter brings tomato juice, saying a tomato is after all a fruit, you have been badly treated and might consider not leaving a tip. If you order a fruit pie and he brings a pizza, he is just in the wrong job: he should seek safer employment.

Unselfishness

Contrasts may be misunderstood even in cases having nothing to do with science, of course.

A: Molly is incredibly unselfish: she is always giving of her time and money to help other people. She just volunteered to take in a whole family of boat people even though she is on a rather tight budget herself.

B: That is not unselfish: she gets a kick out of it. She does it because it makes her *feel good.* It's self-interest really.

B's argument is that if something can be justified by appeal to self-interest, then whatever it is, it cannot be called unselfish. The same point is often made negatively. If someone does something charitable or even heroic, and explains it by saying they would have felt awful or guilty or could not have lived with themselves had they *not* done it, they thereby stand convicted of selfishness. It was in their interest to do whatever it was simply to avoid the awful consequences of not doing it.

In this case we see once again the powerful temptation to think we can tell what job a word has simply by looking at its component parts and how they fit together. 'Self-ish' might sound like it simply covers all self-interest considerations, and hence *un*selfish behavior would have to be something not done in your own self-interest. Some such construction is doubtless at the bottom of B's argument. But this is to fall prey to the tempting but simpleminded view of language we should by now be able to dispense with. 'Unselfish' does not always mean 'not in your own self-interest'—perhaps it does not ever mean quite that; but in any case, that is not the job it has in the sentiment A is trying to express. All A is attempting to say is that Molly gladly makes sacrifices to help other people; and that is precisely what is captured by 'unselfish' in this context. B seized on the 'gladly' part as demonstrating that the sacrifices were in Molly's self-interest, and presumably it does. But the cheerfulness is crucial to the job 'unselfish' does. If Molly gave of herself only grudgingly, bitterly, having to be shamed into it, it would not be clearly unselfish at all. The clearest cases of unselfish acts are ones done happily, and hence, plausibly, done in the doer's self-interest. This is doubtless what B misunderstands about the job 'unselfish' does here, and what the myth of one proper use encourages.

In this case too we may provide some illumination by examining the contrasting possibilities. B's underlying misconception may perhaps best be seen by looking at selfishness. Selfishness has, to be sure, something to do with self-interest. But the lesson of the last chapter is that even rough characterization of the jobs familiar words do requires careful attention to actual applications. And the clearest examples of selfishness are things like taking all the meat from the platter at dinner, butting into a line ahead of those who have been waiting, and refusing to drive three minutes out of your way to help a colleague who needs a ride to work. In none of these cases is the selfish behavior always or clearly in the interest of the selfish person. Eating all the pork chops, for example, is frequently not in the gourmand's interest all by itself. But even if some clear advantage does accrue from such gluttony, it seldom outweighs the social and physical consequences it normally brings down upon the glutton's head. For very few of us is the pleasure of another chop or two worth the hostility, contempt, and other opprobrium that normally results from such an act. But that does not show it was *not* selfish. The concern with one's self manifest in selfish acts is quite typically narrow, blatant, and shortsighted, and hence rather likely to end up not being in the selfish person's best interest. This is why 'selfish' is such a powerful term of reproof.

The self-interest B attributes to Molly is, by contrast, reflective, subtle, all-things-considered. Molly's behavior—her sacrifice—may be in her own self-interest, but it is *not* due simply to a narrow, shortsighted preoccupation with herself. This is the important contrast, and this is why her behavior does not fit the reproving job given 'selfish' in this context. When 'unselfish' is used in the way A uses it, it is intended as an honorific term—a term of praise. But the praise is not for doing something harmful to yourself, just the opposite. It is for the gladness of your self-sacrifice: precisely what makes B question the term. For whatever reason, we as human beings naturally appreciate people who are genuinely pleased to be helpful and charitable. It is very useful to have words to capture this appreciation: 'unselfish' is one that does.

Colors

The basic verbs of a language are always workhorses. The verbs 'to be', 'to have', 'to make', and 'to do', for instance, are pressed into service in a truly immense number of different ways in a wide variety of contexts. Partly as a result, they are subject to more than their share of misconceptions, and are frequent victims of the centipede effect. The case we are about to examine is possibly the toughest of these examples, because it brings to bear all of our great respect for science in an effort to fire a pair of these multipurpose verbs from their normal, practical jobs. The form of the argument is precisely the same as before, but the stark contrast between profound physics and mundane semantics will make that more difficult to display. It concerns when we should say a surface *is* or *has* a certain color: what it is like for something to *be*, for example, green.

> Do you realize that surfaces which appear green are not really green themselves but merely reflect the green part of the light falling on them? An ordinary leaf, for example, has a physical property that allows it to absorb all of the incident light except for some of the green, which it reflects back into your eye. That's why it looks green. If the green light were removed from the incident beam, leaves would no longer even appear green—they'd look black. It is silly to call the *surface* green when it is actually just the light.

The argument will often continue by directing its attention to the other verb ('have'), contending that it is the light, not the surface, that has the color. If there is no light, there is no color. All the surface *has* is the aforementioned physical property governing the reflection of various wavelengths of light.

Of course the reason to resist this argument, to resist firing 'has' and 'is' from their jobs in talk about colored surfaces, is roughly the same as those discussed in the case of sunrise. These are the normal terms we use to refer to obvious chromatic features of our environment, usually without any problem whatever. And in the vast run of contexts the underlying physics is so monumentally irrelevant to the practical point of the reference that muddying up our diction with electrodynamic theory is inexcusable.

> A: Charlie just bought one of the ugliest cars I've ever seen. It's mostly a revolting pea-green, with a brown tufted vinyl top.
>
> B: Did you know that the part which appears pea-green is not really that color at all: it just differentially reflects that part of the spectrum. . . .

B's retort is impertinent; in most settings it would be simply rude. Its tone is reproachful, yet it adds nothing to the ostensible topic of Charlie's taste in cars. A might reasonably write the conversation off as unsalvageable, wondering just how he pushed the wrong button in B's brain.

But most people find B's argument so powerful that resisting it requires a more detailed look at the jobs done here by these two verbs. We may see the irrelevance of electrodynamics more easily by noticing how unproblematic these jobs are, and how natural it is for these verbs to have them. Reshuffling the language gains us nothing here, at a great cost in disruption.

The job given to 'is' and 'has' (the verbs 'to be' and 'to have') in talking about colored surfaces is simply basic predication—one of the fundamental moves in any language. When we say that a car is unstable on rough roads, we attribute the property of rough-road instability to that car: this is to predicate the property of that car. Similarly we attribute beauty to the sunset when we say the sunset is beautiful; we attribute coolness to the evening when we say the evening is cool; we attribute cleverness to Linda when we say Linda is clever. We could have formulated these sentiments using the verb 'to have' as well: the car has a rough-road instability, and so on. It is in this way that we attribute a property to a surface when we say it is blue, has the color blue.

But to think this is incompatible with discoveries in physics about colored light is to misunderstand predication. It is to misunderstand the wide variety of things that can count as properties, and the range of circumstances in which we sensibly attribute these properties to things. We attribute beauty to the sunset, but this is not to *deny* that it has something to do with the clouds—even though they are not explicitly mentioned. "Yes, of course, it's the clouds too; they're all part of it." Talking about a beautiful sunset is simply our way of referring to the whole colorful business. And this way of doing it is normally transparent: nothing could be clearer. Like so much about language, predication—the attribution of properties to things—has many subtle features it is easy to ignore, easy to miss the importance of—features that are a product of our overriding concern with practical communication.

Much of simple predication is dominated by a single practical purpose: *to direct someone's attention to something in a way that will allow the other person to share our perception of it.* This helps explain both why we choose the property we do, and why we attribute it to the thing we do. The "thing" provides an object for attention, the property provides a way of attending to it. Minutely different contexts, containing minutely different aims and interests, will attribute the same property to a variety of different things, and a variety of different properties to the very same thing, all depending on the perception we wish to share. We attribute the instability to the car because we are making a road test of the car, and we have discovered something about the car that readers will find useful. If somebody objects, "It's not really the car, it's the motion that's unstable," he has missed the point of the message. In a way it *is* the motion, but in another way it's the car, and that is what is important here. All we mean in saying the car is unstable is that it reliably exhibits an unstable motion under certain conditions. The different attributions are compatible with each other, they just have distinct uses, make different points.

We attribute beauty to the sunset because that directs attention to the phantasmagoria on the western horizon produced by the setting sun. To object that it is not the sunset but the clouds is to miss the simple point of the attribution. Clouds can be beautiful in many different ways, times, and places. To speak of the beauty of sunset is to direct our attention to one of these: one time, one place, one way of being beautiful. Terribly useful; wholly unproblematic.

So it goes too for colors. In attributing colors to surfaces we are simply directing attention to a feature of those surfaces that most of us find obvious and interesting in normal conditions. What is striking—and obvious—about the car is its hideous pea-green color; this is what reflects on Charlie's taste. The underlying electrodynamics is neither obvious nor of much interest in practical conversation. It is a boring distraction in discussing automotive aesthetics.

Attributing the color to the surface is in its way rather like attributing the beauty to the sunset and the instability to the car. The car has the property 'rough-road instability' even though it only manifests itself when the car is traveling above a certain speed on rough roads. The surface has the property 'blue' even though it only manifests itself when the surface is illuminated in a certain way. The criterion for having the instability is moving in a certain way on rough roads. The criterion for having a certain color is appearing a certain way to normal observers in normal sunlight. That is all it is for the surface to *be* that color. It is not that the surface is not really blue but rather merely reflects the blue light falling on it: it *is* blue *because* it differentially reflects that part of the spectrum. Just as the sunset is beautiful (in part) because of the patterns in the clouds.

The overriding point here is that if we fire 'is' and 'has' from their normal predicating jobs in this case because of something in electrodynamics, then we could just as plausibly fire those verbs from that job in an enormous range of other cases too. It is not the car, it is the motion; it is not Linda, it is what she said; it is not the sunset, it is the clouds. And it is not even the clouds, but rather the light patterns. But besides offering us the inconceivable task of rebuilding vast, devastated chunks of English, this counsel neglects the hard-won insights of the last chapter—namely, that languages are primarily practical tools for communicating our normal, mundane interests; and anything that helps get that done more easily, more clearly, more certainly is not just legitimate but welcome: something to be celebrated.

Before leaving this example, one other point deserves mention. Even more boldly than in the previous exercise, what is being fired here is not simply a pair of verbs, but a pair of contrasts. We normally contrast the color something *is* with the color it *appears to be,* due, say, to abnormal local conditions.

> This suit is really dark blue, although in this light it appears to be black.

Given the run of normal, human interests, this is a useful thing to be able to say on a variety of different occasions.

> If you paint the part between the beams light beige it will appear white, while not glaring back at you as a pure white would.

But if we adopt B's counsel and fire 'is' and 'has' from their predicating jobs here, it would make these sentiments more difficult and complicated to express. For we could no longer speak of something's actually *being* blue, or being beige or being pure white, but only of it *appearing* to be blue or black or green, etc., under a variety of conditions. Instead of saying the suit is blue but appears black, we would have to say that the suit which now appears black *would* appear blue under certain *other* conditions which we might then go on to specify. But it would be very difficult to say exactly what the conditions are under which a blue suit appears blue. So we would doubtless fall back on some formulation such as "normal conditions": normal observers, normal illumination, against a neutral background, some such thing.

But the elaborate conditional circumlocution 'would appear blue to a normal observer in normal illumination against an appropriate background' merely comes to what we usually express by simply saying it is blue. And in most conversations nothing would be gained by substituting the cumbersome ellipsis.

> Charlie just bought a car that a normal observer in ordinary sunlight against a neutral background would find appears to be a nauseating pea-green. Certainly nothing in electrodynamics can make this a reasonable way to talk. The car does not just *appear* to be ugly: it *is* ugly. It is ugly because of its color: it is a nauseating pea-green. Looks like septic phlegm. The sentiment is clear; nobody misunderstands what is meant; and underlying physical theory adds nothing whatever.

Exercise: Each of the following exchanges may be taken to involve the myth of one proper use in one way or another. Comment on each one in a way modeled on the preceding discussions. That is, identify the expression whose normal job is under attack, and the specific misunderstanding that seems to motivate the attack.

◗ 1. MOTORIST: Got any gas?

> SERVICE STATION ATTENDANT: Only air. Everything else is liquid: antifreeze, brake fluid, water, various petroleum products.

> MOTORIST: Oh, for crying out loud! You know perfectly well I meant gasoline!

> SERVICE STATION ATTENDANT: Oh! Gasoline! Why didn't you say so? If you don't talk properly, you can't expect people to understand you.

2. This is a telephone conversation.

> A: Sorry for the late notice, but I can't come to your party tonight. My daughter fell out of a tree just as we were leaving and I think she broke something. I'm going to take her in for an X-ray.
> B: What do you mean you can't come, nobody's forcing you to take her in. You perfectly well *could* come if you wanted to, you just don't want to. I'm not blaming you, it's a perfectly good reason not to come—I wouldn't want to come either. It's just that you shouldn't say you *can't* come when what you mean is you *won't* come.

▶ 3. C: Did you notice how blue the sky was this morning? That was the first time in months it has been that striking.

> D: Of course I didn't; and you didn't either. The sky isn't really blue at all. What happens is that particles in the atmosphere diffuse the sun's light in such a way that the shorter wavelengths, from the blue end of the spectrum, dominate what reaches our eyes on the surface of the earth.

EVISCERATION

In the cases examined thus far, the drive to fire words from their established and unproblematic jobs stems either from a misplaced respect for science or from a simplistic view of language. Sometimes the motivation behind our clamor for reform is not so pure, however. We are occasionally driven to it as a face-saving stratagem: a desperate ploy designed to avoid some awful consequence, which appeared only after we had taken a firm position. After placing my authority behind a statement I begin to see that, under a normal interpretation of the words, it leads inexorably to a falsehood—or something else equally obnoxious. So I begin tinkering with the jobs the words do, thinking that might be just the thing to bail me out. I pretend the problem is with the words, not the ideas. If the listener had just understood my words in the clever and sophisticated way I intended, it would have been obvious that the awful consequence did not follow at all. This bail-out naturally suggests that we should all adopt my clever and sophisticated jobs for those words, and abandon the old, mundane ones that have the awful consequence built into them.

The difficulty in running this line is that the awful consequence is invariably in the view I tried to express, not in the mundane jobs of the words I have chosen to express it. Furthermore, it usually turns out that the only virtue of the new, clever, and sophisticated jobs is that they bail me out—or appear to. As in every case examined so far, there is usually nothing to recommend abandoning the mundane jobs done by our ordinary vocabulary in normal conversation. Doing so is nearly always counterproductive.

Trying Hard Enough

Consider an example. Suppose you are beginning your senior year in high school and wish to attend college. You need financial help in order to attend but do not particularly care whether you get an academic scholarship or an athletic one. For the past two years you have been on the varsity baseball team, but played only occasionally: mostly you rode the bench. The time you spent on baseball has consistently kept you from performing your best academically, but your academic performance is nevertheless very good: very close to scholarship level. You (quite reasonably) decide that unless there is a good chance of playing on the first team this year you will give up baseball and concentrate on coursework.

So you go to your baseball coach for counsel. He knows you personally and has seen you play for two years and should be able to advise you as well as anybody could. He tells you that there is no doubt in his mind that if you try hard enough you will make the first team. It is all a matter of effort.

As a result of this counsel you do not give up baseball. You dedicate yourself to it as never before. All winter long you stay in top shape, bat off a tee, and work on your throwing arm. Your grades suffer slightly, but you arrive at first spring practice in peak form. Through preseason training you take all the practice available, work on fielding and throwing, execution and anticipation, and you swing a bat whenever the opportunity arises. Unfortunately, your hitting and fielding do not improve all that much, and when the first game rolls around, you are once again on the bench. You pinch hit occasionally during the season, and substitute in the field whenever the team has a good lead; but your experience is generally the same as in the previous two seasons. You have sacrificed your chances for an academic scholarship, but an athletic scholarship is now out of the question.

Disconsolate, you complain to your coach. "How could you have been so wrong? You should have known I would never make the team, no matter how hard I tried." The coach replies, defensively, "I was not wrong. You might have tried hard, but you did not try hard enough. Had you tried hard *enough* you *would* have succeeded. That you did not succeed *shows* you did not try hard enough."

The coach's maneuver here is the face-saving stratagem we are discussing in this section. Normally in this context, the "If you try hard enough you will make the first team" means just what you, the baseball player, thought it did. It means that your talents are clearly adequate, making the team is within your grasp, what is required is increased effort and dedication. And this is the claim that has been cast in doubt by the experience of your last season. The most plausible thing for the coach to say is that he was mistaken about your ability: he thought it was within your grasp, but evidently it was not. You certainly did everything within your power, it just did not work out the way he expected. He was wrong, though perhaps understandably. But instead, the coach became defensive and began tinkering with the words he had used. Now he claims that all he meant was that if you try hard enough to succeed, you will succeed, and obviously you did not do that.

But this is a linguistic travesty in several respects. Under its normal interpretation, the coach's advice is clearly helpful. He has seen you play and presumably knows something of your potential. So his saying that it is only a matter of effort is of some value in making your decision: it is a substantial consideration. But in tinkering with the words to avoid admitting his mistake, he turns a piece of substantial advice into something perfectly trivial. "You mean all you were saying was that if I succeeded you would then know I had worked hard enough to succeed? Why do you think I would have been interested in that? Anybody could have given that advice; I thought you were trying to be helpful." The coach "saved" his statement from falsehood only by gutting it of content, by eviscerating it.

Now the coach may be willing to soften his embarrassment by admitting to a trivial sophistry. That is a personal issue of small moment here. Our concern is the suggestion that the words 'if you try hard enough you will succeed' should be given the job of expressing that triviality in the context described above. And of course the suggestion is absurd on its face. There can be no reason to take words that normally express some useful sentiment and restrict them to use in a vacuous word game. But more is involved here than merely wasting words: the coach's suggestion undermines the very foundation of language as a communicative tool. For as we saw in Chapter 6, our linguistic skills, both performance and recognition, key on context-bound plausibility judgments. To communicate, both sides of a conversation must judge the same interpretation of the words to be most plausible. Understanding involves digesting both the linguistic trace-data and all the relevant features of substantive context, to find an interpretation of the words that best accounts for their utterance. Competent performance involves knowing how your words will be understood.

Central to these judgments, you will recall, was the requirement of significance. In settling on an interpretation, one of the central considerations is understanding how that interpretation could be of human significance in the context. So in the normal, sober, polite context, the only plausible interpretation for the words 'if you try hard enough you will succeed' will be roughly the serious advice you took it to be. For trivial word games to be of human significance, the context must be rather special, usually in ways that dramatically change the nature of the conversation. The trivial interpretation would be plausible if the coach were merely expressing his contempt for you (in which case you would not likely take the counsel seriously); or if the coach had a well-known history of lunatic fatuity (in which case you would not have asked his opinion); or if the whole thing were an example in a philosophy classroom (in which case heaven knows what to say). The case described is none of these, however, which is why the coach had to tinker to get his contrived interpretation: there were guts there that had to be removed.

Seeing Stars

With this as background, we are now prepared to tackle a tougher example, as complex and persuasive an application of the myth of one proper use as you are likely to see. In this case a more tempting evisceration combines with our respect for science in a powerful attempt to remove a common word from its most common job. It also illustrates some dangers of hip-shot descriptions in abstract contexts.

The Evisceration

A: Well, you can't see something that doesn't exist: that's true by definition.

B: Gee, that sounds too tough. What about the stars we see at night, for example? Astronomers tell us that the light from many of them left so long ago that some could easily have blown up and vanished in the meantime. Some will still be visible to earthlings for hundreds of thousands of years after they've ceased to exist.

A: Well, you really don't see the star itself, just the *light* from the star, and *that* still exists.

B: But in this respect a star does not differ from any other object: what's in your eye is the light coming from it, not the thing itself. Do you want to say you never really see objects, just the light from them?

A: Yes, strictly speaking you always see just the light.

And once again we have salvage by evisceration. A begins with a reasonable though flawed restriction on things that can properly be spoken of as seen; nonexisting things are ruled out. He ends up defending it by saying that, well, actually we don't see *things* at all, and so of course we can't see things that do not exist. The original restriction looks interesting largely because it distinguishes between things we can and cannot see: some things we actually see, some things we only *think* we see. But in the end it makes no distinction at all: we do not even see the things that do exist, just the light coming from them. The restriction is trivially true of nonexistent things, since it is true of every object of perception, existing or not.

The Firing.   What makes this example so tempting, so difficult, and at the same time so useful is that so much is going on all at once. The case is not a nice, pure evisceration like the previous one. For while A removes the original content of his statement with one hand, he provides wholly different guts with the other. So what is left is not absolutely trivial, as was the coach's eventual defense, it is just trivial as an interpretation of the original statement. A straightforward statement about the *objects* of perception is transformed into a peculiar characterization of the *optics* of perception. The transformation has one set of difficulties, the end product has another; but with a little care we can avoid confusing them.

The evisceration lies in the transformation. The move from objects to optics is a trivial way to defend the original claim. As shown above, the ostensible point of the original statement simply vanishes in the transformation. But the result of the transformation is (as usual) interesting in itself. A's defensive switch from objects to optics is motivated by the reformist misunderstanding we have seen at work in earlier examples. He thinks the expression of a scientific insight requires—or at least encourages—basic reform of the language: here it requires firing 'see' from its usual job in talk about perception. This is why he thinks he can get away with his "defense." But the suggested reform is just as silly and ill-advised here as it was in those earlier cases. In some ways it is worse because the gratuitous damage to our linguistic institutions would be so widespread.

The job done by 'see' in the usual run of contexts simply does apply to objects and their behavior, not to light. What we see are cars and people and movies and fireworks. Being able to talk about our perceptions in this simple way is constantly useful, and largely unproblematic. Usually nothing is gained by alerting everyone to the underlying optics. (In this respect the case is similar to sunrise.) I saw Mary Ann at a party last night. Suppose I tell somebody and he responds, "You know, what actually happened was that some photons from a nearby incandescence bounced off Mary Ann, passed through the lens of your eye and obliterated themselves against your retinas in just such a way as to form an image of Mary Ann." What to say? It looks like he just missed the point of my remark. True, photons were whizzing about, but when it was all over, what had happened was that I had seen Mary Ann. That is all I wanted to say. If he was not interested in whom I saw at the party he could simply have said so.

One thing is clear, however. Nothing in his response suggests I did *not* see Mary Ann: it offers an (unsolicited and rudely irrelevant) account of what probably took place when I did. That the account has light doing interesting things inside my eyeball is no reason to change the job of the verb 'to see'. We can describe those things without destroying any valuable linguistic institutions; and the normal job of 'see' in this context is too valuable to give up. In that (normal) sense I did *not* see the light itself; I did not see anything in my eyeball—that would require mirrors and magnifying lenses. What I saw was Mary Ann. The ordinary job of 'to see' is to help me articulate this fact. Recognizing familiar objects and actions is something we are all pretty good at; and it is something we often wish to convey. That is enough to justify having some linguistic institution to enable us to convey it. That institution in English is the usual job given 'see'.

Yes of course seeing has something to do with light and with eyes. But exactly what it has to do with them is irrelevant most of the time. In fact, we are much better at telling who or what we saw than we are at saying just what happened to the photons. Physicists may even change their minds about the photons, and it will not affect the content of our casual recognitions one scintilla. The valuable but mundane jobs common words do are insulated from scientific discovery in just this way.

What about stars, then: do they raise any special problems? Yes, they do, but only rather minor ones, which may be dealt with soberly. Scientific discoveries were involved in determining the celestial distances and light velocity that revealed the great time lag in our perception of stars. And this is important in characterizing that perception. But it does not *undermine* it. It does not mean that we do not see the stars. The time lag affects only a verb tense in the characterization of what we see: we see the stars not as they are, but as they used to be. And for most practical purposes even this distinction is not very significant.

Celestial cases actually afford the best illustration of how unimportant time lags—and other complexities—are to direct perception. When Voyager I passed close to Jupiter, for example, it allowed us to see detail on that planet's surface which had been invisible from Earth. But what counted as seeing involved digital coding, more than an hour-long trip across the solar system, decoding into still photographs, electronic and photographic enhancement of the image, and construction of a movie out of the stills. In the end we were able to see the counterrotating bands of clouds, the turbulence around the giant red spot, even an erupting volcano on one of Jupiter's moons. And we can describe all this—surface perceptions as well as underlying science—clearly and in great detail, without jettisoning any basic linguistic institutions.

Seeing involves marshaling our estimable visual competence to recognize objects and phenomena. But the underlying character of the marshaling—the exact process of recognition—can be varied and complex. None of the simple pictures captures all that is valuable in it. So when someone appeals to a tempting oversimplification to fire our perception vocabulary from one of its central tasks, we can sympathize, but it is silly not to resist. I knew the storm front had passed through last night when I was able to see stars through my bedroom window. Objecting that I did not really see the stars, just their light, simply misrepresents a valuable chunk of the language.

Another Contrast.   Up to this point, firing 'see' is rather like firing 'sunrise' from its job at dawn. In each case a scientific fact appears to recommend the firing of a useful expression because the practical operation of language is misunderstood. For sunrise, the protestant demands we substitute some astrophysical circumlocution. Here, A demands that we substitute 'see the light from' for the simpler 'see'. Practical communication is made more difficult and less certain by each of these artifices; and the exercises have been designed to show there is no need to suffer the inconvenience and take the risk. When properly understood, existing linguistic practice is perfectly adequate to its mundane but important tasks. The firings were hasty and ill considered.

But the two cases differ in one essential detail. Any astrophysical locution we substituted for 'sunrise' would merely be unusual and perhaps theoretically exotic. It would be unnecessarily puzzling and cumbersome, which of course is bad enough, but it would be only that. The problem is much worse for 'seeing'. The expression A wants us to substitute for 'see' already has a job to do in this context, a *different job.* This makes the substitution more than just strange and puzzling: it is openly misleading.

When we normally speak of seeing the light of or from some object, our seeing the light specifically *contrasts with* seeing the object itself. We often see the light when the object itself is out of view. We see the moonlight on the patio while the moon is out of sight overhead. We see the torchlight on the cave walls, but not yet the torch. We see the beam of light from the flashlight when the instrument itself is lost in the black. This is why 'see the light from x' is such a particularly unhappy substitute for 'see x' in this example. 'See the light from x' already has a job in this context; and it is not only different from the job given 'see x', one of its major features is its contrast with the job of 'see x'. To give 'see the light from x' the job formerly held by 'see x', in addition to its other miseries, obliterates this useful contrast too. In this respect the 'seeing' case resembles the surface-color exercise. What is being fired is not just a single expression, but a contrasting pair.

Once again the moral is: don't tamper with useful language. The mundane jobs of common expressions are often marvelously complex and subtle. And these features invariably develop out of our own human natures. Words get the jobs they do because of what we wish to express in specific contexts, and because of what is required for us to be understood when we do. So we play musical chairs with the jobs words do only at our peril. It invariably makes what we wish to say more difficult to express, and clear communication more difficult to achieve in the practical contexts that dominate our lives. Certainly no application of the myth of one proper use can justify making such a basic human activity more difficult than it is already.

Hip-Shot Definitions.   We may reasonably take A's original statement, the one that launched this discussion, to be a partial job description: an attempt to capture one aspect of the job done by 'see' in this context.

Claiming that it is "true by definition" suggests a concern with language itself. That would also explain the character of the exchange with B that follows the remark. If we adopt this plausible interpretation, the entire preceding discussion simply traces the dangerous temptations of such hip-shot descriptions. Before seriously examining language at work, we may find inconceivable the suggestion that quick, general job descriptions usually miss important detail. So we abandon the detail in defense of the description, and destroy valuable parts of the language. This sounds enough like what A did to justify pursuing this interpretation one step further.

Given what we have learned about language, 'you can't see what doesn't exist' certainly has the ring of a beguiling oversimplification. It is too stark, too categorical to hope to capture an accurate connection between the jobs of 'see' and 'exist' in their workaday contexts. But it does capture something of interest. There is something obviously valuable in A's original observation, and possibly this is what drives A to defend it at such absurd lengths. If A had understood how hard it is to capture such semantic detail *accurately,* he might have defended it in a more plausible and less destructive fashion. Specifically, it may be defended as a helpful oversimplification that may be fashioned into something more accurate (and *less* simple) by adjusting it for contextual nuance. Let us see how this might be done.

First of all there are some contexts, concerning certain kinds of subject matter, in which we may simply accept the substance of A's original statement: you can't see what doesn't exist. In a famous James Thurber short story, a man claims to have seen a unicorn in his garden. When he tells his wife, she replies, "The unicorn is a mythical beast," properly taking this to reject her husband's claim. She feels no need to spell it out in further detail, simply because we do, implicitly, accept A's counsel here. Mythical beasts do not exist, and you cannot see in your garden beasts that do not exist. To see one in your garden it would have to *be* there, and it cannot do that unless it exists. But all this is so obvious there is no need to say it.

We must be careful in applying this principle in other cases, however. For all it does is point out that in this kind of context, the content of a perception must be a *fact.* That is, if we are wrong about what we say we see, then we did not see it—we only *think* we saw it.* And this *is* an important feature of the job 'see' does here. The word simply does not apply when its object is a mistaken diagnosis.

It seems obligatory to reassure the reader at this point that in the run of normal cases this requirement presents no practical problem whatever. As we noted in Chapters 3 and 4, we are very skilled at an enormous range of mundane diagnoses. Our confidence that we saw x happen is often very good reason to think x happened. Some special circumstance is usually required to overthrow this kind of perception. As long as we understand this, and as long as we stay well within the limits of our perceptual competence, we may comfortably identify seeing x with thinking we see x. The point is only that we must give it up when someone produces good reason to think x never occurred. The nonexistence of unicorns rejects the husband's claim only because it shows that what he saw could not have been what he *said* he saw. Whatever it was he saw in the garden, it was not a unicorn. The content of his claimed perception is not a fact.

*This is sometimes captured by saying that 'see' is a *success term* in this kind of context.

But none of this shows that the fact must occur *at the same time* as the perception. The umpire calls the runner out at second: he says he saw the shortstop tag him before he reached the bag. But in slow-motion replays, from three different angles, we see the runner's foot touch the bag before the ball is even in the shortstop's glove. Umpires are usually right, but this time we've got him. And we've got him because of what *we* saw, even though we saw it long after it happened. In the quiet of a comfortable study we see the runner begin his slide, the dirt start to fly, the jolt as his spikes dig into the bag, and we see the white blur snap back the infielder's glove; then everything disappears in an explosion of dust. We see it over and over until we can recognize the trajectories of individual dirt clods from several perspectives. Our perception is better than the umpire's because of the enormous advantage afforded by slow motion, different angles, and knowing exactly what to look for. That our perception occurs long after the fact is irrelevant: it is a perception, and a very good one. (It too may be undermined by further evidence, of course, even further perceptions; but that is enough of a long shot to be reasonably disregarded until something raises our suspicion. In this it is like any other of our best perceptions.)

Something similar is going on when we see turbulence around Jupiter's red spot. Elaborate electronics and a substantial time lapse do not count against our perception. What matters is that we get it right, and the electronic complexity is crucial to our doing that. It is designed specifically to complement our visual skill in the way required to aid our judgment. The result, of course, is that the turbulence we see is not taking place at the instant we see it, but hours or even days before. As long as we get it right, the job 'see' does in this context fits the case perfectly, just as it does the instant replay.

Were we able to see surface detail on the star we began with, that case would be like Jupiter's. But we do not. Of the star, all we see is *it.* And this actually makes it simpler. Because the facts to get right or wrong are merely its existence and direction from earth. So long as the light reaching us now did leave a real star out there in roughly that direction some time in the past, the perception we now form using that light counts as seeing the star. Naturally, we see it as it was then, not as it is now; but that seldom makes any difference in the practical contexts in which we talk of stars. (It makes a lot of difference to physicists and cosmologists; but they see far more in the light than we do just using our eyes.) In this particular context we *can* see things that do not exist any longer; we just cannot see things that never did exist in the first place.

Weasel Words.   As a final comment on this exercise it would be well to note a helpful device popularized by Theodore Roosevelt at the beginning of this century. Appealing to the rural backgrounds shared by most Americans of the day, Roosevelt drew attention to what a weasel often does to an egg. It makes a small hole in the shell and draws out the content, leaving it superficially intact but devoid of content. Some words, he went on to point out, have this effect on sentences, and he dubbed them weasel words. When a weasel word is added to a sentence, it appears to change nothing while stealthily emptying the sentence of content; the sentence is left an empty shell: eviscerated. Roosevelt had other concerns, but we may pirate his terminology for our own ends here.

Adverbs like 'really', 'actually', and 'enough' are the weasel words of our reformist misadventures. Usually they are italicized. We begin with a perfectly sensible sentence which has a few flaws. When the flaws are pointed out, instead of openly refining the sentiment or candidly giving it up, we head for the cover of a weasel word. We offer an empty triviality containing many of the same words, in the hope that no one will notice our devastation. Unfortunately it works too often.

If we were to leave this discussion with one caveat, it would be, beware of weasel words. When, in an exchange like those we have examined here, someone says, "Well, that is not *really* X—I was talking about *real* Xs," a good strategy is to ask, "Well, then, what *would* count as really X?" If the answer is *nothing,* or something absurd, you have identified a weasel word at work. In the present case, when A says you do not *really* see the star, ask "What would count as *really* seeing the star?" He will answer, "Well, you can never *really* see the star," and you should be alerted. Dark happenings are afoot.

Exercise

1. Consider the following exchanges:

   A: All politicians are crooks.
   B: What about Abraham Lincoln? He told a few lies, but you could hardly call him a crook.
   A: Oh, he wasn't really a politician; he was a statesman.

   a. Identify the weasel word.
   b. What word has its job under attack here?
   c. Explain why A's reply to B may be taken to eviscerate his original claim.
   d. What sober, less defensive response would have served A better? That is, what might A have said that would have helpfully reformulated his original point without suspect semantics?

▶ 2. C: I think the immorality among young people today is due mainly to the laxity of educators. They just won't assume responsibility for guiding kids into healthy attitudes about sex, the family, and their place in society.
   D: It's tempting to think that, because schools certainly don't give much attention to such things; but studies have shown that fundamental attitudes like the

ones you're talking about are gotten almost entirely from parents, no matter what the educators do.

C: Well, of course parents are educators too—they teach them before anyone else does. So the point still stands: the problem is with educators.

   a.   What word is being played with here?

   b.   Identify and describe the evisceration.

   c.   What response to D's objection would have been more reasonable?

SEMANTIC INDETERMINACY: THE BORDERLINE CASE

Our temptation to unwise reform of the language encounters a vast new range of applications when we consider unclear cases: words used in certain nonstandard contexts. The cases we have examined so far in this chapter have all been dead standard. The key question in the exercises has been the *legitimacy* of a particular job: Was there any reason to remove a word from some job it has in the context under discussion? Once the legitimacy of the job was conceded no question remained about the particular application. Cars have radiators, the sun does rise, some leaves are green, we can see the star, and the tomato is clearly a fruit in one context, clearly not in the other. In fact, the standardness of the case was actually used in each argument: it showed that the word *had* the job in question, and must be fired if its application is to be refused.

Sometimes the matter is not so clear, however. To help us see why, it will be useful to speak of a term's application as being 'positive' or 'negative' in a certain case according to whether it does apply (positive) or does not apply (negative) in that case. The context determines the term's job; whether the case in question "fits" the job will determine whether the application is positive or negative: go or no-go. At produce counters, when 'fruit' is doing its culinary job, a tomato is not a fruit, a nectarine is. The application of 'fruit' to tomatoes is negative, to nectarines it is positive.

Virtually any job done by any word exhibits this feature. Part of the job consists in drawing a contrast: cases to which it clearly applies contrast with those to which it clearly does not. 'Green', in its normal, chromatic job, clearly applies to many leaves, clearly fails to apply to blood; 'radiator' applies to (something in) all water-cooled cars, but not to (anything in) many air-cooled ones; some stars can be seen (unaided), others cannot; 'sunrise' applies at dawn, not at noon.

But such things are commonly matters of degree. Dawn *gradually* turns into day, green *fades off* into blue, fat becomes slim by *imperceptible stages,* things slowly die. Standard cases gradually fade off into less standard ones; jobs apply less and less clearly, by degrees. This much is perfectly clear of 'green', 'fat', and 'dawn', and only slightly less so of 'death'. But the same point can be made for the usual jobs of a surprising number of words: with a little imagination we can describe (if not actually create) a rich spectrum of cases that provide gradually less and less clear applications of the word in that particular job. To take a very simple example, in one familiar context the jobs done by 'chair' and 'stool' contrast with each other, the major difference being that a chair has a back while a stool does not. Accordingly, if we take a standard, armless chair and whittle away at its back, it will gradually become a less and less clear example of a chair: the term 'chair' will apply less and less clearly. When the back is gone it will not be a chair at all in the sense we are considering. For many chairs, what we have left will be a funny-looking stool—one we could turn into a chair by putting a back on it. (This is not to say that in some contexts the word 'chair' could not properly apply to the funny-looking stool. But when it does it will be doing a different, usually more complicated job than it is here.)

The reason to emphasize the gradualness with which positive application fades off into negative is to draw attention to the troublesome area in between. Even if we are perfectly familiar with the job in question, expertly competent to handle its application in standard cases, there will often be a substantial range of cases "in the middle" about which our judgment is emphatically uncertain. These cases are not clearly positive applications, but they are not clearly negative ones either. Actual physical processes connecting contrasting states provide the best illustrations of this. As a man loses his hair he gradually becomes bald. But there is no precise point at which 'bald' suddenly applies. At the beginning of the process it applies negatively: the man is not bald. At the end of the process it applies positively: the man is bald. But, in the normal case, there will be a number of days or weeks or months toward the end of the process in which it is simply unclear whether 'bald' applies yet. Both positive and negative applications are misleadingly categorical: the most comfortable choice is to decline both. This is called a borderline case.

All manner of developmental processes exhibit borderline cases in the application of certain characterizations, especially if those characterizations are pressed where we normally withhold them. As we gain weight we eventually become fat, but there is no precise point at which the term suddenly applies. Putting together pieces of wood, we eventually construct a chair, but there is no precise point at which the term 'chair' suddenly applies. As we age, we eventually become adults . . . and so on. To say there is no point at which a term suddenly applies in a spectrum of cases is just to say that in a range of these cases the term's application is *indeterminate.* In a range of cases the term does not clearly apply positively and it does not clearly apply negatively. Between a full head of hair and the Telly Savalas look lie a number of configurations for which the application of 'bald' (in its normal job) is simply indeterminate. These are borderline cases of baldness.

As a practical matter the existence of these indeterminate ranges—the fuzzy borderline areas in any job's application—is virtually guaranteed by the nature of our linguistic skill, and the way natural languages result from its operation. Recall from Chapter 6 that our skill is importantly *perceptual.* It requires the *recognition* of standard cases in application, and the ability to *tell* when a context is close enough to standard for words to do the jobs expected of them. Learning the language consists largely in learning to make this judgment. This is how we learn the practical jobs words do, how to recognize them, how to apply them. And it is this judgment that is gradually undermined as we run through a spectrum of increasingly less-standard cases.

This is a misleadingly harsh way to put the matter, however. The existence of semantic indeterminacy, of fuzzy borderlines, is not a problem, it is not something that needs correction. A word's job is useful it if draws a distinction between *some clear* cases. If there are some clear positive applications and some clear negative applications, that is frequently sufficient to make it worth keeping. The fuzziness in other cases is just the inevitable consequence of the way we give words jobs to do: something easily tolerated to allow us to give words interesting jobs. All the examples we have been discussing are like this. The job we give 'blue' is useful not because we can positively or negatively apply it to everything whatever, but because it clearly applies to some things we care about. The job we give 'bald' is useful because of the way it distinguishes between Telly Savalas and, say, Teddy Kennedy. To be able to make that distinction we are quite willing to put up with a whole range of indeterminate cases in between. The same kind of thing may be said of 'fat', 'chair', and the rest.

Moreover, in conceding that a range of cases is indeterminate for one word's job, we do not foreclose the possibility of speaking clearly about those cases. We simply use different words: those cases are not borderline cases of everything. Between blue and green are some clear blue-greens. Between fat and normal lie 'overweight', 'stocky', 'chubby', and, perhaps, 'pudgy'; between Kennedy and Savalas go 'thinning hair', 'balding', and 'bald spot'. On borderlines we simply avoid the troublesome characterization altogether. The ability to recognize borderlines and know how to handle them is a sign of linguistic maturity. "Well, it doesn't look much like a chair yet, but I wouldn't be surprised that's what he's making" or, "I'm not sure you would call the injury severe, but it was enough to take her into emergency to have it checked."

We may simply summarize this long introductory discussion as follows. Let us use the letter X to stand for any word doing a particular job. Now we ask of anything plausible the question "is this X?" (e.g., "Is this [guy] bald?"). (The question may be refined slightly to "is this *an* X?" for nouns and "is this *to* X?" for verbs—but the simpler form will do for each so long as the appropriate articles and prepositions are put where they belong.) It will be apparent that most Xs require (at least) three distinct answers to the question to cover all the cases: "yes," "no," and "unclear."* Ask of every injury "is it severe?" Ask of every tie "is it blue?" Ask of every person "is he or she fat?" Ask of every hump in the earth "is this a mountain?" In virtually every case answers will fall under each of the three headings. This is true even when X marks a distinction that is perfectly clear in its standard applications. It is in fact a natural and easily tolerated consequence of our basic linguistic skills. We find it enormously useful to give jobs to words that are clear in some interesting cases, even though they fade off into fuzzy indeterminacy elsewhere. We avoid problems by avoiding the word except in clear applications.

The Nature of Reform: Use and Abuse

We are nevertheless sometimes tempted to ignore our good instincts and make sharp distinctions where there are none: to draw sharp lines in the fuzzy areas. We say things like "Let us define 'fat' as more than twelve pounds overweight," or "Any gash greater than one inch in length will be called 'severe,'" or "Let us make the blue/green division fall at exactly 5500 angstroms on the monochromatic spectrum." We sometimes say things like this in the frustration of having the answer to "is this X?" come up "unclear." It is important to understand what we are doing when we do this—and even more important to understand what we are *not* doing.

One thing we are not doing is answering the question "is this X?" with which we began. We already have the answer to that question. The answer is that this case is unclear, uncertain, indeterminate. The job X does has a fuzzy edge right there. Its application is useful in *other* cases in which it is clear. To draw a sharp line at this point and give "is this X?" a clear yes or no answer is to give X a different job. (Whether it *needs* a new job will be discussed shortly: that depends on what we have to give up to get it. For now it is important only to notice X does have a new job.) "Is this X?" then asks a different question: same word (X), different job. So of course there can be a different answer. But why change the question just to get the desired answer? How is that useful? We will examine this puzzle shortly, but before we do, it is essential to be clear about the kind of difference involved here, and why it is worth our trouble.

---

*One complexity is worth bearing in mind. A case may be a borderline for *one* of X's jobs, and still a clear case for another. Furthermore, the mere fact that a case *is* a tough one for one of X's jobs will sometimes be enough for X to slide into a slightly different one, in which the case is clear. Some borderline reds, for instance, will clearly fall under 'red' when it refers to a general ruddy contrast. So when somebody uses an unqualified 'red' to refer to a tough case, it will often simply be taken to refer to a general contrast. This is a natural application of Charity II: finding the most plausible interpretation for the words in the context.

In discussing borderlines we will be primarily concerned with what happens when we do *not* change jobs in such a case. The semantic indeterminacy results when a single job confronts a spectrum or array of cases. Explicit notice of this may avoid some confusion.

Sharpening up the fuzzy edge of a common word's job alters the language as an instrument of practical communication in a way that is seldom trivial. Changing to clearly positive cases that were not clearly positive, and to clearly negative cases that were not clearly negative is a fundamental change in our conception of the job: one that would result in communication failure at crucial junctures if adopted without notice.

"Get me the two blue ones and the green one."

"But I only see one blue one and two that are kind of blue-green."

"Oh, I draw a sharp distinction between blue and green. One of the blue-green ones is over the dividing line, so I call it green; the other two are on the blue side."

"Well, how was I supposed to know that? If you play around with the words you can't expect to communicate clearly."

Moreover, as this conversation illustrates, we can usually express what we wish in the fuzzy area without reform by simply avoiding the indeterminate characterization (blue) and using the linguistic resources already available (kind of blue-green).

Not only does borderline reform risk confusion for very little gain, it usually entails substantial loss as well. Much of value in the old job is lost in the revision. That is obvious when precision comes at the expense of great oversimplification, as it does in the reforms of 'fat' and 'severe' suggested above. The normal job given 'fat' concerns not just weight, but height and build as well. Adding twelve pounds to the frame of someone who is four eleven and normally ninety-eight pounds is significant; adding twelve pounds to the average NFL tackle is negligible. Furthermore the distribution is crucial. If it is all in the middle, 'fat' might clearly apply in its normal job; if it is distributed around on the frame, it might clearly not. To fire 'fat' from its old job and give it the new, precise one, we sacrifice whole dimensions of the old job; and it is not clear we gain anything at all. We can always say "twelve pounds overweight or greater" without changing anything. We need not steal 'fat' from its old job to do it. Exactly the same point may be made of 'severe'. Its normal job takes into account not just the length of a gash but depth, location, and associated trauma—all very useful to have lumped into one job, even if it does have a fuzzy edge. The fuzzy edge may be handled in the usual way.

But these are easy cases. The matter is more subtle when precision does not rend whole dimensions from the old job. The loss can nevertheless be significant, far outweighing modest gains. Take 'blue'. Suppose we draw the dividing line near the middle of the blue-greens (however we determine the middle). The change wrought thereby in the job done by 'blue' is fundamental. For part of the old job is to point out that hues near the new sharp line do not quite fit. Some hues that will be just plain blue on the new conception definitely are not just plain blue on the old. Furthermore, ones that will be not blue at all—namely, those just over the line on the green side—definitely do have some blue in them on the old (i.e., normal) conception. In other words, the fact that it fades off gradually toward green is part of our conception of blue: the taper is an essential part of the job. It is a valuable aspect to which we appeal all the time. And it is lost in the reform. Very similar observations apply to 'bald'.

Since sharpening up a fuzzy borderline constitutes such a radical revision of the job, it is also reasonable to ask why we choose just the revision we do. Why do we pick one new job as opposed to any other in this area? Why twelve pounds, not eleven or thirteen, or a hundred? Why the loss, say, of 90% of his hair and not 86.5%? Why cut off blue at one wavelength as opposed to its neighbors? From the point of view of practical communication, there is seldom any general reason to choose one sharp line rather than another. The choice of one particular place to draw the line is largely arbitrary: within the fuzzy range, one place is just about as good as any other. Certainly nothing in the old job dictates a place.

We may now return to our puzzle about changing the question in order to get a different answer. Recall that we begin with the question "is this X?" asked of a variety of things. We came to a range of those things in which the answer is "unclear." Our reformist suggests at this point that we make a sharp distinction among these things so that we always get a clear yes or no answer. But as we have seen, the clear yes or no answers will be to a different question. We will still ask "is this X?" but the 'X' will be doing a different job. So the puzzle is why anyone would want to do this. When is it a useful thing to do? It turns out this is a modestly useful thing to do in certain circumstances, but only modestly: it involves nothing like reform of the language. On the other hand, what most frequently drives us to tinker with borderlines is once again a misunderstanding of the way language works. This one might be called the Myth of Universal Precision: the myth that sharpening up the edges of fuzzy jobs is unequivocal, and always for the best. The contrast between the two motives is instructive.

Useful Precision.   It is legitimately useful to draw a sharp distinction more or less arbitrarily in a spectrum of cases when a practical purpose makes that arbitrariness unimportant. Say you are sending three busloads of schoolchildren to have a group picture taken. It is important that the children arrive roughly in order of height so they can be arranged in a reasonable time. So you divide the group into three: tall, medium, and short—one group for each bus. There is no sharp distinction in the group between tall and medium height or between medium and short. Nevertheless, when the first bus is full the next child in line counts as medium height for your project. Similarly when the second bus is full, the next child in line counts as short. Where you draw the line depends on extraneous things like how many seats are on the bus, the chance distribution of heights in the group, and whether you start with the tall end of the class or the short. It matters very little, however, since

the task is semantically very modest. You have not sharpened up the jobs
done by 'tall', 'medium height', and 'short' in English. You are not saying that
'tall', for example, simply means 'over five foot three' (the tallest kid on the
middle bus), even in this context. You have merely made a convenient division in a group of children by giving these terms arbitrarily precise jobs *in
this specific context.* You can get away with it because the arbitrariness does not
matter here, and because you are doing no damage to the valuable jobs those
terms do elsewhere.

Self-Deception.   Sometimes our drive to sharpen up borderlines has deeper
roots, however. Sometimes we ask the question "is this X?" not for frivolous
or even purely linguistic reasons, but rather because something important
seems to hang on the answer: Are we in a recession? Am I fat? Is it blue? Is
she dead yet? Is it human? These questions can express matters of real
substance. Resolving a substantive issue often simply takes the form of
providing an answer to some such question. The issue and its normal expression (the question) are so intimately bound up with one another that we
mistake them for the same thing. So when the case we care about is on a
borderline, when the answer comes up "unclear," the importance of the
underlying issue encourages us to force the question. "Well, dammit, it's too
important to be unclear. I'll *make* it clear. I'll tell you whether I'm fat or it's
human or we're in a recession or she's dead (choose one): I'll draw in a sharp
line and decide the matter."

But here our earlier discussion makes a telling point. Drawing in a sharp
line changes the question, and that ruins it. We definitely do not want a new
question, we want an answer to the original one. We do not want to know
if this case would be X if we changed X's job, we want to know if it *is* X.
The reason we ask the question using 'X' is because X does the right job. We
change the job and the question becomes suspect. In the borderline area we
can always draw in a line to get either answer, 'yes' or 'no', whichever we
please. There is no semantic reason to prefer one over another. To ignore this
arbitrariness and draw in a sharp line is self-deception here: we pretend we
have discovered an answer when we have only invented a new way of
speaking.

What to do? The remedy is easy, actually, something we do naturally in
our more sober moods. But it requires carefully disentangling the semantic
issue from the substantive one. On a borderline the first thing to do is *concede
the irresolvability of the semantic issue:* the question does not have a clear
answer. Then we try to express your underlying concern in different terms:
what would we have done with an answer had we been able to get one?
Frequently a new way to express the underlying substantive issue will leap
right out. It may then be dealt with unencumbered by borderline semantics.
Let us look at some easy examples.

We ask, "Is Uncle Charlie bald yet?" and the answer comes up "unclear."
So we must consider why we wanted to know. Let us say we asked the

question because we had not seen him in a long time and wanted to be sure we would recognize him. Whomever we had asked the original question might be able to describe just how and where Uncle Charlie's hair had thinned, which might help us recognize him even better than had we gotten a clear answer to the original question. In this way the underlying substantive concern which originally motivated the question may be dealt with while bypassing the troublesome question itself.

A legislator asks an economist, "Are we in a recession?" The economist (often) replies, "Well, it's hard to say. Several indicators are severely depressed, but some others are about normal; one or two are actually a bit better than normal. It's a tough case. I don't really know what to say." All the signs of a semantically indeterminate case. What to do when the best estimate we can get is "uncertain?" Examine why the question was asked in the first place. Suppose the legislator asked because he wanted to know whether to get behind some legislation designed to stimulate the economy. He (or the economist) might be able to deal with the pros and cons of *this* issue, without taking on the tough semantic nut offered by talk of recession. The economist might say, "Well, with inflation running at thirteen percent I wouldn't recommend stimulating legislation even if we were in a recession." On the other hand he might offer, "We should not wait for a recession to begin stimulating the economy. Selective tax cuts would probably ward off a recession without creating undue inflationary forces." The point of this example is not to offer economic counsel. It is to show how we can deal with an underlying substantive issue without resolving the indeterminate semantic issue originally offered as its expression. Divide and conquer. Separate the substantive issue from the irresolvable semantic one if possible. Then deal with the substantive issue in whatever way you can.

For a more difficult illustration, consider the following case. In the years immediately before World War II, some international airlines would fly passengers to island and coastal locations in flying boats. These were relatively ordinary, high-winged passenger planes, except that the bottom was hull-shaped; they could land and take off from water, and hence had access to places without airports. Howard Hughes's *Spruce Goose* is an example of such an airplane. Suppose we ask the question "Is a flying boat a passenger ship?" in a nautical context. This is a useful example for our purposes because in attempting to answer the question we are pulled in both directions. On the one hand, there is something strange about calling a flying boat a passenger ship. The things usually referred to by that phrase in this context are ocean liners: craft much more seaworthy than flying boats, and constrained to travel on the water. On the other hand, a flying boat does have many important features in common with more normal passenger ships. It has a modestly seaworthy hull and is designed to transport passengers or cargo across vast expanses of ocean. It needs a dock to load and unload. And in some circumstances it might even be pressed into water-bound service: taxiing passengers

Culver Pictures

A Flying Boat

from one dock to another. In fact, were oceans mostly shallow—rather like the Everglades—ships generally might have evolved into something like flying boats, using air rather than water as the medium of propulsion, perhaps even using an airfoil for stability.

This example illustrates the most typical and perhaps most frustrating kind of borderline case. The great majority of jobs we give words are like the job 'passenger ship' usually does: they are useful because in the course of our lives they have innumerable clear applications—both positive and negative. We normally handle them effortlessly and unproblematically. We are seldom tempted by troublesome applications. Consequently, when a problematic application first tempts us we are easily frustrated—sometimes even piqued —because it does not fit effortlessly under one application or the other. New possibilities opened up by technological advance or social change are frequently the culprits, raising possibilities and combinations not imagined previously.

Whatever the cause, our best strategy on encountering such a case is to concede its irresolvability.* There is something strange about saying a flying boat *is* a passenger ship; yet it is a great deal more like one than the usual things we would say are not ships. Neither positive nor negative application

*Sometimes the word will change jobs under the impact of new cases. But this is irrelevant to the current argument and may be ignored here.

is happy without qualification. So once again ask: Why do we want to know whether a flying boat is a passenger ship? What made us ask? Is there some underlying issue that may be resolved without forcing the semantic one? Let us suppose the answer is yes. What raised the question was the wording of a charter. A flying boat had landed in a harbor, taxied up to a dock, and unloaded its passengers. Whereupon the authorities in charge of the harbor had demanded a fee for use of the dock. But the airline protested that the harbor's charter specified only that *passenger ships* using the facility were required to pay a fee; and since a flying boat is not, their vehicle was exempt. Now if we are right in classifying a flying boat here as a borderline case of a passenger ship, then it is no more clearly exempt than it is required by the charter to pay: neither answer is right. This is an important point: neither side wins on a borderline. This is why the issue is still to be resolved in different terms.

A standard appeal, when the letter of the law is unclear, is to intent. If the charter's intent was to place the burden of maintaining the harbor on those benefiting from its use, then we might appeal to this in resolving the substantive issue. The flying boat is making the same use of the harbor that a normal passenger ship would, so unless some equally weighty consideration can be found to argue against it, the airline should be required to pay. This is the kind of resolution you often can find when you look past borderline semantics to the underlying issue.

Prospective Reform: Further Difficulties

We have seen that *retrospective* reform is self-deceptive. Answering a question by sharpening a borderline is semantic legerdemain. It involves changing the question, equivocating on the crucial term. Furthermore, the answer that comes up is semantically arbitrary. We may draw in a sharp line on either side of the case we have; we may devise either answer: yes or no. If there is some underlying substantive concern that inclines us to *want* one of these answers rather than the other, then it is far better—and more honest—to deal with that substantive matter directly, and forget about pushing the semantics around.

Prospective borderline reform raises more complicated issues. If we are trying not to answer a question already asked but to change the language for the sake of *future* questions, then no general, formal objection may be lodged against the reform. But, in practice, the simple sharpening of a borderline is unlikely to be helpful, even in framing future questions. It is unlikely to add to the linguistic resources at our disposal. In fact, as we have noticed already, the net impact of such a sharpening can easily be to impoverish the language. For we always lose something of value in the old fuzzy job: sometimes a whole dimension, sometimes just valuable "taper." And often the gain in precision is pointless, because there is other terminology already available to handle the case in question with greater precision.

This last point cannot be overemphasized. When we need to speak precisely about weight, for example, we always have recourse to pounds and ounces. When we need precision about what time of day it is, we may consult a clock. If we ever need great precision in talking about hair loss, we can simply count follicles, or square inches. We can even talk about minute variation along the monochromatic scale by appeal to exact wavelengths of light. And, we can, of course, do all this without firing 'fat' and 'slim', 'dawn' and 'dusk', 'bald', 'blue', and the rest from their practically valuable, though fuzzy-edged, jobs. We can have the best of both worlds: the precision when we need it, the complexity of more basically perceptual predicates when that is more valuable.

This last way of putting the matter raises yet another hazard in the way of casual borderline reform, even if it is only intended prospectively: the newfound precision is usually beyond our perceptual competence in the contexts in which we need the job. The value of many practical jobs that words get lies partly in our easy access to those jobs. Their applications are frequently well within our (unaided) perceptual competence in practical contexts. Normal conversation benefits outrageously from having them around. The reason we appeal to the normal jobs done by 'fat', 'slim', 'blue', 'bald', 'dawn', 'ship', and 'chair' is that they are usefully often applicable on casual inspection. As a result, when we attempt to apply the new, sharpened versions of these jobs the newly imposed precision will often be lost in our uncertain grasp of the application. Normal people in normal contexts simply cannot tell very accurately how many pounds overweight I am, or what wavelength radiation is entering their eye. If being bald is losing exactly 87.4% of one's hair, there will be a whole range of cases in which we cannot be sure without counting, which in practical contexts is simply impossible (not to mention silly and rude). In such cases the fuzziness that used to be part of the job will now inhabit the application. So sharpening up the fuzzy borderline does not even eliminate indeterminacy, it merely transfers it from job to application.

As a final note on this topic, it is worth pointing out that most subjects contain inherent limits past which it does not even make sense to ask for increased precision. A frequent observation in the last few pages has been that if we wish more precision than the words we are using allow in their normal jobs, we can always rephrase the issue in different, more precise terms. If fat and slim won't do, we can switch to pounds and ounces. But in nearly every application, precision, even in appropriate terms, may be pressed past a certain point only at the expense of substantial arbitrariness. It is senseless to ask for my weight in micrograms, because it varies thousands of micrograms every minute due to scrapes, cuts, and evaporation (minus) and accumulation of environmental debris (plus). It is similarly senseless to ask for the length of my house in microinches. This is only partly because the irregularity of the stucco is several hundred thousand microinches. The unevenness of the walls and asymmetry of the whole structure are far greater than that. And variations due to temperature, wind pressure, humidity, and seismic jiggles must also be accommodated. To give an answer accurate to microinches would require arbitrarily distilling a number out of all this. And any number within a million or so of it would be just as good.* My house does not have a length to that degree of precision. The most helpful, even the most accurate answer I could give would be so many feet, plus or minus an inch or so.

Effective Borderlines: Equivocal Fuzziness

The borderline applications we have been examining are all reasonably intersubjective: in practical contexts competent language users would all have reservations about roughly the same range of cases. This is doubtless because the difficult cases of things like fat, blue, bald arise as frequently and neutrally as the clear ones. We all get lots of opportunity to develop a common sensitivity to the indeterminable area, and appreciate the value of the taper.

Some borderlines are not so tidy, however. Some jobs taper off into areas in which cases never or seldom arise. Some have ideological commitments affecting their application in various ways. Still others are subject to parochial influences of local culture or commerce. For a variety of reasons our perceptions may not coincide on the tough cases; as a result the nature of a job—the significance of a word—will vary in small but systematic ways from person to person or place to place.

Although this is a kind of ambiguity, it differs importantly from what we discussed in Chapter 6. For there is substantial agreement on application to the clear, standard, common, easy cases. Difficulty arises only in the troublesome middle ground that is the subject of this section. One person's tough cases are another's easy ones, and perhaps vice versa. But the essential reason to separate this kind of ambiguity from the sort discussed earlier is that resolution of the difficulties to which it leads is, unsurprisingly, very much like resolving any borderline case problem: find the underlying issue and treat it in different terms.

The most innocent example of deviant borderlines might be something like this. Virtually all of us would unproblematically agree on the clearest applications of 'lawn' in the job that word has in landscaping. They would all be

---

*The number might be useful for *something*, of course. Its change might be used to monitor important physical changes in the structure, or it could be used to compute an exact property tax rate. But its usefulness does not show that it is the length of my house, it just shows it is useful. We might coin a new term 'tax-roll length of my house' to stand for a specific function of precisely determinable lengths of walls and things. But this would be a new job and deserve a new term here. It would not be the length of my house.

This is in a way just one more reflection of the arbitrariness of resolving borderlines. To microinches, length is semantically indeterminate when applied to large, coarsely constructed objects. (It is even indeterminable when applied to carefully machined blocks of steel, but less elaborately so.) We may sharpen up the borderline however we please: from the point of view of the job done by 'length', any possible answer is as good and as bad as any other.

plots of grass of various kinds. A front yard covered with desert weeds—spurge, Russian thistle, wild poppies, oxalis—would not be a clear case of a lawn, even if it were kept down with a mower. It would be a difficult case: rather like a lawn in important respects, but distinct from it in perhaps the *most* important respect. Yards of ordinary weeds and wild flowers are at best borderline lawns. Yet it is easy to imagine a community in which grass is unusually difficult to maintain, and as a result virtually everybody grows whatever will survive and keep down the dust in the yards surrounding their homes. It would be quite natural in such a community to jimmy the semantics a little and refer to their weed-covered yards as their lawns. The community might adopt this as orthodox usage. A borderline lawn for most of us would simply be a lawn for them, which is a way of saying they have a different conception of lawn. But the difference is not dramatic, it is very subtle. And it is common enough to be accorded special treatment if we can bring to bear what we have learned in this section.

Of course, the lawn example is so innocent that no interesting reasoning problems are likely to arise from it. Only when something important seems to hang on the equivocal characterization do interesting problems arise. When our personal commitments move the indeterminate areas around, then characterizational issues generate heat. Is a Toyota Celica a sports car? Is *Rhapsody in Blue* classical music? Could a robot be conscious? When a substantive dispute centers on such a question the best strategy is to uncover the underlying substantive issue, express it in terms all parties can agree on, and deal with it independently of the semantic controversy. In other words, as long as the semantic disagreement falls in our 'troublesome middle area' it is best to regard the entire area of disagreement as semantically indeterminate, and treat the dispute as though it concerned a standard borderline case.

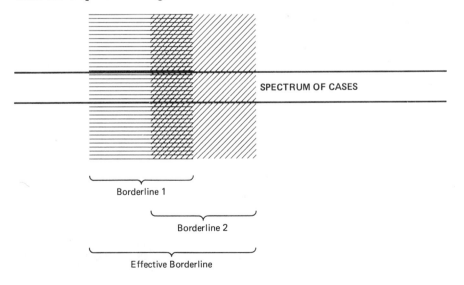

SPECTRUM OF CASES

Borderline 1

Borderline 2

Effective Borderline

One such controversy currently raging concerns whether or not a (human) fetus is a human being. For many it is a borderline case: there are pulls in both directions. But others have decided the case one way or the other; and because it is bound up in personal, religious, and ideological issues, hostility has focused on this disagreement, and it has caused some very hard feelings. It will accordingly make a good illustration of the recommended strategy.

Consider a familiar argument:

1. The deliberate killing of an innocent human being by another person is murder.
2. A fetus is a human being.
3. Abortion is the deliberate killing of a fetus.

Therefore, abortion is murder.

If we accept the three statements, this is a pretty good argument.* It is clear in the context that 'fetus' refers to a human fetus, that fetuses are presumably innocent, and that abortions are carried out by 'persons'. So the pieces of the argument fit together in the proper way. But not everyone subscribes to the clear truth of all three statements. In particular huge controversy rages around the second. And if the second goes, so does the argument. What to do?

Consider for a moment two people whose conception of 'human' differs very slightly, but just enough to cause disagreement about this statement. A accepts it, B thinks fetuses are only borderline human beings and hence withholds clear assent. They give 'human' slightly different jobs, which show up only in tough cases like this. Notice how silly (or self-deceptive) it is to try to resolve a substantive matter by pushing the semantics around.

Assume, reasonably, that the underlying substantive issue concerns how we should treat abortion, and abortionists, in the law. A offers the above argument to support his view that abortion should be forbidden: we should treat abortionists as murderers. Presumably A and B could agree that the underlying issue is whether or not we should forbid abortion. Now suppose A goes back to his argument and attempts to secure B's agreement by semantic means. Notice what can happen. A will insist that B change the job he gives 'human' so that the second statement is true. B relents. Unfortunately for A, this move cannot be isolated from the rest of the argument. For if B had originally assented to the first, he did so before he changed the job he gave 'human'. So now the first says something slightly different, and he must reassess it. What he is likely to say, of course, is that murder covers human beings only as he *used* to use the term. In its new job, 'human being' includes

---

*In fact, if we merely make explicit a few of the assumptions presupposed in the context of the argument, it will be deductively valid. Nothing in the following discussion requires such a strict interpretation, however.

some things the killing of which is not clearly murder as he understands it. His conception of murder is tied to his former conception of human, not the new one.

Not yet seeing the futility of attempting a semantic resolution of a substantive disagreement, A might further insist that B change the job he gives 'murder'. Let us say that B agrees to use 'murder', as A does, to cover the killing of human beings in the newly agreed-upon application of 'human being'. This glues the argument back together: abortion is murder for both A and B now. But the expense has been to raise a question about the connection between semantic and substantive issues. Before adjusting the jobs done by 'human' and 'murder', B doubtless conceded the importance of A's argument because of the connection between its conclusion and the substantive issue. Characterizing something as murder sounded like an important consideration in deciding whether to allow it or forbid it. But now that 'murder' has a different job, B may well want to reassess the argument's substantive impact.

Once again it is reasonable to expect B to think changing jobs vitiates the connection. In its new job B might well feel not all murders should be forbidden; in its new job some murders are permissible: for B 'murder' drops its perjorative force. What's in a word if you play around with its jobs. The point is that if, for whatever reason, people have different conceptions of 'human' and hence different conceptions of 'murder', it is very likely also that they will have different perceptions of permissible behavior and reasonable social policy. Such perceptions may well be amenable to argument. But, if they understand what is going on, it is silly to expect moving the semantics around to have much effect on their settled views. They can always keep their views and express them in the new terminology. In any case *we must avoid the fatuity of moving a borderline to fit our preconception* on some matter, *and then trying to use the adjusted semantics to justify the preconception.*

So we are led inexorably to direct confrontation with the substantive issue: should abortion be forbidden? It is by no means simple to deal with—it may be beyond general resolution. But any direct consideration is more honest, and offers more promise than semantic sleight of hand.

Exercise
1. Some years ago the NCAA declared Lonnie Shelton ineligible to play varsity basketball for Oregon State University because he had signed a contract to play professional basketball. The NCAA did this in spite of the fact that Shelton had decided not to play professionally, returned to Oregon State, and never received any money under the contract. The NCAA argued that since he had *signed* the contract, he was no longer, strictly speaking, an amateur; hence he was ineligible to play on an amateur team.
   a. What is the semantic issue?
   b. What is the underlying substantive issue?

    c. What is the problem with the NCAA ruling as articulated above?

    d. How might they have dealt differently with the substantive issue to avoid this problem?

▶ 2. What is wrong with asking for the duration of World War II in microseconds?

3. Write a paragraph arguing as well as you can that the case of the hunter and the squirrel, examined in Chapter 6, should be considered a borderline case of going around something, not clearly negative as argued there.

▶ 4. When (in what context, for what purpose) might it make perfectly good sense to divide cars into three precisely specified price ranges: low-priced, medium-priced, and expensive? What would be wrong with requiring those terms ('low-priced', 'medium-priced', and 'expensive') to specify those exact price ranges in every automotive application?

GENERAL EXERCISES

1. Several topics discussed in this chapter are relevant to the following exchange between an attorney defending a woman accused of bigamy, and the prosecutor. Comment in as much detail as you think required.

ATTORNEY: While my client's husband was being operated on all his life signs (heartbeat, respiration, etc.) vanished for nearly ten minutes; therefore he was technically dead. According to the law, marriage is terminated by death. So it was perfectly legal for my client to marry somebody else.

PROSECUTOR: Nonsense, death is *permanent,* by definition. The accused's husband did not die, he *almost* died—and almost doesn't count in the marriage law.

▶ 2. There is an old philosophic conundrum that goes, "If a tree falls in the forest and nobody is around to hear it, does it make a sound or not?" This seems puzzling because there is a significant distinction between sound and sound *waves* (i.e., pressure waves in the air). Write a short essay in answer to the above question using whatever you take to be relevant from this chapter and the last.

3. What do you think of Mr. Briggs's attempt to define 'natural' in the article below. [There are a number of things worth mentioning.]

Use of 'Natural' by Food Firms Leaves Bad Taste

MILWAUKEE (UPI)—At a time when many products on the supermarket shelf are labeled "all-natural" or "made with natural ingredients," nutritionist George M. Briggs thinks the word should mean something.

"I'm not a natural nut, but I want the truth," he said.

"Advertisers—in their world of their own—picked up the word 'natural' to help sell their products," said Briggs, an internationally known scientist and educator whose work led to the discovery of vitamin B-12. He also is coauthor of a widely used textbook on nutrition.

"People are looking for natural products because of an interest in health foods. I think it is a word being misused terrifically, and I've been speaking out about this.

"We have a rule of thumb—if you have to use the word 'natural' in advertising, although it is on the food package it probably isn't natural," he said.

That may change later this year when the Federal Trade Commission defines "natural" in a proposal to regulate advertising in the food business, said Briggs, assistant dean of the college of natural resources at UC Berkeley.

Briggs was one of three nutritionists who made national headlines recently in testimony to the FTC that the "natural" beer ads used by Anheuser-Busch, Inc., St. Louis, are inaccurate and deceptive. The conclusions were part of a memorandum filed by the Miller Brewing Co. of Milwaukee. Miller has asked the agency to halt such presentations.

"I'm not pushing beer, I'm pushing truth in advertising. I was contacted by Miller because I'm an expert in the field. I consult for any food company that comes to me," he said of his testimony.

"Anheuser-Busch beer isn't natural, but neither is Miller's. Just because a thing is traditional doesn't mean it is natural. The beer people have this problem."

Briggs, interviewed while in Wisconsin to visit relatives, said he opposes banning use of the word "natural" in food advertising.

"It is a good word and means something," he said. "It ought to be used. It is an honest word that is part of the English language. I'd rather define it."

His definition of "natural" would require a food to be "derived from nature and look something like the original food." It would allow minimum processing after harvest, such as cutting, grinding, drying and packaging, but would not permit such foods to contain artificial flavorings, color additives or chemical preservatives or to have two or more ingredients.

"Under that definition, any food with sugar in it could not be called natural," he said.

Consumers also need to be better educated, he said.

▶ 4. Comment on the following exchange:

A: You only do what you want to do; that's true by definition.
B: No, I often do things I *hate* to do. Do you think I wanted to go to my niece's piano recital? I went knowing I was going to hate it, and I did hate it. If you think I wanted to go, you're crazy.
A: Well, if you went, and you went voluntarily, then you must have wanted to go.

8

Mischaracterized Insights: The Perils of Pedantry

Most of us exaggerate for effect now and then. We quite commonly say things like, "He hit it a mile," or "I have a million things to do," or "I thought I was going to die," in circumstances in which a literal reading of them would be clearly false. One of the most interesting observations to make about hyperbole like this is that we are almost never misled by it. In normal contexts we virtually always understand exaggerations *as* exaggerations, and are able to see through them to the sober sentiment they are intended to express. In saying things like "It was the worst night of my life," or "He is the fattest person in the world," or "It seemed to go on forever," or "I wouldn't take one as a gift," we seldom wish to be taken literally, and that is usually understood. The transparency of exaggeration allows it to form the basis of a great deal of humor; it also assures it a serious role in communication.

The two (humor and communication) are sometimes not independent. When a road tester says, "The brakes on this car are so bad you have to count telephone poles to know whether you're slowing down," the two go together. It is amusing, but it also expresses some of the frustration—or terror—you might experience driving the car. And this is the communicative task hyperbole tackles best. We exaggerate to express the great degree of something which may be far more difficult to express literally. The terror might simply not come through in the data table's cold listing of 419 feet as the stopping distance from sixty miles per hour. The easy, clear, succinct expression of extreme degree is what we are after when we say of a boring lecture "it seemed to go on forever" or when the man in the antacid commercial says ". . . thought I was gonna die." Literal exaggeration provides clear, graphic expression of just how bored we were, or just how bad he felt. This is usually obvious; and this is also why it is usually silly to respond, "Really? Forever?!" or "You didn't really think you were going to die—you would have screamed for help or called an ambulance." No, of course not; the statements are not to be taken literally. Anyone who responds in this way has missed their point.

Our natural tendency to exaggerate for effect does occasionally get us into trouble, however. On some topics and in some contexts we are easily seduced by our own hyperbole: we end up taking it literally and insisting on statements that are literally outrageous. Something like this probably explains what enthusiasm we have for the more outrageous suggestions examined in Chapter 7, and others like them. Each of these statements—surfaces don't have colors, we never really see the star, and the rest—may be understood as the exaggerated expression of some insight into the nature of things. And as with any exaggeration, there is a more modest, more literally defensible expression of the insight available in each case. We say:

> It doesn't take much thought to be considerate; it's stupid to call that 'thoughtful'.

But there is a more sober way to put the point.

> Isn't it interesting that the job given 'thoughtful' concerns the amount or degree of thought only in one narrow context; in one common application it involves thinking of others in a certain way.

But the modest formulation lacks zing, it does not have the ring of profundity we seem to require. This makes us suspicious of it.

It is interesting to compare this case with an unproblematic exaggeration like "I've got a million things to do." This is hyperbolic for "I'm very busy." On any orthodox way of counting, even when I am very busy, the distinguishable things I have to do may come to six. But saying "I've got six things to do and that will more than use up the day" does not capture the panic, and dead-run preoccupation of the pending schedule that "I've got a million things to do" seems to. The difference between these two cases is that, when pressed, we naturally concede that 'a million' literally exaggerates the number of things on the schedule, that the exaggeration is for effect. By contrast, we are far more reluctant to abandon the 'it's stupid' formulation of the insight about thoughtfulness, even though what it rejects is clearly *not* stupid: it is an absolutely normal complexity in the linguistic duty of 'thoughtful'. The difference is doubtless due to the subject matter. Our casual familiarity with things like daily schedules allows us to reformulate the exaggeration confidently with no sense of substantial loss. We are comfortable with the practical equivalence of the two ways of putting the matter. We are not nearly so secure, however, when dealing with something as tenuous and abstract as an insight. Insights are by their nature often elusive and difficult to capture. So when we lose the zing of the exaggeration, we may think we have lost the insightfulness too. The modest formulation seems to demean the insight, seems to suggest that it is not such a big deal after all. So we cling to the overstatement in spite of its ludicrousness, even at the expense of hobbling the language.

The remedy is to recognize that even modest-sounding insights may be important and valuable to us. Modest insights are often all we can hope for on certain subjects; we must learn to appreciate what we can get and not try to blow it up into something it can never be. Unexaggerated insights can have an important impact on our perception and understanding, in spite of their modesty. In fact, accuracy is usually more essential to their value as insights than zing. So it is worth cultivating some enthusiasm for modest expression here. With a little care we can have the best of both worlds: the insights and the linguistic resources we are tempted to destroy in their behalf.

Because we have such trouble handling it soberly, the overstatement of insights is not the generally helpful device that exaggeration for effect normally is: it is a threat to reasoning, and even to sensible linguistic practice. We must try to get over our dependence on it, to shake the habit. That is the aim of this final chapter: to allow us to see how much enthusiasm for ill-considered linguistic reform results from the mischaracterization of simple insights. Each of the suggested reforms we examined in Chapter 7 may be viewed as a mischaracterized insight. If the treatment given any of those cases seemed vaguely dissatisfying, it may be because the insight the reform was attempting to capture peeped through the hyperbole. In this chapter we will examine some of those same cases—as well as others like them—from this importantly different perspective. We will try in each case to discover the underlying insight and express it more accurately. A more defensible characterization usually eliminates altogether the attraction of the proposed reform.

NONSCIENTIFIC INSIGHTS

Insights from science, especially those concerning the underlying explanation of familiar phenomena, require a systematically different treatment from the treatment of more general insights. Scientific insights will be taken up shortly. It is better to begin with a brief look at more general ones, those not particularly connected with the perspectives and preoccupations of science. We can then treat the scientific or explanatory insights by merely adding a layer of complexity.

Recall that in the last chapter we discussed a complaint against standard cases of unselfishness that had the following form:

> Charitable behavior, what is sometimes called 'self-sacrifice', is actually selfish if it is done for the personal rewards the charitable person gets from doing it. Molly's generosity—contributing to charities, taking in boat people, and the like —is not really unselfish because of the direct personal reward—the sense of fulfillment—she derives from them.

The insight underlying this complaint is that actions like Molly's could well be—probably are—in her own self-interest. As charitable as they are, they are also prudent. Further evidence is provided by the fact that they are often explicitly defended in such locutions as "Oh, I just *love* helping other people, it's what makes my life worthwhile," or "I just couldn't have lived with myself if I had turned them down." So on a cold, costs-benefits analysis it is plausible to say that Molly does what she does simply because the benefits for her outweigh the costs. Her satisfaction is worth the sacrifices. This makes it sound rather calculating, and encourages us to move from 'self-interest' to 'selfish.' So we arrive at a formulation guaranteed to attract attention:

> Molly is really being selfish!

But we have already seen in elaborate detail what is wrong with putting it this way: the job done by the selfish/unselfish distinction is not simply to mark the contrast between what is in one's own self-interest and what is not. In this context the two contrasts are radically distinct. Some *kinds* of self-interest are selfish, others are not. An unselfish person just is someone who derives personal satisfaction from being generous and helpful, someone who naturally, happily, gladly does things for people in need. Molly's generous actions are unselfish precisely because her self-interest involves—perhaps even requires—such charity to others. So the exciting, splashy, jazzy-sounding expression of the insight is also perversely misleading: it egregiously mischaracterizes the insight.

The best formulation of the insight at the bottom of this discussion is some version of the modest one with which we began:

> Sometimes it is in your own self-interest to be unselfish.

If we can grow to appreciate the accuracy of such modest formulations, we might lessen our predilection toward the attention-grabbing outrageous ones.

Accuracy is, after all, of some value intrinsically. But, as in this case, there is sometimes a further payoff as well. For as soon as we allow that unselfishness may be prudent, we can more easily appreciate the converse possibility: that selfishness may be *im*prudent. Understanding that selfishness is not just self-interest, but a rather narrow preoccupation with one's self, allows us to see how easily it can be harmful to our own self-interest. This in turn may clarify the value of the term in child rearing and social awareness generally. In short, a modest-but-accurate formulation might well lead to a cluster of insights having an appeal nearly as great as the fancy one-liner we had to abandon to get them. And it has the additional benefit of preserving the valuable bits of language the mischaracterization would encourage us to scrap.

Less striking mischaracterizations of less profound insights may be found every day. Consider part of a radio advertisement:

All hypnosis is really self-hypnosis.

Suppose this is defended by arguing that successful hypnosis requires the subject's cooperation, and since this makes the subject a kind of participant in his own hypnosis, it is self-hypnosis. The best that can be said for such a construction is that it is just a bad way to put the point. (It does not matter here whether we agree or disagree with the suggestion: *this* is a bad way to make the point.) For self-hypnosis openly suggests the subject's participation in his own hypnosis is *active:* he is doing it himself, it is his own activity, his own technical competence. But this is the very opposite of what happens in most hypnosis: participation consists in relatively passive acquiescence, the subject does not even know *how* to do it, it requires the active administration of a hypnotist, of somebody else who knows what to do. To call such cases self-hypnosis is to mischaracterize confusingly a modest insight that may be put much more clearly. In fact, it was put more clearly above in the "defense":

Successful hypnosis requires the subject's cooperation.

or, negatively,

You cannot be hypnotized if you resist.

These reformulations express the ostensible point of the original statement, without the misleading hyperbole. They are still very interesting, but they avoid the mistaken implications.

Exercise: Treat each of the following as mischaracterized insights. First explain what it is about them that exaggerates or otherwise misrepresents the point they are trying to make, and then provide a more accurate formulation of that point.

1. Lake Erie is not really a freshwater lake; you can't drink the water and it kills the fish.
2. Buddhism is not really a religion because it does not require belief in a supernatural being.
3. An anthology is not a genuine book because it does not have an author, just an editor.
4. If guns are outlawed, only outlaws will have guns.
5. In California the geranium is a weed; if you don't keep after them they will take the place over.

SCIENTIFIC INSIGHTS

Those applications of the myth of one proper use inspired by misplaced respect for science are, from the perspective of this chapter, of two importantly different kinds; that is, they may result from mischaracterizing scientific insights in two distinct ways. The first are mischaracterizations resulting from the technical use of a term that also has a nontechnical job. Second is mischaracterization of the underlying scientific explanation of familiar phenomena.

Technical Terms

The General Case. In general, when science has found it useful to use in a technical way a word that also has a nontechnical job, we must treat it rather as we did the case of 'thoughtful'. As long as both jobs are useful, and we can handle them in their respective contexts, the mere fact that both jobs involve the same word is an orthographic curiosity, but certainly no objection to either one. This is so not just of 'radiator', which we have examined, but of 'energy', 'inertia', 'field', 'gravity', and many others like them. Because of the different jobs these words do, we can always come up with some jazzy-sounding formula by making what amounts to a pun.

> Even though he is dramatically more active, Johnny doesn't really have more energy than Jimmy, because they both have the same mass and chemical constitution.

But this *is* a pun, and it would be perverse to take it seriously. All energy comes to in this context is the incessant jumping around Johnny seems driven to; it does not matter in the least that the underlying physiological story does not appeal to net differences in chemical or kinetic energy.

So once again all we are left with is some modest remark about the different jobs done by 'energy'.

> Isn't it interesting that Johnny has more energy than Jimmy in one sense but not the other?

Maybe it is interesting, maybe not, but it at least has the virtue of reasonable sobriety. And the literal accuracy of the more sober formulation is a real virtue here: it helps avoid the confusion and perplexity encouraged by the dramatic mischaracterization. It also preserves some useful linguistic institutions.

Pirated Words.   One particular kind of technical application deserves special mention, however. This is the technical application of a word with a well-established nontechnical job, when the word is chosen for its technical job *because of* some feature of the nontechnical one. Words like 'fruit', 'fish', 'element', 'work', 'probability', 'star', and 'clock' have been pirated from their various (and enormously useful) jobs in normal conversation to mark technical distinctions in various sciences. Sometimes the rationale is a plausible metaphor (clock), but usually the word is chosen because the technical distinction bears some more complicated relation to a slice of the original job (work, fish, star, probability).

The reason this class of terms needs special attention is that the rationale of the technical application adds to our normal temptation to think science has discovered that the old job should be run out of the language. So we get miscast insights such as

> A tomato is a fruit, not a vegetable.

Now, botanists doubtless picked the word 'fruit' to do its current job in structural taxonomy because of something in one of that word's nontechnical jobs. The word 'fruit', when used with the preposition 'of' or the verb 'to bear', can mean something like offspring. So if we are interested in the propagation or evolution of plants, it is natural to focus attention on the fruit *of* plants, the part playing an offspring's role in propagation, as central to those activities. In this way we might come to use the unqualified word 'fruit' simply to label that part of a plant's structure, quite independently of any other jobs that word might have. But this provides no reason at all to fire it from any of those other jobs. Specifically, it provides no reason to prevent its continued marking of the distinction between fruits and vegetables at produce counters and in kitchens. Both jobs are perfectly good jobs, but they are distinct. Confusion results only when we run them together, as in the mischaracterization of the tomato. A more sober expression of the insight is simply that some vegetables fall into the botanical category of fruit by virtue of their place in the structure of the plant. They are vegetables nonetheless. The usual distinction between fruits and vegetables is both perfectly clear and constantly useful in its standard employment. And that is all we can require of a distinction to welcome it in the language and protect it from unreflective attack.

Our skill in discriminating various substantive contexts is what allows 'fruit' to handle these closely related jobs without much confusion. If this were not so, however, if we could not reliably keep the two jobs straight, it would be reasonable to ask botanists to find a new word for their technical distinction rather than to fire 'fruit' from its culinary task. For it is comparatively easy for an organized discipline to change technical jargon; and if the alternative is muddying up a distinction of value to the conduct of our lives, we should insist. Fortunately we do not have to make the choice: we are up to the task of using the word both ways, if only we can resist the temptation to issue mind-numbing mischaracterizations.

The word 'fruit' represents only the clearest example of an established term being pirated by science to mark a technical distinction. It is clearest in part because the natural mischaracterization (saying that things like tomatoes are fruits not vegetables) is a wholly senseless thing to say in virtually *any* context. There are pirated-word cases that are not so blatant, however, and require greater care to uncover. These are cases in which the sentence expressing the natural mischaracterization also has a different and *sensible* application in some other context, usually within the technical discipline itself. That is, it sometimes expresses a mischaracterized insight, sometimes not, depending on which job the pirated word is doing at the time. Examples of such sentences are:

Venus is a planet, not a star.
A whale is a mammal, not a fish.
Inventing tensor analysis did not require much work, just a lot of thinking and writing.

Each of these sentences expresses something true and even insightful within the narrow confines of its respective technical discipline. We are often not content with such constraints, however, and that is where trouble begins. For outside technical contexts, outside contexts in which a particular technical distinction is relevant, each of these sentences represents roughly the same confusion as the one we just explored concerning 'fruit'. 'Star', 'fish', and 'work' have been pirated from other contexts to function in the technical taxonomy of their respective disciplines. And although the jobs are related, they are very far from identical. The job done by 'star' in astrophysics is different from that done by it in normal reference to the nighttime sky; the job of 'fish' in zoology is distinct from its job in Melville, the Bible, and nearly everywhere else; the job of 'work' in mechanics is actually rather remote from the one it does in talk of employment or human activity in general.*

Frequently, the technical distinction will be *within* the class of things covered by the term in its nontechnical job. That is, some nontechnical term 'X' will cover an entire class of things represented by the circle in the diagram below.

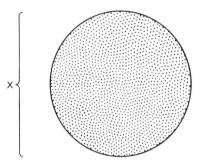

But some important distinction will be discovered by scientific investigation to exist in this class. Some of the things, say, have property α, others property β.

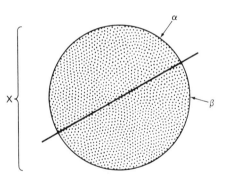

The discipline involved will then (sometimes) mark this distinction using the same term 'X', thus giving it a technical job. The Xs with α, say, are Xs in this technical sense, the Xs with β are not. So we might be tempted to say

Only the αs are *really* Xs.

---

*The opposite process is going on all the time too, of course. An enormous amount of technical jargon finds its way into the ordinary vocabulary of natural languages, often, initially, for metaphorical employment. Examples are 'neurotic', 'supernova', 'quantum', 'radiate', and 'symptom'. When a word ends up with several different jobs in *this* way, the same remarks apply. If each job is useful, and each reasonably clear in its special context, there is no reason to fire the word from any of them.

But this mischaracterizes the insight: it is openly misleading. All that's happened is that we have given 'X' another job to do. Both αs and βs are Xs in the everyday sense. Only the αs are Xs in its technical sense. But notice that in saying this we do not need the adverb 'really'. In saying that only the αs are Xs in its technical sense we are merely describing the job. Saying only αs are *really* Xs suggests that the other job is illegitimate—and that is the mistake. The sober expression of the insight is that there is an important distinction among Xs (in the everyday sense) which science has chosen the term 'X' to mark. Some things properly called Xs in everyday contexts, are not properly called Xs in special technical ones.

The point is that in the normal, everyday, nontechnical sense of 'star', for example, astronomers have not discovered that Venus is not a star, any more than botanists have discovered the tomato is a fruit, in the culinary sense of that term. In its everyday employment,* Venus is one of the stars: sometimes the morning star, sometimes the evening star, often the brightest star in the firmament. What modern astronomy has discovered is that there is a huge and striking difference in the physical makeup of the various bodies that dot the nighttime sky, particularly in the nature of their illumination. Some are rather like the sun, others more like the moon, especially in the latter respect. This is a far less misleading way to capture the insight in most contexts. And certainly there is nothing in this discovery—as important as it is—that says we should not have a word referring indifferently to all the venerable dots in the night sky, lumping them all together when the astrophysical distinctions are unimportant. That is, the more sober expression of the insight allows us to see that there is no reason to fire 'star' from its long-established job, the one it has in expressing sentiments like "Aren't the stars beautiful tonight?" It would be a pedantic embarrassment to add, "Yes, and the planets too!" The distinction is gratuitous here: 'star' covers them all.

In fact, because they are brightest, the planets—what the Greeks called the wandering stars—are the stars we talk about most often. Besides the morning star and the evening star, they include the only stars visible during the day (if you look hard enough), namely Jupiter and Venus. The planets are what Cassius refers to when he tells Brutus that the fault lies "not in our stars, but in ourselves. . . ." In smoggy climates, the planets often constitute a majority of the stars visible at all. So when astronomers use the word 'star' to *contrast* with 'planet', it should be clear they are using it to mark a technical distinction of little relevance to much of our common talk about stars. The distinction is enormously important in some contexts of course; but this fact, as should be transparent by now, provides no reason at all to rob us of the useful job done by 'star' in less technical circumstances. The choice of terms to mark

---

*Actually, astronomers often employ it in this "everyday" job even when they do astronomy. They speak of the parallax of the fixed stars, presumably contrasting with the "other" ones. And Copernicus entitled his earth-shaking treatise *De Motibus Stellae Martis.*

the astronomical distinction is, as always, relatively arbitrary. There is little about the word 'star' that makes it singularly appropriate for this astronomical job. Astronomers might just as well have used the word 'sun' (as one Greek suggested, long ago) and characterized the revelation as discovering that most of the stars are actually *suns.* But they did not: they used the word 'star' to make the distinction. And so we have to be just a bit more careful about the context when we use that word, so we understand which of its two closely related jobs it is doing at any moment.

This case reflects the risk we take whenever science commandeers an established, nontechnical word to do an important, technical job, especially when the old job somehow suggests the new one. It invites confusion; and it invites just that mischaracterization of the technical insight that tempts us to fire the word from its original job, simply because it is not the technical one. Science is unlikely to stop pirating established terms to mark its exotic distinctions; and as long as we are adequately sensitive to the subtly different jobs words can do in subtly different contexts, we may encourage science in this practice. Scientists do nevertheless bear a special responsibility in this enterprise: to take some pains not to rob us of a useful concept just to have a flashy or suggestive way to make a scientific point. If, following the currently jocular idiom of microphysics, the next subatomic particle is named the 'smithereen', we may soon be faced with:

> You didn't really blow it to smithereens, just to bits and pieces and fragments and splinters.

It would be a sad loss, and one we could avoid simply by resisting the hyperbolic mischaracterization of scientific insights.

Exercise: Describe a plausible context in which each of the following sentences would involve the misapplication of a technical term, like the ones just discussed.

1. The whale is a mammal, not a fish.
2. Strictly speaking, a runny nose and fever are not symptoms of a cold, they are actually signs of a cold: physicians reserve 'symptom' for subjective indicators.
3. I thought you were going to play *classical* music. That's Brahms, he belongs to the *romantic* period, not the classical.

Underlying Explanations

The various scientific disciplines routinely offer, in their own theoretical terms, explanations of familiar features of our everyday lives. They explain why light-colored clothing is cooler than dark; why tides are higher at one time than another; why the sky is blue; why certain places have more earthquakes than others; why binoculars make things look closer; why your ears pop when you change altitude; how camera film registers an image—and countless other things just like these. Such explanations provide the theoretical story underlying things we are all more or less familiar with.

The characterizational difficulty that arises in such cases may be generally described as follows. Call the phenomenon being explained A and the underlying, scientific account B. B explains A. The standard, neutral way to express the relationship between A and B is something like this:

What makes A happen is B

or, perhaps,

When B occurs, what you get is A

or, more generally,

When A occurs, what is happening is B.

We have a phenomenon and an explanation, and the two are linked together in some such way as this. The phenomenon, A, is something described in the nontechnical terms of everyday conversation: cooler, closer, blue, pop, earthquake, and the like. The explanation, B, on the other hand will usually appeal to the theoretical terms of a scientific discipline: radiation, index of refraction, photon, precipitate, geological plate. Because of this difference in terminology we are tempted, in a whole range of these explanations, to mischaracterize the explanatory insight in the way that results in the unwarranted destruction of valuable language we encountered in the last chapter. In place of the relatively modest formulation listed above, we are tempted to offer

A is not really happening at all, what is *really* happening is B.

Because A is cast in everyday language and B invokes the awe-inspiring concepts of science, we are tempted to think A is just a crude way of saying B, and should be dispensed with.

But this is all a misunderstanding—precisely the misunderstanding behind some of our worst reformist temptations. When B explains A in this way, it virtually never explains it *away*. Thermodynamics explains the relative coolness of light-colored clothing by appeal to its more efficient reflection of incident radiation. But it would be absurd to capture this by saying "light-colored clothing isn't *really* cooler, it just reflects more of the incident radiation." This would perversely mischaracterize the insight. The sensible way to put it is "light-colored clothing *is* cooler *because* it reflects more of the incident radiation." When geologists explain earthquakes as elastic vibrations in the earth's crust induced by slippage along a fault, they do not show that there really are no earthquakes, just vibrations induced by fault slippage. That is just what earthquakes *are.* These are (in each case) two different ways of talking about the same thing, each perfectly satisfactory in its own context. They happen to come together in an explanation, but the explanation eliminates neither one; it simply displays the relationship between them. It is "A *because* B," not "B instead of A."

This is perhaps easier to accept when we notice that the different terminologies in A and B have different kinds of jobs to do, different purposes. The terms of A is useful in our everyday lives, and terms of B is useful in scientific theory. The jobs of the scientific terms are explicitly crafted to aid in scientific investigation and explanation. The more mundane vocabulary has been shaped and selected to aid in conveying the practical matters of our pedestrian existence. These two endeavors are so disparate it would be astonishing if the same terms, the same jobs, the same distinctions would do for both. The fact that they come together in an explanation is a relatively minor incident in the lives of the various terms involved.

To be suited for practical, everyday conversation, language must be geared to our practical needs, rudimentary physical abilities, largely unaided perceptual skills, and a wide variety of interests other than scientific explanation. This is why we have terms for rather coarse divisions in the visible spectrum of light, rough and ready distinctions such as 'up' and 'down', 'hard' and 'soft', 'loud' and 'quiet', 'smooth' and 'rough', 'bitter' and 'sweet'. This is also why we attribute the characteristics we do to the objects we do. The best practical language is whatever helps us communicate our basic concerns clearly and quickly.

The language of scientific theory, on the other hand, is primarily geared to displaying systematic interrelationships among different phenomena in an explanatory way. As a result, some of its most important terms refer to nonexistent idealizations ('mass point', 'inertial reference', 'black body', 'ideal gas') or to entities the discrimination of which is difficult or expensive or both ('photon', 'neutrino', 'wavelength', 'geological plate', 'moment of inertia'). As a result, things that are simple to communicate in our everyday vocabulary are frequently beyond our practical ability even to *characterize* in the language of underlying scientific theory. "It smells rather like cantaloupe," or "The best ones are slightly asymmetrical," or "The rich mixture of dissonance and harmony can move you to tears," or "Stay on the main road until the pavement begins to deteriorate, then take the next left: it will be obvious." Sometimes we would not even know how to begin a theoretical recharacterization of such a mundane sentiment.

But even if we *could* begin, there is usually no point in it. In choosing what to wear it is sometimes useful to understand that light-colored clothing is cooler than dark. It is perfectly clear what this means, as is its occasional impact on our choice. Nothing is to be gained at this level from burdening our sartorial reflections with bits of thermodynamic theory: it would be rather like insisting on an astrophysical characterization of sunrise. Similarly for earthquakes. What normally matters in the conduct of our lives is the shaking and breaking and swaying and toppling, not mechanical models of the earth's crust. In short, we have a phenomenon (A), described in one set of terms, and a scientific account (B), described in another. The relation between these two things is simply that one (B) explains the other (A). We must resist the temptation to think the explanation gets rid of what it is trying to explain.

Note that none of this means the underlying science is of no relevance to our everyday lives. It is. Thermodynamics lies behind much of the technology we depend upon in our work and in our homes. Our growing understanding of plate tectonics will doubtless make life less hazardous in seismically unstable regions. But our gratitude to science for all these things does not require that we disrupt our conversations to rephrase everything we can in terms of the underlying principles. When the underlying science is not relevant, as it often is not in our mundane affairs, it is usually silly to mention it at all. Worse, mentioning it gratuitously complicates the characterization and distracts from the point of a remark, thus making getting the point across more difficult. It is often hard enough to make ourselves understood without adding a layer of irrelevant esoterica.

Applications. The main reason to single out this particular kind of mischaracterization is that it lies behind several of the unwarranted firings discussed in the last chapter. We are sometimes tempted to fire the terms in A because we thoughtlessly slip from "A because B" to "B instead of A." We sometimes talk as though in explaining something science explains it *away*. Accordingly, it will be useful now to turn to some of those examples, and others like them, to see how this observation can lessen our temptation to do destructive things to the language.

Consider first the suggestion that we actually do not see stars—or any other objects for that matter—just the light coming from them. This may be most naturally appreciated as a mischaracterized insight. For we sometimes think —and talk—of our seeing as though our eyes somehow reached out to grasp the things we see, searching out in various places and directions until the object of our perception is finally apprehended. The ancients actually developed theories of sight precisely along these lines.

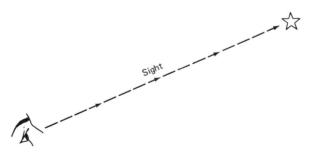

So it certainly is an 'insight into the nature of things' to notice that this is a mistaken picture; it misrepresents the mechanics of sight. Our insight consists in substituting a better picture for the mistaken one. What happens when we see things (the underlying account) in one way or another involves light coming *from* the object (often the same light) entering your eye, and forming an image on your retina. In the simplest case the picture looks like this.

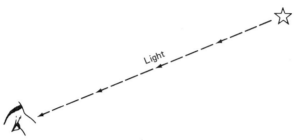

But when a picture such as this captures our imaginations we sometimes "read things off" that are not there. Here we might notice that what is in our eye—what we actually make contact with—is the light; so we might think we can simply "read off the diagram" that what we see is the light, not the object it came from.

We have seen in elaborate detail what is wrong with this move linguistically. Now we can see what is wrong with the picture that gives rise to it. The underlying optics does not tell us *whether* we see things, it explains how: it tells us what goes on when we do. To say we do not really see things, just have light-sketched images on our retinas, simply mischaracterizes the new picture. (In fact, this suggests we have not yet freed ourselves of the *old* picture, and still think seeing something requires making physical contact with it.) The sober rendering of the insight is that we see things precisely *because* light sketches images on our retinas. The picture above simply *is* a picture of seeing the star: it shows how we manage it. But it is important not to exaggerate the insight: that can damage both our understanding and the language. Seeing the star's light (which we can sometimes do under the right conditions) typically has a different picture.

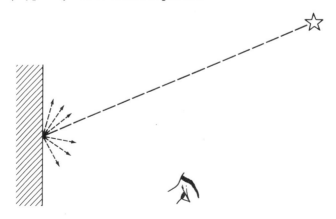

It is easy enough to extend this treatment to other examples discussed in Chapter 7. So let us richen our repertoire somewhat by considering two we have not yet examined. Earlier in this century Sir Arthur Eddington popularized a spectacular-sounding statement, which he claimed was an insight into the nature of things, provided by physics. The statement was that *there really are no solid objects.* His support for this surprising contention was that "modern physics has by delicate test and remorseless logic assured me" that what we think of as a solid object—a rock, a table, a hockey puck—is *actually* only a swarm of sparsely scattered electric charges: mostly emptiness. The books and papers on my desk, for example, are not supported by the substance of a solid object, but rather by "a series of tiny blows from the swarm underneath." Our belief in solid objects, Eddington complained, is simply a popular myth we cling to out of an ignorance of physics, and some innate hardheadedness.

But, of course, this is all a mistake: just the mistake we should now be so familiar with. The job done by 'solid' in this context simply is to invoke the well-known property shared by desks and rocks and hockey pucks: they hold their shape, hurt when they hit you hard, support things in a characteristic way (e.g., without a dent), and such. That is just what it is to be solid. Thus 'solid' may be employed to point out an impressive contrast in a bucket of ordinary tap water before and after it sits out all night in a Minnesota winter. When it is drawn from the tap it is not solid, after sitting out all night it is. It is terribly convenient to have a word mark this particular contrast, and 'solid' is the one that does.

Moreover, nothing in physics denies that there are things which hold their shape, hurt when you bump them hard, or support things without a dent, as we suppose solid objects to do. Physics does not deny the familiar difference between water and ice. There is nothing in physics to recommend firing 'solid' from its immensely useful job in practical contexts. So once again we arrive at our recurring observation. 'Solid' and 'swarm of charges' normally go in different contexts: they belong to radically different ways of talking about the objects of our experience. They may come together in an explanation, but it is important to understand what happens when they do. To say that a desk is actually a swarm of charges goes no way at all toward denying that it is also a solid object in the usual sense. But it does suggest that we might reasonably try to *explain* its solidity by appeal to the kind of charge swarm it is.

The insight Eddington was trying to express, put soberly, is simply that if physics is right, everything—all matter—consists in a swarm of charges of one sort or another. But nothing in this conflicts with the well-established properties of matter we are all familiar with in our daily lives. If it did, it would be the physicists who would have to worry. For the best reason to think matter is a swarm of charges is that the charge-swarm theory looks capable of *accounting for* the familiar properties of matter. If the charge-swarm theory could not account, say, for the obvious change in the water when it freezes, that would count heavily against the theory. This sort of thing happens all the time, in fact. The current version of the charge-swarm theory arose precisely because the previous theory could not account for some familiar phenomena on the level of everyday phenomena. In other words, if the charge-swarm theory could not explain why some swarms are solid objects and others not, *that* would be a very bad sign for the theory.

For a final illustration of this type of mischaracterization let us briefly consider the spectacular-sounding claim that black is really not a color. A slightly more elaborate phrasing of it will allow us to begin to see what is going on here. Consider

Black is really not a color at all; it is the absence of all color.

Such a claim might be defended in the following way:

Look, colors are just different wavelengths of light, ranging from long wavelengths at the red end of the spectrum, through green in the middle, to the shortest wavelengths at the violet end. Black isn't *any* wavelength: it is not on the spectrum at all. Black is what you get when there *isn't* any light. Black surfaces are merely those that absorb (virtually) all the light falling on them.

This reasoning represents yet another application of the by now familiar pattern. A phenomenon is confused with its explanation, and that confusion is used to argue that a word ought to be fired from (part of) a useful and unproblematic job. To begin with this last point, even if we grant everything in the argument just offered, it provides no reason at all to change the job of the word 'color' as it is normally employed in our conversation, so that it no longer covers black. In most circumstances, when we concern ourselves about the color of something, what we are interested in is a surface property among the variations of which is black. When the police ask what color the getaway car was, when a dermatologist asks what color a mole is, when the clerk at the tuxedo rental asks what color tux you want, one of the possible answers is "black." That answer is usually perfectly clear, and the underlying electromagnetic theory is beside the point, a pedantic distraction at best. At worst it cripples communication. If you tell the clerk you want a tux that has no color, you may end up going to the prom in the latest see-through fashion; if you tell the dermatologist that your mole has no color, you deserve the misdiagnosis that will inevitably result. The point, once again, is that it is silly to abandon useful and unproblematic language no matter what science tells us is going on behind the scenes.

This naturally leads us back to the physics itself, to find, once again, that it has been badly characterized. Physics does not tell us colors are wavelengths any more than it tells us desks are not solid. Even if colors *could* be perfectly correlated with specific wavelengths (or ranges of wavelengths), to say that colors *are* wavelengths would be, again, to confuse a phenomenon (color) with its explanation (wavelengths of light). Monochromatic light of a certain wavelength *is* light of a certain color—that much is true. But the color and the wavelength are different things—they may be determined independently.* We simply discovered that they go together. So it should not be surprising that some colors do not go together with wavelengths (black is just one; brown, gray, and white are others). Colors like black simply have a different electromagnetic explanation than the monochromatic colors of the spectrum. This is the insight behind the hyperbole: black is a color with a distinctive electromagnetic account. But the peculiarity at this level does not even bear on the question of *whether* black is a color. That question concerns how we find it convenient to group the superficial characteristics of our everyday, mundane world, and the linguistic institutions that have grown up in that rich soil.

Exercise

▶ 1. The following cases, which were used in Chapter 7, may also be thought of as mischaracterized insights. In each case, reformulate the insights in the way suggested in this section.
   a. The sky is not really blue; it is just that particles in the atmosphere are diffusing light (exercise on p. 215).
   b. The sun does not really rise; it stands still while we rotate into its light (discussion begining on p. 206).
   c. Surfaces do not really *have* colors; they just differentially reflect various wavelengths of light (discussion begining on p. 211).
2. The statements below also mischaracterize underlying scientific insights, but in novel ways. Explain the mischaracterization in each case, and then restate the insight in a less misleading way.
   a. Dinosaurs are not really extinct; they are still with us in their direct descendants, the birds.
   b. Epilepsy isn't a single thing at all. What we call epilepsy is actually the result of at least four distinct neurophysiological disorders.

THE MYTH OF AN ULTIMATE CONTEXT

The hyperbolic mischaracterization of certain insights is sometimes defended against the criticisms we have just made by invoking a special context, one in which interest lies in (what is sometimes called) 'the final analysis'. This defense finds the criticism offered in this chapter quite congenial, as far as it goes. Nothing justifies routinely disrupting our conversations to impose

---

*In fact, we can usually duplicate nearly any shade using a variety of mixtures of wavelengths. So the independence is not merely conceivable.

an irrelevant layer of esoteric complexity. Nevertheless (this defense continues), in the special context in which we look for *ultimate* truths, seek what is true in the final analysis, the hyperbolic characterization is sometimes just the right one. The very same sentence, the one expressing the pernicious mischaracterization in normal contexts, may provide just what we need in the more exotic philosophical context. The exaggeration is fraudulent and dangerous only when this is misunderstood and it is employed in everyday conversation.

So perhaps it is only "in the final analysis" that there are no solid objects, we do not really see the stars, the sun does not rise, all prudent action is selfish, and the rest. But what can it mean to say there really are solid objects, *except* in the final analysis? On the one hand, we have the everyday job of 'solid' in which talk of solid objects is clear and unproblematic. On the other we have the modest (i.e., accurate) formulation of the underlying insight from physics, couched in different language. What is left for the exaggerated formulation to express? What other "analysis" is there, and in what sense is it privileged as "final"? The two "analyses" mentioned above are each final in their way. In the semantic final analysis there are solid objects, quite independent of microphysics. In the physical final analysis, everything consists of charge swarms, some of which form solid objects. What other final analysis could there be, in which there are not any solid objects, only charge swarms?

We may begin to see what is happening here by recalling the role of context, and of charity, in our understanding of the jobs words do. When someone says something superficially contradictory, or incoherent, or paradoxical, we naturally grope around for a context in which a plausible interpretation may be placed on their words. In the worst of cases we are forced to give their words unusual, even wildly metaphorical jobs. But with a little imagination we can usually "make some sense of" nearly any sentence, no matter how intractable and opaque it seems at first. This is the second principle of charity at work.

So in the present case, confronted by the stupefying 'there really are no solid objects', we are naturally open to the suggestion that there is *some* context in which it may be made sense of—perhaps even express something true. The ultimate-context devotee explicitly encourages this suggestion by saying that it is not in everyday contexts but only in a very special one that his sentence makes any sense. And this unravels the mystery. For in making sense of the sentence in this way we simply change what it expresses to avoid the stupefaction. Specifically, since we are no longer in the context in which 'solid' gets the job Eddington was attacking (in which we all think of, e.g., desks as solid objects), the word is now free to shift away from that job in our attempt to give the sentence sense. In the abstract, philosophical contexts of ultimate truths and final analyses, we are emphatically no longer constrained by those mundane features of our environment that make the solidity of furniture and hockey pucks so important to our everyday lives. That a pound of ice dumped on one's head hurts more than a pound of water seems irrelevant to anything important in those contexts. For just this reason, words like 'solid' cannot get enough of a foothold to do their usual, practical jobs in the sketchy and unfamiliar context of ultimate truths and final analyses. So, given the nature of our linguistic skills, and especially our automatic charity, they normally fall into some metaphorical role only distantly related to their mundane occupations. As happens to 'hand' in 'the hands of fate', to 'house' in 'seventh house of the celestial sphere', or to 'tree' in 'family tree', 'solid' is forced by the unusual context to break substantial literal ties with its familiar mundane roots.* Asking 'solid' to maintain its relevance to the water/ice distinction in this context would be like requiring the hands of fate to have five fingers each, or the family tree to shade us from the sun.

In any case, when we are forced to make sense of the sentence in this way, 'solid' no longer has its usual job in the expression 'solid object', and the paradox vanishes. For, in spite of appearances, the sentence is not denying the existence of the ordinary solid objects with which we are so familiar. It is saying something else. And we can now see the trouble caused by simply offering Eddington's statement as "the final analysis." For it is not even competing with the semantic and physical "final analyses" already given. It is an analysis of something else. Hiding all this under the honorific label 'ultimate' sets us up to be taken in by a pun on 'solid'.†

Worse, the pun is far from innocuous. It encourages a silly misconception about the value of various linguistic structures and institutions. To say that there is something ultimate about talking of charge swarms instead of solid objects suggests that the (theoretical) purposes served by the vocabulary of physics are intrinsically more important than the (practical) ends served by our everyday conversation. It is worth noting that from one perspective a

---

*The most plausible rendering of what 'solid' might be doing in this context is actually a metaphorical application of (probably) two other jobs we give 'solid' in practical, everyday contexts. The sort of internal uniformity indicated by 'solid' in 'solid color', or when it contrasts with 'hollow' ('solid door', 'solid handle') may be metaphorically extended to refer to a uniformity of substance on microscopic examination. This is metaphorical, since the sort of uniformity implied by solid color or solid door is not the least bit troubled by microscopic structure or grain. 'Solid' merely rules out an obvious kind of macroscopic structure: that indicated by 'patterned' or 'variegated' for colors and 'hollow' for doors.

In the exotic context, these contrasts are naturally extended to cover any microscopic structure or nonuniformity. That is, the metaphor simply is a rejection of all common and plausible analyses of the nature of matter. Microphysics is incompatible with the applicability of the metaphor in this respect.

†Sometimes final analysis buffs do perversely suggest that the job 'solid' finds in the abstract, philosophical context is a better, purer, more important one, and should be the one we give 'solid' in other contexts too. But it is hard to see why a job that has no practical applications (there are none) is to be preferred to one that has very important practical applications. In any case, the burden is on them to show why we should embrace such an imprudent-looking recommendation.

good case may be made for the opposite position: for our survival and social structures—two major factors governing the shape of practical language—are crucial to the very existence of physics; whereas they got on quite well for centuries before theoretical physics came to be. But of course the most sensible position is that the purposes of theoretical physics are sometimes very important, and the purposes of practical conversation are sometimes very important, and the trick is simply to recognize which are more important when. Since the "final analysis" hyperbole suggests that one (physics) is absolutely more important, it is best to avoid it altogether. Certainly the insight provided by physics into the microscopic structure of matter may be adequately captured without saying something so dangerously misleading.

To be fair, advocates of ultimate contexts do not try to salvage every mischaracterization produced by human imagination. Some, such as those we have discussed, may be too obviously beyond saving. There are others they do try to save by this stratagem, however. And these hold precisely the same dangers as any mischaracterized insights. It is worth looking at the most tempting of them to locate one last semantic snare lurking in the careless exaggeration of our insights: the ultimate-context device of lumping or splitting.

Lumping and Splitting

It is sometimes insightful to point out similarities in things we commonly think of as quite distinct, and equally insightful to point out differences among things we think of as very similar. Coming to see a previously unnoticed analogy or disanalogy frequently refines our perception of something, aids our understanding of it. To think of the Milky Way as made up of millions of distant suns, for example, can have a dramatic impact on our appreciation of our place in the universe. And understanding the common cold as the effects of any one of hundreds of different viruses allows us to appreciate better both its commonness and its intractability.

But virtually never does a newfound similarity eliminate previously dominant distinctness—or vice versa. It may change our view of it, but it does not get rid of it. The sun may be only one of the stars in the Milky Way, but it is still the only one near enough to do us much good. And colds may be due to a number of distinct agents, but they still are similar in miserable symptoms and prudent precautions. When two things share some features and differ in others, whether the similarities or differences are most important usually depends on what is at issue. It will vary from one context to another. And when one set (similarities or differences) is so clear that it has dominated our perceptions up to now, the sudden discovery of something from the other side (differences or similarities) virtually never obliterates our interest in the first. Sometimes it does not diminish it at all.

Accordingly, when we express such insights by simply lumping together distinct things, or splitting apart similar ones, we must be careful to make clear that the lumping or splitting is not (almost ever) absolute, but depends on the context: on what is at issue. In easy cases this is not difficult. Lumping the sun together with the other stars in the firmament hardly obscures its crucial difference in distance. And splitting colds into several hundred etiologies hardly confuses us about carrying a handkerchief or checking our temperature when we begin to feel lousy.

Nevertheless, we are occasionally tempted in these cases, too, to exaggerate our newfound insight. We express the lumping or splitting in such a way as to suggest that it is *really* the only or most important way to put the matter, quite independent of context. "Ultimately they're all alike." "In the final analysis they're actually distinct." We will say these things with a flourish, suggesting that the contrasting features (differences or similarities) are categorically less important, perhaps insignificant. And this is almost always a mistake. What has happened is that we are so taken with our new insight that we get swept away. No hyperbole is too good for it. No competing insight should diminish its luster. So we sacrifice other perfectly sensible observations and insights to our (hopefully temporary) euphoria.

It is as important to resist hyperbole here as it is in the expression of any insight. Someone says "All companies are, ultimately, in the same business: making money." Certainly we may concede the insight: the profit motive is a fundamental driving force in virtually any business. In this respect such enterprises are importantly similar. But there is nothing about this similarity that makes it intrinsically more interesting than the enormous variety among companies in their size, structure, product, and a million other things. In most contexts the business a company is 'in' concerns its product (cars, clothing, cleaning service). For most purposes these distinctions are far more important than coarse-grained similarity in underlying motivation.

If the suggestion is that to understand businesses—how they work, how they fit into our lives or into our society—we must think of them as 'in the same business' in this way, that too substantially misrepresents the case. There are similarities among businesses that may well be accounted for by such coarse-grained considerations as the profit motive. But there are obvious differences among them too. And *they* will doubtless be accounted for by dissimilarities. Whether the differences or similarities are more interesting, more impressive, more useful, will depend on the context, on our immediate concerns. Even an understanding of how a company operates requires as much attention to its particular market and the idiosyncrasies of its product line as it does to the general profit motive.

In fact, because "making money" is such a vague and general attribute, it will be intrinsically *un*interesting in most contexts. Lumping companies in this way is rather like insisting that all fires are ultimately caused by oxygen. This would be a boring fatuity in most applications, precisely because the presence of oxygen is so general. The differences among fires are what is interesting: Was it a short circuit or spontaneous combustion? Was negligence involved, or was it beyond human control? Mention oxygen to the arson squad and you will be laughed out of the room. Similarly for businesses. For relatively few purposes will the underlying similarity of motive be even worth mentioning by comparison with salient differences. So it is perfectly natural that we should employ the phrase 'the business a company is in' to direct our attention to some of those differences, namely product or service. To the extent that it obscures the overriding practical legitimacy of employing the word 'business' in this way, the all-companies-are-in-the-same-business epigram is a destructive thing to say.

Sources and Types of Energy.   A more serious example of a modest insight run amok in this way is a product of our energy crisis.

The energy we derive from burning wood is, actually, *solar* energy.

The defense of this claim consists in pointing out that the combustion process releases energy installed in the wood by photosynthesis when it was a growing plant. And photosynthesis, as the name suggests, is a process energized by the sun. So the warmth of the hearth may be traced back to the energy of the sun's rays. It is, we might be tempted to say, ultimately solar energy.

Now, there is no question that we find some insight in noticing the pervasive debt we all owe to the life-giving rays of the sun. But the hyperbolic way of putting the point in this instance tends to blur or obliterate some important distinctions within the typology of energy. And for most of our interests and purposes, these distinctions are far more important than the insight to which they are sacrificed in this instance. For on the rationale presented here, the energy provided by all fossil fuels is solar too: the energy released in burning coal, gasoline, fuel oil, and natural gas may be traced to the sun in the same way. In fact, most fossil fuels came from ancient vegetable matter, the energy of which is directly traceable to the very same process as firewood: photosynthesis.

Furthermore, other sources of energy not involving combustion are energized by the sun even more directly than wood. Wind currents, which may represent an important source of energy in coming decades, are created by the rising of sun-warmed air. And hydroelectric power takes direct advantage of the fact that the sun's warmth continuously evaporates water from low-lying bodies and wafts it aloft to fall as rain on the higher elevations, and run back down through the water turbines, turning the generators. The energy of the sun is what keeps this cyclic process going. So in virtually the same way as wood burning, all these sources of energy are "ultimately" solar.

Of our major sources of energy, that leaves nuclear reactors and, perhaps, geothermal steam as not solar. Geothermal steam is traceable to the warmth of the earth's core, which is maintained by the decay of radioactive substances within the earth. So it is, ultimately, nuclear energy. If we accept the reasoning behind the "wood burning is solar energy" epigram, then we seem destined to say that, ultimately, all energy is either solar or nuclear. But, of course, the sun's energy comes from nuclear reactions, so it is nuclear too! Suddenly we find that all energy is, ultimately, nuclear. And this illustrates the pointlessness of lumping (or splitting) without any specific purpose.

For it is our practical purposes in everyday contexts that give words like 'solar' and 'nuclear' their usual jobs in talk of energy sources. That is why those jobs require substantially more direct connection to the sun and to nuclear reactions, respectively, than most of those traced in the ultimate-source story above. In its standard applications, one central feature of solar energy is its *contrast* with fossil fuels and nuclear energy, as well as hydroelectric power and wind. Similarly, nuclear energy is contrasted with solar energy, fossil fuels, geothermal, and the rest. The distinctions among these various sources of energy are far more important, for nearly any interest we have, than the tenuous, indirect connection of the ultimate-source story. Whether we lump them together, and how we do if we do, will depend on whether we are interested in immediate availability, environmental impact, renewability, social consequences, expense, specific business interests or investment profile, or some long-range prospects. Invariably our concerns will include a number of these considerations, weighted for importance in one way or another. And this will determine which sources are "essentially the same" and which "importantly distinct."

The trouble with the "ultimately solar" epigram is that it takes a term whose major function in the context is to draw a contrast and paradoxically suggests the contrast is, ultimately, illusory. But it is not only not illusory, it is in practice one of the paramount features of the term's occupation. The illusion of illusoriness is due simply to an unfortunate insistence on expressing the matter in inappropriate terms. For none of this should obscure the legitimate insight that without the sun, many *other* forms of energy would simply not exist.

Exercise: Explain why each of the following epigrams is an ultimate-context mischaracterization. That is, describe the contexts or purposes for which it would be a helpful thing to say, and contrast those with contexts or purposes for which it would be silly, obscurantist, or just false.

▶ 1. The ultimate product of the television networks is not programming, it is audiences. Audiences are what they sell to sponsors.
  2. In the final analysis, every human being is unique.
▶ 3. Except in unusual or particularly violent cases, every death is, ultimately, by suffocation. For no matter what else has happened, the vital functions of the body cease only because the cells are deprived of oxygen.

Retrospective

The dominating aim of this text has been to refine and organize our natural, human skills so that we may bring them to bear on some important reasoning problems we encounter in the course of our lives. The structures provided here are intended to extend those skills from applications in which they are effortlessly reliable to those requiring care and attention. Much of the self-conscious application initially required to deal with these structures will eventually become natural and effortless, too: habits of thought. This is as it should be. They will be *good* habits, habits of good thinking, as long as we stay alert for signs of trouble: evidence the habits are leading us astray, symptoms of a skill pressed past its limits. Then it is time to return to the slow, careful, self-conscious deliberation on which the habit is grounded.

The most important habits to cultivate in each part of the text may each be epigrammatically captured by a simple question. So, as a quick retrospective sketch of our progress, we will close with a brief description of those habits by appeal to the relevant questions and the circumstances in which they should naturally arise.

PART ONE

The representative question for Part One is the one we asked of trace-data in a diagnostic argument:

What is the best explanation of that?

Developing the habit of asking this question is helpful in at least three distinct contexts.

A. The most obvious is when we simply notice some puzzling or otherwise striking phenomenon. Long, black skid marks cut diagonally across the interstate toward a heavily damaged guardrail; the coffeepot perks but the water stays clear and colorless; a healthy tree suddenly turns brown and lifeless; there's a flash in the sky or an ominous bump in the night. Given the nature of our lives and of human curiosity, we naturally take these things to be significant: to be evidence of—traces of—something. But *what* we take them to be evidence of is sometimes misguided in a way that could be avoided with a little patience and well-directed imagination: we jump to conclusions. Somebody killed the tree; the bump in the night is a burglar. If, instead of jumping, we ask of each of these things, "What is the best explanation of that?" we will be guided naturally into a diagnostic inquiry. And our model of diagnostic induction contains just what we need to insulate us from hasty oversight. Fleshing out the list of rival accounts encourages us to think of the competing possibilities; and looking around for something to raise hurdles for the rivals helps us notice relevant data we might otherwise overlook. None of this guarantees we will get it right, of course, nor even that we won't overlook something important. But it will increase our effectiveness and efficiency in dealing with puzzling (or auspicious or ominous) phenomena.

B. We sometimes jump to conclusions even when it is not clear what we are jumping from. We simply make the judgment—in a broad sense, have the perception—that something-or-other must be the case, even though we can say nothing very helpful about what makes us think so. I simply think it will rain shortly, that the teacher hates me, that we should bear right at the fork in the road. Here we should naturally ask our question of the judgment itself: "What's the best explanation of my thinking that?" The best account may be that I have data (perhaps ignored until I asked the question) that is best explained by my belief. Or it could just be that I am demonstrably reliable in making this judgment, even when I cannot specify the relevant data. But we must always consider the possibility that the judgment results in part from bias or misunderstanding, which would, of course, undermine it. Thinking through the rival possibilities will, once again, reduce the chance we have overlooked an important consideration.

C. Our diagnostic question gets more complex exercise when an issue rather than a phenomenon guides the investigation. Do large doses of vitamin C prevent colds? Is cantaloupe more nutritious than escargot? Can we hear the difference a digital recording makes? Will increasing the defense budget make war less likely? The complication lies in the need to look around for things to explain, to *discover* data to ask our question about. Finding evidence for or against a thesis like those above consists in finding data the explanation of which bears in one way or another on the thesis. The diagnostic question guides the investigation.

The structures and schemata into which we have forced this Part One question may, from the most general perspective, be understood as providing guidelines for extending our perceptual/diagnostic skill past its current natural limits. We have no need for that apparatus in the easy cases in which our skill is clear and effortless: we simply can tell what's going on. As complexity increases and familiarity wanes we need more and more help, however; and that is what this text attempts to provide. Diagnostic inductive argument represents a relatively simple extension of our skill: it allows us to tell what's going on (or has gone on) more broadly, it extends the range of our perceptual competence. Nondiagnostic argument yields a more complex extension, covering in addition what *will* go on and what *ought to* go on. This of course involves appeal to our consequence-drawing skill as well.

PART TWO

The representative question for Part Two is the second principle of charity in action.

What is the most plausible interpretation of that?

This question, asked in the service of understanding a bit of language, should arise naturally in at least the following contexts.

A. Most common is the case, parallel to the first case above, in which we are honestly puzzled. We have a word, a phrase, or a sentence in front of us, but do not know how to "read" it: no compelling interpretation springs readily to mind. The range is large: from momentary lapses in conversation to intractable exegetical problems in ancient texts. But the procedure is formally the same. We must find something in the surrounding circumstances that counts as evidence for one interpretation or another. It might be more language: other things just said, other uses of the word or phrase in question, or some point of dialect. But the clues might be extralinguistic: a raised eyebrow, an embarrassed look, or historical information on the author.

Much of what counts as evidence in this endeavor will be something to be explained by an interpretation, and hence will be trace-data in a diagnostic argument. The interpretation will explain the raised eyebrow, the look, some of the other things said. So the two questions are not independent: the second is a version of the first. The most plausible interpretation is simply the one accounting best for the relevant trace-data, the one soundly inferred from the available information.

This principle—Charity II—is simply an extension of our usual practice—what we do automatically all the time. But we do not have to depart very far from effortless conversation before it becomes a useful slogan. Sometimes all we need is a gentle reminder: *that* is what we do to make sense of something. We can usually take it from there.

B. The more interesting and useful application of Charity II is not when words find no interpretation at all, but rather when the interpretation we fall on is bizarre, absurd, trivial, or inconsistent. These interpretations are by their nature antecedently implausible and need very special circumstances to sustain them. They *can* be justified, but we should develop an automatic suspicion of them. If there is some mundane, practical sentiment that looks as though it might be put in those words, that is probably what they are expressing, no matter if confusedly, clumsily, or paradoxically.

What impressed us as confusion or paradox, however, is often enough just our own misunderstanding, our failure to grasp what the language is up to. Myths about how the language works can make the perfectly ordinary expression of a wholly unproblematic thought seem weird and mindless, can prompt us to reject the expression in favor of some ideologically purified circumlocution. But the expectations of language raised by our abstract ruminations are not just outrageous, they are typically at odds with the mundane facts of practical human communication, which are the driving force behind the shape and structure of natural languages. The communicative significance of most words, phrases, expressions in general is relatively modest—at least compared with our abstract pictures of them. Their value for us may be understood only by seeing how that communication, that significance is of practical value to us in the course of our lives.

Appendix A

(Examination of the Argument on Page 35)

This argument allows a more complicated study of semantic elimination at work. Along the way it also illustrates the plausibility difficulties often encountered in casting substantive arguments deductively.

If we reconstruct what happened, characterizing the data in a plausible and idiomatic way, we get a pretty good inductive argument.

S_1' The Russell mansion was robbed.

S_2' Nobody heard a violent entry.

S_3' The usually reliable and alert guard saw nothing suspicious.

C_1 It was an inside job.

The implicit question is something like "How did it happen?" so the natural rivals would be:

C_2 The robber (somehow) got past the guard and got into the mansion quietly.

C_3 The robber got past the guard and broke in, but the noise was obscured by other noise or distraction.

C_4 The robber got past the guard and broke in but nobody was within earshot to hear.

Notice that at least three other rivals are semantically eliminated:

C_5 The missing valuables were removed noncriminally.
C_6 The guard was in on it and lied about not noticing anything.
C_7 Somebody heard the break-in but lied about it.

These are, of course, super-rivals, naturally split into a number of subrivals. Each of these is, naturally, eliminated too.

Now, in ordinary inductive arguments, there are usually a number of bizarre possibilities not clearly covered by (that is, included in) any rival on the list. They are so implausible that we automatically and rightly ignore them. If some consideration later recommends that we take one of them seriously, it may easily enough be formulated at that time; but in normal circumstances they all may be safely ignored. The first difficulty in a deductive casting of substantive arguments arises at this point. In order to eliminate semantically all of our conclusion's competition, we must make sure all possibilities—even bizarre ones—are covered by the rivals we eliminate. In the Russell mansion robbery, we must be sure the support claims conflict with possibilities such as somebody's living undetected in the mansion for twenty-five years, taking the valuables, and then teleporting himself out of the solar system, all without the complicity of a servant. To do this, to make sure everything of this sort has been semantically eliminated, requires some terminological artificiality; but it will be unproblematic if we are careful not to abuse it.

The trick is to begin with logically exhaustive super-rivals (typically, C and not-C), and then subdivide them into exhaustive subrivals in a way that allows whatever support claims we have to bear directly on them. This will, of course, usually take us some distance from the natural diagnostic rivals. In the Russell mansion example, the most convenient beginning (given the support claims) is to divide the (super) rivals into break-ins versus everything else:

C = Robber broke into the mansion.
not-C = Robber did not break into the mansion.

In this context not-C is naturally taken to include all the possibilities not covered by C.

Both C and not-C may be exhaustively subdivided in the following way:

$$C = \begin{cases} C_1 & \text{Robber broke in by smashing the door.} \\ C_2 & \text{Robber broke in by picking the lock.} \\ C_3 & \text{Robber broke in in some other way.} \end{cases}$$

$$\text{not-}C = \begin{cases} C_4 & \text{Robber did not break in but had an accomplice among the servants.} \\ C_5 & \text{Robber did not break in but had no accomplice among the servants.} \\ C_6 & \text{Robber did not break in but had several accomplices among the servants.} \end{cases}$$

C_6 is included here merely because the conclusion we seek refers to a single accomplice. We might take the conclusion as an idiomatic way of saying '. . . at least one accomplice . . . ' but it is simpler to keep it literal; and nothing much hangs on this. C_2 must be further subdivided to allow the elimination we seek:

$$C_2 = \begin{cases} C_{2A} & \text{Robber broke in by picking the lock and fooled the guard.} \\ C_{2B} & \text{Robber broke in by picking the lock and did not fool the guard.} \end{cases}$$

And since the deductive argument's first support claim (S_1) characterizes the robber as 'some criminal'—that is, semantically eliminates everybody but those properly so characterized—we may safely adopt this characterization in the list of rival conclusions. (It will shortly be clear why this is a convenient thing to do.) So the complete list looks like this:

C_1 Some criminal broke in by smashing the door.
C_{2A} Some criminal broke in by picking the lock and fooled the guard.
C_{2B} Some criminal broke in by picking the lock and did not fool the guard.
C_3 Some criminal broke in in some other way.
C_4 Some criminal did not break in but had an accomplice among the servants.
C_5 Some criminal did not break in but had no accomplice among the servants.
C_6 Some criminal did not break in but had several accomplices among the servants.

Now, looking down the list of support claims (S_{1-9}) in the argument we can see the following semantic conflicts:

S_5 and S_6 together eliminate C_1, since they explicitly reject any smashing that was heard and any that was not.

S_8 eliminates C_{2B}.

S_3 eliminates C_3 by explicitly ruling out all 'other' ways of breaking in.

S_2 eliminates C_5 by direct conflict: S_2 says the robber either broke in or had an accomplice among the servants, C_5 says "no, neither."

S_2 also eliminates C_6, if we take 'several' to conflict with 'an' accomplice as we have here. Interpreted that way, C_6 says "no, neither" too.

Finally, S_4, S_7, and S_9 together eliminate C_{2A}. Because S_4 and S_7 require that the criminal in C_{2A} be both an expert locksmith and a convincing actor; while S_9 conflicts directly with this.

We have thus semantically eliminated all but C_4: Some criminal did not break in but had an accomplice among the servants. Since the original conclusion, 'Some criminal had an accomplice among the servants', is explicitly contained in C_4, it is an obvious deductive consequence of it. So the overall argument is deductively valid.

On the sort of evidence we would normally have in a robbery investigation, many of the deductive argument's support claims (S_{1-9}) would be pretty shaky. Together they would provide very little support for the conclusion. This is due almost entirely to the peculiar nature of the statements we require to eliminate substantive rivals semantically. They must often be indefensibly categorical, such as S_8 and S_9, or offer peculiar combinations, such as S_2, or both, such as S_3. The peculiar device of referring to the robber as a 'criminal' was probably employed for just this reason. If 'no criminal' in S_9 were replaced by 'nobody' or even 'no robber' it would probably sound more ridiculous than it does in its present form. Only because 'criminal' severely restricts the class of people we must consider does S_9 have the little surface plausibility it does. And that is not very much. Furthermore, what little plausibility accrues to S_9 through this artifice is doubtless lost to S_1 in the exchange. For if 'criminal' in S_9 is read more significantly than as a slightly hysterical synonym for 'robber', then (keeping the same sense) S_1 says more than it seems to, and is concomitantly riskier.

This leads us directly to the risk inherent in the terminological artificiality we so easily fall into when forcing substantive arguments into deductive form: namely, equivocation. For it *is* perfectly natural to read 'criminal' in S_1 as merely an abrasive way of referring to the robber of the mansion; while in S_9 'criminal' seems to be doing more than that. So we are naturally tempted to give 'criminal' two different senses in those two statements—*not* to keep them the same. But this would ruin the deductive argument—our semantic elimination procedure required that 'criminal' mean the same thing in both places.

So the rule to follow in casting substantive arguments is simply to do it the most natural way in each case. Sometimes we will naturally eliminate all competing rivals by semantic means alone; but only in very special circumstances should we *expect* to do so. Usually the argument we get naturally will be inductive. We should then make the best of it, because if we try to force it into deductive form, we are likely to end up with a weaker argument and open up to much semantic risk along the way.

Appendix B

The distribution of red and white jelly beans may be derived as follows. Recall the small populations we discussed briefly in Chapter 4. If we have a population of, say, five jelly beans, two red and three white (r_1, r_2, w_1, w_2, w_3), then there are six different ways to draw a sample of one red and two white:

$$r_1 \ w_1 \ w_2$$
$$r_1 \ w_1 \ w_3$$
$$r_1 \ w_2 \ w_3$$
$$r_2 \ w_1 \ w_2$$
$$r_2 \ w_1 \ w_3$$
$$r_2 \ w_2 \ w_3$$

As this list illustrates, if we can determine how many ways we can get the red part of the sample from the red part of the population, and how many ways we can get the white part of the sample from the white part of the population, then merely multiplying these two numbers together gives us the result we wish: the total number of ways to draw the sample from the population. Here there are just two ways to draw one red from the population, but there are three ways to draw two white. So the total number of ways to draw a sample of one red, two white is two times three or six.

Fortunately, there is a general combinatory formula for determining the two numbers we wish to multiply here. If the population contains R red jelly beans and the sample contains r, then the number of ways to draw r from R is

$$C^R_r = \frac{R!}{r!\,(R-r)!} \text{ *}$$

Similarly, if the population contains W white jelly beans and the sample contains w the number of ways to draw w from W is

$$C^W_w = \frac{W!}{w!\,(W-w)!}$$

So to get the total number of ways to draw the sample $(r + w)$ from the population $(R + W)$ we just multiply these two numbers together.

$$C^R_r \cdot C^W_w = \frac{R!}{r!\,(R-r)!} \cdot \frac{W!}{w!\,(W-w)!}$$

In the example above, $R = 2$, $W = 3$, $r = 1$, and $w = 2$. Substituting in the formula we get,

$$C^2_1 \cdot C^3_2 = \frac{2!}{1!\,(2-1)!} \cdot \frac{3!}{2!\,(3-2)!}$$

$$= \frac{2}{1\,(1)} \cdot \frac{6}{2\,(1)} = 6$$

That is, as we discovered by listing them all, there are six different ways to draw a sample of one red and two white jelly beans from a population of two red and three white.

This is the formula used to generate the following computer printout, from which the graph and the first line in the table on page 132 were derived.

*R! (R-factorial) is merely the symbol for the series of multiplications R x R − 1 x R − 2 x R − 3 . . . all the way down to 1. E.g. 7! = 7 x 6 x 5 x 4 x 3 x 2 x 1 = 5040. (Zero-factorial (0!) is taken to be 1)

(Similar printouts were used for the lower rows in the table.) Each row of the printout represents one possible population (jar) of 1000 red and white jelly beans. The number of red ones (R) is given in the left-hand column; the rest (1000-R) are white (W). The second column is C_6^R, the number of ways to draw six reds from the population. The third column is C_4^W, the number of ways to draw four whites. The fourth column is the product of these two numbers. The last column gives the percentage of all possible samples (from all 1001 jars) that this product represents; that is, it divides the number in column four by the sum of all the numbers in column four. As a sample calculation, consider the peak of the first distribution: R = 600, W = 400, r = 6, w = 4. The number of ways to draw a 6r, 4w sample from a population of 600r, 400w is

$$C_6^{600} \cdot C_4^{400} = \frac{600!}{6! \, (600 - 6)!} \cdot \frac{400!}{4! \, (400 - 4)!}$$

$$= \frac{600!}{6! \, (594!)} \cdot \frac{400!}{4! \, (396!)}$$

$$= \text{(approximately)} \; 6.6402 \times 10^{22}$$

Jar Number	R	C_6^R	C_4^W	(Product) $C_6^R \times C_4^W$	(Cumulative Probability) %
1	0	0	--	0	0
2	1	0	--	0	0
3	2	0	--	0	0
4	3	0	--	0	0
5	4	0	--	0	0
6	5	0	--	0	0
7	6	1	40430556376	40430556376	0.0000000000002
8	7	7	40267857960	281875005720	0.0000000000013
9	8	28	40105651080	1122958230240	0.0000000000060
10	9	84	39943934745	3355290518580	0.0000000000200
11	10	210	39782707965	8354368672650	0.0000000000549
12	11	462	39621969751	18305350024962	0.0000000001312
13	12	924	39461719115	36462628462260	0.0000000002834
14	13	1716	39301955070	67442154900120	0.0000000005647
15	14	3003	39142676630	117545457919890	0.0000000010551
16	15	5005	38983882810	195114333464050	0.0000000018691
17	16	8008	38825572626	310915185589010	0.0000000031662
18	17	12376	38667745095	478552013295720	0.0000000051626
19	18	18564	38510399235	714907051398540	0.0000000081451
20	19	27132	38353534065	1040608086251600	0.0000000124863
21	20	38760	38197148605	1480521479929800	0.0000000186628
22	21	54264	38041241876	2064269949159300	0.0000000272746
23	22	74613	37885812900	2826677415790770	0.0000000390674
24	23	100947	37730860700	3808817195082900	0.0000000549572
25	24	134596	37576384300	5057631021242800	0.0000000760568
26	25	177100	37422382725	6627503980597500	0.0000001037057
27	26	230230	37268855001	8580408486880200	0.0000001395017
28	27	296010	37115800155	10986648003882000	0.0000001853362
29	28	376740	36963217215	13925522453579000	0.0000002434311
30	29	475020	36811105210	17486011196854000	0.0000003163799
31	30	593775	36659463170	21767472743767000	0.0000004071902
32	31	736281	36508290126	26880360362261000	0.0000005193306
33	32	906192	36357585110	32946952766001000	0.0000006567798
34	33	1107568	36207347155	40102099073769000	0.0000008240792
35	34	1344904	36057575295	48493977244547000	0.0000010263880
36	35	1623160	35908268565	58284865203965000	0.0000012695428
37	36	1947792	35759426001	69651923889340000	0.0000015601191
38	37	2324784	35611046640	82787991451926000	0.0000019054969
39	38	2760681	35463129520	97902387866403000	0.0000023139295
40	39	3262623	35315673680	115221729208860000	0.0000027946155
41	40	3838380	35168678160	134990750875780000	0.0000033577746
42	41	4496388	35022142001	157473139027590000	0.0000040147264
43	42	5245786	34876064245	182952369551520000	0.0000047779734
44	43	6096454	34730443935	211732553849310000	0.0000056612866
45	44	7059052	34585280115	244139290766350000	0.0000066797953
46	45	8145060	34440571830	280520523989660000	0.0000078500805

Jar Number	R	C_6^R	C_4^W	(Product) $C_6^R \times C_4^W$	(Cumulative Probability) %
47	46	9366819	34296318126	321247404252660000	0.0000091902716
48	47	10737573	34152518050	366715155695690000	0.0000107201465
49	48	12271512	34009170650	417343945741520000	0.0000124612364
50	49	13983816	33866274975	473579757855800000	0.0000144369328
51	50	15890700	33723830075	535895266572800000	0.0000166725992
52	51	18009460	33581835001	604790714177110000	0.0000191956859
53	52	20358520	33440288805	680794788442370000	0.0000220358491
54	53	22957480	33299190540	764465500838240000	0.0000252250727
55	54	25827165	33158539260	856391064627000000	0.0000287977945
56	55	28989675	33018334020	957190772281240000	0.0000327910360
57	56	32468436	32878573876	1067515871664200000	0.0000372445356
58	57	36288252	32739257885	1188050440423900000	0.0000422008854
59	58	40475358	32600385105	1319512258062700000	0.0000477056722
60	59	45057474	32461954595	1462653675153400000	0.0000538076213
61	60	50063860	32323965415	1618262479181400000	0.0000605587446
62	61	55525372	32186416626	1787162756505600000	0.0000680144919
63	62	61474519	32049307290	1970215749935900000	0.0000762339060
64	63	67945521	31912636470	2168320711437700000	0.0000852797812
65	64	74974368	31776403230	2382415749482400000	0.0000952188255
66	65	82598880	31640606635	2613478670571600000	0.0001061218261
67	66	90858768	31505245751	2862527814473100000	0.0001180638184
68	67	99795696	31370319645	3130622882715200000	0.0001311242591
69	68	109453344	31235827385	3418865759895000000	0.0001453872013
70	69	119877472	31101768040	3728401327365600000	0.0001609414747
71	70	131115985	30968140680	4060418268876800000	0.0001778808678
72	71	143218999	30834944376	4416149867751400000	0.0001963043143
73	72	156238908	30702178200	4796874795189400000	0.0002163160822
74	73	170230452	30569841225	5203917889300000000	0.0002380259665
75	74	185250786	30437932525	5638650924471200000	0.0002615494851
76	75	201359550	30306451175	6102493370695000000	0.0002870080776
77	76	218618940	30175396251	6596913142473600000	0.0003145293076
78	77	237093780	30044766830	7123427336943300000	0.0003442470678
79	78	256851595	29914561990	7683602960857900000	0.0003763017879
80	79	277962685	29784780810	8279057646084100000	0.0004108406464
81	80	300500200	29655422370	8911460353269500000	0.0004480177844
82	81	324540216	29526485751	9582532063350500000	0.0004879945225
83	82	350161812	29397970035	10294046456577000000	0.0005309395809
84	83	377447148	29269874305	11047830578741000000	0.0005770293020
85	84	406481544	29142197645	11845765494293000000	0.0006264478755
86	85	437353560	29014939140	12689786926062000000	0.0006793875667
87	86	470155077	28888097876	13581885881274000000	0.0007360489471
88	87	504981379	28761672940	14524109263588000000	0.0007966411276
89	88	541931236	28635663420	15518560470881000000	0.0008613819940
90	89	581106988	28510068405	16567399978503000000	0.0009304984452
91	90	622614630	28384886985	17672845907758000000	0.0010042266340
92	91	666563898	28260118251	18837174579327000000	0.0010828122093
93	92	713068356	28135761295	20062721051434000000	0.0011665105616

Jar Number	R	C_6^R	C_4^W	(Product) $C_6^R \times C_4^W$	(Cumulative Probability) %
94	93	762245484	28011815210	21351879642465000000	0.0012555870703
95	94	814216767	27888279090	22707104437853000000	0.0013503173526
96	95	869107785	27765152030	24130909780982000000	0.0014509875152
97	96	927048304	27642433126	25625870747892000000	0.0015578944076
98	97	988172368	27520121475	27194623605598000000	0.0016713458772
99	98	1052618392	27398216175	28839866253797000000	0.0017916610270
100	99	1120529256	27276716325	30564358649775000000	0.0019191704737
101	100	1192052400	27155621025	32370923216342000000	0.0020542166088
102	101	1267339920	27034929376	34262445232585000000	0.0021971538608
103	102	1346548665	26914640480	36241873207299000000	0.0023483489588
104	103	1429840335	26794753440	38312219234892000000	0.0025081811977
105	104	1517381580	26675267360	40476559333639000000	0.0026770427055
106	105	1609344100	26556181345	42738033766106000000	0.0028553387103
107	106	1705904746	26437494501	45099847341605000000	0.0030434878106
108	107	1807245622	26319205935	47565269700545000000	0.0032419222450
109	108	1913554188	26201314755	50137635580536000000	0.0034510881642
110	109	2025023364	26083820070	52820345064122000000	0.0036714459034
111	110	2141851635	25966720990	55616863808020000000	0.0039034702560
112	111	2264243157	25850016626	58530723253757000000	0.0041476507482
113	112	2392407864	25733706090	61565520819581000000	0.0044044919136
114	113	2526561576	25617788495	64724920073562000000	0.0046745135699
115	114	2666926108	25502262955	68012650887771000000	0.0049582510951
116	115	2813729380	25387128585	71432509573452000000	0.0052562557048
117	116	2967205528	25272384501	74988358997109000000	0.0055690947299
118	117	3127595016	25158029820	78684128677411000000	0.0058973518946
119	118	3295144749	25044063660	82523814862871000000	0.0062416275947
120	119	3470108187	24930485140	86511480590196000000	0.0066025391764
121	120	3652745460	24817293380	90651255723283000000	0.0069807212149
122	121	3843323484	24704487501	94947336972778000000	0.0073768257934
123	122	4042116078	24592066625	99403987896160000000	0.0077915227822
124	123	4249404082	24480029875	104025538878310000000	0.0082255001169
125	124	4465475476	24368376375	108816387092500000000	0.0086794640776
126	125	4690625500	24257105250	113780996441830000000	0.0091541395670
127	126	4925156775	24146215626	118923897481000000000	0.0096502703885
128	127	5169379425	24035706630	124249687318460000000	0.0101686195240
129	128	5423611200	23925577390	129763029498870000000	0.0107099694107
130	129	5688177600	23815827035	135468653865960000000	0.0112751222181
131	130	5963412000	23706454695	141371356405620000000	0.0118649001238
132	131	6249655776	23597459501	147475999069350000000	0.0124801455885
133	132	6547258432	23488840585	153787509578040000000	0.0131217216307
134	133	6856577728	23380597080	160310881206070000000	0.0137905120998
135	134	7177979809	23272728120	167051172545710000000	0.0144874219491
136	135	7511839335	23165232840	174013507251950000000	0.0152133775067
137	136	7858539612	23058110376	181203073767660000000	0.0159693267462
138	137	8218472724	22951359865	188625125029210000000	0.0167562395553
139	138	8592039666	22844980445	196284978152430000000	0.0175751080041

Jar Number	R	C_6^R	C_4^W	(Product) $C_6^R \times C_4^W$	(Cumulative Probability) %
140	139	8979650478	22738971255	204188014099190000000	0.0184269466112
141	140	9381724380	22633331435	212339677324360000000	0.0193127926084
142	141	9798689908	22528060126	220745475403450000000	0.0202337062042
143	142	10230985051	22423156470	229410978640800000000	0.0211907708456
144	143	10679057389	22318619610	238341819658450000000	0.0221850934780
145	144	11143364232	22214448690	247543692965750000000	0.0232178048030
146	145	11624372760	22110642855	257022354509750000000	0.0242900595356
147	146	12122560164	22007201251	266783621206500000000	0.0254030366576
148	147	12638413788	21904123025	276833370453210000000	0.0265579396705
149	148	13172431272	21801407325	287177539621440000000	0.0277559968455
150	149	13725120696	21699053300	297822125531440000000	0.0289984614715
151	150	14297000725	21597060100	308773183907570000000	0.0302866121009
152	151	14888600755	21495426876	320036828815060000000	0.0316217527931
153	152	15500461060	21394152780	331619232078080000000	0.0330052133551
154	153	16133132940	21293236965	343526622679270000000	0.0344383495803
155	154	16787178870	21192678585	355765286140810000000	0.0359225434843
156	155	17463172650	21092476795	368341563887200000000	0.0374592035380
157	156	18161699556	20992630751	381261852589710000000	0.0390497648982
158	157	18883356492	20893139610	394532603492760000000	0.0406956896352
159	158	19628752143	20794002530	408160321722280000000	0.0423984669576
160	159	20398507129	20695218670	422151565576210000000	0.0441596134343
161	160	21193254160	20596787190	436512945797100000000	0.0459806732127
162	161	22013638192	20498707251	451251124827240000000	0.0478632182353
163	162	22860316584	20400978015	466372816046120000000	0.0498088484514
164	163	23733959256	20303598645	481884782990610000000	0.0518191920268
165	164	24635248848	20206568305	497793838557780000000	0.0538959055495
166	165	25564880880	20109886160	514106844190760000000	0.0560406742323
167	166	26523563913	20013551376	530830709047450000000	0.0582552121120
168	167	27512019711	19917563120	547972389152530000000	0.0605412622445
169	168	28530983404	19821920560	565538886532770000000	0.0629005968973
170	169	29581203652	19726622865	583537248335760000000	0.0653350177373
171	170	30663442810	19631669205	601974565932360000000	0.0678463560155
172	171	31778477094	19537058751	620857974002790000000	0.0704364727474
173	172	32927096748	19442790675	640194649606840000000	0.0731072588902
174	173	34110106212	19348864150	659991811238060000000	0.0758606355154
175	174	35328324291	19255278350	680256717862270000000	0.0786985539778
176	175	36582584325	19162032450	700996667940510000000	0.0816229960799
177	176	37873734360	19069125626	722218998436590000000	0.0846359742332
178	177	39202637320	18976557055	743931083809450000000	0.0877395316138
179	178	40570171180	18884325915	766140334990460000000	0.0909357423153
180	179	41977229140	18792431385	788854198345870000000	0.0942267114962
181	180	43424719800	18700872645	812080154624610000000	0.0976145755234
182	181	44913567336	18609648876	835825717891540000000	0.1011015021113
183	182	46444711677	18518759260	860098434446470000000	0.1046896904562
184	183	48019108683	18428202980	884905881729000000000	0.1083813713662
185	184	49637730324	18337979220	910255667209470000000	0.1121788073864

Jar Number	R	C_6^R	C_4^W	(Product) $C_6^R \times C_4^W$	(Cumulative Probability) %
186	185	51301564860	18248087165	936155427266180000000	0.1160842929199
187	186	53011617022	18158526001	962612826049040000000	0.1201001543431
188	187	54768908194	18069294915	989635554329950000000	0.1242287501171
189	188	56574476596	17980393095	1017231328340000000000	0.1284724708940
190	189	58429377468	17891819730	1045407888593600000000	0.1328337396177
191	190	60334683255	17803574010	1074172998700300000000	0.1373150116209
192	191	62291483793	17715655126	1103534444163600000000	0.1419187747161
193	192	64300886496	17628062270	1133500031167700000000	0.1466475492817
194	193	66364016544	17540794635	1164077585352000000000	0.1515038883436
195	194	68482017072	17453851415	1195274950574200000000	0.1564903776509
196	195	70656049360	17367231805	1227099987660600000000	0.1616096357467
197	196	72887293024	17280935001	1259560573146600000000	0.1668643140337
198	197	75176946208	17194960200	1292664598004100000000	0.1722570968347
199	198	77526225777	17109306600	1326419966359500000000	0.1777907014467
200	199	79936367511	17023973400	1360834594199900000000	0.1834678781914
201	200	82408626300	16938959800	1395916408068900000000	0.1892914104585
202	201	84944276340	16854265001	1431673343752500000000	0.1952641147444
203	202	87544611330	16769888205	1468113344954300000000	0.2013888406854
204	203	90210944670	16685828615	1505244361960900000000	0.2076684710852
205	204	92944609660	16602085435	1543074350298000000000	0.2141059219365
206	205	95746959700	16518657870	1581611269377000000000	0.2207041424373
207	206	98619368491	16435545126	1620863081131500000000	0.2274661150016
208	207	101563230237	16352746410	1660837748646100000000	0.2343948552641
209	208	104579959848	16270260930	1701543234775900000000	0.2414934120790
210	209	107670993144	16188087895	1742987500757000000000	0.2487648675136
211	210	110837787060	16106226515	1785178504809700000000	0.2562123368356
212	211	114081819852	16024676001	1828124200732700000000	0.2638389684947
213	212	117404591304	15943435565	1871832536490500000000	0.2716479440979
214	213	120807622936	15862504420	1916311452792000000000	0.2796424783799
215	214	124292458213	15781881780	1961568881663200000000	0.2878258191662
216	215	127860662755	15701566860	2007612745011500000000	0.2962012473313
217	216	131513824548	15621558876	2054450953184500000000	0.3047720767505
218	217	135253554156	15541857045	2102091403520700000000	0.3135416542452
219	218	139081484934	15462460585	2150541978895200000000	0.3225133595231
220	219	142999273242	15383368715	2199810546258700000000	0.3316906051113
221	220	147008598660	15304580655	2249904955170500000000	0.3410768362843
222	221	151111164204	15226095626	2300833036326300000000	0.3506755309845
223	222	155308696543	15147912850	2352602600080500000000	0.3604901997383
224	223	159602946217	15070031550	2405221434963100000000	0.3705243855641
225	224	163995687856	14992450950	2458697306192600000000	0.3807816638759
226	225	168488720400	14915170275	2513037954182900000000	0.3912656423792
227	226	173083867320	14838188751	2568251093047200000000	0.4019799609614
228	227	177782976840	14761505605	2624344409097200000000	0.4129282915763
229	228	182587922160	14685120065	2681325559338500000000	0.4241143381211
230	229	187500601680	14609031360	2739202169962000000000	0.4355418363083
231	230	192522939225	14533238720	2797981834833000000000	0.4472145535309

Jar Number	R	C_6^R	C_4^W	(Product) $C_6^R \times C_4^W$	(Cumulative Probability) %
232	231	197656884271	14457741376	2857672113976100000000	0.4591362887209
233	232	202904412172	14382538560	2918280532057900000000	0.4713108722021
234	233	208267524388	14307629505	2979814576867100000000	0.4837421655359
235	234	213748248714	14233013445	3042281697791600000000	0.4964340613616
236	235	219348639510	14158689615	3105689304294600000000	0.5093904832293
237	236	225070777932	14084657251	3170044764388200000000	0.5226153854274
238	237	230916772164	14010915590	3235355403105100000000	0.5361127528036
239	238	236888757651	13937463870	3301628500970000000000	0.5498866005765
240	239	242988897333	13864301330	3368871292469100000000	0.5639409741492
241	240	249219381880	13791427210	3437090964519200000000	0.5782799489051
242	241	255582429928	13718840751	3506294654935800000000	0.5929076300061
243	242	262080288316	13646541195	3576489450901800000000	0.6078281521804
244	243	268715232324	13574527785	3647682387434900000000	0.6230456795054
245	244	275489565912	13502799765	3719880445856500000000	0.6385644051833
246	245	282405621960	13431356380	3793090552260300000000	0.6543885513107
247	246	289465762509	13360196876	3867319575981700000000	0.6705223686421
248	247	296672379003	13289320500	3942574328068300000000	0.6869701363466
249	248	304027892532	13218726500	4018861559751900000000	0.7037361617581
250	249	311534754076	13148414125	4096187960921300000000	0.7208247801198
251	250	319195444750	13078382625	4174560158597500000000	0.7382403543217
252	251	327012476050	13008631251	4253984715410900000000	0.7559872746320
253	252	334988390100	12939159255	4334468128080000000000	0.7740699584220
254	253	343125759900	12869965890	4416016825893300000000	0.7924928498851
255	254	351427189575	12801050410	4498637169194200000000	0.8112604197490
256	255	359895314625	12732412070	4582335447867800000000	0.8303771649816
257	256	368532802176	12664050126	4667117879832100000000	0.8498476084912
258	257	377342351232	12595963835	4752990609532100000000	0.8696762988193
259	258	386326692928	12528152455	4839959706438000000000	0.8898678098287
260	259	395488590784	12460615245	4928031163546700000000	0.9104267403836
261	260	404830840960	12393351465	5017210895888000000000	0.9313577140250
262	261	414356272512	12326360376	5107504739039000000000	0.9526653786387
263	262	424067747649	12259641240	5198918447631600000000	0.9743544061181
264	263	433968161991	12193193320	5291457693881300000000	0.9964294920201
265	264	444060444828	12127015880	5385128066109000000000	1.0188953552150
266	265	454347559380	12061108185	5479935067272900000000	1.0417567375307
267	266	464832503058	11995469501	5575884113057000000000	1.0650184033903
268	267	475518307726	11930099095	5672980532657900000000	1.0886851394436
269	268	486408039964	11864996235	5771229562846600000000	1.1127617541933
270	269	497504801332	11800160190	5870636351011700000000	1.1372530776140
271	270	508811728635	11735590230	5971205951478300000000	1.1621639607662
272	271	520331994189	11671285626	6072943324526000000000	1.1874992754039
273	272	532068806088	11607245650	6175853334965600000000	1.2132639135763
274	273	544025408472	11543469575	6279940750723500000000	1.2394627872234
275	274	556205081796	11479956675	6385210241432900000000	1.2661008277665
276	275	568611143100	11416706225	6491666377034100000000	1.2931829856917
277	276	581246946280	11353717501	6599313626382000000000	1.3207142301283

Jar Number	R	C_6^R	C_4^W	(Product) $C_6^R \times C_4^W$	(Cumulative Probability) %
278	277	594115882360	11290989780	6708156355862400000000	1.3486995484217
279	278	607221379765	11228522340	6818198828016900000000	1.3771439456999
280	279	620566904595	11166314460	6929445200176600000000	1.4060524444343
281	280	634155960900	11104365420	7041899523104800000000	1.4354300839957
282	281	647992090956	11042674501	7155565739649500000000	1.4652819202038
283	282	662078875542	10981240985	7270447683404500000000	1.4956130248713
284	283	676419934218	10920064155	7386549077381400000000	1.5264284853428
285	284	691018925604	10859143295	7503873532690800000000	1.5577334040277
286	285	705879547660	10798477690	7622424547233800000000	1.5895328979282
287	286	721005537967	10738066626	7742205504404600000000	1.6218320981615
288	287	736400674009	10677909390	7863219671803000000000	1.6546361494764
289	288	752068773456	10618005270	7985470199958200000000	1.6879502097656
290	289	768013694448	10558353555	8108960121063700000000	1.7217794495713
291	290	784239335880	10498953535	8233692347723300000000	1.7561290515867
292	291	800749637688	10439804501	8359666967171709300000	1.7910042101519
293	292	817548581136	10380905745	8486894762731300000000	1.8264101307444
294	293	834640189104	10322256560	8615370167218400000000	1.8623520294651
295	294	852028526377	10263856240	8745098307112500000000	1.8988351325189
296	295	869717699935	10205704080	8876081478674800000000	1.9358646756902
297	296	887711859244	10147799376	9008321851304000000000	1.9734459038137
298	297	906015196548	10090141425	9141821466368500000000	2.0115840702407
299	298	924631947162	10032729525	9276582236050400000000	2.0502844362994
300	299	943566389766	9975562975	9412605942204100000000	2.0895522707519
301	300	962822846700	9918641075	9549894235227000000000	2.1293928492452
302	301	982405684260	9861963126	9688448632944900000000	2.1698114537587
303	302	1002319312995	9805528430	9828270519510500000000	2.2108133720461
304	303	1022568188005	9749336290	9969361144316700000000	2.2524038970735
305	304	1043156809240	9693386010	10111172162092300000000	2.2945883264523
306	305	1064089721800	9637676895	10255352925999000000000	2.3373719618687
307	306	1085371516236	9582208251	10400255898277000000000	2.3807601085078
308	307	1107006828852	9526979385	10546431237527000000000	2.4247580744741
309	308	1129000342008	9471989605	10693879503541000000000	2.4693717702074
310	309	1151356784424	9417238220	10842601115134000000000	2.5146047078948
311	310	1174080931485	9362724540	10992596349161000000000	2.5604640008782
312	311	1197177605547	9308447876	11143865339549000000000	2.6069546305855
313	312	1220651676244	9254407540	11296408076346000000000	2.6540811082950
314	313	1244508060796	9200602845	11450224404785000000000	2.7018495498011
315	314	1268751724318	9147033105	11605314024363000000000	2.7502649995369
316	315	1293387680130	9093697635	11761676487936000000000	2.7993327675968
317	316	1318420990068	9040595751	11919311200838000000000	2.8490581615945
318	317	1343856764796	8987726770	12078217420003000000000	2.8994464860438
319	318	1369700164119	8935090010	12238394253115000000000	2.9505030417358
320	319	1395956397297	8882684790	12399840657773000000000	3.0022331251130
321	320	1422630723360	8830510430	12562555440669000000000	3.0546420276393
322	321	1449728451424	8778566251	12726537256785000000000	3.1077350351678
323	322	1477254941008	8726851575	12891784608612000000000	3.1615174273040

Jar Number		C_6^R	C_4^W	(Product) $C_6^R \times C_4^W$	(Cumulative Probability) %
	R				
324	323	1505215602352	8675365725	13058295845380000000000	3.2159944767669
325	324	1533615896736	8624108025	13226069162308000000000	3.2711714487458
326	325	1562461336800	8573077800	13395102599878000000000	3.3270536002558
327	326	1591757486865	8522274376	13565394043116000000000	3.3836461794881
328	327	1621509963255	8471697080	13736941220898000000000	3.4409544251597
329	328	1651724434620	8421345240	13909741705279000000000	3.4989835658581
330	329	1682406622260	8371218185	14083792910827000000000	3.5577388193852
331	330	1713562300450	8321315245	14259092093992000000000	3.6172253920970
332	331	1745197296766	8271635751	14435636352478000000000	3.6774484782419
333	332	1777317492412	8222179035	14613422624649000000000	3.7384132592953
334	333	1809928822548	8172944430	14792447688940000000000	3.8001249032930
335	334	1843037276619	8123931270	14972708163301000000000	3.8625885641613
336	335	1876648898685	8075138890	15154200504647000000000	3.9258093810455
337	336	1910769787752	8026566626	15336921008339000000000	3.9897924776358
338	337	1945406098104	7978213815	15520865807679000000000	4.0545429614908
339	338	1980564039636	7930079795	15706030873421000000000	4.1200659233602
340	339	2016249878188	7882163905	15892412013314000000000	4.1863664365040
341	340	2052469935880	7834465485	16080004871652000000000	4.2534495560111
342	341	2089230591448	7786983876	16268804928851000000000	4.3213203181155
343	342	2126538280581	7739718420	16458807501048000000000	4.3899837395106
344	343	2164399496259	7692668460	16650007739711000000000	4.4594448166628
345	344	2202820789092	7645833340	16842400631285000000000	4.5297085251227
346	345	2241808767660	7599212405	17035980996840000000000	4.6007798188353
347	346	2281370098854	7552805001	17230743491756000000000	4.6726636294485
348	347	2321511508218	7506610475	17426682605422000000000	4.7453648656213
349	348	2362239780292	7460628175	17623792660952000000000	4.8188884123291
350	349	2403561758956	7414857450	17822067814930000000000	4.8932391301701
351	350	2445484347775	7369297650	18021502057170000000000	4.9684218546686
352	351	2488014510345	7323948126	18220892105020000000000	5.0444413955788
353	352	2531159270640	7278808230	18423822930575000000000	5.1213025361876
354	353	2574925713360	7233877315	18626696705685000000000	5.1990100326159
355	354	2619320984280	7189154735	18830703856621000000000	5.2775686131201
356	355	2664352290600	7144639845	19035357536538000000000	5.3569829773927
357	356	2710026901296	7100332001	19242090730843000000000	5.4372577958624
358	357	2756352147472	7056230560	19449456257114000000000	5.5183977089942
359	358	2803335422713	7012334880	19657926765030000000000	5.6004073265887
360	359	2850984183439	6968644320	19867494736332000000000	5.6832912270814
361	360	2899305949260	6925158240	20078152484799000000000	5.7670539568424
362	361	2948308303332	6881876001	20289892156250000000000	5.8517000294754
363	362	2997998892714	6838796965	20502705728566000000000	5.9372339251171
364	363	3048385428726	6795920495	20716585011738000000000	6.0236600897367
365	364	3099475687308	6753245955	20931521647934000000000	6.1109829344363
366	365	3151277509380	6710772710	21147507111584000000000	6.1992068347502
367	366	3203798801203	6668500126	21364532709501000000000	6.2883361299467
368	367	3257047534741	6626427570	21582589581008000000000	6.3783751223284
369	368	3311031748024	6584554410	21801668698101000000000	6.4693280765347

Jar Number	R	C_6^R	C_4^W	(Product) $C_6^R \times C_4^W$	(Cumulative Probability) %
370	369	3365759545512	6542880015	22021760865626000000000	6.5611992188446
371	370	3421239098460	6501403755	22242856721481000000000	6.6539927364795
372	371	3477478645284	6460125001	22464946736843000000000	6.7477127769085
373	372	3534486491928	6419043125	22688021216416000000000	6.8423634471533
374	373	3592271012232	6378157500	22912070298700000000000	6.9379488130951
375	374	3650840648301	6337467500	23137083956286000000000	7.0344728987826
376	375	3710203910875	6296972500	23363051996172000000000	7.1319396857407
377	376	3770369379700	6256671876	23589964060101000000000	7.2303531122816
378	377	3831345703900	6216565005	23817809624922000000000	7.3297170728164
379	378	3893141602350	6176651265	24046578002979000000000	7.4300354171694
380	379	3955765864050	6136930035	24276258342516000000000	7.5313119498928
381	380	4019227348500	6097400695	24506839628107000000000	7.6335504295846
382	381	4083534986076	6058062626	24738310681110000000000	7.7367545682072
383	382	4148697778407	6018915210	24970660160147000000000	7.8409280304086
384	383	4214724798753	5979957830	25203876561598000000000	7.9460744328457
385	384	4281625192384	5941189870	25437948220129000000000	8.0521973435095
386	385	4349408176960	5902610715	25672863309233000000000	8.1593002810527
387	386	4418083042912	5864219751	25908609841803000000000	8.2673867141200
388	387	4487659153824	5826016365	26145175670721000000000	8.3764600606801
389	388	4558145946816	5787999945	26382548489473000000000	8.4865236873611
390	389	4629552932928	5750169880	26620715832788000000000	8.5975809087880
391	390	4701889697505	5712525560	26859665077298000000000	8.7096349869232
392	391	4775150900583	5675066376	27099383442220000000000	8.8226891304098
393	392	4849391277276	5637791720	27339857990067000000000	8.9367466939177
394	393	4924575638164	5600700985	27581075627372000000000	9.0518101774934
395	394	5000728869682	5563793565	27823023105446000000000	9.1678832259116
396	395	5077860934510	5527068855	28065687021151000000000	9.2849686280317
397	396	5155981871964	5490526251	28309053817698000000000	9.4030693161561
398	397	5235101798388	5454165150	28553109785470000000000	9.5221881653933
399	398	5315230907547	5417984950	28797841062864000000000	9.6423279930231
400	399	5396379471021	5381985050	29043233637162000000000	9.7634915578670
401	400	5478557838600	5346164850	29289273345415000000000	9.8856815596606
402	401	5561776438680	5310523751	29535945875362000000000	10.008900638431
403	402	5646045778660	5275061155	29783236766361000000000	10.133151373879
404	403	5731376445340	5239776465	30031131410348000000000	10.258436284762
405	404	5817779105320	5204669085	30279615052818000000000	10.384757828283
406	405	5905264505400	5169738420	30528672793829000000000	10.512118399487
407	406	5993843472981	5134983876	30778289589025000000000	10.640520330656
408	407	6083526916467	5100404860	31028450250689000000000	10.769965890711
409	408	6174325825668	5066000780	31279139448080000000000	10.900457284617
410	409	6266251272204	5031771045	31530341712170000000000	11.031996652799
411	410	6359314409910	4997715065	31782041429479000000000	11.164586070552
412	411	6453526475242	4963832251	32034222850489000000000	11.298227547464
413	412	6548898787684	4930122015	32286870087168000000000	11.432923026841
414	413	6645442750156	4896583770	32539967114878000000000	11.568674385136
415	414	6743169849423	4863216930	32793497773579000000000	11.705483431387

Jar Number	R	C_6^R	C_4^W	(Product) $X_6^R \times C_4^W$	(Cumulative Probability) %
416	415	6842091656505	4830020910	33047445769056000000000	11.843351906654
417	416	6942219827088	4796995126	33301794674162000000000	11.982281483464
418	417	7043566101936	4764138995	33556527930093000000000	12.122273765267
419	418	7146142307304	4731451935	33811628847679000000000	12.263330285885
420	419	7249960355352	4698933365	34067080608691000000000	12.405452508979
421	420	7355032244560	4666582705	34322866267181000000000	12.548641827516
422	421	7461370060144	4634399376	34578968750836000000000	12.692899563235
423	422	7568985974473	4602382800	34835370862356000000000	12.838226966136
424	423	7677892247487	4570532400	35092055280848000000000	12.984625213957
425	424	7788101227116	4538847600	35349004563252000000000	13.132095411665
426	425	7899625349700	4507327825	35606201145778000000000	13.280638590957
427	426	8012477140410	4475972501	35863627345366000000000	13.430255709756
428	427	8126669213670	4444781055	36121265361172000000000	13.580947651724
429	428	8242214273580	4413752915	36379097276068000000000	13.732715225777
430	429	8359125114340	4382887510	36637105058168000000000	13.885559165604
431	430	8477414620675	4352184270	36895270562370000000000	14.039480129194
432	431	8597095768261	4321642626	37153575531921000000000	14.194478698375
433	432	8718181624152	4291262010	37412001600004000000000	14.350555378349
434	433	8840685347208	4261041855	37670530291338000000000	14.507710597244
435	434	8964620188524	4230981595	37929143023810000000000	14.665944705665
436	435	9089999491860	4201080665	38187821110113000000000	14.825257976257
437	436	9216836694072	4171338501	38446545759412000000000	14.985650603275
438	437	9345145325544	4141754540	38705298079032000000000	15.147122702153
439	438	9474939010621	4112328220	38964059076156000000000	15.309674309093
440	439	9606231468043	4083058980	39222809659551000000000	15.473305380650
441	440	9739036511380	4053946260	39481530641312000000000	15.638015793332
442	441	9873368049468	4024989501	39740202738618000000000	15.803805343200
443	442	10009240086846	3996188145	39998806575513000000000	15.970673745484
444	443	10146666724194	3967541635	40257322684709000000000	16.138620634198
445	444	10285662158772	3939049415	40515731509398000000000	16.307645561768
446	445	10426240684860	3910710930	40774013405093000000000	16.477747998669
447	446	10568416694199	3882525626	41032148641474000000000	16.648927333061
448	447	10712204676433	3854492950	41290117404268000000000	16.821182870444
449	448	10857619219552	3826612350	41547899797135000000000	16.994513833315
450	449	11004675010336	3798883275	41805475843576000000000	17.168919360829
451	450	11153386834800	3771305175	42062825488858000000000	17.344398508478
452	451	11303769578640	3743877501	42319928601959000000000	17.520950247772
453	452	11455838227680	3716599705	42576764977523000000000	17.698573465924
454	453	11609607868320	3689471240	42833314337844000000000	17.877266965556
455	454	11765093687985	3662491560	43089556334854000000000	18.057029464398
456	455	11922310975575	3635660120	43345470552136000000000	18.237859595008
457	456	12081275121916	3608976376	43601036506951000000000	18.419755904491
458	457	12242001620212	3582439785	43856233652282000000000	18.602716854237
459	458	12404506066498	3556049805	44110413788910000000000	18.786740819654
460	459	12568804160094	3529805895	44365439017400000000000	18.971826089922
461	460	12734911704060	3503707515	44619405840376000000000	19.157970867752

Jar Number	R	C_6^R	C_4^W	(Product) C_6^R x C_4^W	(Cumulative Product) %
462	461	12902844605652	3477754126	44872921064443000000000	19.345173269146
463	462	13072618876779	3451945190	45125963852400000000000	19.533431323179
464	463	13244250634461	3426280170	45378513315364000000000	19.722742971782
465	464	13417756101288	3400758530	45630548514915000000000	19.913106069532
466	465	13593151605880	3375379735	45882048465270000000000	20.104518383458
467	466	13770453583348	3350143251	46132992135462000000000	20.296977592852
468	467	13949678575756	3325048545	46383358451535000000000	20.490481289087
469	468	14130843232584	3300095085	46633126298756000000000	20.685026975451
470	469	14313964311192	3275282340	46882274523837000000000	20.880612066982
471	470	14499058677285	3250609780	47130781937176000000000	21.077233890321
472	471	14686143305379	3226076876	47378627315105000000000	21.274889683564
473	472	14875235279268	3201683100	47625789401256000000000	21.473576596136
474	473	15066351792492	3177427925	47872246913338000000000	21.673291688662
475	474	15259510148806	3153310825	48117978536427000000000	21.874031932858
476	475	15454727762650	3129331275	48362962934271000000000	22.075794211423
477	476	15652022159620	3105488751	48607178747103000000000	22.278575317947
478	477	15851410976940	3081782730	48850604594866000000000	22.482371956828
479	478	16052911963935	3058212690	49093219079559000000000	22.687180743193
480	479	16256542982505	3034778110	49335000787580000000000	22.892998202835
481	480	16462322007600	3011478470	49575928292095000000000	23.099820772159
482	481	16670267127696	2988313251	49815980155404000000000	23.307644798135
483	482	16880396545272	2965281935	50055134931331000000000	23.516466538262
484	483	17092728577288	2942384005	50293371167619000000000	23.726282160544
485	484	17307281655664	2919618945	50530667408327000000000	23.937087743477
486	485	17524074327760	2896986240	50767002196258000000000	24.148879276038
487	486	17743125256857	2874485376	51002354075372000000000	24.361652657693
488	487	17964453222639	2852115840	51236701593228000000000	24.575403698415
489	488	18188077121676	2829877120	51470023303426000000000	24.790128118704
490	489	18414015967908	2807768705	51702297768062000000000	25.005821549623
491	490	18642288893130	2785790085	51933503560187000000000	25.222479532849
492	491	18872915147478	2763940751	52163619266280000000000	25.440097520722
493	492	19105914099916	2742220195	52392623488725000000000	25.658670876318
494	493	19341305238724	2720627910	52620494848302000000000	25.878194873519
495	494	19579108171987	2699163390	52847211986677000000000	26.098664697105
496	495	19819342628085	2677826130	53072753568909000000000	26.320075442851
497	496	20062028456184	2656615626	53297098285955000000000	26.542422117634
498	497	20307185626728	2635531375	53520224857191000000000	26.765699639550
499	498	20554834231932	2614572875	53742112032931000000000	26.989902838047
500	499	20804994486276	2593739625	53962738596360000000000	27.215026454061
501	500	21057686727000	2573031125	54182083369070000000000	27.441065140169
502	501	21312931414600	2552446876	54400125207598000000000	27.668013460747
503	502	21570749133325	2531986380	54616843011976000000000	27.895865892143
504	503	21831160591675	2511649140	54832215725282000000000	28.124616822861
505	504	22094186622900	2491434660	55046222233680100000000	28.354260553750
506	505	22359848185500	2471342445	55258841884582000000000	28.584791298210
507	506	22628166363726	2451372001	55470053458008000000000	28.816203182403

Jar Number	R	C_6^R	C_4^W	(Product) $C_6^R \times C_4^W$	(Cumulative Probability) %
508	507	22899162368082	2431522835	55679836200364000000000	29.048490245484
509	508	23172857535828	2411794455	55888169311415000000000	29.281646439831
510	509	23449273331484	2392186370	56095032049980000000000	29.515665631293
511	510	23728431347335	2372698090	56300403736518000000000	29.750541599447
512	511	24010353303937	2353329126	56504263755705000000000	29.986268037868
513	512	24295061050624	2334078990	56706591559029000000000	30.222838554405
514	513	24582576566016	2314947195	56907366667371000000000	30.460246671470
515	514	24872921958528	2295933255	57106568673604000000000	30.698485826343
516	515	25166119466880	2277036685	57304177245178000000000	30.937549371478
517	516	25462191460608	2258257001	57500172126720000000000	31.177430574826
518	517	25761160440576	2239593720	57694533142626000000000	31.418122620171
519	518	26063049039489	2221046360	57887240199658000000000	31.659618607470
520	519	26367880022407	2202614440	58078273289541000000000	31.901911553209
521	520	26675676287260	2184297480	58267612491558000000000	32.144994390768
522	521	26986460865364	2166095001	58455237975147000000000	32.388859970798
523	522	27300256921938	2148006525	58641130002499000000000	32.633501061606
524	523	27617087756622	2130031575	58825268931151000000000	32.878910349553
525	524	27936976803996	2112169675	59007635216579000000000	33.125080439467
526	525	28259947634100	2094420350	59188209414793000000000	33.372003855055
527	526	28586023952955	2076783126	59366972184929000000000	33.619673039340
528	527	28915229603085	2059257530	59543904291832000000000	33.868080355097
529	528	29247588564040	2041843090	59718986660864800000000	34.117218085309
530	529	29583124952920	2024539335	59892200119406000000000	34.367078433625
531	530	29921863024900	2007345795	60063525921590900000000	34.617653524838
532	531	30263827173756	1990262001	60232945228758000000000	34.868935405366
533	532	30609041932392	1973287485	60400439373029000000000	35.120916043748
534	533	30957531973368	1956421780	60565989980774300000000	35.373587331149
535	534	31309322109429	1939664420	60729578109979000000000	35.626941081878
536	535	31664437294035	1923014940	60891185983122000000000	35.880969033912
537	536	32022902621892	1906472876	61050795259426000000000	36.135662849435
538	537	32384473329484	1890037765	61208387902557000000000	36.391014115388
539	538	32749984795606	1873709145	61363946010138000000000	36.647014344025
540	539	33118652541898	1857486555	61517451816292000000000	36.903654973484
541	540	33490772233380	1841369535	61668887694170000000000	37.160927368367
542	541	33866369678988	1825357626	61818236158476000000000	37.418822820330
543	542	34245470832111	1809450370	61965479867987000000000	37.677332548684
544	543	34628101791129	1793647310	62110601628065000000000	37.936447701007
545	544	35014288799952	1777947990	62253584393154000000000	38.196159353767
546	545	35404058248560	1762351955	62394411269284000000000	38.456458512950
547	546	35797436673544	1746858751	62533065516549000000000	38.717336114709
548	547	36194450758648	1731467925	62669530551591000000000	38.978783026013
549	548	36595127335312	1716179025	62803789950067000000000	39.240790045312
550	549	36999493383216	1700991600	62935827449106000000000	39.503347903207
551	550	37407576030825	1685905200	63065626949763000000000	39.766447263141
552	551	37819402555935	1670919376	63193172519456000000000	40.030078722086
553	552	38235000386220	1656033680	63318448394393000000000	40.294232811251

Jar Number	R	C_6^R	C_4^W	(Product) $C_6^R \times C_4^W$	(Cumulative Probability) %
554	553	38654397099780	1641247665	63441438981997000000000	40.558899996797
555	554	39077620425690	1626560885	63562128863304000000000	40.824070680556
556	555	39504698244550	1611972895	63680502795369000000000	41.089735200772
557	556	39935658589036	1597483251	63796545713639000000000	41.355883832841
558	557	40370529644452	1583091510	63910242734335000000000	41.622506790066
559	558	40809339749283	1568797230	64021579156804000000000	41.889594224423
560	559	41252117395749	1554599970	64130540465868000000000	42.157136227330
561	560	41698891230360	1540499290	64237112334157000000000	42.425122830438
562	561	42149690054472	1526494751	64341280624428000000000	42.693544006415
563	562	42604542824844	1512585915	64443031391873000000000	42.962389669757
564	563	43063478654196	1498772345	64542350886407000000000	43.231649677596
565	564	43526526811768	1485053605	64639225554945000000000	43.501313830521
566	565	43993716723880	1471429260	64733642043668000000000	43.771371873414
567	566	44465077974493	1457898876	64825587200266000000000	44.041813496286
568	567	44940640305771	1444462020	64915048076167000000000	44.312628335129
569	568	45420433618644	1431118260	65002011928759000000000	44.583805972774
570	569	45904487973372	1417867165	65086466622358100000000	44.855335939763
571	570	46392833590110	1404708305	65168398636510000000000	45.127207715220
572	571	46885500849474	1391641251	65247797055924000000000	45.399410727745
573	572	47382520293108	1378665575	65324649584847000000000	45.671934356304
574	573	47883922624252	1365780850	65398944543085000000000	45.944767931134
575	574	48389738708311	1352986650	65470670469333000000000	46.217900734660
576	575	48899999573425	1340282550	65539816123269000000000	46.491322002413
577	576	49414736411040	1327668126	65606370487629000000000	46.765020923960
578	577	49933980576480	1315142955	65670322770265000000000	47.038986643849
579	578	50457763589520	1302706615	65731662406174000000000	47.313208262548
580	579	50986117134960	1290358685	65790379059523000000000	47.587674837409
581	580	51519073063200	1278098745	65846462625639000000000	47.862375383628
582	581	52056663390816	1265926376	65899903232988000000000	48.137298875217
583	582	52598920301137	1253841160	65950691245125000000000	48.412434245989
584	583	53145876144823	1241842680	65998817262635000000000	48.687770390542
585	584	53697563440444	1229930520	66044272125038000000000	48.963296165260
586	585	54254014875060	1218104265	66087046912684000000000	49.239000389313
587	586	54815263304802	1206363501	66127132948618000000000	49.514871845676
588	587	55381341755454	1194707815	66164521800427000000000	49.790899282141
589	588	55952283423036	1183136795	66199205282062000000000	50.067071412352
590	589	56528121674388	1171650030	66231175455640000000000	50.343376916838
591	590	57108890047755	1160247110	66260424633215000000000	50.619804444052
592	591	57694622253373	1148927626	66286945378535000000000	50.896342611427
593	592	58285352174056	1137691170	66310730508764000000000	51.172980006430
594	593	58881113865784	1126537335	66331773096192000000000	51.449705187626
595	594	59481941558292	1115465715	66350066466990800000000	51.726506685749
596	595	60087869655660	1104475905	66365604217457000000000	52.003373004784
597	596	60698932736904	1093567501	66378380186463000000000	52.280292623048
598	597	61315165556568	1082740100	66388388486235000000000	52.557253994283
599	598	61936603045317	1071993300	66395623489339000000000	52.834245548753

Jar Number	R	C_6^R	C_4^W	(Product) $C_6^R \times C_4^W$	(Cumulative Probability) %
600	599	62563280310531	1061326700	66400079833151000000000	53.111255694352
601	600	63195232636900	1050739900	66401752421373000000000	53.388272817712
602	601	63832495487020	1040232501	66400636425534000000000	53.665285285323
603	602	64475104501990	1029804105	66396727286453000000000	53.942281444652
604	603	65123095502010	1019454315	66390020715681000000000	54.219249625277
605	604	65776504486980	1009182735	66380512696910000000000	54.496178140022
606	605	66435367637100	998988970	66368199487358000000000	54.773055286094
607	606	67099721313471	988872626	66353077619120000000000	55.049869346234
608	607	67769602058697	978833310	66335143900497000000000	55.326608589867
609	608	68445046597488	968870630	66314395417288000000000	55.603261274262
610	609	69126091837264	958984195	66290829534055000000000	55.879815645691
611	610	69812774868760	949173615	66264443895362000000000	56.156259940602
612	611	70505132966632	939438501	66235236426978000000000	56.432582386788
613	612	71203203590064	929778465	66203205337052000000000	56.708771204566
614	613	71907024383376	920193120	66168349117255000000000	56.984814607964
615	614	72616633176633	910682080	66130666654389300000000	57.260700805901
616	615	73332067986255	901244960	66090156678990000000000	57.536418003385
617	616	74053367015628	891881376	66046818871331000000000	57.811954402707
618	617	74780568655716	882590945	66000652757486000000000	58.087298204641
619	618	75513711485674	873373285	65951658262785000000000	58.362437609651
620	619	76252834273462	864228015	65899835602278000000000	58.637360819096
621	620	76997975976460	855154755	65845185281646000000000	58.912056036447
622	621	77749175742084	846153126	65787708098088000000000	59.186511468499
623	622	78506472908403	837222750	65727405141174000000000	59.460715326593
624	623	79269907004757	828363250	65664277793658000000000	59.734655827839
625	624	80039517752376	819574250	65598327732265000000000	60.008321196342
626	625	80815345065000	810855375	65529556928435000000000	60.281699664431
627	626	81597429049500	802206251	65457967649038000000000	60.554779473893
628	627	82385810006500	793626505	65383562457053000000000	60.827548877206
629	628	83180528431000	785115765	65306344212209000000000	61.099996138779
630	629	83981625013000	776673660	65226316071594000000000	61.372109536192
631	630	84789140638125	768299820	65143481490226000000000	61.643877361438
632	631	85603116388251	759993876	65057844221586000000000	61.915287922171
633	632	86423593542132	751755460	64969408318118000000000	62.186329542947
634	633	87250613576028	743584205	64878178131693000000000	62.456990566483
635	634	88084218164334	735479745	64784158314029000000000	62.727259354897
636	635	88924449180210	727441715	64687353817082000000000	62.997124290968
637	636	89771348696212	719469751	64587769893398000000000	63.266573779388
638	637	90624958984924	711563490	64485412096419000000000	63.535596248016
639	638	91485322519591	703722570	64380286280765000000000	63.804180149138
640	639	92352481974753	695946630	64272398602465000000000	64.072313960717
641	640	93226480226880	688235310	64161755519156000000000	64.339986187662
642	641	94107360355008	680588251	64048363790242000000000	64.607185363078
643	642	94995165641376	673005095	63932230477015000000000	64.873900049527
644	643	95889939572064	665485485	63813362942736000000000	65.140118840293
645	644	96791725837632	658029065	63691768852673000000000	65.405830360636

Jar Number	R	c_6^R	c_4^W	(Product) $c_6^R \times c_4^W$	(Cumulative Probability) %
646	645	97700568333760	650635480	63567456174109000000000	65.671023269054
647	646	98616511161889	643304376	63440433176296000000000	65.935686258544
648	647	99539598629863	636035400	63310708430384000000000	66.199808057860
649	648	100469875252570	628828200	63178290809299000000000	66.463377432773
650	649	101407385752600	621682425	63043189487584000000000	66.726383187328
651	650	102352175060850	614597725	62905413941200000000000	66.988814165101
652	651	103304288317230	607573751	62764973947285000000000	67.250659250458
653	652	104263770871260	600610155	62621879583872000000000	67.511907369810
654	653	105230668282740	593706590	62476141229567000000000	67.772547492864
655	654	106205026322390	586862710	62327769563182000000000	68.032568633877
656	655	107186890972520	580078170	62176775563332000000000	68.291959852908
657	656	108176308427660	573352626	62023170507982000000000	68.550702570655
658	657	109173325095190	566685735	61866965973963000000000	68.808809001755
659	658	110177987596070	560077155	61708173836431000000000	69.066245291923
660	659	111190342765400	553526545	61546806268300000000000	69.323008383298
661	660	112210437653160	547033565	61382875739618000000000	69.579087583634
662	661	113238319524790	540597876	61216395016912000000000	69.834472253943
663	662	114274035861910	534219140	61047377162478000000000	70.089151809732
664	663	115317634362930	527897020	60875835533641000000000	70.343115722230
665	664	116369162943750	521631180	60701783781960000000000	70.596353519622
666	665	117428669738380	515421285	60525235852396000000000	70.848854788265
667	666	118496203099640	509267001	60346205982440000000000	71.100609173916
668	667	119571811599790	503167995	60164708701182000000000	71.351606382942
669	668	120655544031200	497123935	59980758882835800000000	71.601836183538
670	669	121747449407050	491134490	59794371473333000000000	71.851288406931
671	670	122847576961930	485199330	59605562034054000000000	72.099952948586
672	671	123955976152570	479318126	59414346195950000000000	72.347819769406
673	672	125072696658450	473490550	59220739930792000000000	72.594878896924
674	673	126197788382510	467716275	59024759495507000000000	72.841120426496
675	674	127331301451820	461994975	58826421430949000000000	73.086534522482
676	675	128473286218200	456326325	58625742560624000000000	73.331111419428
677	676	129623793258960	450710001	58422739989370000000000	73.574841423239
678	677	130782873377520	445145680	58217431101990000000000	73.817714912344
679	678	131950577604100	439633040	58009833561849000000000	74.059722338864
680	679	133126957196410	434171760	57799965309412000000000	74.300854229763
681	680	134312063640300	428761520	57587844560752000000000	74.541101187998
682	681	135505948650440	423402001	57373489805998000000000	74.780453893667
683	682	136708664171000	418092885	57156919807750000000000	75.018903105140
684	683	137920262376360	412833855	56938153599443000000000	75.256439660192
685	684	139140795671720	407624595	56717210483664000000000	75.493054477125
686	685	140370316693860	402464790	56494110030428000000000	75.728738555884
687	686	141608878311750	397354126	56268872075404000000000	75.963482979166
688	687	142856533627270	392292290	56041516718103000000000	76.197278913518
689	688	144113335975900	387278970	55812064320009000000000	76.430117610435
690	689	145379338927370	382313855	55580535502674000000000	76.661990407437
691	690	146654596286380	377396635	55346951145763000000000	76.892888729154

Jar Number	R	C_6^R	C_4^W	(Product) $C_6^R \times C_4^W$	(Cumulative Probability) %
692	691	147939162093270	372527001	55111332385058000000000	77.122804088390
693	692	149233090624700	367704645	54873700610407000000000	77.351728087184
694	693	150536436394340	362929260	54634077463636000000000	77.579652417861
695	694	151849254153600	358200540	54392484836416000000000	77.806568864075
696	695	153171598892230	353518180	54148944868073000000000	78.032469301840
697	696	154503525839120	348881876	53903479943368000000000	78.257345700557
698	697	155845090462910	344291325	53656112690219000000000	78.481190124027
699	698	157196348472700	339746225	53406865977385000000000	78.703994731454
700	699	158557355818790	335246275	53155762912098000000000	78.925751778444
701	700	159928168693300	330791175	52902826837655000000000	79.146453617986
702	701	161308843530940	326380626	52648081330964000000000	79.366092701428
703	702	162699437009650	322014330	52391550200041000000000	79.584661579441
704	703	164100006051340	317691990	52133257481464000000000	79.802152902972
705	704	165510607822560	313413310	51873227437780000000000	80.018559424189
706	705	166931299735200	309177995	51611484554873000000000	80.233387997410
707	706	168362139447220	304985751	51348053539276000000000	80.448089580025
708	707	169803184863310	300836285	51082959315447000000000	80.661199233405
709	708	171254494135650	296729305	50816227022997000000000	80.873196123797
710	709	172716125664540	292664520	50547882013873000000000	81.084073523216
711	710	174188138099180	288641640	50277949849495000000000	81.293824810311
712	711	175670590338330	284660376	50006456297850000000000	81.502443471234
713	712	177163541531000	280720440	49733427330542000000000	81.709923100484
714	713	178667051077240	276821545	49458889119794000000000	81.916257401748
715	714	180181178628740	272963405	49182868035414000000000	82.121440188722
716	715	181705984089630	269145735	48905390641702000000000	82.325465385925
717	716	183241527617150	265368251	48626483694331000000000	82.528327029495
718	717	184787869622360	261630670	48346174137170000000000	82.730019267977
719	718	186345070770860	257932710	48064448909069000000000	82.930536363091
720	719	187913191983520	254274090	47781455890640000000000	83.129872690494
721	720	189492294437160	250654530	47497102000768000000000	83.328022740521
722	721	191082439565300	247073751	47211455093630000000000	83.524981118919
723	722	192683689058870	243531475	46924543004947000000000	83.720742547559
724	723	194296104866890	240027425	46636393973873000000000	83.915301865142
725	724	195919749197260	236561325	46347035463771000000000	84.108654027883
726	725	197554684517400	233132900	46056496510127000000000	84.300794110186
727	726	199200973555040	229741876	45764805365562000000000	84.491717305301
728	727	200858679298910	226387980	45471990067194000000000	84.681418925967
729	728	202527864999460	223070940	45178081221623000000000	84.869894405041
730	729	204208594169580	219790485	44883105953700000000000	85.057139296108
731	730	205900930585350	216546345	44587093950356000000000	85.243149274078
732	731	207604938286750	213338251	44290074433057000000000	85.427920135772
733	732	209320681578370	210165935	43992076758756000000000	85.611447800479
734	733	211048225030190	207029130	43693130416044000000000	85.793728310512
735	734	212787633478240	203927570	43393265021268000000000	85.974757831738
736	735	214538972025380	200860990	43092510314601000000000	86.154532654095
737	736	216302306042030	197829126	42790896156080000000000	86.333049192092

Jar Number	R	c_6^R	c_4^W	(Product) $c_6^R \times c_4^W$	(Cumulative Probability) %
738	737	218077701166860	194831715	42488452521598000000000	86.510303985292
739	738	219865223307580	191868495	42185209498864000000000	86.686293698780
740	739	221664938641610	188939205	41881197283319000000000	86.861015123610
741	740	223476913616880	186043585	41576446174020000000000	87.034465177241
742	741	225301214952530	183181376	41270986569476000000000	87.206640903948
743	742	227137909639640	180352320	40964848963460000000000	87.377539475219
744	743	228987064942000	177556160	40658063940772000000000	87.547158190141
745	744	230848748396810	174792640	40350662172975000000000	87.715494475755
746	745	232723027815460	172061505	40042674414085000000000	87.882545887402
747	746	234609971284230	169362501	39734131496236000000000	88.048310109052
748	747	23650964716508 0	166695375	39425064325300000000000	88.212784953607
749	748	238422124096330	164059875	39115503876479000000000	88.375968363194
750	749	240347470993480	161455750	38805481189855000000000	88.537858409433
751	750	242285757049870	158882750	38495027365916000000000	88.698453293690
752	751	244237051737520	156340626	38184173561039000000000	88.857751347311
753	752	246201424807800	153829130	37872950982944000000000	89.015751031836
754	753	248178946292200	151348015	37561390886116000000000	89.172450939192
755	754	250169686503100	148897035	37249524567191000000000	89.327849791871
756	755	252173716034500	146475945	36937383360315000000000	89.481946443085
757	756	254191105762780	144084501	36624998632468000000000	89.634739876907
758	757	256221926847430	141722460	36312401778758000000000	89.786229208382
759	758	258266250731850	139389580	35999624217688000000000	89.936413683628
760	759	260324149144060	137085620	35686697386386000000000	90.085292679916
761	760	262395694097460	134810340	35373652735815000000000	90.232865705721
762	761	264480957891610	132563501	35060521725946000000000	90.379132400769
763	762	266580013112970	130344865	34747335820909000000000	90.524092536044
764	763	268692932635670	128154195	34434126484113000000000	90.667746013795
765	764	270819789622230	125991255	34120925173340000000000	90.810092867503
766	765	272960657524380	123855810	33807763335815000000000	90.951133261846
767	766	275115610083780	121747626	33494672403242000000000	91.090867492626
768	767	277284721332380	119666470	33181683786830000000000	91.229295986690
769	768	279468065595260	117612110	32868828872277000000000	91.366419301819
770	769	281665717487230	115584315	32556139014745000000000	91.502238126605
771	770	283877751917760	113582855	32243645533801000000000	91.636753280298
772	771	286104244089660	111607501	31931379708341000000000	91.769965712638
773	772	288345269500290	109658025	31619372771494000000000	91.901876503667
774	773	290600903942270	107734200	31307655905497000000000	92.032486863512
775	774	292871223504320	105835800	30996260236559000000000	92.161798132154
776	775	295156304571970	103962600	30685216829694000000000	92.289811779173
777	776	297456223828380	102114376	30374556683551000000000	92.416529403467
778	777	299771058255060	100290905	30064310725208000000000	92.541952732961
779	778	302100885132690	98491965	29754509804958000000000	92.666083624279
780	779	304445782041870	96717335	29445184691080000000000	92.788924062408
781	780	306805826863900	94966795	29136366064589000000000	92.910476160328
782	781	309181097781560	93240126	28828084513971000000000	93.030742158631
783	782	311571673279870	91537110	28520370529903000000000	93.149724425112

Jar Number	R	C_6^R	C_4^W	(Product) $C_6^R \times C_4^W$	(Cumulative Probability) %
784	783	313977632146890	89857530	28213254499968000000000	93.267425454335
785	784	316399053474500	88201170	27906766703344000000000	93.383847867186
786	785	318836016659160	86567815	27600937305487000000000	93.498994410396
787	786	321288601402690	84957251	27295796352807000000000	93.612867956045
788	787	323756887713080	83369265	26991373767327000000000	93.725471501040
789	788	326240955905260	81803645	26687699341334000000000	93.836808166581
790	789	328740886601850	80260180	26384802732024000000000	93.946881197589
791	790	331256760734000	78738660	26082713456136000000000	94.055693962125
792	791	333788659542160	77238876	25781460884583000000000	94.163249950783
793	792	336336664576840	75760620	25481074237073000000000	94.269552776053
794	793	338900857699400	74303685	25181582576726000000000	94.374606171674
795	794	341481321082900	72867865	24883014804691000000000	94.478413991956
796	795	344078137212810	71452955	24585399654751000000000	94.580980211079
797	796	346691388887840	70058751	24288765687938000000000	94.682308922378
798	797	349321159220750	68685050	23993141287135000000000	94.782404337595
799	798	351967531639090	67331650	23698554651687000000000	94.881270786115
800	799	354630589886040	65998350	23405033792005000000000	94.978912714178
801	800	357310418021200	64684950	23112606524180000000000	95.075334684070
802	801	360007100421360	63391251	22821300464593000000000	95.170541373284
803	802	362720721781320	62117055	22531143024530000000000	95.264537573671
804	803	365451367114680	60862165	22242161404809000000000	95.357328190560
805	804	368199121754640	59626385	21954382590404000000000	95.448918241855
806	805	370964071354800	58408520	21667833345080000000000	95.539312857115
807	806	373746301889960	57211376	21382540206036000000000	95.628517276607
808	807	376545899656930	56031760	21098529478561000000000	95.716536850340
809	808	379362951275310	54870480	20815827230693000000000	95.803377037075
810	809	382197543688320	53727345	20534459287895000000000	95.889043403312
811	810	385049764163610	52602165	20254451227745000000000	95.973541622256
812	811	387919700294020	51494751	19975828374635000000000	96.056877472761
813	812	390807439998440	50404915	19698615794489000000000	96.139056838254
814	813	393713071522600	49332470	19422838328949600000000	96.220085705629
815	814	396636683439840	48277230	19148520392862000000000	96.299970164132
816	815	399578364652000	47239010	18875686363580000000000	96.378716404212
817	816	402538204390170	46217626	18604360181216000000000	96.456330716357
818	817	405516292215500	45212895	18334565540729000000000	96.532819489905
819	818	408512718020040	44224635	18066325847294000000000	96.608189211838
820	819	411527572027570	43252665	17799664211172000000000	96.682446465552
821	820	414560944794360	42296805	17534603442583000000000	96.755597929599
822	821	417612927210020	41356876	17271166046622000000000	96.827650376422
823	822	420683610498330	40432700	17009374218196000000000	96.898610671057
824	823	423773086218030	39524100	16749249836990000000000	96.968485769817
825	824	426881446263640	38630900	16490814462466000000000	97.037282718959
826	825	430008782866300	37752925	16234089328893000000000	97.105008653325
827	826	433155188594590	36890001	15979909534041000000000	97.171670794965
828	827	436320756355330	36041955	15725853066612500000000	97.237276451743
829	828	439505579394420	35208615	15474382735250000000000	97.301833015911

Jar Number	R	c_6^R	c_4^W	(Product) $c_6^R \times c_4^W$	(Cumulative Probability) %
830	829	442709751297660	34389810	15224704232274000000000	97.365347962681
831	830	445933365991570	33585370	14976837092172000000000	97.427828848757
832	831	449176517744240	32795126	14730800495664000000000	97.489283310865
833	832	452439301166110	32018910	14486613264501000000000	97.549719064252
834	833	455721811210850	31256555	14244293856811000000000	97.609143901167
835	834	459024143176140	30507895	14003860362483000000000	97.667565689329
836	835	462346392704560	29772765	13765330498591000000000	97.724992370369
837	836	465688655784350	29051001	13528721604880000000000	97.781431958258
838	837	469051028750300	28342440	13294050639294000000000	97.836892537710
839	838	472433608284560	27646920	13061334173555000000000	97.891382262575
840	839	475836491417460	26964280	12830588388798000000000	97.944909354208
841	840	479259775528380	26294360	12601829071262000000000	97.997482099823
842	841	482703558346550	25637001	12375071608034000000000	98.049108850823
843	842	486167937951900	24992045	12150330982851000000000	98.099798021124
844	843	489653012775930	24359335	11927621771968000000000	98.149558085449
845	844	493158881602490	23738715	11706958140080000000000	98.198397577616
846	845	496685643568660	23130030	11488353836312000000000	98.246325088801
847	846	500233398165580	22533126	11271822190273000000000	98.293349265789
848	847	503802245239290	21947850	11057376108175000000000	98.339478809208
849	848	507392284991590	21374050	10845028069025000000000	98.384722471745
850	849	511003617980850	20811575	10634790120880000000000	98.429089056352
851	850	514636345122900	20260275	10426673877185000000000	98.472587414427
852	851	518290567691820	19720001	10220690513173000000000	98.515226443993
853	852	521966387320840	19190605	10016850762351000000000	98.557015087849
854	853	525663906003160	18671940	9815164913056600000000	98.597962331715
855	854	529383226092800	18163860	9615642805098000000000	98.638077202362
856	855	533124450305470	17666220	9418293826475600000000	98.677368765726
857	856	536887681719400	17178876	9223126910185000000000	98.715846125011
858	857	540673023776170	16701685	9030150531107100000000	98.753518418775
859	858	544480580281640	16234505	8839372702985100000000	98.790394819008
860	859	548310455406710	15777195	8650800975490500000000	98.826484529198
861	860	552162753688260	15329615	8464444243138080000000	98.861796782379
862	861	556037580029930	14891626	8280303683750800000000	98.896340839176
863	862	559935039703040	14463090	8098390873378600000000	98.930125985829
864	863	563855238347400	14043870	7918709666169900000000	98.963161532218
865	864	567798281972210	13633830	7741265250701100000000	98.995456809869
866	865	571764276956880	13232835	7566062335864700000000	99.027021169950
867	866	575753330051930	12840751	7393105148617600000000	99.057863981266
868	867	579765548379820	12457445	7222397431836400000000	99.087994628235
869	868	583801039435820	12082785	7053942442279600000000	99.117422508862
870	869	587859911088910	11716640	6887742948660800000000	99.146157032704
871	870	591942271582580	11358880	6723801229834000000000	99.174207618823
872	871	596048229535760	11009376	6562119073093500000000	99.201583693738
873	872	600177893943630	10668000	6402697772590600000000	99.228294689367
874	873	604331374178530	10334625	6245538127869800000000	99.254350040964
875	874	608508779990820	10009125	6090640442525700000000	99.279759185050

Jar Number	R	C_6^R	C_4^W	(Product) $C_6^R \times C_4^W$	(Cumulative Probability) %
876	875	612710221509750	9691375	5938004522984000000000	99.304531557337
877	876	616935809244300	9381251	5787629677408900000000	99.328676590650
878	877	621185654084100	9078630	5639514714737500000000	99.352203712849
879	878	625459867300270	8783390	5493657943846600000000	99.375122344735
880	879	629758560546320	8495410	5350057172850800000000	99.397441897967
881	880	634081845859000	8214570	5208709708538000000000	99.419171772966
882	881	638429835659170	7940751	5069612355940400000000	99.440321356828
883	882	642802642752730	7673835	4932761418048400000000	99.460900021222
884	883	647200380331430	7413705	4798152695665000000000	99.480917120300
885	884	651623161973780	7160245	4665781487407000000000	99.500381988602
886	885	656071101645960	6913340	4535642589853100000000	99.519303938957
887	886	660544313702640	6672876	4407730297842800000000	99.537692260397
888	887	665042912887900	6438740	4282038404927800000000	99.555556216057
889	888	669567014336110	6210820	4158560203979000000000	99.572905041096
890	889	674116733572830	5989005	4037288487951300000000	99.589747940603
891	890	678692186515630	5773185	3918215550809200000000	99.606094087519
892	891	683293489475060	5563251	3801333188615600000000	99.621952620562
893	892	687920759155480	5359095	3686632700786300000000	99.637332642149
894	893	692574112655960	5160610	3574104891513500000000	99.652243216336
895	894	697253667471210	4967690	3463740071360000000000	99.666693366756
896	895	701959541492380	4780230	3355528059028100000000	99.680692074567
897	896	706691853008060	4598126	3249458183304600000000	99.694248276408
898	897	711450720705090	4421275	3145519285185400000000	99.707370862365
899	898	716236263669470	4249575	3043699720183200000000	99.720068673945
900	899	721048601387290	4082925	2943987360819200000000	99.732350502062
901	900	725887853745600	3921225	2846369599303600000000	99.744225085031
902	901	730754141033280	3764376	2750833350406300000000	99.755701106579
903	902	735647583941980	3612280	2657365054521900000000	99.766787193862
904	903	740568303567010	3464840	2565950680931100000000	99.777491915506
905	904	745516421408220	3321960	2476575731261200000000	99.787823779648
906	905	750492059370900	3183545	2389225243149900000000	99.797791232009
907	906	755495339766710	3049501	2303883794113900000000	99.807402653966
908	907	760526385314540	2919735	2220535505626400000000	99.816666360655
909	908	765585319141470	2794155	2139164047405700000000	99.825590599086
910	909	770672264783600	2672670	2059752641919200000000	99.834183546273
911	910	775787346187030	2555190	1982284069103600000000	99.842453307393
912	911	780930687708720	2441626	1906740671307500000000	99.850407913959
913	912	786102414117380	2331890	1833104358456200000000	99.858055322012
914	913	791302650594450	2225895	1761356613449900000000	99.865403410345
915	914	796531522734950	2123555	1691478497761400000000	99.872459978742
916	915	801789156548380	2024785	1623450657341800000000	99.879232746247
917	916	807075678459690	1929501	1557253328663600000000	99.885729349449
918	917	812391215310130	1837620	1492866345078200000000	99.891957340811
919	918	817735894358230	1749060	1430269143386200000000	99.897924187005
920	919	823109843280630	1663740	1369440770659700000000	99.903637267294
921	920	828513190173060	1581580	1310359891313900000000	99.909103871931

Jar Number	R	C_6^R	C_4^W	(Product) $C_6^R \times C_4^W$	(Cumulative Probability) %
922	921	833946063551240	1502501	1253004794431800000000	99.914331200594
923	922	839408592351800	1426425	1197353401345400000000	99.919326360854
924	923	844900905933160	1353275	1143383273476700000000	99.924096366671
925	924	850423134076510	1282975	1091071620441800000000	99.928648136928
926	925	855975406986700	1215450	1040395308422000000000	99.932988493996
927	926	861557855293130	1150626	991330868804520000000	99.937124162342
928	927	867170610050740	1088430	943854507097530000000	99.941061767162
929	928	872813802740880	1028790	897942112121790000000	99.944807833068
930	929	878487565272240	971635	853569265483290000000	99.948368782801
931	930	884192029981800	916895	810711251330160000000	99.951750935990
932	931	889927329635740	864501	769343066397420000000	99.954960507957
933	932	895693597430350	814385	729439430343320000000	99.958003608557
934	933	901490966993010	766480	690974796380800000000	99.960886241070
935	934	907319572383050	720720	653923362207910000000	99.963614301130
936	935	913179548092730	677040	618259081240700000000	99.966193575711
937	936	919071029048170	635376	583955674152510000000	99.968629742154
938	937	924994150610240	595665	550986640723250000000	99.970928367246
939	938	930949048575540	557845	519325272002620000000	99.973094906346
940	939	936935859177320	521855	488944662790980000000	99.975134702571
941	940	942954719086380	487635	459817724441690000000	99.977052986030
942	941	949005765412070	455126	431917197988930000000	99.978854873109
943	942	955089135703170	424270	405215667604780000000	99.980545365822
944	943	961204967948870	395010	379685574389480000000	99.982129351210
945	944	967353400579670	367290	355299230498910000000	99.983611600807
946	945	973534572468360	341055	332028833613200000000	99.984996770159
947	946	979748622930920	316251	309864481750530000000	99.986289398409
948	947	985995691727510	292825	288724188430110000000	99.987493907947
949	948	992275919063350	270725	268633898188430000000	99.988614604119
950	949	998589445589730	249900	249547502452870000000	99.989655675005
951	950	1004936412404900	230300	231436855776850000000	99.990621191271
952	951	1011316961055100	211876	214273792440510000000	99.991515106076
953	952	1017731233535400	194580	198030143421310000000	99.992341255066
954	953	1024179372290600	178365	182677753738620000000	99.993103356426
955	954	1030661520216500	163185	168188500176530000000	99.993805011018
956	955	1037177820660400	148995	154534309389300000000	99.994449702586
957	956	1043728417422500	135751	141687176393520000000	99.995040798040
958	957	1050313454756400	123410	129619183451490000000	99.995581547825
959	958	1056933077370400	111930	118302519350070000000	99.996075086360
960	959	1063587430428400	101270	107709499079480000000	99.996524432567
961	960	1070276659550600	91390	97812583916326000000	99.996932490481
962	961	1077000910814800	82251	88584401915424000000	99.997302049948
963	962	1083760330757100	73815	79997768814836000000	99.997635787402
964	963	1090555066373100	66045	72025709358614000000	99.997936266743
965	964	1097385265118700	58905	64641479041816000000	99.998205940297
966	965	1104251074910900	52360	57818586282334000000	99.998447149871
967	966	1111152644129100	46376	51530815024130000000	99.998662127905

Jar Number	R	C_6^R	C_4^W	(Product) $C_6^R \times C_4^W$	(Cumulative Probability) %
968	967	1118090121615800	40920	45752247776520000000	99.998852998712
969	968	1125063656677900	35960	40457289094137000000	99.999021779827
970	969	1132073399087100	31465	35620689502275000000	99.999170383449
971	970	1139119499081400	27405	31217569872326000000	99.999300617985
972	971	1146202107365900	23751	27223446252046000000	99.999414189698
973	972	1153321375113500	20475	23614255155448000000	99.999512704463
974	973	1160477453966300	17550	20366379317108000000	99.999597669628
975	974	1167670496036300	14950	17456673915743000000	99.999670495983
976	975	1174900653906500	12650	14862493271918000000	99.999732499845
977	976	1182168080631700	10626	12561718024793000000	99.999784905254
978	977	1189472929739600	8855	10532782792844000000	99.999828846281
979	978	1196815355231900	7315	8754704323521000000	99.999865369459
980	979	1204195511584800	5985	7207110136834900000	99.999895436330
981	980	1211613553750600	4845	5870267667921600000	99.999919926115
982	981	1219069637158300	3876	4725113913625600000	99.999939638508
983	982	1226563917714600	3060	3753285588206700000	99.999955296595
984	983	1234096551805000	2380	2937149793295800000	99.999967549898
985	984	1241667696294600	1820	2259835207256100000	99.999976977556
986	985	1249277508529300	1365	1705263799142400000	99.999984091635
987	986	1256926146336600	1001	1258183072482900000	99.999989340566
988	987	1264613768026700	715	904198844139100000	99.999993112734
989	988	1272340532393500	495	629808563534770000	99.999995740191
990	989	1280106598715300	330	422435177576050000	99.999997502521
991	990	1287912126756300	210	270461546618810000	99.999998630842
992	991	1295757276767000	126	163265416872640000	99.999999311958
993	992	1303642209485600	70	91254954663993000	99.999999692659
994	993	1311567086139000	35	45904848014866000	99.999999884166
995	994	1319532068443500	15	19792981026653000	99.999999966739
996	995	1327537318606000	5	6637686593029800	99.999999994430
997	996	1335582999324800	1	1335582999324800	100.00000000000
998	997	---	0	0	100.
999	998	---	0	0	100.
1000	999	---	0	0	100.
1001	1000	---	0	0	100.

Answers to Selected Exercises

CHAPTER 1

Review Questions

2a. When 'must' is a flag term it signals the argument's conclusion. The basic form is this: since A and B are true, C must be too. Here A and B are offered in support of C.

b. The air safety official's argument in *2a* below, under Arguments, provides an example of 'must' as a flag term.

c. 'Must' is not a flag term in sentences such as, "I simply must find a place to live before the tourist season begins."

Arguments

2a. S$_1$ Both pilots unemotionally acknowledged the presence of another plane.

S$_2$ There was plenty of time between acknowledgment and collision to allow them to avoid each other.

S$_3$ Neither made any attempt to avoid collision.

==================================

C There was a third plane near the two rapidly approaching aircraft, situated so that each pilot thought it represented the danger to be avoided, but clearly representing a threat to neither plane.

b. S$_1$ Ivan Potter's car crashed through a freeway guardrail and rolled into the adjoining field.

S$_2$ Examination of Ivan's corpse at the crash sight revealed no broken bones or external injuries.

==================================

C The crash occurred because Ivan died at the wheel.

c. Not an argument: nothing offered in support of anything else.

d. S$_1$ Most of what AJS imports are fountain pens.

S$_2$ Every fountain pen imported by AJS is defective.

S$_3$ Most of what AJS imports is from China.

==================================

C At least one fountain pen from China is defective.

e. [Charitable reconstruction.]

S$_1$ There is little reason to prefer any one of the major-party candidates for president to the others.

S$_2$ A "none-of-the-above" space on the ballot would allow people to participate in an election and express their opinion without flattering some candidate with a least-of-evils vote.

==================================

C The ballot should contain a "none-of-the-above" space.

4a. : 3

b. : 3

c. : 1

d. : 3
e. : 2
f. : 1
g. : 3

Concerning *e*, the argument does not require that conservation be the *only* way out of our crisis, on any of the reasonable interpretations of that phrase. The argument need hold only that conservation is an important part of any of the best ways out of the crisis: that any substitute would be more painful, more dislocating, more expensive.

CHAPTER 2

Review Questions

2. It is difficult to find something that is good substantive support (e.g., the normal sort of evidence), which is *also* general enough to semantically eliminate every rival but one. When your schematization of a substantive argument does end up deductive, that usually means you misrepresented the support: put something above the line that doesn't belong there. Sometimes the culprit will simply be a deceptive restatement of the conclusion tangled up among the support claims. But occasionally the trouble will lie in a subtle feature of the way in which some bit of support is expressed. And this is sometimes hard to see.

4. First, we would naturally be interested in an independent inductive argument for that conclusion if it provided the conclusion with greater support than the deductive one. This would occur when the inductive argument's looser link was more than compensated by more plausible support claims.

Second, the support provided by a deductive argument very often is itself indirectly inductive. For (again) the strength of that support depends on the plausibility of the support claims, which usually rests on inductive arguments (e.g., reconstructed perceptions).

Arguments

2a. C_2: The satellite never was in any trouble, but the Soviets were about to attempt a risky ICBM test, and they manipulated the satellite and exploited the reports to provide a cover in case the test failed. It then did fail, producing the fireball and radioactive debris, but with much less adverse reaction than would otherwise have been possible. The satellite is presently circling the earth in ghostly silence, and the Soviets are trying to figure out how to get rid of it without attracting any further attention.

C_3: A meteorite entered the atmosphere near Baker Lake just as the satellite was returning to earth. The meteorite's enormous streak across the sky was so bright that it completely obscured the flash made by the reentering satellite. The radioactive debris on the river is part of the satellite.

b. The possibility of such a hoax is semantically eliminated by S_2, on its most natural reading.

c. Simply reformulate S_2 to refer to the reports rather than the actual fireball. For example, a fireball was reported over Baker Lake by many local residents at just about the time the satellite's orbit would have carried it over that part of northern Canada.

d. The controlling consideration in this case is that we (and any investigation) must deal with a number of things (events, phenomena) which seem clearly to be related to each other. So, helpful implicit questions will be those allowing all the interestingly distinct stories relating those items to be reasonably direct answers (that is, rival conclusions). Appealing to the fireball is a natural and convenient way to do this. But if that option is foreclosed, as it is here, the best procedure would be to move toward the general diagnostic question: "What's going on here?" Perhaps (slightly more specifically): "What explains all these seemingly related phenomena?"

4a. Deductive. It is just a reworking of the syllogism we discussed in the chapter.

S_1 A is true
S_2 When A is true, B is always true

C   B is true

Since all rivals to C must be incompatible with it, must say B is *not* true, they have been crudely but effectively eliminated by S_1 and S_2.

b. S_1 All the important economic indicators are good

===

C   The short run future of the economy is rosy

c. Such an item of information from the past would show that S_2 in the deductive argument is false. And since the argument cannot get along without S_2 and still be deductive, this information ruins the deductive argument altogether: it (as a deductive argument) provides no support at all.

On the other hand, as pointed out in an argument discussed briefly in Chapter 1, economic indicators may be important, useful and worth our reliance, even if they are occasionally mistaken. So a single incident from the past such as this will do little if anything to diminish the support offered by the argument cast inductively. It (and much more) will have already been taken into account.

6. A useful first step toward schematization (even more useful in complicated cases) is to write down a very coarse oversimplification of the inference being made. Here Steve concludes he's found a pioneer trail, and the *reason* he thinks so (that is, the support he offers) has something to do with the bones. So we have,

S   Bones
========
C   Pioneer Trail

The next step is to simply line-out the relatively pure padding, such as the cool autumn afternoon and the racing of Steve's heart. And finally, the rest must be condensed into economical statements of the argument's substance. Condensation and the elimination of redundancy is one of the trickiest parts of schematization: it requires careful reading and real understanding. Here, for instance, nearly everything following the exclamation point is a restatement, embellishment, or celebration of the conclusion. So, a schematization adequate for our purposes would be

a. S_1 Old animal bones litter the trail Steve has been following through the Nevada desert.

   S_2 The bones were (his anthropologically-trained eye told him) those of large, domestic animals.

   ==

   C The trail is an ancient pioneer route to California.

   [This is a median-schematization: how much detail and how complex a structure to provide are largely practical matters. We could here collapse the support into one carefully worded sentence. But we also could expand S_2 into another argument all by itself (the parenthetical part is support for the rest of it).]

b. The question Steve is trying to answer in making his inferences is 'What are all these bones doing here?' (Alternative: 'How did they get here?')

c. C_2: This was the route along which nearby cattle ranchers drove their marketable stock to a railroad depot during the late nineteenth century.

   C_3: Knowing he would be hiking along this trail, some of Steve's friends scattered old bones along it to trick him into thinking he had discovered an old pioneer trail.

CHAPTER 3

Review Questions

2. A diagnostic inductive argument is an inductive argument in which the support contains some trace-data for the rival conclusions to explain. Such arguments will inevitably have diagnostic implicit questions, that is, questions which are literally diagnostic, such as 'What happened?', or 'What's going on here?' So a rough rule of thumb that works most of the time is: a diagnostic inductive argument is one with a diagnostic implicit question. This will mislead you only in those rare cases in which none of the support produced contains trace-data.

4. This is virtually answered by number 2, above. If the support offered for an explanatory conclusion contains no trace-data, that is, nothing for the conclusion to explain, then the argument for that conclusion, constructed with that support cannot be diagnostic. If it is inductive, it must be nondiagnostic.

6. Changing the support claims changes the argument, of course; so, when you add new data to an argument you get a different argument. Moving from argument to argument by accumulating data in this way is just what produces an investigation. And since any bit of data may come into an investigation in a variety of ways, as part of a number of different arguments, it is perhaps better to say the relevance is to the investigation, rather than any particular argument.

   Part of what allows a collection of arguments to form an investigation is that they are all directed to something like the same implicit question: usually what launched the investigation. And this underlines the point of the previous paragraph. For what determines the relevance of a bit of data here is how it effects the plausibility of the rival answers to the implicit question.

8. Some aspect of a case, some fact about it, is an explanatory hurdle for a particular rival if that rival has difficulty explaining it. Typically the rival will be able to get around (or over) the hurdle only by supposing that something implausible took

place: this is what the difficulty is. Since the relation is explanatory, explanatory hurdles are always trace-data. *Other* aspects of a case that raise difficulties for specific rivals (normal background information, for instance) can never be explanatory hurdles. (You may wish to think of them as hurdles of another kind, perhaps.)

10. We are constantly called upon to make decisions on matters we do not know enough about, to act on limited information. The evidence we have provides some order among the rivals, but the one at the top is still not very plausible. Here it is often reasonable to go with the best bet, even though it is not very good. The argument is weak, but it is a valuable guide to action.

    Another place weak inductive arguments may be useful is during the early stages of an investigation. Initial data may be far from establishing one of the rivals, while still valuable in eliminating others and providing some order among those at the top of the ranking. The investigation proceeds by looking for data to explanatorily differentiate among the top few. Investigations are easier—sometimes only possible—if they can narrow down the list of live possibilities at the outset. This can (and sometimes must) be done with very weak arguments.

12. We may test a particular rival by looking for traces of it. In such a case we will know enough about the matter to know what to look for, and a bit about where to look; so we test the rival by looking around to see if the trace in question occurred where it should have or not. An asymmetrical test is one in which one of these results would have substantially greater effect on the plausibility ranking than the other. Finding the trace would strongly support the rival, for example, but failing to find it would leave things pretty much as they were. If the bills Joe just gave you for a purchase are the marked ones taken in a robbery, that strongly supports the rival claiming Joe is the robber. If they are not marked, that hardly changes anything either way: Joe could easily have other money to spend, even if he were the robber.

14. In this context it is reasonable to assume that a broken starter is simply one that won't turn the engine over. If so, that possibility contradicts one of the support claims and is thus eliminated semantically. A dead battery, on the other hand, does not conflict in this way with anything in the support. A dead battery is ruled out in the plausibility ranking. As soon as the starter turns the engine over, the possibility of a dead battery drops so low in the ranking that it is no longer a matter of practical concern. But it is not eliminated semantically: some weird new data could rescue it from oblivion without abandoning anything currently in the supporting statements.

Arguments

2a. *Rivals:*

C_2 Neither pilot took seriously the warning about another plane; they issued perfunctory acknowledgments to placate the ground controllers.

C_3 The pilots were, with calm determination, settling a long-standing grudge in an aeronautic joust.

C_4 The controls of both planes were mysteriously locked but both pilots happened to be extremely impassive personality types.

C_5 There was a third plane, but only one of the pilots saw it and mistook it for the one he was to avoid. The other pilot was an abject incompetent who wouldn't have recognized an imminent collision with the earth itself, and whose calm acknowledgement merely signaled stupefying ignorance.

b. *Trace data:*

T_1 The lack of emotion in the pilots' voices.
T_2 The failure to attempt an avoidance, in spite of adequate time.

C_2 accommodates T_1 and T_2 together by offering that the pilots did not think a collision was imminent.

C_3 accounts for them separately: T_1 by making the pilots calmly determined; T_2 by making the collision intentional.

C_4 explains T_1 with stoic pilots and T_2 by appeal to locked controls.

C_5 is more complicated. It breaks both T_1 and T_2 in half and accounts for the actions of one pilot as in C_1 and the other in a new way. T_{1a} and T_{2a} are explained because the first pilot thought there was no danger of collision (hence unemotional and unswerving). T_{1b} and T_{2b} are explained as the product of simple ignorance of the danger.

c. C_3 might be so elevated by uncovering a history of growing antipathy between the pilots, a copy of the schedule and rules for an airborne joust, and observation of partisan throngs on the ground watching the proceedings with intense interest. The first of these three items would be background information; the second and third would be trace-data.

C_2 would rise to the top if it were found that air traffic controllers in that area are famous for issuing collision warnings rather generously, even when the danger of planes coming close to one another is only very slight by normal standards. You might wish to add that the crews of both aircraft were intimately familiar with local controllers and had remarked on the fatuity of heeding their advice on collisions.

4a. It was a suicide, prompted by the loss of her car.

b. C_2: She was unintentionally killed during a mugging in a nearby town, and her body was dumped at the bottom of the freeway embankment. Her car was stolen just prior to the mugging and happened to be involved in the flaming crash at the top of the same embankment.

C_3: In the night and the fog she was unable to see just how steep the bank was. So when she stepped over the guard rail in her attempt to flee the developing inferno, she also stepped off into space.

6a. C_1: Herman is trying to prevent his roof from catching on fire (alternatively, prevent his house from burning down).

b. C_2: Herman is watering his lawn, which he finds it easier to do from his roof.
C_3: Herman has just lost in a weird party game that requires the loser to do something difficult, dirty, and mildly insane.

c. S_A: Herman always waters his lawn from his roof, which is made of fireproof tile.

d. S_B: Before scrambling up the ladder, Herman deliberately disconnected the hose from the spiggot. And his performance is being cheered on by a crowd of slightly inebriated people dressed in implausible-looking costumes a lot like Herman's.

8. S_1 Seventy-five percent of all living species, including the dinosaurs, were wiped out simultaneously about sixty-five million years ago.

   S_2 At the same time some iridium deposits were laid down in Denmark, Spain, and Italy.

   S_3 Iridium is abundant in meteorites.

   S_4 A huge meteorite (e.g., modest-sized asteroid) would kick up enough debris to obscure the sun for several years if it collided with the earth. This would kill off plant life and whatever depended on it.

   === d

   C The dinosaurs were wiped out when an asteroid collided with the earth sixty five million years ago.

   a. C_2: The dinosaurs were wiped out by changes in the climate due to the oceans' retreating from the continental shelves.

   C_3: Same as C_2 except that the climatic changes were due to the massive invasion into the oceans of fresh water from the arctic basins.

   Lump: The dinosaurs were wiped out by climatic changes to which they could not adjust.

   b. The fact that unusual iridium deposits were laid down at the same time the dinosaurs were wiped out.

   c. The age of the deposits (and the time of extinction too, of course).

   d. Some flexibility is possible in interpreting this request. The conclusion offered in the schematization above represents the narrowest construction of the argument, based on the preoccupation of the headline. So, rivals to this conclusion would have to account merely for the dinosaurs' extinction.

   C_4: They were wiped out by some virulent and highly contagious virus.

   You could take the implicit question to concern more of the trace-data than this, however. The rivals would then have to be rival explanations of more than just the dinosaurs' extinction; and this would make them more interesting as well as more difficult to generate.

   e. C_4 would rise in plausibility relative to the other three if it were discovered that the dinosaurs died out over several hundred years, rather than all at once. This is so because although C_1, C_2, and C_3 could account for this finding, they would have to further complicate already complicated hypotheses to do so; whereas, it would be perfectly natural for a virus to take a long time to work its way through the dinosaurs' extended and not very mobile population.

10a. That six or eight have died each summer for the past few years.

   b. S_1 Six or eight of a majestic stand of shade trees have died each summer lately.

   === d

   C_1 The trees are suffering from some mysterious disease.

   A_1 The city refuses to take the problem seriously.

   ===================================

   C_2 All of the trees will soon be gone.

   c. Besides A_1, it might be worth mentioning that Eleanor is assuming that no other kind of agency, public or private, has responsibility for or interest in saving the trees. A less interesting assumption is that the trees won't be cured naturally through some accident or quirk of nature.

   Note: one thing that is *definitely not* an assumption at this stage is that the problem with the trees is a disease. Eleanor does not *assume* this, she *infers* it: that is what the diagnostic step is all about.

   d. C'_1: The grove has been losing members of its original, ancient population, allowing room for the second- and third-generation trees to prosper.

   e. Eleanor's grove is substantially the oldest of such trees in the city. And none of the other groves—including some nearby—are suffering serious disease or mortality problems.

12. The trick here is to see that some kind of diagnostic picture is interposed between observation and prediction to make the prediction seem reasonable.

   a. S_1 Southern California has not had a very large earthquake in more than a century.

   == d

   C_1 The local fault system is locked together quite firmly, thus preventing the motion that produces earthquakes.

   A_1 When this happens, stresses build up within the fault system and eventually become more than the locked rock can resist.

   A_2 Along the main fault system in Southern California, this process takes about a century.

   ===

   C_2 Southern California will soon have a very large earthquake.

   b. The difference lies, of course, in the diagnostic step. The best explanation of the recent absence of great earthquakes in South Dakota is not a locked fault system. It is the basic lack of seismic activity in that part of the world: the earth's crust is boringly stable beneath South Dakota. So, recent quiescence will not lead to an earthquake prediction there, with *any* plausible set of assumptions.

CHAPTER 4

Review Questions

2. The difference is between deception and self-deception. In the first stage a motive will be offered (C_2) as showing the testimony was disingenuous. In stage two, even though the testimony is ingenuous, a motive might still be relevant in challenging the testifier's perceptual or judgmental competence. Perception is sometimes distorted by hopes and desires.

   4a. No, a representative sample cannot be biased. If a sample accurately represents a population in a certain respect, it is in that respect not distorted. There is nothing for a distorting feature of the sampling procedure (C_2) to explain.

   b. No, a random sample cannot be biased either. A sample is random only if all connection has been broken between the sampling procedure and the property of concern. This categorically eliminates the possibility that the sample's having P might be due to some feature of the sampling procedure.

   c. Of course. A random sample may be unrepresentative just by chance. No matter how well you stir the jar of red and white jelly beans, and no matter how judiciously you select a sample you still may get all red ones just by chance.

   d. Yes, in many ways. If you know the composition of a population already you may (nonrandomly) construct a representative sample by contrivance. If you know the jelly beans are half red and half white you pick two reds and two whites and have a representative sample of four. More interestingly, even when you do not know the population's composition in advance, a representative sample may (sometimes easily) be obtained through an emphatically nonrandom procedure. You could just get lucky, or you could have good reason to believe the nonrandom aspects of your sampling procedure are not related to the property P you're concerned with. A streetcorner survey may well yield a representative percentage of left-handed people.

6. The *characterization* of a modus operandi will typically be background information, just as in criminal investigations. But the *evidence* we have that a certain modus operandi is at work will be the traces of a suspect. The rival offering X as the cause will explain all the data that could be evidence of X's modus operandi. These modus operandi considerations are, accordingly, trace-data.

8. Many things would do, of course. An autopsy revealing massive cerebral hemorrhage as the cause of death would make the death-caused-crash direction reasonably certain. A verdict of death by ruptured spleen and other internal injuries would, on the other hand, make a very strong case for the opposite direction.

10. The only general rule is to treat it all—direct and indirect—as evidence, on a categorically equal footing. That rival is best which squares best with all of it. In a diagnostic step eyewitness reports are trace-data to be accounted for along with everything else. Sometimes they are easy to explain away, sometimes nearly impossible. It all depends on the case, which is to say it depends on everything else, including the indirect evidence.

Arguments

2a. The most serious difficulties could be raised under C_2 (deception) and C'_{2a}. Under C_2 the company doubtless has strong motivation to see prices decontrolled whether or not that would result in greater production. Accordingly, a motivational account of the executive's statement might be made plausible. In some cases, such an account might be hard to distinguish from one under C'_{2a}, for strong motivation is precisely what leads to self-deception when principles conflict. The executive might have convinced himself of what he told the subcommittee, in spite of the absence of any substantial reason to think it was true. It was so important it just had to be true.

b. The other three rival headings on the checklist are joke (C_2), unreliability (other than motivational), and inadequate access to information (last two C'_2). The context counts heavily against a joke-rival, and the resident expertise of the oil companies make the other two less plausible places to raise questions with the testimony.

c. Perhaps the most straightforward revelation would be that this executive has a reputation for damn-the-consequences candor. She has succeeded within the company in part because her reputation allows her to demand absolute honesty from those she supervises. This virtue is so widely appreciated that she constantly receives attractive job offers from outside the industry.

Anything to neutralize the motivational considerations for a normal human being would work as well. But there is a different kind of consideration that would have the same effect, only by circumventing the entire argument. This would be to offer a different argument—even some other (less suspect) testimony—for the same conclusion. If we find other evidence that decontrol would spur production, this would lessen the plausibility of deception rivals in the original argument. Such a move would normally be less interesting than a direct attack, however.

4a. It is plausible to claim that students unhappy with their grades would be distinctly more likely to come see Professor Ogden about the course during the last week than those quite satisfied with their progress. So a rather plausible C_2 rival would explain the high proportion of disgruntled students in the sample as due to the natural tendency of disgruntled students to come see Professor Ogden, not the general unhappiness of the population. (This is sometimes called the problem of self-selection.)

b. Quite.

c. Go through the class roster alphabetically each year, choose every thirteenth name, and interview that student.

6a. A is drinking a great deal of coffee; B is suffering a heart attack

b.   i. Drinking a great deal of coffee, through some physiological reaction to the caffeine, makes the body more prone to heart attacks.

ii. Heart attacks might cause increased coffee consumption if coffee becomes part of the postcoronary therapeutic program. Alternatively, a craving for coffee might be the direct result of a coronary.

iii. Long hours and inadequate rest might cause (stress-related) heart attacks and, independently, results in excessive coffee drinking (say, trying to stay awake).

iv. 'Chance' just means that there is no causal connection between the correlates; so, the explanatory challenge is to explain away the correlation. This is typically done by attributing it to some freak of nature or (good or bad) luck—anything that would break the explanatory connection between A and B.

c. ii. B→A would look best if it were discovered that the precoronary coffee consumption of heart attack victims was just about average: their consumption was higher only when postattack consumption was included.

iii. Eliminate from the statistics all those whose lives involve long hours and high pressure; that is, study the coffee consumption of heart attack victims who do not fit the common-cause profile of *iii*. Then, if the coffee consumption of those who remain is average or less, that would promote the common-cause thesis in *iii* to the top of the list.

iv. Elevating chance is (as it often is) more complicated. *i* and *ii* might be eliminated by discovering that the ingredients in coffee are actually good for the heart, helping it work through a long and trouble-free career by dissolving cholesterol and improving the muscle tone. But common causes may only be eliminated one by one, by examining all the plausible ones and rejecting them individually.

8. This is a trick question. If we were willing to characterize the data as Dr. Atlas wishes us to, the answers would be easy. A would be being a symphony conductor, B would be having greater than average life expectancy. He thinks the best explanation of the A/B correlation is A causes B. A decent rival would be a common-cause thesis appealing to early childhood environment or genetic and cultural background. The two rivals (A→B and common cause) are fairly close in plausibility. But the common-cause hypothesis could be elevated by discovering a remark-

able similarity among the cultural, ethnic, and economic backgrounds of a majority of the conductors, and, further, that men with that background tended to live significantly longer than average whether or not their lives had anything to do with music.

But we cannot accept the Atlas characterization. The life-expectancy figures he offers are not comparable in the way he suggests. The expectancy figure he gives for American men (68.5 years) is *at birth*. But since symphony conductors, or potential symphony conductors, are not labeled at birth, the figures do not describe the same phenomenon: they cannot be directly compared. The major reason for this is that part of the 68.5 figure is due to those who die of the usual childhood diseases and accidents in the first two or three decades of life. Since you must have already lived to be thirty or forty to even become a symphony conductor (Atlas only counted *major* symphony conductors), you would have already survived the hazards of youth, and the 68.5 figure would no longer be a valid comparison. That is, the differences in the sort of data represented by the two figures might account for their difference just as well as any characteristics of the subject matter.

In fact it is even clearer than this. Since surviving to thirty or forty is a precondition of being a (major) symphony conductor, the comparable life expectancy would be that of American men who have already made it that far. And in *this* comparison there turns out to be almost no difference at all. The same actuarial tables Atlas appealed to tell us that American men of forty can expect, on the average, to live *past* 73.4. In other words, music not only doesn't seem to help, it may shorten your life.

CHAPTER 5

Review Questions
2. Constructing a straw man usually wastes time and energy, and it risks misleading yourself about the nature and strength of the position you are criticizing.
4. To understand whether an argument presupposes 'what's at issue' in a question-begging way requires that we know something about the context in which the issue is raised and usually something about the perspective of the disputants too. This is most naturally achieved in conversation. If you attempt to apply the notion of begging the question in more formal contexts, you will very likely have to manufacture substitutes for the missing conversational detail.

Arguments
2a. False dilemma.
  b. and c.
  This way of putting the matter paints the alternatives as clear and opposed in a way those who disagree with the sentiment would simply never accept, for two reasons. First, the epigram claims our criminal justice system has located itself at an objectionable place on a simple, continuous scale that runs from favoring the criminal at one extreme to favoring the victim on the other. But since the very existence of such a simple relationship is rejected by many parties to this debate, the question of just *where* we are on the scale cannot be sensibly raised at this stage. In other words, it may be that treating suspects and prisoners less

humanely will decrease crime, but it is a very controversial point, not one to be dismissed in a characterization. Second, much of what is usually included under 'protecting the criminal' is treatment of suspects following arrest, during interrogation and trial. But to refer to these individuals as criminals further damages the credibility of the epigram's dilemma, for these individuals are not unambiguously criminals: some are actually innocent. So, treating them badly would under the *best* of conditions not be merely redressing the balance with the victims of crime. It would also be creating a new class of victims. Framing the criminal justice issue in the simple and monolithic way suggested by this epigram seriously misrepresents a very complicated matter.

CHAPTER 6

Here, and in the next two chapters, some of the "answers" will be short essays. In every case there will be an indefinitely large number of other essays just as good as the one offered; it is offered only as a sample, one sketching the major point or points your essay should contain.

Page 177
   a. 1. We can't play football here until the field dries.
      2. Sally learned how to play the violin before she was ten.
      3. I am stumped. I just don't know what card to play.
   b. 1. I tried unsuccessfully to pass the car ahead.
      2. The quarterback tried (also unsuccessfully), to pass the ball to his running back.
      3. Tom was arrested for trying (again unsuccessfully) to pass a bad check.
      4. It was so bad I thought I might pass out.
   c. 1. Did you turn on the light?
      2. Did you put on your shirt?
      3. Did you put it on the counter where it belongs?

Page 179
   a. 1. His handshake was firm but not painful.
      2. Because he was unable to maintain a firm grip, the rope tore through his hands, burning them severely.
      3. The deeply driven piles provided the building with a firm footing.
   b. 1. Whip the cream until it's firm.
      2. Make sure the gelatin is firm before removing the molds.
      3. The walls cracked because the earth was not firm under the foundation.
   c. 1. Exactly where were you on the night of March 13?
      2. Exactly where did you leave your keys?
      3. You must mark the point on the yardstick exactly or the piece we order won't fit.

Page 186
A comment on this exchange should mention that important aspects of our skillful performances can easily escape our notice, that we can do things well without being

able to accurately describe what we do. And this does not detract at all from the performance.

One application of this is language. The jobs important words do in communication are complex and dependent in elaborate ways on subtle features of the context. Our skill in using them develops only through practice in the contexts, with a heavy debt to the feedback we get from others. To discover whether somebody can handle a certain job—knows what a word means—we observe his or her performance in actual applications: identification, exchanges with others under varying conditions, and the like. On the other hand, to describe a job in any interesting detail is often wholly beyond our patience, time, and skill. In short, to know what a word means is not the same as being able to say what it means in any interesting way.

Page 193

1. Charity II exhorts us to *choose* the most plausible interpretation in the context. The five headings of Section 2 represent five different *kinds of choice* we have in normal conversation, choices we make by appeal to the context. Sometimes we must choose among a number of substantially different jobs a word might be doing. Sometimes we know the job, in the coarser sense, but must settle on a particular nuance within that job. Occasionally a job is laden with contrast, in which case we must decide just what contrast is being drawn. Just as frequently the job is comparative, so we need to understand the application in some detail in order to assign a specific value. And sometimes a word is clearly being used in a metaphorical way and we must determine what the metaphorical employment is up to. The argument of Section 2 is that the best thing to do in each of these decisions, determinations, and assignments is to be charitable. It is reasonable to choose whatever job, or aspect of a job, is most plausible in the context.

Page 195

The equivocation is on 'outlaw': to make the slogan plausibly true 'outlaw' must do one job, but its antigun control clout requires a different job. This may be seen as follows. If we construe 'outlawing guns' to mean that to own or carry a gun is illegal, then the bumper slogan would be true if an outlaw is simply *anybody who has broken the law.* Then, anyone having a gun will thereby be in violation of the gun law, and ergo an outlaw in this sense. On the other hand, the clear intent of the epigram is to draw a threatening picture of normal civilized people, in their homes, disarmed and thus at the mercy of the armed outlaw. But the job 'outlaw' is doing *here* is quite different. Here an outlaw is not just anybody who has broken a law; rather, it is limited to burglars, rapists, muggers, and the like, who would use force to have their way with you and your possessions. This emphatically does not include those whose most grievous offense is to violate the gun law or the speed limit.

CHAPTER 7

Page 201

2. It is best to begin by conceding that there is a grain of truth in the peculiar claim about 'valuable'; that is, that it covers subjective values. With a little care something may be usefully characterized as valuable in virtue of sentimental associa-

tions it has for a single person. For example, "That ugly little mutt was the most valuable thing in the old man's life." But it is important to quickly point out that this is so only in a very specific context, and that the standard used to distinguish the valuable from the worthless depends heavily on substantive context, rather like comparative and contrasting terms. In some contexts what is valuable is a simple matter of price: if it costs a lot it is valuable, if not, not. But in other contexts cost is not directly relevant: "A climber's most valuable possession is a good, waterproof pair of boots" (even if his watch is far more expensive).

So, the basic error in the incautious generalization about 'valuable' is its neglect of the essential pragmatic component in value talk. Whether something is valuable or worthless depends in large measure on what's at issue in the conversation, and this will vary from place to place and purpose to purpose. The above generalization seems anxious to destroy a valuable aspect of value talk by saying that if something is valuable in any context it must be valuable in all. But a team leader is quite justified in rejecting a pair of leaky boots as worthless independent of any sentimental attachments the owner might have to them. To add "well they aren't worthless to me, they were my father's" is an embarrassing irrelevancy in most circumstances. To insist that it is the only proper thing to say is to gratuitously attack an important and useful linguistic institution.

Page 214

1. This is just a crass application of the myth of one proper use that were it not for his second response we would unhesitatingly dismiss what the attendant said as an egregious pun. But he does genuinely seem to think there is something about 'gas' which makes it "incorrect" as a shortened form of 'gasoline' (perhaps because of its colloquial origins, perhaps because the competing job is older). What needs to sink in is simply that 'gas' has done both jobs competently for some time now and that they are usually easy to keep distinct in specific contexts. There is danger of confusion only in a few cases, and even here our linguistic skills are usually up to the challenge if we exercise the slightest care. And in all this 'gas' is just like thousands of other words that do double, triple, or multiple duty in the language. In short, there are no reasons to reject the motorist's formulation; and in his business, the attendant has all the reason in the world to adjust to the idiom.

Page 215

3. This case is a little more complicated than the mere misunderstanding of what job a word is doing. D's retort at first suggests that the problem is with 'blue'. But the problem is not simply *whether* something is blue, but rather in characterizing what it is that *is* blue. After noticing this, however, the issue is a rather natural extension of the one we were exploring under 'predication' in the preceding section. Saying the sky is blue conveys something absolutely straightforward in the vast run of applications. Attributing blueness to the *sky* tends to direct others' attention in a way that allows them to share a perception we find it useful to share. That attribution tells us where to look and what to look for, and most of us get the hang of it right away: intersubjectivity is easy to achieve. The fact that it is hard to give a characterization of the sky from some points of view and disciplines is indeed interesting, but it raises not the slightest difficulty for the bulk of normal talk about

the sky. All that talk requires is a bit of intersubjectivity and interest. To translate it all into the underlying physics would be gratuitously puzzling, sometimes even worse than that.

> After being confined below decks for two days by an insanely raging storm, a sudden lull tempted the first mate to pull himself off the debris and vomit-strewn floor and up the four steps to the door to the deck. He struggled with it briefly, got it open, stuck out his head and gasped, "My God, Captain, there's blue sky out here."

The message is clear, and worries about the objective nature of the sky and the paths of light rays are clearly beside the point. If the captain responded with speculations about diffusion and wavelength, that would be evidence of delirium. The mate should assume command.

In short, when we say the sky is blue, the sentiment is nearly always clear and useful, and injecting the underlying physics is at best irrelevant. All of which justifies our saying to D: "Now you know perfectly well what I meant when I referred to the blue sky. It was a very modest sentiment clearly expressed. I neither intended nor needed to say anything exotic. You raised a question only because you have been taken in by an understandable but deeply confused picture of how the language works, about what features of our experience we are "allowed" to address and how we must address them. It is a picture you had better try to free yourself of or you will find greater and greater difficulty in talking to other people."

Page 224

2a. 'Educators'.

b. The evisceration is the standard one in which an interesting-but-risky statement is turned into a less-interesting-but-less-risky statement by allowing a key term to vary its job to include troublesome cases. C originally attributes our youths' immorality to educators, with that word doing a clear and orthodox job. It's picking out the people in the field of education, in schools; it does not include parents (except those in education, of course). C's response to the objection is to expand 'educators' ' job to include parents and thus parry the objection. The problems with this are basically two. First, it incorrectly suggests that D should have known 'educators' was supposed to include parents originally. Second, and worse, it suggests that the job of 'educators' may be sufficiently flexible to gobble up any refuting case. If so, C will not have given us an account of anything, but rather an empty formula which can be made to fit the facts, whatever they are.

c. A clearer and more helpful response by C would go something like this.

> Yes, you're probably right: parents do have enormous influence. But educators are still very important in this. And since they are more directly accessible to anyone interested in reform, their role is worth emphasizing. We can do very little about parents in the short run.

Page 240

2. Even the end of a war is not determinate to that degree of precision, but the beginning is many times worse. What counts as World War II began rather gradu-

ally, picking up national involvements one by one, reaching a sustained climax, and winding down to the final signing of the treaties with the Japanese, which itself took several million microseconds to accomplish. To choose any one of several starting points weeks or months apart as *the* beginning would be relatively arbitrary. So, an answer in microseconds should probably include the caution "plus or minus a month or two," which would make the precise number look deservedly ridiculous.

Furthermore, even if we did choose one nation's declaration of war the *real* beginning, saying just when *that* was accomplished, to microseconds, is just as arbitrary. You can say just when certain votes were taken, and when certain officials did things, and when messages were sent and announcements made. But which of these is taken to constitute the declaration is arbitrary: any might be dismissed as a mere formality. "Gentlemen, may I remind you that we are already at war." And even if one of these activities were chosen, it certainly could not be pursued down to millionths of a second without further arbitrariness.

The point of all this is that if you want an answer in microseconds, you can have practically any answer you please, within an absolutely enormous range. Which is to say that, as an answer to the original question, none of them is at all significant. A significant answer would have to include a sense of its difficulty and arbitrariness. Perhaps the most reasonable course would be to give the shortest and longest reasonable durations, rounded to weeks or months, and add a sketch of the sort of decisions that would have to be made to narrow the range at all. Or perhaps say, "Tell me what made you ask the question that way in the first place, and I'll try to give you a better question to ask." The request for precision might be perfectly legitimate. It might only be the object of the precision that is misidentified.

4. Periodicals testing automobiles commonly use charts and tables to compare the one being tested with others. To make the comparisons interesting, these periodicals usually restrict the comparisons to cars the one being tested is competing with in the marketplace. The divisions must be coarse to allow enough cars in the comparison group; so we get "economy cars", "expensive cars", and those in between, with the divisions drawn exactly. And this is a perfectly reasonable thing to do in that context. But nobody—certainly not automative journalists—would contend that adding a minor option to a car just below the "expensive" cutoff suddenly makes it expensive, when it was not before. The point is that it is natural to usurp 'expensive' for precise duty in the road test reports only because it has its everyday (fuzzy-edged, tapered) job, to which it reverts in nearly every other context. To abandon *this* one would not just destroy a valuable resource, it would diminish the value of the precise one. That is, part of the value of using 'expensive' for the top category is due to its other job.

Pages 240–241

2. This puzzle may be approached in a number of different ways, but an interesting one that ties in with our discussion goes something as follows. In our normal talk about sounds—in which we exercise 'sound' in its usual auditory job—both of the conditions mentioned are satisfied. That is, somebody had a sound-sensation and that sensation was the result of some external physical cause—"sound waves" in the passage quoted here. So when asked to consider a case in which only one of the two is present, we are at first bewildered, as the hunters were by the squirrel,

because the departure from the run of comfortable cases is clearly relevant, but it is just not clear how. Most natural attempts to work out of the puzzle run immediately afoul of our penchant for hip-shot definitions, which in this case only deepen the mystery. For, shooting from the hip, we seem to have only three alternatives: sound simply consists in the waves in the air, or it is just the auditory sensation itself, or perhaps it is both together, each being necessary for something to be a sound.

The first alternative will give us the happiest answer to the original question—the tree does make a sound—but it misrepresents the job done by 'sound'. In the dead-normal context we are discussing here, we do not hear sound waves any more than we see light waves. What we hear are sounds—or, perhaps, objects that make sounds; just as what we see are colors and shapes—or perhaps objects with color and shape. Sound waves do push our tympanic membrane around, but that is the underlying explanation of our hearing sounds, not a simple redescription of it. (Once again the parallel with seeing and light is instructive.) So we can adopt this alternative (sound = sound waves) only by changing the job done by 'sound' in the context under examination. But if we were willing to make this move, we need not have come so far to do it: we could have adopted it at the outset and avoided the problem altogether.

Of course, we didn't do it then for the same reason we cannot do it now: it goes no way at all toward helping us with our puzzle. The puzzle concerns a feature of the normal auditory employment of the word 'sound', and tinkering with that employment in the middle of the inquiry is a kind of displacement behavior—self-deceptive delusions brought on by frustration. So let's look at the two other alternatives. These of course are in trouble immediately because they require a negative answer to our original question. Each requires a sound sensation in somebody, before anything can be a sound, so the tree falling in an unpopular forest makes no sound, no matter how it falls.

But this is to make a substantial modification of 'sound' 's employment too, and is unacceptable for the same reasons brought against the first alternative. For the way 'sound' works, the heart makes a thumping sound all the time, even though it requires a stethescope to hear it. And we can tell the lamp knocked over by the deaf burglar must have made one hell of a racket, even though the house was empty at the time. To say it fell without making a sound would be either to misunderstand the facts, or (more likely in this case) to have talked yourself out of some of your linguistic facility.

So none of the alternatives help: what to do? Recall that we were led to think of these alternatives as the only reasonable ones by an understandable but mistaken view of our ability to handle language. The ease with which we talk about sounds encourages us to think we must be able to give a helpful general characterization of sounds—a helpful description of 'sound' 's linguistic occupation. But as we've seen, the one doesn't follow from the other; in fact, job descriptions are frequently enough beyond our resources. Therefore, the thing to learn from this conundrum is that puzzles and paradoxes arise when we forget where our linguistic skill lies: in application, in specific contexts, not in abstract characterization of the jobs words do.

Although it need not, this discussion may be carried one step further. The proper sequence in this case would be this. First note that denying that the tree makes a sound here is based on accepting 'somebody being around to hear it' as a necessary precondition for something to be a sound. That's the only reason you'd be tempted; that's what creates the puzzle. Second, appeal directly to the best, most reliable source of information available, your ability to talk about sounds in boringly normal contexts (watching out for the centipede effect). Third, note that being heard by somebody is not required for something to be a sound (see cases above), and hence cannot be an objection to saying the tree mentioned makes a sound. Fourth, the (obviously important) role of hearing in talk about sound might better be caught conditionally (or subjunctively). Part of what we mean to convey when we say something made a sound is that if somebody (or, perhaps, some animal) with the proper hearing apparatus was (or had been) in the right place, then he, she, or it did (or would have) heard the sound. This is only a rough approximation, and it only concerns one aspect of the job done by 'sound'. But it does allow us to see why the three alternatives originally offered are not forced on us. And that addition to this discussion might allow the puzzle to fade away forever.

4. Hip-shot definitions run amok once again. 'Want', in the context offered here, is one of those basic words with a very complicated job. It would be a freak if a one-liner like this were even true of it, much less captured anything of interest. And sure enough, although doing and wanting are interestingly related in a number of contexts, the relation is not the simple one offered here. In fact the reply by B appeals to just the sort of data we need here: examples of the words engaged in their workaday occupations, where we are reasonably competent to handle them. And in those specific applications little can be clearer than that we sometimes do things we do not want to. It's a clear and dramatic part of life. All A can be suggesting, therefore, is that we not be allowed to use the words in this way, that we christen other words to express these facts, that we change the job of 'want' to fit his epigram. But why do it? Why destroy valuable linguistic institutions that express in a clear way things we're interested in, for the sake of somebody's pet one-liner? There is no reason. But we must stay clear about where our linguistic competence lies if we are to avoid falling into the trap.

CHAPTER 8

Page 247

2. The insight being mischaracterized here is that Buddhism departs from the vast majority of religions in not being organized around a supernatural deity. But that doesn't make it not a religion, just an unusual one. A better way to make the point might be, "You have to remember that Buddhism is not like the run of Western religions with which you are familiar: it has no supernatural being."

4. The insight here is perhaps that making gun ownership illegal would provide much less incentive for criminals to give up their guns than for law-abiding citizens to do so. The exaggeration is obvious.

Page 252

2. In normal conversation 'symptom' includes all those things physicians call signs: symptoms are roughly just the indicators of a state that is not apparent. The

symptom/sign distinction is not made in these contexts. The fact that it *is* made in a doctor's diagnosis is interesting and doubtless useful, but it provides no reason to modify our normal conversation about diseases. The job we give 'symptom' exposes our mundane concerns perfectly well, and physicians presumably can keep the contexts straight.

Page 259

1a. The sky is blue because of the way particles in the atmosphere diffuse sunlight.
 b. The astronomical account of sunrise and sunset appeals to the whirling of the earth on its axis. (You might want to add something about the practical considerations which govern the selection of a reference frame for the description of motion, as we did in the discussion of this case in Chapter 7.)
 c. The color of a surface is determined by the way it differentially reflects the various wavelengths of light falling on it.

Page 265

1. This might be a useful thing to say to help somebody understand sweeps weeks, Nielsen ratings, and the regrettable state of television programming. But this should not obscure the fact that in most contexts 'product' doesn't work that way. In most contexts the product of the networks is programming—in just the sense that the product of car companies is cars. It's what they do, what they devote their time to, what their expertise is organized around, what they produce. The distortion about audiences is helpful in the narrow context in part because 'product' does its normal job almost everywhere else. So, insisting on the distortion everywhere is not only confusing and destructive of other institutions; it also undermines itself. For most purposes, the product of the networks is programming.

3. This might be of some value in a physiology class, or perhaps in coming to understand something in forensic medicine or emergency care, but only if great care is exercised. For it is in many ways rather like the energy case discussed in the text. The job 'suffocation' has in describing the causes of death contrasts importantly with a long list of other causes: poison, electrocution, gunshot, decapitation, heart attack, kidney failure, and the like. To insist in normal contexts that the accident victim actually died of suffocation (via a ruptured spleen) is just perverse. It deliberately obscures the distinctions and contrasts which are of primary interest in the context. The underlying story about the sustenance of cells is interesting and relevant only in a very few places. It is senseless to disrupt our mundane conversations about death and its causes with constant, irrelevant references to cell physiology. It does not help, but merely obscures what we wish to say. None of this is to say that the physiology is not interesting and valuable in all sorts of ways. That is beyond question.

Index